STRINGHOPPERS A

# STRINGHOPPERS AND RABBITHOLES

## *Letters of a Wayfarer*

by

Sāmaṇera Bodhesako

(a.k.a. Robert E. Smith, Bob, Mikhail Medvedovsky, V, Vināyadhāra, Ñāṇasuci, Sadhu, etc., etc.)

EDITED BY HŪM

Path Press Publications

First edition: May 2013
Path Press Publications
ISBN 978 94 6090 006 8

Path Press Publications
*www.pathpresspublications.com*

# Contents

# Foreword

At Ellis Island, the Russian Jewish immigrant, Morris Medvedovsky, aware of the American penchant for short names, when asked his name at the hiring window, replied, "Name's Med." *Smith* was how the man heard it, as he seemed to hear a lot of other names, so yet another of that illustrious family was launched in America.

Bob Smith was born in Detroit, Michigan in 1939. He grew up in a middle-class, secular Jewish household. Coming of age in the early 60's, the wanderlust bloomed in his blood, fueled by the time, and his own search for a more satisfactory life that the USA could offer him: the verities of the Eisenhower years imploding in the prophetic paeans to a missing vision conjured up by the poems of Allen Ginsburg and the novels of Jack Kerouac, then an assassinated President, Civil Rights, Vietnam, LSD, and all the rest, as America wrestled with the painful prospect of an existential adolescence.

By the time Bob Smith got his BA in English from Wayne State in Detroit, then went to the Writer's Workshop in Ames, Iowa, he'd been involved in the Civil Rights movement, and his appetite to experience a more—if we can dissolve the patina on the word—'holistic' way of life, had been whetted by the best literature of that complaint. 'The land of Opportunity offers opportunities I don't seek'—Bob Smith.

So he set off to Europe, just about a half-step ahead of droves of other young Americans also jumping the reeling if not sinking ship of the, perhaps, fatally flawed American Promised Dream. After an unexceptional year on the continent breathing in its world weariness, weight of history, and rich cultural claustrophobia he, skeptical idealism in tow, hide himself to the Promised Land. After a couple of years on kibbutzim in the Galilee and the Negev, he ended up squatting on the then—undeveloped beach of Eilat, on the southern reach of Israel. The local gendarmes, in their wisdom, burnt out the 'beatnikim', and, on a trumped up charge, threw him in jail briefly and beat him up. When he got out, he still had some sore love for the land (he had seriously considered permanently settling at the Negev kibbutz, Ein Gedi), but he'd been disabused of any Zionist idealism and much affection for the State of Israel.

At this time he came into the possession of a slim, dog-eared paperback called The Way of the Compassionate Buddha. His ordeal with the Israeli police and the desertion of his Danish girlfriend at the same time no doubt made him a more sensitive reader, but it also struck a deep chord of destiny. In the Buddha's Teaching was the most trenchant explanation of the essential problem of the human condition, as well as a way to solve it, that he'd ever encountered. No overnight convert, he still had some thinking and experiencing to do, but the seed had been sown in him.

Leaving Israel, rucksack on his back, he headed overland to India. In Nepal the seed sprouted. From his sojourn in Katmandu he visited me in Shantiniketan, Bengal, and, thence, to Calcutta, where, at a Buddhist monastery on December 18, 1966, he was ordained as Vināyadhāra Sāmanera, a novice Buddhist monk. (Vināyadhāra means Keeper of the Discipline in Pāli, the language of the original Buddhist scriptures. Sāmaṇera means novice.)

As India wasn't a Buddhist country, his preceptor suggested he go to either Thailand or Sri Lanka to further his study and practice and to live the life in a more sympathetic environment. And so he did, in Sri Lanka, for the next five years.

The Path is not a straight one. At that point he felt his progress was obstructed by too much unfinished business to remain a monk. (By that time he had taken his higher ordination and was Ñāṇasuci Bhikkhu.) So he trekked back to India, then Nepal, where, in Katmandu, he disrobed.

He returned to the USA, but found it, as ever, a Land of Opportunity offering opportunities he didn't seek, and, after a few years, he hit the road again.

A year in a Guatemala village, where he could live a simple life, think, and write, shook him out of his stateside blues (almost shook him out of more than that in the earthquake of February, 1976), and he was soon winging back to Asia.

In Thailand he took the robe again and was ordained Bodhesako Sāmaṇera. A line from Edward Albee's The Zoo Story explained it all, he explained: 'Sometimes you have to go a long way out of your way to come back a short way.'

Bob once said to me he felt he was 'always moving toward Nepal'. It's not surprising that that portion of earth where Siddharta Gautama was born and died should have held such an attraction for him. And again it was in Nepal—Katmandu—that he unexpectedly died. He was 48 years old.

From Thailand Bob returned to Sri Lanka, where he lived the last six years of his life. When he died in Katmandu, after emergency intestinal surgery, he was on his way back to the USA to celebrate his father's 80th birthday and also to publicize a book he'd long labored on and finally electronic type-set and published himself. The book is called *Clearing the Path*[1] and is a compilation and annotation of the Buddhist philosophy writings and related letters of an English Buddhist monk, Ñāṇavīra Thera, who died in Sri Lanka in 1965. The discovery, or rather re-discovery, *recognition*, of Ñāṇavīra's unpublished writings by Vināyadhāra in 1967, helped to clear the novice monk's path.

What I've tried to do in this pastiche of letters (written by Bob to myself or his father) is no more than to suggest a man and his search for meaning; what he may have found, or ghosts of what may be found. In no way does it purport to be a biography—or autobiography—in any other sense.

I've centered the narrative of the letters in Sri Lanka--now and then pulling from the past in other places—because it's there that he spent almost twelve years as a Buddhist monk. Much of that time he lived in a fashion which hasn't been seen in the West since medieval times when mendicant friars wandered through Europe. In his last years, he had simple but modern digs on the tea-estate of an English couple near Bandarawela in the southern highlands of Sri Lanka, where, along with his begging bowl and a few books he had the personal computer, which, with no instruction, he programmed for the difficult diacritical demands of *Clearing the Path*.

Bob was always up for a new mental challenge. Despite his deeming it necessary for himself to be cut off from much of the technological trivia that imprisons most people in the modern world, he kept as keen and curious an eye on science and technology as literature and philosophy,

1. Reprinted by Path Press Publications, December 2010.

and politics, for that matter, although he considered that a minor vice. But the journalist, even war-correspondent, still perked a little in his blood, as a few of his lengthy letters describing Sri Lanka's communal strife clearly demonstrated.

When I think back to Bob on the road in the 60's, with Walden and Civil Disobedience in his rucksack, tinkling in my ear is a song he loved then: Bob Dylan's Tambourine Man.

> 'Though you might hear laughin', spinnin',
> Swingin' madly 'cross the sun,
> It's not aimed at anyone,
> It's just escapin' on the run,
> And but for the sky there are no fences farin'.
> And if you hear vague traces
> Of skippin' heels of rhyme,
> To your tambourine of time,
> I wouldn't pay it any mind,
> It's just a shadow that you're
> Seein' that he's chasin'.'

A couple other quotes flicker through my head that the man said in a manner that made me suspect he'd realize them in his bones.

> 'The ability to give up what one would keep: that is freedom.'
> —Marianne Moore

> 'We don't so much solve our problems as get over them.'
> —Bob Smith

So... to the story then... as Bob sometimes ended his letters: 'To begin at the beginning, as the White Knight instructed Alice...'

In this case, it's more like the middle.

Hūm
Sooke, British Columbia
September, 1989

February 23, 1989

My dear Hūm,

Your letter of inquiry about my son Bob arrived today. It is with great sadness that I must tell you that Bob died last August 15th in Katmandu, Nepal. He was on his way here to help celebrate my 80th birthday. Even though I hadn't seen him in 10 years, we had spoken to each other by phone. In Katmandu he became severely ill and placed himself in the local hospital where surgery was performed from which he never recovered. According to the hospital they removed a section of gangrenous bowel from a strangulated hernia, he developed pneumonia and died of sepsis. He was 48. He was cremated there with a foreign service national employee from the Embassy attending the simple but nontheless impressive ceremony. Their words. Burial in Nepal is prohibited and shipping the remains here would be prohibitively expensive and politically impossible.

The Embassy in both Katmandu and Colombo have been extremely cooperative operating through the Departement of State, but the process of closing out his affairs has dragged on now for 6 months, but hopefully it will soon be completed.

Should you desire any additional information, please don't hesitate to inquire.

Alan Smith

* * *

March 6, 1989

Dear Mr. Smith,

First please accept my belated but no less heart-felt condolences for the loss of your son. I'm a writer but wracking my brains can I come up with any first sentence better than that numbing old mouthwash? Which already points up how hard it's going to be to write this letter.

You're a man near the end of your own life, with eighty years of memories, a good many as a husband and father, with your plate already full enough with suffering, and, no doubt, some wisdom. Late in the game to be dealt this blow: your son, barely a middle-aged man, dying in a strange, foreign place, under who knows what conditions, after living a life, which, although I'm sure he expressed to you his belief in its value, must still appear somewhat alien, even inimical to the usual human affections and preoccupations.

You had not seen him in 10 years (neither had I)—and not a lot in the last 25 I'd think. Yet however separated your lives, I'm sure particularly in these last few years you'd grown closer to a Bob we both knew (I called him V, after Vinãyadhãra, his name after his first taking of the robe in Calcutta in 1966, with a winking reference to *V*, the title of a novel by Thomas Pynchon).

Despite his 'ascetic job' as he called it, typically with no frills, he was a warm-hearted and affectionate man, more a Pooh bear than a stony saint; as gentle, kindly, and sensitive a soul as I've known, and one of the wisest. But to me he was much more. It yawns like an impossible gulf before me, this trying to express the inexpressible, about what he was in my life. But for my benefit, probably more than for yours, you'll forgive me if I try, filling my first pages about it, not knowing if either of us will make head nor tail of it.

As when starting off on any unimaginable journey—like life itself—certainly in the great relationships, the great creations, of our lives—simplicity is doubtless of the essence. Suffice to say that Bob was the brother of my life; he was there at the creation (and I with hin), so to speak, in that odyssey geographically eastward, and psychologically inward, that irrevocably altered and transformed our lives.

For us it didn't begin with, nor end with, the Beatles. Though old Kerouac gave us a nudge. But it became, for both of us, the imperative of living. That is to get to the nub of the nonsense.What was it that caused this itch of dissatisfaction, this numbing ache of unknowing at the heart of being? Even the blandishments of pleasure, the coercions of pain, even the buttress of faith, the oblivion of nihilism, hardly dent it. Was there a way to solve the problem or was it unsolvable? Was it even no problem (that's a tough fantasy to sustain)? These were the questions that obsessed Bob and myself, and although he took the robe and lived in the East and I tried to live like a monk in the world of the West, our lives for 25 years have been parallel streams of consciousness, an ongoing dialogue with the Dhamma, in particular, and life, that pop-goes-the-political-weasel, in general (he had a most unmonastic eye for it). Nothing warmed my heart and head more than getting one of his wry little letters in my box; our idiom established we just went on with our talk, slightly to one side of time and space. I was always surprised that his missives navigated the physics. But always it was a communion of kindred spooks; unpretentious, poking gentle fun at ourselves as well as the world that takes itself so seriously with such disastrous consequences.

I don't know if Bob spoke much of our commen history, but it went something like this. We sort of met in passing in Israel in 1965 ('I don't remember seeing you, but I remember being seen by you,' were Bob's words, a twinkle in his eye, with the impeccable timing of a stand-up comic.). The Israel experience for both of us was catalytic. We went there with some ideals (delusions). Much of the best of the Jewish spirit was, indeed, in evidence, but also much, too much, was that spirit under bitter siege by the Israelis themselves. It hit us in the spiritual solar plexus and knocked us eastwards. We actually met on a rickety bus crossing from Iran into Afghanistan. At a late night stop in a dim-lit, smoky (hashishy) cafe in Khandahar he narrowed his eyes down a long wooden table at me and nodded at his neighbour, 'What's he on?' 'Pencils,' I chirped back. We grinned, our eyes glinted, and our bond was forged, a bond of spirit for life. Nascent Dharma-Bums that we were. That night, our sleeping bags unrolled on the floor of a Sikh temple, I thumbed by candle-light through a notebook of his while he snoozed (an incredibly deep sleeper he was!) and came across a poem he'd written about the Negev desert which moved me, spoke to me, in my own language, of that piece of ground and state of mind.

This initial intimation would bloom 15 years later, when we rewrote a novel of mine, *Worthy Bones*. The cussed book, the first draft of which I completed in the late 60's has yet to see the light of print, in spite of having been revised about as many times as the Bible. Anyway, about 10 years ago Bob wrote me from Bali that the book still gave him an itch. He just couldn't forget the story (perhaps, because it was, in fact, the story of our lives, in a slightly fabulous form). With my leave, he said he'd love to try to scratch it. One of the most scratchable drafts had been sulking for years on my shelf, so I said sure—not merely to the query of an editor, but a soul brother, a co-defendant of the accused fable; moreover, although my way with words could be more extravagant, our styles could also mesh without insult or injury, and our fine print of philosophy and compassionate irony was identical.

After he took the robe again in Thailand, he settled down to work on the book at the hermitage in the south, Wat Suan Moke. Winging our words between Sooke and Wat Suan Moke was a transcendent time: as if it were now neither my book nor his book, but that some dubious muse with a weakness for prolonged practical jokes had used first me, then Bob, then, as it turned out, me again, to finish the book. Bob got to a point, after going at it quite inspired, where he just ran out of gas, he said, he was pushing the words like dead weights. So once again, oddly, working from what he'd done to be working from myself, the culpable muse grabbed me and we wrapped it up. What surprised me (though it shouldn't have) was how much Bob's work resembled not the draft of the book I'd sent him but an earlier draft only *better*. He'd pruned the jungle into an exotic garden. Hence, the author, neither Hūm nor V, but HMV, His Master's Voice (an antediluvian pun, but not lost on us old fogies).

In sum, that book made us as we made it, much more than, before and after, the mere siege of writing it.

What I've been thinking about now is my own modest memorial to my friend: a narrative composed of his letters over the years, perhaps with a little commentary. Not a biography or anything—the letters should speak for themselves. But any letters you have of his to you over the last couple decades, which you think would add to the broth, and that you wouldn't mind parting with temporarily, I'd appreciate seeing; also any anecdotes from Bob's childhood or youth that come to mind which you think might have some bearing on the man he became. I realize, sir, that at 80 years of age you're probably not crazy to get mixed up with more papers than those winding up Bob's affairs, so if all this strikes you as bother, or an invasion of your privacy, your grief, I apologize and understand. In any case, if I finish the work, and my track record as a perfectly unpublished writer doesn't hold, any proceeds from it are yours. More than just a testament, I think there's a good book in those letters; a serial, epistolary novel, which just might breathe new life into those defunct forms.

Could you tell me what you know about what happened to Bob between July, when I received my last letter from him from Sri lanka, and August, when he died in Nepal? I'm mostly in the dark. What precipitated his decision to come home? The political situation in Sri Lanka? Your age and health? His? Had he disrobed? Temporarily, indefinitely? Were his plans to return to Sri Lanka or not set? A selfish sadness, is, of course, how close I myself was probably to a visit from him.

Although the circumstances of his death would strike anybody as regrettable—a lonely, painful, not entirely explicable, passing in a faraway place—I feel impelled to enlarge on this, perhaps to no enlightenment for you, but necessary for me.

Hero is a word that Bob would tweak with his considerable resources of irony, in particular if it was applied to himself. Certainly the word, washed in blood and iro, seems to have connotations not becoming a humble monk. There are many kinds of heros, however, big and small, disputable all. Only one hero, to me, is beyond dispute: he who sees, or strives to see, the fundamental problem of existence, and solves, or tries to solve, it with devotion and dedication. That's precisely what Bob's life, so far removed, so dimly alien, so finally incomprehensible, to the hurlyburly of the wordly in general, and many of the cherished notions of Western Civilazation in particular, was about. And that makes him a hero in my book. He never ceased struggling with, being obsessed with the essential desperate predicament and untenable premise of human existence; its incomparable contradictions and its inexorable collapse were a wound which remained fresh, as it does in every authentic man, and no man more authentic than the Buddha impelled by it to seek a healing in understanding. Not an easy nor a common task, and, for that reason, few undertake it as the work of their life—one can certainly be a fine and decent person without doing so—but it's the pursuit of the true hero because there is no victory or that victory has no laurels in this world or any other.

I don't know if you have any interest in the Buddha's Teaching, apart from the fact of its making him and breaking him into an instrument to realize it. Along with some respect or at least acceptance, it would be understandable if you also had an ache of some bitterness that it consumed him, that it so separated you from him and the life you know. I'm sure over the years Bob tried to express to you his reasons in this regard. I'm sure you know that he loved you—and your late wife, his mother (the loss of her—with him so far away—was doubtless difficult for you all). If there be a greater love, however, it is in striving to discover in oneself the source of fear and delusion, which begets all unloving, as often as not in the guise of the opposite. Hence, the Buddha's Teaching. We often, regrettably, must choose between what we see as a smaller immediate good and a larger, long-term good. Not that it's ever so clear, or the choice *should* be anything but difficult. I can't think of any 'larger' smaller good than having a close and caring relationship with one's family. A few years ago I was with my father in his last illness to death. I wrote Bob about it and he was quite moved. I later send him a recorded tape of me reading a passage from a novel I wrote about it and a small book of letters my father wrote me over the years and he was equally moved. Perhaps these communications may have in some small way worked in him to decide to make his last ill-fated trip to see you. But Bob, On the road pal, brother on the Path, even an enthusiast of my decidedly unpopular and seemingly unpublishable prose, helped me to grasp something greater than these: a spiritual engagement for life.

*Sotapanna* in Pali, the language of the Suttas, means 'stream-attainer'. One who attained the stream leading to Nibbāna, to the extinction of the ignorance of the Four Noble Truths, of the nature of this ache at the heart of creation which spawns all manner of dis-ease. For most of us this extinction isn't even begun. For a Buddha this extinction is complete. A *sotapanna* stands between the two, perhaps, in some ways, crucified between them, but therefore his great compassion is evoked. Except for a Buddha and a couple other preliminary stages there is no greater spiritual attainment, no more thorough transformation of heart and mind, than that realized by the *sotapanna*. He can fall off the wagon, so to speak, but immediately recognizes he has, and jumps back on again. Unlike most of us who've fallen off the wagon and don't even recognize we've fallen, let alone the wagon, and the Buddha, who recognizes the wagon and the fall perfectly, and will never again fall off. in other words, the *sotapanna* can break any of the Five Precepts and stumble on the Eight-Fold Path, but he quickly realizes he has and rights himself. What he *can't* do is this: *not* directly and constantly see the reality of the Four Noble Truths and the Three Characteristics, namely the nature of dis-ease, the nature of impermanence and the nature of the assumption of self. In my view, Bob attained or came near to attaining *sotapatti*.

Whether this means anything to you or not, I hope it will help shed a little light on the dark picture you must have in your mind of his seemingly miserable death in that Katmandu hospital. The Buddha is said to be a man who has 'done what has to be done'—he has seen the problem and solved it. Your son, my friend, nearly did too. For this reason, with all the others, I salute you, sir, and I love you, for siring a noble son, a noble man, and, yes, a noble Jew. I'm like Mohel, the protagonist of *Worthy Bones*, merely a 'wandering, wondering gentile', but, perhaps, with some probably disreputtable proclivity for the Jewish soul. Or a kind of Jewish soul—the kind that breathed from Bob. I know for much of Bob's life he had very mixed feelings about his spiritual heritage. (Very Jewish!) But he didn't cease to be a Jew because he became a Buddhist. *Because* he was a Jew, a noble Jew, that is one obsessed with the intractable human condition, railing against it, yet wracked by compassion for it, rejecting the false easy solution, indeed, seeking, in the name of the true, the most difficult, perhaps, the impossible solution. With these best of Jewish qualifications, he became a Buddhist, or, rather, it became him. Because he was this kind of Jew he had, perhaps, both a better and worse chance of realizing it. Because he'd never stop questioning it, testing it, doubting it, even as he gave himself heart and soul to it, even as he attained what he attained. Like the Just Man of Jewish lore, he can only truly be a Just Man who does not know he's a Just Man; entertaining any conception of one's uncommon worth is not the requisite of humility.

When I think of Bob the picture that comes to mind is of a certain fateful air about him, a kind of clear fog, the inexpressible in his so expressive big brown eyes, and the strong profile, an ancient regal cast to it somehow. I loved his eyes and profile and could watch them as if they were live classic sculpture. Sometimes he had a sort of ineffable sadness about him that could bring tears to my eyes; not the small sadness of the deflated ego, but the big sadness at the tragic absurdity called life. Yet this gravitas, this seriousness of soul, didn't repress the delight and wonder that perked from him so charmingly at the simplest pleasures: being with a good compagnion, witnessing any gesture of gentleness, humility, or grace, the sight of the sky, the green growing earth, the meekest creatures, a modest meal prepared and offered with affection, a well-told joke, well-tempered words spoken or written, a piece of fine music (he once told me, with not too much tongue-in-cheek, that what he missed most as a monk was Mozart, the horn quartets, in particular; though he didn't argue against the seemingly archaic and unreasonable stricture against listening to music: *not* to be transported, one could say, was the gist of the Buddha's Teaching), and, of course, in a reflective mood, his surpassing gratitude for 'the gift that excells all gifts', the Dhamma.

Well, I've gone on far too long, and far too foolishly, and could go on longer and foolisher. I don't know you at all, except as the featureless 'father' of my friend, yet something of you leaks through your simple, unembellished words. And I know that because you are an old man facing your own imminent end, you *have* to be more aware of the concerns about certain questions which pursued Bob through life, to life, and finally to death, and surely, you must have some empathy for his grappling with these concerns with such constancy and endurance.

I thank you for indulging my own need for this letter; a kind of verbal spasm from some deep place in me, my first reaction to the belated news of a watershed in my life, as I now begin to unreel the meaning of Bob's life and death from my own. If it has lit the smallest candle for you to see infinitesimally more clearly your loss—and what sorrow, regret, or bitterness you may feel or have felt—that's enough.

If your eyeballs haven't rolled into your head, or up to heaven, by this time, or even if they have, bless you, sir, bless you for being the father of this man, this friend, this brother, irreplacable in my heart, where, indeed, he will ever live.

The perfection of one thing can't escape me—perhaps I know as few others how perfect it is, for Bob: he died near the Buddha's birthplace and On the Road…

Hūm

## AMERICAN YOUTH ENTERS BUDDHIST ORDER

A 27 year-old American traveler, Mr. Robert E. Smith, will be ordained today (Sunday) as a Buddhist sāmaṇera (novice) by Ven. Dharmapala, Vihar Secretary of Dharmankur at 1, Buddhist Temple St., Calcutta. The ceremony will be held at about 6:30 PM.

Mr. Smith of Detroit (Michigan State), U.S.A., left his homeland about four years ago. Since then he has lived in Europe and the Middle East.

Wishing to explore the land of many religions, he began his India-bound journey early this year, traveling through Turkey, Iran, Afghanistan, and West Pakistan before entering India via the Ferozepur checkpoint in August. He came to Calcutta two weeks ago.

THE SUNDAY HINDUSTAHN STANDARD
18 December 1966

# A Letter From a Monk

December 31, 1966
Calcutta, India

Dear Steven Michael,
My congratulations to you on the happy event of your birth. Though you have received prior attention from relations less distant, and shall certainly receive future attention from others (particularly, you will find, from those who want to convince you that your happiness is dependent upon owning *their* product), my congratulations are sent to you as an uncle's to his first nephew. As such, I await the day when you will be able to reply.

It's fitting, perhaps, that this letter, written at the end of a year eventful for both of us, should be sandwiched between the messages of others, for your birth was similarly sandwiched between two other events. The day following it was the second wedding anniversary of your parents (and I hope you will give them my congratulations), while the day preceding it was the day I was ordained as a monk of the Buddhist Order—also a sort of birth, if you care to look at it that way.

I have no concern for your future success, Stevie (is that what you will be called?), for I know that that will be difficult enough for you to avoid. My concern, and what I shall be watching for, has not to do with what you will make of yourself, but of what you will not make of yourself, for this must be a guideline to life in your America. In a country where everything is ready-made, pre-cooked, pre-tested, and pre-decided, I caution you against being pre-pared. Keep your skin to yourself, both physical and mental, and you will be better able to avoid that complex of naturally and artificially produced desires that carries with it, *at the least*, those vague fumes of dissatisfaction that rise from the sanitary corners of every American household. Don't allow yourself to be made to admire and seek that which is most ephemeral and thus you will remove yourself from that sphere of ephemerality also. Ignore the pleas that to possess more—material, status, fame, etc.—is the only way to be happy, for you and I know that this isn't even one of the ways. He is richer who needs less. Don't be duped. Don't be committed. It makes little difference whether you are committed to an office, a factory, or a prison. None of them are of use, except to kill time. As if you could kill time without injuring eternity (not to mention yourself)!

Live a life that is praiseworthy, not merely praised. Remember that there is no quantity of *things* that can be possessed that can bring about a real and stable satisfaction. The only way to that lies within us, and we know—don't we?—that desire (one of the dominant factors on which American civilization literally depends), which arises from ignorance, is the source of that dissatisfaction you/we see everywhere around us, but which you—and I—know how to avoid.

Finally, question most closely those ideas which are most frequently and insistently presented to you.

I introduce myself to you with this subject because of my own present happiness, and because that happiness is the most basic thing that can be achieved. Since I've spent all my years before your birth in discovering its source, I wished to inform you at once: You can achieve happiness to no greater degree than you can extinguish ignorance, craving and egotism.

Now, with the completion of this little lecture, and before the completion of this little aerogramme, let me offer you an exchange. If you'll ask your parents to send me a photo of you I shall, in return, send you a photo of myself as a monk. My robes will be saffron-color rather than white and a bit larger than your diapers, but of the same material, of the same squarish shape, and for the same purpose. We are, I expect, equally bald. All of us, then, begin in the same Order.

May your achievements in that Order be of a high degree.

With fondness and hope,

from your uncle, Bob

… As he continued down the road, he
looked around at all the universe not
yet encumbered by the hopes of man…

from *A Foreign Retreat*
an unfinished novel by Robert E. Smith

# PART I

# A Contemporary Journal of a Very Minor Journey

December 1, 1967—5:00 AM boat leaves Dodanduwa Hermitage, I go to main road and turn south. It's just becoming light, but dawn comes very fast in the tropics and it becomes light quickly. I walk until 7:00 towards Galle. All the way to Galle is an unbroken line of villages, and it's necessary to keep robe done in such a way that both shoulders are covered. With baggage, this is very uncomfortable. Baggage becomes heavy. I am carrying; 1 alms bowl; 1 light outer robe; 1 inner robe (in addition to the ones I wear); 1 upper covering for chest; 1 bathing cloth, 1 towel, and 2 handkerchiefs; a few simple medicines, candles, and a Japanese paper lantern; 3 small books; a thermos flask; sandals, razor, soap, toothbrush and paste, matches, and other assorted minor items. How does it all fit? Very tightly, very tightly.

* * *

The ordination went off well. Mostly it just involved my requesting to be given robes, reciting the Ten Precepts (vows), and ritual acceptance in the Order, but they made a bit of a fuss over it, and a lot of people attended. Every evening people came to visit me, which is very funny. They venerate me, since I'm a Venerable (Venerable Vināyadhāra Sāmaṇera, to be exact), which means bowing down before me. The men touch my feet. I'm not supposed to have any contact with women though. All the time they're venerating I'm hoping my robes stay up, because they're pretty tricky things to wear. Done up properly, they look nice, and saffron is a nice color. One fellow thinks he's being very Western by calling me Reverend instead of Venerable. I know he means merely 'one who's revered', but I can't help smiling and picture Santa Claus and Thanksgiving and Sunday morning sermons to brightly scrubbed young faces... And, of course, they give me everything I could possibly use and many things I could never use: 3 blankets, shawls, a thousand billion sticks of incense, a lifetime supply of candles, all my meals, and what do I give in return?—my blessing. If that sounds like a con job, I'm not surprised, yet if this robe, if not what's in it, makes them feel this way, is it really?...

There is only one rule (out of 227 that monks follow) that gives me any trouble. That is the rule against singing. I'm just used to humming; it's in my blood. I'm getting the better of it, though; now that I've learned a few Pāli chants I've set them to little melodies and whenever I feel an irrepressible urge to burst out singing I launch into a little chant...

* * *

7:00—car stops; it's the car of the dentist in Galle who pulled my tooth. I accept his offer of a ride to Galle. He offers, as well, breakfast and a ride to Kottawa, where there is an <u>arañña</u> (forest hermitage), which is today's goal. I decline both, since it is my custom to take only one meal a day, and since I wish to walk. Ride to Galle accepted only to get beyond this long unbroken unpleasant village area. Today is new moon, when religious laymen observe the eight sīlas (or precepts) of abstinence from 1/killing 2/stealing 3/incelibacy 4/lies 5/intoxicants 6/eating after midday 7/use of luxury or vain items 8/attendance on shows, dancing, etc. (This is an extension of the normal 5 precepts-1,2,4,5, plus abstinence from sexual misconduct—but not requiring total celibacy—which laymen are expected to always observe.) There are special early morning religious programs on the radio on these new—and full moon days. Surprising both how many radios are tuned into them and how loudly (though there are other stations available).

* * *

...When laymen have told me that they lighted candles at the altar to achieve happiness I've always smiled inwardly with the knowledge that this popular superstition was not really part of Buddhism. Several evenings ago I suddenly realized that they were right, and I looked at the candles which I had purposelessly lighted and realized that they would make me happier. This is a very good thing to know, that you will become happier, and this knowledge filled me with joy, and suddenly I *was* happier, and it worked. So simple, once the method is mastered, I suspect this 'popular superstition' is a more essential part of Buddhism than all the scholarly studies made about the state of *Nibbāna* by people who ain't been there...

* * *

7:30—reach turn-off just past Galle; I set out on foot again. "Dentist tells me it is 7 miles; am offered ride/bus fare several times, by various curious people. About 8:00 AM am offered a cup of tea—accepted; am asked if I have had hil dāna—morning meal—and say no. It is promptly brought; refused. I do not want it and was not asked if I wanted it. I drink tea, answer questions, start walking again. Villages: no chance to go 'one-shouldered', which is far more comfortable.

* * *

A New Yorker has been staying at the monastery for some days while making arrangements to return to the States and, apparently, to be drafted, and he, it seems, is my first convert. I gather from him they're drafting everything that moves. Now that I've passed the magic age of 26, I can now even claim a clerical exemption. Imagine them sending me, in my robes, to Vietnam! What would they say if I tried to join the Army as a clergyman for duty in SVN?...

* * *

8:30 begin collecting alms—finished (bowl full-and it's a big bowl) by 9:30. Sit down on a log in shade on a hill off road and inspect contents. Very different from Colombo alms. No rice at all. Everything is wrapped in newspaper, so there is not really as much—a lot of space between parcels: 8

packages of sugar (useless); 3 packages of tea (even more useless); 4 tiny cupcake type sweets; 3 wrapped pieces of candy; 2 unwrapped candies; 2 flat pastry things and 6 bananas. ABSURD! I discard sugar and tea; eat the rest—still hungry. Am brought tea by one of the people staring at me from the road. Set out again; continue on alms. Much better this time: some rice cakes, 2 pieces of fantastically spicey and foul fish with sauce; 1 slice bread and about 1/8 pound butter to go with it; several indescribables. No sugar, tea. By now it is getting late; meals end at midday. I find a quiet shady place and begin eating when: leeches are everywhere! Depart hurriedly; don't sit down on damp, low ground. I'm becoming disheveled and my baggage is mixed up; discomfort; trying to find some place to eat; find a nice tree. Man comes and warns me against leeches; invites me to his home. I go and eat there, most comfortably, finish just after 11:00 and set out again.

* * *

We start dying the moment we are born. Birth is the cause of death. All circumstances which may bring about actual death are but its occasions. How *can* one be at one's ease in the interval? The Buddhist point of view will appeal only to those who are completely disillusioned with the world as it is, and with themselves, who are extremely sensitive to pain, suffering, and any kind of turmoil who have an extreme desire for its surcease, and a considerable capacity for renunciation. According to the views elaborated by Scheler, Freud, Heidegger, and Jaspers, there is in the core of our being a basic anxiety, *a little empty hole*, from which all other forms of anxiety and unease draw their strength. In its pure form this anxiety is experienced only by people with an introspective and philosophical turn of mind, and only then rarely. If one has never felt it oneself no amount of explanation will convince. If one has felt it, one will never forget, however much you may try. It may come upon you when you have been asleep, withdrawn from the world; you wake up in the middle of the night and feel a kind of astonishment at being there, which then gives way to a fear and horror at the mere fact of being there. It is then that you catch yourself by yourself just for a moment against the background of a kind of nothingness all around you, and with a gnawing sense of your powerlessness, your utter helplessness in the face of this astonishing fact that you are there at all. Usually we avoid this experience as much as possible because it is so shattering. We try to avoid this by trying to keep busy as much as possible, to always be doing something; thus, do we incessantly run away from this experience of the basic and original anxiety, and rely on something else than this empty center of ourselves to inform our lives. The Buddhist contention, however, is that we will never be at ease before we have overcome this basic anxiety, and that we can do that only by relying on nothing at all. It is in the nature of things that intimate knowledge of the Path is discovered only by those who walk it.

The Buddha's description of (and prescription for) the problem is summed up in the Four Noble Truths: 1) Life is bound up with *dukkha* (dis-ease, dissatisfaction, suffering, grief, etc.). 2) *Dukkha* arises from desire. 3) the Way to break the hold of *dukkha* is to break the hold of desire. 4) to break the hold of desire is to follow the Eight-Fold Path—and the Three Signata: 1) All is impermanent (*anicca*). 2) All is unsatisfactory (*dukkha*). 3) All is not-self (*anattā*)—that is, the ego is a delusion (or a delusional complex)...

* * *

11:10—huge snake on the road, 7 or 8 feet long, slithering everywhere very quickly, very close to me. I step back quickly as well. Villagers go by curiously looking at me, paying no attention to snake. One man throws a stick at snake, which disappears—harmless, apparently—certainly startling, however. Walk for a while. Rearrange baggage. Becoming tired; feet hurt; pavement is hot—can't wear sandals in villages, which are now scattered but still too frequent to take out sandals or go with one shoulder bare, tired, hot, wet, dissatisfied. Have already gone 10 miles, according to mile posts. Arrive at Kottawa village—am told hermitage is first junction to the left: walk on and find small foot path with turnstile entrance. Is this the place? Path is on the left; there is a signpost but only in native script—can't read it. Enter. It's a beautiful park, with shady jungle paths—altogether pleasant. Is it the place? Uncertain. Walk on. No sign of anyone anywhere. Perhaps there is a dry place? Downhill is a gentle river, a quiet marsh. Mosquitos? Uphill—too dense to sleep under a tree. Better find hermitage—and not try any 'by the root of a tree' sleeping business just yet. Leave park—if that's what it is—and proceed. Eventually come to real junction precisely 11 miles from Galle, on road to Udugalla, turn left—shortly another left onto a dirt road, walk on another mile across a river, then a sharp left, short walk—and there is the hermitage. There were several attractive places, along the way, but they can't compare with this: a fine river; hills, beautiful jungle, clean, well-kept, isolated, looks nice; arrive at 1:00. Am shown to a fairly nice kuṭi (a native hut)—given a cup of tea—welcome, but fortunately not overly-welcome. Then a delicious long bath in the icy stream, where tropical fish of many colors circle my legs or nibble my toes. Wonderful; wash off blood—probably from the leech bites. On my right foot I cool a few blisters. Everything is fine again. Return to kuṭi; straighten it up; make first entry in this record. Night: there is an insect—or perhaps a bird?—which sounds exactly like a power saw being flicked on and off, rapidly speeding up and slowing down; there are several mongooses here as well—perhaps more—but they will not come to me, nor let me get close to them. There are a great many paths, and I have yet to learn my way around. One path leads to a cetiya (shrine) on top of a hill which has a magnificent view for many miles, north and east. My first impression of the place itself is that it is primarily devotional. We'll see how much formal devotion is required of me. (I have no objection to devotion; a great deal to formal devotion.) Mosquitos are bad, and no screens or nets--I think this is the worst time of year in this part of Ceylon—but even so, not nearly so bad as Island Hermitage (where they are worse in number—though not in viciousness—even as Ein Gedi in the Negev)

* * *

Essentially, the Buddha's Teaching is a meditative system with a rather specific—and attainable—goal, and not the system of priest-preaching-laymen that is practiced here under the name of Buddhism but not in accord with the Teaching of the Buddha. The latter is a practice and the only way to understand it is to practice it. Study alone won't suffice. More than a practice, it's an experience. More than an experience, it's meditation. More than meditation, it's an attainment, and for me it is the means which I've been searching for since before I left the US. I can look back on what I was when I became a monk and I can see the difference, and it's a very desirable difference, and since I can see a difference I know that, as opposed to all the other things I've tried—with the exception of the kibbutz—for the last 7 years or so, as a Buddhist monk, some progress is being made…

* * *

December 2—Mosquitos are much worse today: a great distraction to all attempts at meditation (and, of course, that's all there is to do—the books are not 'reading' types but 'consultation' types). It's either do or die: I've removed myself from the distractions which were available to me at Island Hermitage. There are, it seems, 4 monks at this _araññа_—3 novices and a _Bhikkhu_. The head of the place is a novice. He was a _bhikkhu_, he tells me for 33 years—then chose to become a novice again. He speaks very little English and no one else any at all, so any real conversation—if either of us were so inclined—is impossible. I have learned of him, though, from another source: there is a book at Island Hermitage called Saints, Sages, and Seers, by a California professor P. Hopkins, in which he describes his various experiences in the East; in 1950 he was in Ceylon, and at Island Hermitage, for a short time, and at one other place for a longer time. That place, I learn now, was here. His opinion was that this place was chiefly devotional and meditational, while Island Hermitage was chiefly intellectual, which, in 1950, was probably true. I read the book chiefly for its Island Hermitage references, paid little attention to the Ven. Saranatissa's hermitage at Kottawa, and recalled it only when he came last evening with a lantern and a few questions. (He possesses, it seems, the amazing ability of waiting for some hours after having first met me before inquiring of my nationality—a phenomenon I have not previously encountered from an Asian). Food is, of course, not so good as at Island Hermitage, but healthy and satisfying and sufficient. Meal was taken alone here—a vast improvement—and actually it's only the mosquitos which will, within a few days, drive me away—that, and of course, the goal of the whole trip, which is to visit Ñāṇasumāna (another American monk) in Bundala. It rained last night, is very hot today. Relief at night from the mosquitos too—they leave at sunset via the western window—if I use no light, and remain in darkness until dawn, which is further meditational incentive.

* * *

With regard to begging, I don't glorify it. I've done some of it before I was ordained, and I know that it's a rather tiresome business. (Though in Asia it's not considered dishonorable in any way.) What I *do* glorify is the generosity, the devotion, even the faith, if you will, of the people who consistently give me far more than I need or, for that matter, could possibly use. *They* know I can't use what they give me, but when someone *runs* half a block to catch up with me to be able to offer me something without any expectation of even so much as a 'thank-you' (monks observe silence when on their alms-rounds) then *that* is worth glorifying. If I serve no other purpose here I am worthwhile in simply being an object to whom things may be given. I think, though, that most Westerners would have to see this for themselves to understand the attitude and the way of giving that these people have...

* * *

Afternoon—Having been exploring, it turns out that relief is possible except for the mid-part of the day, when there is no shade, there's a nice wall near the cetiya on the hill which will leave one shady side, and where there is a brisk, though sporadic, breeze and an extensive view which gives me an impression of vast aloneness and is fine for meditation—I suppose any hilltop of the sort would be. For walking about there is the sandy area of the cetiya itself. There is a flat rock, right next to the river—at the bottom of the hills—where a brook feeds the river as it bends sharply—which should be fine for meals. I'll try tomorrow. That leaves only a few hours at midday to deal with the mosquitos. Other natural phenomenon noted; some very fine trees (no coconut trees, though, and therefore no coconut milk), containing the odd monkey or two, and a great variety of colorful birds—parrots, cockatoos, etc., and also a handsome old rooster. The place is very extensive—miles of paths—with some very attractive spots. There must be 15 to 20 kuṭis, most of them falling apart through disuse.

* * *

...The Island Hermitage is 65 miles south of Colombo (a 4.5 hour train ride) and is situated on two jungle islands (connected by an earthen embankment) in the middle of a lagoon, about a mile from shore. There are paths encircling both islands, close enough to shore to catch glimpses through the stands of coconut and bamboo, beyond the vines and bushes alive with sounds of birds, small animals, and insects—out into the waters, where bright tropical fish swim past. Along the shore of the 'mainland' lies only jungle growth broken by an occasional thatched-roof house.

On the island are a few German and Sinhalese monks—usually, I'm told, about 10, but 7 at the moment. 3 of them live on this island—the smaller of the two, about half mile around—and the rest on the other island (which is, I think, a bit over a mile around). So there is enough room here so that each monk's *kuṭi* or hut can be placed as to be out of sight of all the others, and afford a greater measure of that solitude for which the Hermitage was created. Also living on the island (aside from wildlife) are 3 or 4 dogs, an indeterminate number of cats, and 2 mongooses, neither of whom seems very friendly. (The mongooses, whose job is to control the snake population are tame, but so far they have only hurried past me, seemingly bent upon pursuing their duties, and have paused only long enough to sniff my toes. Just making certain, I suppose, that I'm not a snake in disguise, they are indistinguishable, but it doesn't really matter since both of them have the same name.) Meals, by the way, are brought from the mainland for there is no possibility of collecting alms...

* * *

December 3—At night the insects take over, and have a real jam session—very far out and very real jazz. They have a strong rhythm section, a superb brass section (which blows a strong muted staccato, always in tune); their strings, however, are poor, and, while the woodwinds are good, proper use of them is seldom made. What a gas to listen to them, though, from twilight to dawn! Very few fireflies here—unlike Island Hermitage—which is too bad; of all the insects they are the only ones whom I have a liking for—though I wouldn't want my sister to marry one. It rained again last night, and today is bright, sunny, and, it seems, very native weather.

* * *

...The clouds cast a dim and diffuse light here; the lagoon fills from the torrential rains (the channel to the sea is kept closed until the flood waters are impossibly high), and I rest briefly from the long hours of strenuous effort involved in developing *samathabhāvana*—calm concentration. After six months of hard—very hard—work, a few words of the language of wisdom have been learned—though perhaps the grammar necessary for this mental development may still be a long way off. I have found my solitude: it is totally internal.

Yes, I was aware that Lama Govinda (I assume you were referring to him) was at the Hermitage for a while—and I'm not surprised that he found the horizon for a poet-painter limited. The Buddha left no instructions for success in any of the arts, and if one wishes to practice the arts one may well find the Buddha's Teaching limiting. The Buddha's Teaching *is* limited: 'Two things only do I teach, Monks. What is *dukkha*, and the path leading to the cessation of *dukkha*.'

No, I hope I did not suggest that Tibet, Zen, Ch'an, etc. have nothing to offer. They may have quite a bit to offer; but what they do *not* offer is the Buddha's Teaching. That teaching is, of course, not just *Vinaya* and *Sutta*. (It's not at all Abhidhamma, which is a scholastic invention having nothing to do with the Buddha's Teaching—or with anything else.) Meditation is an integral and necessary part of the Teaching—and the part which is generally neglected in *Therāvada*—without which attainment is not possible. But: (1) There are many types of meditation, only a few of which are suitable for practice of the Buddha's Teaching. (2) Meditation, while necessary, is not sufficient, and a grasp of the subject on an intellectual level, to some degree, is also necessary. The teachings of Mahāyana and Tantric, whatever be their value, do not lead to an understanding of the Buddha's Teaching. There are a number of very basic points in which they are totally at variance with the Teaching. The meditations taught by them are, generally, not the meditations which lead to that reflexive view of reality, constant mindfulness, which is needed to realize the Teaching. But, after all, most people, in their heart of hearts, do not want to believe that the Teaching can actually succeed. If they knew that today, in Ceylon, there might be someone still living who had actually attained some part of the Path, they would surely be shocked and outraged. They want their Dhamma on easier terms, and so turn to mysticism to get it. But—'nuff said.

Except for a rather fruitless month in Colombo when I arrived—a month filled with the despair that can only be known by one who walks the hollow corridors of officialdom—I've been here at the Island Hermitage since arrival, It's far from being the best place for me, but I can say this about it—it's the only place for me, at least, in Ceylon. The only real trouble is it's so terribly overpopulated. When I first arrived here there were 5 dogs, 4 Sinhalese, 3 Germans, 2 mongooses and an elderly Yugoslavian ex-philosophy professor who has been a *sāmaṇera* for a year and will not take his higher ordination because he doesn't want to have to eat dirty food. There is an ocean filled with fish, a sky filled with birds, a jungle filled with snakes and a well filled with tadpoles. Hardly a day goes by when someone doesn't speak to me. Kierkegaard, for instance, has been saying a lot, all of which I've found well worth listening to, though, it's necessary to dodge the occasional theological snowballs he throws out. But they melt rapidly in this climate.

Climate? The monsoon lasts, apparently, 10 months of the year. The mosquitos last 12. The fireflies are holding out strong also.

The solution is a permanent retreat—my novel, by the way, has the impermanent title of *A Foreign Retreat*—into *samathabhāvana* (calm concentration), which, in spite of all the nonsense I picked up in Calcutta, really works. That is, it's useful.

Yes, I've found my Guru: the Buddha. But I've also found a present-day Guru. Unfortunately, he's been dead for two years now. He was an English *Bhikkhu*[1] (Oxford, Intelligence W.W.2, etc.), who lived in the jungles south of here, and attained *sotāpatti* (stream-winner: one who has entered the stream leading to liberation; i.e. limited rebirths before attaining it). He left a manuscript, letters, notes in the margins of books he'd read, scraps of paper, etc.—all of which I've been collecting and compiling and which is proving to be a fantastic document. Without his papers I would still be quite lost, but with them as a guide I'm getting somewhere?

The novel? It's in the States now, being read by various people. I don't give a damn about it really—publishing that is—and am not making any effort at all. If others want to, that's their account. Since then I've written some pages on the theme of identity-searching, which I gave up as being poorly conceived. Also I've been doing some drawings, which are fun because I don't have any inclination to take them seriously. A few poems revolve in my head. Whatever I do is just for the doing of it now. If something were published it would be as pseudonymous as hell. Whatever solitude I've got (and it's gotten by meditation, not by running away), I'm not about to give up.

Give up? Rather, after having given up everything else, I've found that the vacuum created is peace. It cannot be given up, but only dispersed by not giving up other things—hell—you know all this anyway.

V.

* * *

7:30 PM—sitting on the cement meditation seat outside the <u>kuṭi</u> (very nice with a pillow), listening to the cicada concerts, and writing by the light of a candle balanced delicately inside a partly—burnt red paper lantern, while a

1. Ven. Ñāṇavīra Thera. ed.

faint drizzle taps on the corrugated iron roof so rapidly it is almost steady drone (a sort of audio version of a newspaper photo, which is comprised of individual dots). I record the following events of the day: dāna (food offering) was presented today by a very large group of villagers. I assume news of my presence has spread and was the immediate cause of the dāna, for everyone stared but none asked questions. They must have known a white monk—an American yet—was there, and just wanted to see for themselves. A pilgrimage, perhaps, to the zoo? (Do you have The Zoo Story, by Edward Albee, there?) At any rate, at 10:00 I went to the building by the entrance to the hermitage, covered in both shoulders, my bowl was taken from me and I was shown a seat. I sat and waited until 10:25, when two old monks came, whom I had seen before engaged in devotional flower arrangements and gossip —betel-nut mouth, teeth red and rotted and widely spaced— the sort of old men the village makes into monks and supports because they have a certain faith and are good for nothing else, yet must be supported anyway, using the Order as an old-age home. (It's also used as a reformatory, on the other end of the age scale.) Anyway, the three of us sat down, our bowls were returned filled with food, and one of the men, the one who seemed the brighter of the two, took a large alarm clock, placed it next to him, and waited until it was exactly 10:30, then he gave the Five Precepts to the villagers. Then he began to give a sermon interspersed with ritual chants, when the other old monk joined him. Absent from all of this was both Ven. Saranatissa and the young monk, whom I've only seen once. About 10:40 the handsome old rooster strutted in, picking up and setting down his legs in a military fashion even when standing still. He seemed to look over the crowd, found them uninteresting, pecked slightly without any real enthusiasm at the floor, and finally turned to face the three monks, myself included, sat down and listened. Very slight power of concentration. He quickly discovered that a vagrant flea had illegally taken residence in his feathers, and tried for some time to evict the wee fellow. Finally succeeded or gave up, sat down and closed his eyes. I too was unimpressed with the sermon. A fly was having a very intimate affair with my left eyeball, and simply would not be discouraged. At precisely 11:00 the sermon ended, we rose, took our bowls and left, the rooster close behind us

I know, of course, that when people hear that the Dhamma has spread so far and been accepted to the extent that an American should appear here in robes, it's good for increasing the faith, the devotion, their respect, and their donations to the arañña. And besides Ven. Saranatissa—who is a very good person—has probably not had an American here since 1950, when Dr. Hopkins was visiting (as a layman), 17 years back. I know, not only that the monks here don't often get as fine a meal as they did today (it approached Island Hermitage standards, though I'm perfectly content with the standards of yesterday's meal), but also that the people don't often have the occasion available to give it, and can therefore well appreciate the motives in using me for this purpose, even though I don't particularly like it, even find it detrimental to my efforts to practice the Buddha's Teaching. Well, it is detrimental, so I don't like it. Still, it must be tolerated. Nothing else seems to be expected of me.

But I didn't eat my meal sitting on a mossy rock by the bend of a shady jungle river with my feet in the water. I ate it in the company of the two old monks in a hot, unaesthetic, unfunctional building with flies, mosquitos, and discomfort, with farcical ritual in a village—priestly atmosphere. I prefer to be alone, and so to eat alone, but if I must eat with others, then let them be urban and urbane types—to whom I'm accustomed and can therefore ignore—rather than village monks with village manners. They were very nice, of course, and tried to be friendly, bustling about trying to arrange things the way they thought I'd like best, which was, of course, what I liked least, and plagued me with petty favors. Very trying, annoying, but the food, though terribly spicey, was edible, and I survived the experience and, perhaps, even learned from it.

* * *

...Yes, there is, it seems, a present you could send: some permanent dye. The bark dye is simply terrible. If I perspire—as one must in the tropics—the dye gets on me, runs into splotches on the robes, etc., looks bad and ruins the cloth as well. It washes half out in plain water, let alone soapy water. I'm enclosing a few threads. These are approximately the right color—even darker would not hurt. If you could send—using your experience as an artist—the right combination of dyes to match this color (approximately) it would be very welcome...

* * *

In the afternoon I went up to the cetiya on the hilltop and watched the clouds slowly gather in the east, until, forces mustered, they marched westward toward me and the sun, blurring distant details, and finally, victoriously, forced me to retreat back to the kuṭi at 5:00 in the face of a light rain, which continues even yet.

Before I went to the hill, while at the kuṭi, after dāna, I watched some men come with a very large box of little clay lamps which, it seems, they distributed at intervals along all the paths of the araññā, up to the cetiya itself. Behind them came a man with a 2-gallon tin of coconut oil; then a man with an infinite number of cloth wicks; then two fellows with matches, trying to light the lamps. It was a bright day. One of the last of the fellows, with matches, wore trousers rather than the native sarong, which means that he can speak English: anyone who could not speak English and yet put on airs by wearing trousers would be ridiculed. So I asked him if he spoke English. 'Yyyyyyyesss!' he replied, with a terrible nervous stutter, which I noticed was not present when he spoke to his companions in Sinhalese—and I asked what the purpose of the lamps might be. They were lighting them, he informed me, because his brother wanted to have a baby. Oh? And did they believe that by lighting coconut oil in a hermitage they would be helping his brother to give birth? Yyyyyesss! Indeed, native beliefs and customs do take some peculiar turns! But, it turned out, the lamps were not for the brother, but for the brother's wife who, it seem, has already just had a baby. This was a celebration. I gathered too, from other signs, that they wanted to thank Lord Buddha for having granted them—her—a son. This is, of course, completely contrary to the whole concept of the Buddha's Teaching: it is almost undisguised god-worship. Such things may well be expected from a generally uninformed laity, but it is not unreasonable to expect a Buddhist arañña to refrain from encouraging such mistaken ideas by the simple expedient of not participating in them, if, as it seems, preachings from 10:30-11:00 AM don't manage to get the message across.

* * *

...While it's true the snake doesn't ever win, it's *not* true that the mongoose never loses—sometimes they kill each other, in which case they both lose...

* * *

There are—at least—three mongooses here, and I must admit they are even cuter than those at Island Hermitage, though not at all tame. Other animals here: chipmunks (not at Island Hermitage) and king iguanas (lizards 6-8 feet long, with a long thin blue forked tongue that flicks out regularly like an automatic suspender—also found at Island Hermitage). Also an odd sort of gecko (small lizards about 6 inches full grown), puffy in parts, and skeletal in others—not at all like the sleek variety we enjoy at Island Hermitage—and seeming to be parodies of something, though I'm not sure of what.

* * *

Kierkegaard is a fascinating writer. One statement which I found very relevant is: 'Whatever is great in the sphere of the universally human must not be communicated as a subject for admiration, but as an ethical requirement.' Elsewhere he says: 'Precisely because the negative is present in existence and present everywhere (for existence is a constant process of becoming) it is necessary to become aware of its presence continuously, as the only safeguard against it. In relying upon a positive security the subject is merely deceived.' As far as I've gone in his Concluding Unscientific Postscript it seems, taking due account of his Christian background, to apply full face to Buddhism...

* * *

December 4—No crowd of dāyakas today. Took dāna at 10:30 from the building at the arañña entrance, where it's presented, and went to the mossy rock by the stream; sat beneath a low and shady branch—it is, however, a cloudy day and the branch was, therefore, no more than decorative—and, with my feet in the water, I ate my rice with a few not-too-highly-spiced vegetables. I suppose I was meant to go to the dining hall and eat with the others, where I would have been given fruits, curds, and the other necessities of the village monk's life—but I gladly exchanged them for the stream. So far no complaints.

* * *

...Your black and red letter arrived, delivered by our steward here (who looks like a stumble-bum anarchist), from a very foreign port, indeed. It has taken me some days to read it, as it takes me, of late, some days to do anything. Action involves anticipation (in three directions), removing presence from the present by means of the root addiction: to being (and, in the same sense, not-being). I'm still a junky—every drop of blood contains, in its very fluidity, addiction to change (which demands a background of sameness); every vein, in its solidity, contains addiction to sameness (which requires a background of change). Infinite hierarchies lurk everywhere: the world contains an infinite number of them, hierarchically structured. The world *is* an infinite number of structures of infinite structure. One learns to live every moment as arises, endures, and fades—each event an impossible surprise—which, as you well-put it, is a very simple, often tedious, moral exercise. When it's accomplished, it is accomplished alone, no matter how many (or few) other people are about; no matter how closely. Solitude cannot be shared. Immediacy is here-now, where there is only room for one, at most, and infinity, at least; *not ten*. Communion afterwards is shelter on a cold dark bough.

I have been very slowly dyeing my robes russet (the color of the *Vinaya*) with bark-dye, which has very weak adhesive powers. It gets on everything, and I sit on Sinhalese newspapers. Some arbitrary gust of wind—perhaps a passing poltergeist—dusted my empty bookshelf free of your letter, which took residence upon the news of the day, hiding, possibly as a legal notice, upon which I sat. Your letter is, consequently, black, red, and russet, and all crinkled up, and a bit more difficult to read than before. (The lines themselves are clear as Burl Ives—single spacing suits your style—but there is so little space between the lines that I can hardly make out what's going on there.) Your blessing is clear, however, and so that you need not retain dross (and lest I forget or run out [T̤35] of paper before another chance arises), you have my blessings—right now.

It is now six days since I have begun this letter. I stopped last time unable to decide upon the appropriate blessings, or on anything else, for that matter. Having nothing original and striking, I give you, simply: Blessings: of virtue, of vision, of wisdom of the Way. Of pleasure, joy in understanding of serenity in equanimity; of anticipation of the unsurpassable final extinction of delusion: of having done what is to be done, with no further task in sight.

Mahāyāna has it beauty. I don't deny it has its value. I don't deny it its truth. What I *do* deny is that it has the *same* truth, the *same* value, as that which is in the Pāli Vinaya and Sutta piṭākas (note that I make no reference to Theravādins, about whom most charges are valid). By putting Ven. Ñāṇatiloka Mahāthera into a tomb modeled after Lenin's tomb, one has not in any way created a dead red *bhikkhu* (though the effect, I admit, is rather disconcerting to the few who know). The Pāli is not, of course, an authoritative collection (but who is the authority?), but the Kanjur-Tanjur, in its all-inclusiveness, however authoritative, and historical it may be, is also: comic, in Kierkegaard's sense, and *precisely* absurd in Camus'. It may also be useful. If they have the Pāli canon and the Mahāyana; how do they reconcile them? They don't? Because mysticism (which they are) allows such incomprehensibilities? And even though the Pāli texts don't, there is still only a higher mystery? Fine—but where does it get you? I know where the absurdity lies for exactly the same reason as you know the absurdity of someone trying to unite, say, your novels with mine, or as Shostakovitch would if someone tried to unite his music with Ives (Charles not Burl): the public, the 'they', the observers who are not intimately involved with their being in and as their subject—those whose existence is considered as an objective object—the scientists and scholars, the hobbyists—can combine, mix, jumble, until they have a fantastic salad with an unbelievable dressing; but the concerned individual, who cares about his occupation with an infinite concern can never allow himself the sensuality of doing so, must always eat his carrots whole, raw, and unpeeled, and must rigorously discriminate and discard simply because it is concerned in and for his own immediate and subjective being. In a word: apply your experience with your novels to my position. You will immediately understand how it is both possible and necessary for you to appreciate and use each bit of Buddhism you discover that fits into the non-Buddhist 'thing' you are building; how it is both possible and necessary that I do likewise with all the non-Buddhist 'things' for the 'thing' I am building, but how we both must differentiate carefully, closely, and always to prevent our 'thing' from becoming, through osmosis, generalities, and no longer *ours*. 'Nuff.

I'm sorry/happy to hear that your/my rucksack has been lost by Qantas: may it long continue on its journeys, an itinerant container to the world.

I myself shall continue on my journey very shortly. After 9 months on the island, leaving it only under compulsion or need, I find that the foetus has grown nicely, but expect that birth will be easier outside, and therefore propose to leave, in a few weeks, for a few months, wandering on foot in jungles and finding, hopefully, a solitude without the many breaks required here. Perhaps it will be a stillbirth, or a monster. I suspect, however, that it will merely be a female receptacle which must also be impregnated and cared for nine months or so until... another hierarchy is born. Anyway, we shall see; we shall see...

By now a number more days have passed—I'm not even sure how many (but the moon was waxing when I began this letter, and now is waning)—and so unless I become inspired between now (evening) and tomorrow (when mail is posted), shall say no more.

Inspiration! *Mettā* (loving-kindness) is *the* popular way of signing letters, pretending to meditate on such, etc., and is very appealing to the slovenly positivistic commonsense common mind. The Buddha, however, has said that, of the four Brahma-viharas (Divine Abidings—of which *mettā* is the first), the last *upekkhā* (equanimity, onlooking) is the best. I agree, therefore, fully aware that *most* people would be grossly insulted at the idea, unable to comprehend the beauty and necessity of negative thinking, I shall limit application of this beautiful and necessary attribute, without which one can only half exist—I shall limit my use of it to those who fully exist.

With *upekkhā*,

Vināyadhāra

* * *

December 5—Rain most of the morning: if it's clear tomorrow I shall leave. It's too bad I came here first, for I rather suspect that this will turn out to be the best araññа of the trip. If it had been the last, I could stay on as I liked; but with the trip just begun, and with a definite goal and eventual purpose, lingering at this point seems slightly absurd, I may never arrive. At any rate, I can return here whenever I wish, for it will not be far from Island Hermitage. I shall go either North or South—I must get details from Ven. Saranatissa before deciding.

* * *

...I've been told now by several people that I reminded them of a character in a novel: Maugham's Razor's Edge. I don't know, as I haven't read it, but even if I had it would probably take me a book-length reply to qualify it, and even then it would be nothing more than a justification, which I don't need. To paraphrase T.S. Eliot, I must do what I must do and there's no doing anything about it...

* * *

2:30 PM—I shall probably go North. I have just learned, by the way that leeches, though perhaps rare, are to be found here; for I just removed one from my left calf. There is no pain involved in a leech bite at all: just disgust. Also the tiny wound bleeds for a long and messy time. Big dāna today, and the farce of 2 days ago repeated, with a few variations on its central theme. There are monkeys in the trees outside--I've seen three: two adults and one baby clinging to one of the adults, presumably female. Other monkeys are indicated by crashes, flashes, leaps, vague figures dark between dappled leafy shadows, barely seen or not seen at all. The strange thing, though, is that the presumptive female monkey is, or at least, seems as if, perhaps—well—to be wearing short trousers. Most peculiar.

* * *

...In order to develop proper meditation it's necessary to also develop *sīla*, a word loosely translated as virtue. It involves establishing a mental state of non-opposition, an accord, a state in which it is no longer possible for conflicts to arise which could hinder meditation. Both meditation and *sīla* are developed—one gets more and more proficient, one's activities and perceptions more and more refined. The use of money is, inevitably, a disrupting action, and this is why monks are not permitted to use it...

* * *

December 6 night—Left this morning beneath an uncertain sky. Ven. Saranatissa gave me a towel and some foil-wrapped aspirins (greatly prized here) and an invitation to return: very nice. I regretted not being able to give him anything; but all I could have given him was my old towel, which would hardly do. If and when I return I shall give him a tin of Nestomalt, which would always find a warm reception anywhere except at Island Hermitage's overstocked storeroom.

* * *

...Yes, the moon grows for 10 days. It waxes (and wanes) in 14 day periods—a full cycle is 28.5 days. In Ceylon rest-days (called *poya* days) are based on the moon—each full and new moon and the intervening quarter moons are as Sunday in the West. Pre-*poya* day ('Saturday') is a half day. Thus *poya* days are usually 7 days apart, but sometimes 8 (since the moon takes an extra half day per revolution). Since on full and new moons there are special observances, I always know the date in relation to the moon, but since I have no contact with the outside world (no newspapers, etc., or other distractions) I am not sure of the date. It's early April, I believe. I've left the Hermitage once since arriving. That was several evenings ago. There is a temple in the village and an old monk died, so we went to pay our respects. The cremation is in a few days and I'm curious how it will differ (not in effect) from what I witnessed at the burning ghats of Benares. (He was 80-some years old—monks seem to have long life-spans.)

* * *

Set off North. Udugama the day's goal. Alms fairly decent: rice cakes, stringhoppers (a kind of fried patty of rice spaghetti; tastey), bananas, a few curries, some bread, all topped off, at the very end, by a great glob each of honey and coconut oil poured liberally everywhere. Ate in comfort. The route was mostly uphill, past many rubber-tree estates, fewer tea-estates. Slight drizzle. Fifteen miles to Udugama village. The height of the hills was most unprepossessing and unimpressive until I'd climbed half a dozen of them, by which time they looked awe inspiring indeed. It began raining at 11:00 in earnest, and I took shelter a number of times for the next few hours beneath friendly roofs, where I was stoked with endless cups of tea. Finally only a mile and a half to go, I tried to make it, got absolutely soaked, and arrived at Udugama with a trail of dye dripping behind me. Hard day; great strain, tension; am staying the night in a small temple where one of the two resident monks is absent, none speak English, everyone is very friendly, and I am exhausted, sore, etc. Very nice building, but I don't feel up to going into details now. Mosquitos a nuisance.

* * *

...Essentially the Buddhist Order is supported just like any church, shul, etc.—by donations from the laity. Since monks don't (or, at least, ought not to) handle money there are a few differences. But the Hermitage is supported by a committee (in Colombo) which makes all the arrangements needed. They fix dates on which supporters (called *dāyakā*—*ā*=plural) can bring us a prepared meal—there is apparently something of a waiting list—and in addition provides salary for the servants, pays taxes, provides whatever else is needed—i.e. postage, fuel, books, etc. When a *dāna* (offered meal) is given—which tends to be an elaborate affair and, curiously, *always* includes a dish of curds and honey—often some small item will be given each monk—as, for example, a towel, a bar of soap, a spool of thread (pillows are an unexpectedly popular item), simple medicines, etc. (There are numerous restrictions on giving robes to individuals but none on giving to the Order so robes, along with other items, are given to the Order and when a monk needs something of this sort it is given to him from 'stock').

In addition to this if a layman wishes he may offer to support a monk individually—if a monk wishes to live in seclusion other than at a hermitage or meditation center he almost certainly needs this—as does Ñāṇasumāna, the other American monk, who lives alone in the jungle—and those monks who cater to the laity—i.e., who function as priests rather than as monks—often have such *dāyakā*, after some years. (I have two *dāyakā* myself—one in Calcutta and one in Ceylon—but that's only because of status involved in supporting a Western monk—native monks have a more difficult time of it.) Since monks are not allowed to ask for anything until they have been invited to do so (with the immediate family excepted) this system is necessary. So my simple needs are more than satisfied (if I sunk all the soap I've stored up into the lagoon the suds would clean out San Francisco bay)—with the exception of a few products not available here or many of inferior quality...

* * *

December 7, 5:00 PM—I left Udugama this morning, feeling much refreshed after a good night's rest, at about 7:00. My robes were almost dry, and quite a few shades lighter as well. (I prefer wearing the heavier robes while traveling, for they wear better and, being older, are both more dispensable and more comfortable, like shoes.) Actually the temple I stayed at rated another star—I was excellently received: the whole difficulty was my lousy attitude towards being 'wet, cold, and alone', but had I been more inclined to listen to advice (I was warned it would rain hard), it would not have happened. That, however, is past. Today it was a 9 mile walk from Udugama to Hiniduwa village along a road which gradually deteriorated as there came to be fewer estates, more hills, less people. A forest officer helped me greatly. Alms consisted largely of cakes, sweet rolls, and bananas; the sky consisted of fragments of sunshine mixed with fragments of misty rain: almost fine. The whole day can be described as fragmentary and almost.

* * *

## From the Wilderness: Peace

Having received your letter (on my birthday: a welcome stiff); having flown the coop the following day; having tramped along an erratic dotted line (on the edge of a 150 mile-long box of Ritz Crackers); having, after many unrefreshing pauses in as many empty shrines, perched myself atop Karmagala (a shrineless emptiness), the only nameworthy hill within a day's walk of here, I can now look down onto the sporadic dull green of the dry jungle, whose leaves lay about like forgotten dandruff, broken by a rare farmhouse and irregular fields where farmers tend scant paddy. Before me, a thin line beneath the sky: the sea, sharp and bright; behind me, a thin line above the land: the Upcountry peaks, vague and dark; both far away. Closer, suddener, birds dart about, catching the incessant wind in arrowed wings, disappearing like sparks; chimpanzees stare moodily, greedily, hoping for the remains of the rice I collect daily at the nearest village, a 40 minute trek away.

I live in a large cave—a gap, actually, formed by the imperfect juncture of two gargantuan boulders one atop the other. The entrance is puckered up, as if to kiss me, or perhaps devour me. The roof (which is 15 feet of solid rock) bears faint traces of an ancient artist: a hand is visible; other lines define nothing at all, for every rock, every tree, every day, every cloud, every thought, frog and accident occurs the same as every other.

Repetition is important, and must be understood. Nevertheless, because, atop the peak of Karmagala I can see too the peak of Kataragama, I think this; because it is December 31st, I write this.

Your letter was very poetic, very human, thoughtful, sane, and—essentially—mystical. This is fine for a writer, for a mystic. I must be now, as usual, mundane and dull enough to point out a mere fact. I hope this will not affect you, or even that you will find some way of transforming it into something better than the base metal of mere factuality.

*So loko so attā*: thus the Pāli says, time and time again: 'This, the world, is this, the self.' And so you, too, write: *'I am the universe.'* The difference being as follows: the Pāli ascribes the view to the *asutvā puthujjana*, the untaught commoner, who has not grasped the Dhamma. Then, invariably, the text goes on to record the attitude held by the *sutvā ariyasāvako*, the instructed disciple of the Noble One, which is: 'This is *not* mine, I am *not* this, this is *not* my self.'

This is a fundamental tenet of the Pāli teachings (and the *experience* of the *sutvā ariyasāvako*) and is a phrase which occurs hundreds of times in the texts. You will note that it is the exact opposite of your views, which is the view, by and large, of the Mahāyānists. Therefore one cannot-except by a prodigious effort of doublethink—hold to both the Pāli and the Mahāyāna texts. I do not suggest you do so, but rather that you have been either uninformed or misinformed as to the nature of the Pāli texts.

Beginning with the basic idea that we are, each of us, individuals, units, *one*, while our universe is infinite (the end is not to be found). The Mahāyānist takes the basic dilemma of the equation $1=\infty$ (which is the human condition) and tries to resolve it by squaring it, $1^2=\infty^2$. But this only raises the dilemma to a higher power. The Tantricist tries to multiply both sides by zero—a very illegitimate procedure—to prove, like some Hindus, that nothing *really* exists.

The Buddha does not alter either the 'one' or the 'infinity': His discovery was that the fault of the equation is not amenable to tinkering: it is the equal sign itself that is the mistake; it's the *relationship* which is false. Tantric merely denies our humanity (which all too obviously *does* exist); Mahāyana tries to raise it to a higher power; the Pāli shows us how to give up this too-cherished delusion. The aims are different; the means are different; the conceptions are different: the deception is the same: $1=\infty$, The equal sign means 'is', part of 'to be', and so the Pāli defines *nibbāna*, the 3rd Noble Truth, as *bhavanirodha*, cessation of being (being that delusion). Is that the same as what you tell me Nirvana is?

The following is from Kafka (a dialogue between two of his various selves):

'I've had some experience and I don't mean it as a joke when I tell you it is like being seasick on dry land. It is a condition in which you can't remember the real names of things and so in a great hurry you fling temporary names at them. A poplar tree in the field, which you called 'the tower of Babel', since you either didn't know or wouldn't know, that it was a poplar, stands wavering anonymously, again, and so you have to call it 'Noah in his cups'.'

Neither pain nor joy in themselves, can produce anything beyond themselves; but the two combined form the teaching experience; and the intensity of the pain (in a jugular vein), combined with the vast minuteness of the individual moments when a ray of light bounced right have taught me much—too much for the remaining sixth of this page, not enough for even a sentence. It is, I have learned from Jerry in The Zoo Story, necessary to go a long distance out of your way in order to come back a short distance correctly. There is an inherent honesty in the jungle—an honesty which is much more sudden than that of the desert—which is the only justification for its occasional luxuriance. Concomitant with our refusal to recognize this honesty is the attempt to relate ourselves to it. This is what is meant by the Parable of the Raft.

Tomorrow I shall leave here-traveling to a place two dozen miles off to the East, and shall post this on my way. Shall, surely, return to the island soon enough. I find that now I can live there: I can live anywhere.

Like the light shining through a hurricane lamp, we have to escape from within the structure: we have to get rid of what we think of as freedom in order to see the deception and to see that, for every existing individual, there is a way out...

* * *

About 11:00 AM I reached a little group of buildings, where there was a Mahā Bodhi Estate (125 acres of rubber trees). The Mahā Bodhi Society is the leading Buddhist missionary group in India and Europe (especially Germany), and was founded by a Ceylon 'hero', in co-operation with Col. Olcott, an American who came to Ceylon 80 years ago and did a lot of rehabilitation of Buddhism in Christian missionary-ized Ceylon. This estate belonged to the society (whose monks, by the way, are not only very worldly, but also very mercenary—at least those I've met). The manager (a layman, of course) had seen me walking when he passed me in a truck of goats, and apparently assumed I was going to his estate for dāna; so when I arrived I was led to the bungalow. I, of course, didn't know what was happening, but was more or less decided, after yesterday's mess, to 'follow advice'—and was given a seat. The grounds were beautiful and green with very steep jungle hills as backdrop and a rushing jungle river as sound effects: lovely. A huge bowl of rice was brought, along with curry sauces, but since I'd already had enough from alms for the day, I explained that I could not accept more without eating what I had, it would hardly be proper, etc., but took a few ceremonial spoonsful of the manager's offering. I ate my meal, but the manager seemed put off that I had allowed him to go to the trouble of preparing a meal for me and then refusing it. Of course, I had not 'allowed' it, for I had not known of it—but the whole incident seemed very Mahā Bodhi-ish. (I had some experience with them both as a layman and a monk in India): very well done, very nicely set up, etc., but very unwanted.

* * *

...The razor blades you sent are excellent (the local ones barely get through a shave before they're dull and corroded). We are required to shave at least once every two months (face *and* head), and that rule suits me fine. Mundane repetitive tasks have absolutely *no* interest for me, and never have. That includes shaving daily.

I'm quite certain that no amount of 'Jewish education' would have made a difference in my views. I can recall specifically not believing what little I was taught as I was taught it. I remember as a Safety Boy stationed at Joy and Wildemere, I was involved in an argument with Macey P. about God—I didn't believe then and I never have. Besides, the Buddha's Teaching is not religious—at least as religion is conceived in the West. The Teaching is basically instruction on the examination of the here-now (and is strongly opposed to *any* speculation, whereas a religion is in *essence* a speculation—you can never *really* be sure, as you can about your own immediate experience—I *know* I'm writing a letter, here and now). But—I'm not interested in criticizing other beliefs (and have much good to say about much of the Jewish tradition)—besides, you should see how Judaism is practiced in Israel—it might change your own opinions…

* * *

I went on to the village of Hiniduwa, where there was, I learned, a wedding. A number of pseudo-sophisticated government employees spoke to me. Also a man in yellow clothes who was both the ayruvedic (native) medicine pharmacist and the coroner. Well, if the first trade is unsuccessful, never mind; there is always another possibility. He seemed very wealthy and bejeweled. I was asked—it was about 1:00—if I would like a 'late lunch'. I was told it was the custom here: the place is, it seems, corrupt. There is a large and very well built Catholic church here as well—the first I've seen in Ceylon outside of Colombo—and Catholicism seemed to be thriving. No wonder. I was assured, of course, that there were 'only a few' Catholics: who, then, paid for the fine church? Rome? When the Buddha's Teaching is allowed to fall into corruption not only in its teaching of wisdom, not only in its teaching of mindfulness, but in the simple virtues of keeping a vow which one has voluntarily undertaken, then it is no wonder that another religion thrives. These people were terribly complacent, as well they might be, for they have no understanding of what the Buddha actually taught. They want the Dhamma on easy terms; but it cannot be had easily; so they accept what can be so had.

I refrained from commenting to them, of course: it would be of no use to tell them that they couldn't be Buddhists so easily, and besides, I am not a missionary nor am I fit to be a missionary; it's my general policy not to point out to people how complacent they are about such things

* * *

The rains, as I think I mentioned, occur at sunset, presumably due to the cooling air not being able to hold so much moisture. I'm told there is a 4-month rainy season as well beginning about June when it rains almost all the time. This is, after all, 'tropical rain forest'. Things not used get moldy, but that takes some time. Books, especially, deteriorate rapidly and become worm-eaten as well (wouldn't moth balls work?), and have to be rebound frequently. (The Hermitage has an excellent library.) The worst thing about the damp is that perspiration never evaporates. The best thing is that there is very little temperature change. Always between 65-85 (at the *extremes*)...

* * *

I finally reached a turn-off, where I had to take a foot-path to today's goal: Nugagala Araññа. The foot-path is not quite 3 miles: the trip takes—took—over 2 hours. It is the hardest path I have ever walked: up and over huge hills, with jungle closing in, over streams unbridged and leech-infested, higher and higher. I only barely made it—that's no exaggeration. Even when the arañña was, after a long long time, actually in sight, I still only barely found the last reserve of energy to struggle up a water-spill slippery rock and up steep stone steps to reach it—farther still

* * *

...Miles Davis once said, 'Man, if you don't *know* what jazz is, then no one can tell you'—meaning that jazz can only be understood as an experience. Not only does this also apply to the Buddha's Teaching, but to just about everything else as well. An experience can only be communicated to one who has had a similar experience—and the closer the experience the more meaningful the communication. Since the experience involved in practicing the Buddha's Teaching (which, by the way, is a very different thing from 'Buddhism') is foreign to the Western experience one shouldn't really expect a book on the subject to say much to one. Perhaps, though, it will give you an idea of what to look for in your own experience to find as analogous a situation to mine as is possible...

* * *

But here I am—and this place is real jungle Bridge on the River Kwai type: on one side a wall of solid green rises almost perpendicularly 60 feet; on the other side thick and impenetrable undergrowth has—if I may so put it—overgrown all, and only other huge jutting hills of solid green can be seen. The place looks like jungle, sounds like M-G-M jungle, and smells like jungle—damp, mosquito-ridden, absolutely uncivilized. The price to reach it is great—damned near fatal in fact—but it is—almost—worth it. Thank god the trip back's downhill

* * *

...There was a typhoon a few days ago, which was rather spectacular. The coconut palms were bent over at 45° angles, but they amazingly sprung back, none of them blown over, apparently...

* * *

The arañña is kept by an elderly monk and two novices. The elderly monk speaks English, which is a great relief (I was assured several times that he didn't), and made me quite welcome. One of the novices fanned me—presumably I was bordering on heat stroke. My robes were torn and soaked as if it had been raining. The other novice prepared a wonderful glass of orange juice. My guide, a villager, who was neither educated nor pseudo, seemed hardly fazed by the trip. The elderly monk has told me there are three elephants and a tiger hereabouts, but they have caused no trouble at all; so far, I assume; so far, this is in addition to the usual hazards. There are, on the other hand, no hazards from car accidents, lung cancer, etc., so it all balances out.

* * *

...Last full moon day was the anniversary of the birth/enlightenment/*parinibbāna* (i.e. bodily extinction—'death' is a term not applicable to one who has attained *nibbāna*, since upon the attainment there is no longer any 'self' to die) of the Buddha—the 2,511th according to the reckoning of some schools (though Western orientalists usually consider this as 56 years too early)—and there was, apparently, a lot of festivity on the mainland, judging by the distant noise. Here, though, there was no special group observance—only, for each a 'sane and happy' observance. There is no reason to celebrate the fact that we are getting farther and farther away from the Buddha's Teaching…

* * *

Night—this place smells like a huge greenhouse, slightly steamy, slightly moldy: decay is as evident as growth. There is one huge rock, about 50 feet high, and a 100 feet across, with one sheer face. Part of it overhangs, and beneath this overhang has been built a <u>dhammasala</u>—a preaching hall—and temple. The roof, then, and one wall are solid rock, and produce a solid and sonorous bass echo when <u>suttas</u>—discourses—are chanted. It is here that <u>pūja</u> is performed. This is a thing—the performance of <u>pūjas</u>—not done at Island Hermitage, so this evening I saw, and participated in, my first full-scale <u>pūja</u>. The word is derived from the Pāli verb <u>pūjeti</u>, to worship and consists of the recitation of <u>suttas</u>—which in itself is quite appropriate and salutary when performed for the purpose of reviewing the teachings—but, in a <u>pūja</u>, raised—or lowered—to the level of a sideshow, or ritual designed to satisfy the devotional needs of the laity. The <u>dāyakās</u> stay overnight it seems—I can't imagine anyone making the round trip in a day, carrying food, etc.—and this evening, for about two hours, there was this chanting, along with preaching and assorted gimmicks, all designed to make people think that they were actually <u>doing</u> something. What it is that they are doing is to make a mockery of the teachings: to think that in worship, and recitation they are doing enough, when they are, in fact, not doing what is required, which is the development of wisdom and mindfulness for the purpose of escape from the round of rebirths rather than they think, collecting merit for a better rebirth. I didn't recite the gibberish sections of the <u>pūja</u>, but my presence is evidently expected, and since there are two pūjas a day—at 4:00 AM and 6:00 PM, of two hours each, and perhaps a third one—I don't know yet—during the day—and since there will undoubtedly be a lot of other nonsense expected of me as well, all of which will make the serious and difficult task of meditation impossible—therefore my stay here will not be long. A shame, for the setting is fine, and if it were possible to actually be physically left alone, it would be a good place to practice solitude (which is a mental, not a physical, condition). I have been made very welcome, given a kuṭi to myself—absolutely necessary, of course—but only at the price of knowing that the two novices are sharing a room. They may not mind this, of course, but I am thus unavoidably imposing upon them, which gives them a right to impose upon me by expecting me to participate in their way of practicing the teachings which, right or wrong, is nevertheless not only not my way, but inimical to my way. Therefore, I can't stay long, and shall, as of now, plan to leave the day after tomorrow: to stay only long enough to see the full extent of their life here throughout one day, and to rest my feet and shoulders (which are sore from carrying my bag: a rucksack would be very easy, for I haven't much; but it seems it's not possible to use a rucksack with robes: it just wouldn't fit.)

Night sounds: insects and raindrops.

* * *

...Re your comment on the Kierkegaard quote: you seem to consider creative work as the important aspect of existing, and you say that 'the living part of it comes incidental'. This seems to be putting things backwards, since there can be no creative work without life. At any rate, *creative* work is not 'working for a living'. A salesman, for example, works for a living, but I don't think he could be said to be 'creating' anything—whatever other function he may have. If one *wishes* to create there is indeed satisfaction in its completion; but in the matter of getting a living there is no completion at all, for we have *always* to be getting a living—therefore the work of getting a living becomes a drudgery: something without end cannot have purpose, for the purpose is the end.

If there be a purpose to existence it must, of necessity, involve the ending of existence. (This does *not* mean 'annihilation'—there is, of both logical and evidential necessity, a state that does not *involve* existence—but it can only be understood, of course, by one who has attained it. (Just as the flavor of an orange can only be known by one who has tasted it. Though this does not mean that we can't know anything about the state—indeed quite a bit can be said about it, and especially how to attain it—but that is not the same as attaining it. The taste of an orange can also be well-described, but it's not the same as the taste itself.)

Another quote from K: 'The best proof for the wretchedness of existence is the proof that is derived from the contemplation of its glories.' A bit overdrawn, and written in a bitter moment, but the point is well-made. To wit, I haven't quit writing, but I am not close to finishing anything. This, however, does not mean that I am not creating: I'm creating within myself certain mental states and abilities which seem likely to become the most *useful* thing I have ever created: calmness, mindfulness, and a concentration which is directed and, thus, can be used as a powerful tool... K again: 'If I were to wish for anything, I should not wish for wealth and power, but for the passionate sense of the potential.'

* * *

December 8—rain last night: got up at daybreak, about 5:45. Dreamt I was being called at 4:00. Was the dream real? I don't know; but I certainly needed the sleep; no one said anything. There was a short worship at 7:30-8:00 this morning; otherwise I am left alone. I found a vantage point where I could look down into the valley, covered in steam this morning, which very slowly dispersed and reassembled above us, finally resulting in a slight misty rain. Finally the clouds moved out and new ones came in, at our level, and suddenly the whole place was enchanted: a silence descended, broken only by one song-bird, and outlines became indistinct, and everything not immediate seemed remote—all very fine. This place could be great; but it is merely comic: that people should expend such a great effort to build a place so far from everything, only to have flocks of dāyakās coming daily and overnight, with things so arranged that isolation is quite difficult and often impossible—that is comic, like one man digging a hole and another filling it up. Besides, except for the dhammasāla—which is the araññā's raison d'etre, the place, in comparison with the jungle it is within, must be termed squalid: mud rooms with corrugated tin roofs. Couldn't they use some of the trees to build a timber hut? Or would termites destroy it? There are some araññas, I hear, where the kuṭis themselves are caves, finished with wooden walls where there is no rock, or even stone walls. (Anuradhapura is constantly mentioned in this respect, and I shall have to visit it some day.) Upon reflection the place could only partially be termed squalid—there are some redeeming features as well. But it is the layout that is unfortunate: everything is too close together for a hermitage, and also there are no fine long paths to walk on. (Though I fully appreciate the difficulty of cutting a path through this jungle.) There is a walking area outside this kuṭi, a real requirement of any meditator—a long narrow prepared strip of land—but unfortunately the former occupant of the room has put a clothesline up over it so it can't be used. That shows the real purpose of this place more than anything: show. They must have a walking area, for it is a need of a meditator, but they don't go so far as to even pretend to use it, let alone actually do so.

Dāna was, of course, a farce, and not very pleasant—the surroundings that is—but I hardly expected anything else.

* * *

...I've just returned from flood-ridden Colombo to flood-struck Dodanduwa. The monsoon has begun. Colombo is under 2 or 3 inches but I was told that while I was gone the outlet from the lagoon to the Ocean here got blocked up with rubble, it rained for 4 days and nights, and the water rose 4 feet! It was necessary to swim between the two islands, since the foot-path was totally submerged. (Fortunately, the houses are all on high ground.) For meals the monks made do or did without. No reports of ducks in robes washed ashore...

* * *

December 10—Yesterday: I left Nugagala immediately after noon dāna, but not before I came face to face with a cobra. I was about to open a gate opening onto the porch of the kuṭi, when I saw it—black-grey, with indistinct white markings—coiled on the pillar right next to the gate, resting its head on the gate itself. It more or less ignored me for a while, then finally slid off the post to the porch floor, went once around the porch, out the partly-opened gate and away. All very polite, no threats, but not friendliness either. We both seemed perfectly willing to simply leave each other alone and this, from what I have been told, is the normal attitude of snakes, who will only bite if attacked (or if they think they will be attacked).

I was a bit sorry to leave, since the place was great: only the manager, so to speak, left something to be desired. Mahāthera—Ven. Sarānadoti (Sarāna, by the way, is Pāli for 'refuge'), who is a very active 72 years old, gave me an umbrella which I have since discovered to be a more useless item than I formerly thought, since it is awkward to carry about. But I could not refuse: he was scandalized to learn that I didn't have one, for in Ceylon one is hardly considered; a real monk without such props. Now I'm stuck with it, unless I can find a monk who will accept it—it would be improper to give it to a layman (it's yellow, considered a monk's color), and wrong to discard it.

I left with the dāyakās, taking a different route out, which brought me to the other side of the bend in the road through a much easier path, which gradually disintegrated from very fine jungle to jungle, then to scrub, and finally marsh through which we had to wade—very muddy. At last we came to a high ridge which looked down on the valley through which the road ran—splendid view—and then we descended to the valley floor, with its rice fields and civilization

* * *

...I left the island 2 weeks ago at 5:30 AM, arriving in Colombo by 8:30 AM. (On the return trip I left Colombo at 12:25 PM and arrived on the island at 6:00 PM *the following day—never* take a slow train in Ceylon. The distance, by the way, is 65 miles.) My passport was renewed promptly with no difficulty by a Mr. Rosenblatt, formerly of Haifa, with whom I had a pleasant chat on the subjects of Israel and cremation (a natural couple?). The visa is handled through the Ceylon Government and so that, of course, will take some months, in spite of the fact that it's only a renewal of a visa issued only 3 months ago...

'Working for a living cannot be the meaning of life, since it would be a contradiction to say that the perpetual production of the conditions of subsistence is an answer to the question about its significance, which, by the help of this, must be conditioned.'

(Kierkegaard, Either/Or)

* * *

I continued on my way, reaching the village of Opata about 4:00. Fantastic reception: everyone came to stare at me. But it was very friendly, and I have been told of some good jungle nearby. Also was told that there is not an arañña at Morawahea, where I had been heading in the belief that there was: change of plans, then; which makes my travels shorter by some days. Therefore I decided to stay the next day—today—here and look over the jungle, mostly because a friend at Island Hermitage is looking for a place to live alone, and this seems promising for him: good jungle, friendly people, not too big, the richest village in the area, etc. Some disadvantages discovered as well. But that's for Ñāṇasiha to decide; if he's interested. Spent the night at the local temple, which seems to have its share of corruptions of both practice—assuming there is any practice at all here—and 'doctrine', but not, apparently, more than its share. This part of Ceylon seems, in fact, rather benighted—possibly because of the many estates in foreign—i.e. English—hands, which take no interest in developing the area. Perhaps other reasons as well. I find the more important things that are happening now are internal, not external, and much more difficult to pin down. Entries will probably become shorter, but a summary of internal events at the end will be attempted

* * *

...The package has arrived in Colombo, and from the looks of things seems likely to remain there, I am now—as they say—'in communication with the Authorities', which is always a frustrating business. It is useless to use logic with them, since they follow only their regulations, which are not logical. Every time I'm forced to deal with the government I find myself more and more in agreement with Thoreau—not only his statement that that government is best which governs not at all, but also his remark that no person had ever caused him serious harm nor given him much difficulty, except those people who represented the State...

* * *

December 12—This record is becoming rather un-contemporaneous. I'll try to catch up. I spent a day at Opata, where there is some formidable jungle (lions, bears, tigers, etc., I'm told). There are some caves, I was informed, half a mile into the jungle, but it takes over 2 hours to reach them. This sounds like formidable jungle, indeed. There was a pleasant fast river where I spent the afternoon, and the evening I spent talking with the villagers, most of whom are very ignorant, but not at all stupid—their questions were on a very basic level and showed only the slightest acquaintance with the Dhamma, but the questions had the incomparable advantage of being relevant to their own lives. Unfortunately, they have not, and will not, receive the proper guidance from the resident monks, who seem uninterested in anything but their own finances. Still, it is a promising location for one who wants to live alone in the jungle, the main doubt being whether support would continue on a permanent basis, which would depend largely, but not entirely, on the monk

* * *

...Well, the package finally got here, complete with all items, which is more than I expected. That, however, is probably why it did happen. The mantel bread was very good and enjoyed by all. The Mahā Thera enjoyed it also (Mahā Thera means, literally, 'Great Elder' and is a term properly used toward any monk with 20 years or more standing from his higher ordination. In common usage, however, it refers to the chief resident monk—the 'abbot'. In fact, there are two 'Mahā Theras' here, but only one of them is referred to as '*the* Mahā Thera'. The other one is known as the 'crazy monk', because he is insane.) I've now read the Razor's Edge, and think it worth the reading, though there is a lot wrong with it. (Esthetically and structurally, I mean—to hope for philosophical accuracy or relevance from Maugham would be absurd.) It mentions, at the end, that Larry's book consists of essays about the same length as Lytton Strachey's Eminent Victorians. By one of those odd coincidences, Eminent Victorians was the book I read immediately before reading the Maugham, and I found it to be one of the most enjoyable and best written I've read in a long time. It obviously has nothing to do with the Buddha's Teaching, so I can safely recommend it to you without fear of being considered a 'missionary'...

* * *

Leaving Opata yesterday morning I walked as far as 3 miles north of Akuressa where, I discovered, there is a temple-school where I spent the night. The village is very pleasant, well laid-out fields, seems thriving. The temple is several hundred years old. The monks here function as teachers. There was a broad muddy river where I had a pleasant bath—the color of the river seems to have no relationship to its ability to cleanse—and spoke to the Pandit Thera (Pandit = teacher; Pandit Thera is, in this case, the Principal), who acted like a schoolmaster and always kept a large wad of betel nut and leaf in his mouth. They had a library which included books donated by the Asia Foundation, including a selection of Dr. Seuss books (which are great), college English books, and the 10 volume Grolier set of Science Books, of which he was especially proud.

I was well received, of course, and the quietness of the place was stressed. Unfortunately, a little while later a generator was turned on to provide electricity for the lights—a feature which they thought more highly of than I did—and it rained well into the night. Mosquitos were bad—slept poorly because of them. I had to share a room, and the roommate was a monk who had no business at all being a monk--a teacher who earned a salary and conducted himself in all ways like a layman. He was, in fact, a layman in monk's robes, and, though he taught Dhamma, he had no understanding of its purpose. The laity are taught Dhamma here like children are taught maths in the States—as a mere collection of data having no relationship at all to their lives. I discovered this both in talking to the 'monk'-teacher and in talking with one of the school's products, a fellow who simply did not understand that the Dhamma was something to be used. Here there was almost no attempt at even maintaining the Discipline (Vinaya) of the Buddha, let alone the teachings. (The araññas, at least, do maintain the Vinaya.) They wanted me to stay longer, but not even Dr. Seuss could induce me to remain in that farce—and worse than farce, it totally misleads any who might otherwise find the Dhamma of use. I learned, also, that there is an official Government exam which all children must pass—an exam on Buddhism—to graduate. By reducing the Dhamma to the level where a child can understand it well enough to pass an exam they distort the teachings so that it simply no longer has anything to do with reality. The whole thing would be comic if it wasn't so sad. The temple contained Hindu gods. When asked the Pandit Thera seemed embarrassed—he knew, of course, that it was a very misleading thing—but excused himself on the grounds that the 'laymen want it'. This place is, then, a Business with a Product (Buddhism), which they Sell, and for as great a Profit as possible. They are the worst sort of leeches I've yet discovered

* * *

...Last full moon day marked the start of Vas, which is the three month rainy-season retreat, during which time all monks with higher ordination must stay within one residence. (They may go out during the day, of course, as many of them must to collect alms-food, etc., but they must spend the night in the same residence. Thus *carika*—wandering—is limited to nine months of the year. Not having taken my higher ordination this rule does not apply to me, and I am free to come and go as I please—though it's not likely at any rate that I shall leave the Hermitage at all during this time. The Vas is calculated, somewhat illogically, according to the rainy season of the Ganges River area, where the Buddha lived, rather than adjusted to local conditions. This Vas there are 8 monks in residence here—4 Sinhalese (3 of them *bhikkhus*—i.e, having received higher ordination), 3 Germans (2 of them *bhikkhus*; 1 of them a *thera*—with 10 or mere Vas seasons since receiving higher ordination), and myself. The Yugoslav is spending Vas at Bandarawela.

The weather here the last week certainly went along—rain most of the day, and at night so cold a blanket is necessary. This part of Ceylon—that is, about a 30 square mile area—has the reputation of having the worst weather in the country, and I believe it…

* * *

Today I set out about 7:00 AM, and reached Akuressa, after a brief encounter with a small—18 inches—yellow-brown snake with squarish black markings, about as thick as my thumb. It was crossing the road as I approached; but a truck was also approaching and I tried to shoo the snake off the road before it got run over. The tires missed it by no more than an inch, and it quickly dove (?) onto a pile of stones. It turned out to be a very deadly sort and all, but I stood a while watching it, and it made no attempt to harm, or even threaten me. I am becoming more and more convinced that snakes are really very polite and don't deserve at all their bad reputation.

Akuressa does deserve a bad reputation: how can people actually desire to live amidst all the filth, noise and general unpleasantness of a town? Alms was peculiar: lots of buttered toast. Yesterday there was a glut of honey rolls. Tastes change. Few hills now, much more rice paddy fields. I was refused alms more times today than all the other days of the journey combined: don't know why, but I suspect it's just the general ignorance of the laity combined with their growing disrespect for monks through seeing un-monkish behavior in their local village priests. Difficult road: feet sore. It began to rain about 1:30, which was welcome, since the asphalt tends to get a bit sticky on bare feet about then, and the rain cooled it off. The umbrella, it seems, has a use after all. (Its main use is as a sunshade, but I have excellent tolerance of the sun-even at Bin Gedi I never wore a cap in the fields—and don't really need it for that.)

Finally reached the turnoff for Dediyagala Araññа—where I am now—about 2:30, where I met a monk who was properly dressed: the first one I've seen properly dressed since leaving Nugagala. Stopped to rest a minute, given a cup of tea (usual), and asked questions (usual) by someone whose English was rather curious and uncertain (usual). Finally at the end of his questions, the fellow said (uncertain of his grammar): 'Am I off? Am I off?' 'I don't know,' I replied. 'Are you off?' He hesitated a moment, then said, 'I am off. I am off.' I agreed. He was off. I, too, was off, down the cart track, which passed through a very long stretch of rubber-tree estate—rubber trees, en masse, are a pleasant sight, reflecting the usual muted and subtle beauty of Ceylon. Guideless, I continued, into rice land, brush, and finally jungle. At about 4:00, getting tired, having been alone in the jungle for some time, I heard, about 20 feet from me, and very unmistakably, a deep, long growl. Then silence. Then rustling, and I saw dark vague movements. Silence. I didn't know whether to stand or run, so I 'just kept walking', slightly—very—nervous, and thought of the tiger at Nugagala, the lions and bears at Opata. The sounds became more distant; I never found out what had caused the noise, but I was attacked by nothing more than the usual number of leeches. I must retract my statement, by the way, that leech bites do not hurt. There are, I have discovered, different varieties.

Finally, just when I was wondering whether I was lost, and perhaps on the wrong path—about 4:30—I arrived at the araññа. The place seems quiet—it's certainly remote—but the jungle doesn't really compare (from the little I've seen) with the jungle of Nugagala. There are at present only 3 novices—the other resident(s) being away for an uncertain time—none of whom speak English. Two are young and one is closer to my age. This, more or less, and rather absurdly, puts me 'in charge' of them, I being the eldest, until the other(s)—which will be (include) their teacher—return(s). These 3 seem very well trained, with excellent manners and monk-like conduct, following the Discipline closely. Very good. I have been put in a kuṭi—a nice one—where I am alone, but only, apparently, because the resident is absent. There was a pūja this evening, but a reasonable one, with no lay folks about, a minimum of fuss, emphasis on meaning, and not absurdly repetitious and drawn-out. The place seems spacious, clean, well laid-out. Two questions remain: (1) How much is expected of me in the way of group participation? (the less the better), and (2) How long will I have the aloneness of a room to myself? (sharing will oblige me to leave). We shall see.

* * *

...I've learned that the outlet from the lagoon to the sea is normally kept closed, for apparently inexplicable reasons, which explains why the level of the lagoon fluctuates so oddly. It seems that when it reaches flood level and becomes necessary to wade from one island to the other they finally open the channel and the water level drops 3 or 4 feet in one day...

* * *

December 13—night. Not much night-jazz here, but lots of fireflies: medium jungle, I suppose. Mosquitos are medium also, but there's something yet undetected that raises quite a bothersome welt. This evening a monk showed up—it turned out to be the properly dressed monk I had seen yesterday. I don't know why I didn't realize yesterday that he was from the hermitage—I wasn't sure, when I saw him whether I was even close to the hermitage yet. Any way, that accounts for his proper conduct, and since he is a bhikkhu his presence relieves me of my unwanted leadership.

It was difficult at dāna, for example, to initiate all procedures when the procedures here differ from those of other places. (Every place has its own way of doing certain things.) I gathered, from a very fragmentary conversation in Pāli, that there are 5 novices and 2 bhikkhus regularly here. One more novice appeared mysteriously this morning, leaving 2 still absent—a novice and a bhikkhu.

I gathered also that Ñāṇasiha is expected here on the 17th. Very mysterious: they seem to know all about Ñāṇasiha, who is one of the German monks, a very nice person, and informed me that he was in Colombo, and had taken his higher ordination at Anuradhapura in June, etc.; whereas the Ñāṇasiha I know was last at a hermitage and has never taken his higher ordination at all. Yet they say he is a German; there could not possibly be 2 German monks in Ceylon with the same name, yet they were quite certain of their facts; very peculiar. I am very much inclined to remain here until the 17th, not only to meet Ñāṇasiha, but to find out just who they were referring to, and if their information is correct. It hardly seems possible, since I had a long talk with him just last month about taking higher ordination. Another reason for remaining is that this is a very nice place.

I haven't explored yet—the day was spent in meditation—but there is a fine stream where I bathed, and everyone conducts himself pleasingly, and also I am left alone in a pleasant kuṭi. (The roof, by the way, is tiles; the ceiling is old robes tacked onto the rafters: unusual, but not ugly.) The discipline here is generally good—a few lapses and actions contrary to what is set forth; it seems, though, to be based on a different attitude than at Island Hermitage. At Island Hermitage there is, I think, a sort of grim determination to keep the rules, whereas here they are used as a pleasant aid: actually far preferable than at Island Hermitage.

I have been expected to participate only in evening chanting, which is simple and honest, and therefore quite nice, lacking the razzamatazz of Nugagala and the formality of Island Hermitage both—though there are pictures of Hindu gods next to the Buddha image, it's not too important, for everything is too casual for importance to enter, and a relaxing congeniality is the attitude of the chanting.

The place is, then, very pleasing, with only a few objections. No one here goes any further than the discipline into the practice of meditation, but that could hardly be expected of the younger novices, and the older one and the bhikkhu only could be expected to practice: perhaps they will develop a practice someday. Late now: to sleep

* * *

...I receive no periodicals or papers here, but I was told, via letters from Europe, of the Arab-Israeli war. I suppose, too, I'll hear about it if either pushes the other into the sea. As for books, there is a library here, but almost all the books, save the Pāli texts, are totally useless (including most of the commentaries on the Pāli texts). They were all contributed free, of course, and by people who had, apparently, vested interests in the books they gave—a large share of the books are about flying yogis and such things, whereas I'm interested in learning to walk...

The riots in Detroit, from your description, sound as bad as the Watts riots in L.A. I can't say it surprises me—though one might have hoped that with a liberal council it could have been avoided. Or is the government no longer liberal? Maybe riots don't know the difference?...

* * *

December 14—Explorations: there is one easy path leading into the arañña, about 3 miles from the village, as I discovered when I came here; the place has only 4 kuṭis, but only 2 of them are in use (and I'm using one of those two); the sāmaṇeras sleep in an addition beside the dining hall, en masse. They study, but the bhikkhu, who is a friendly person, practices meditation (though, I suspect, not very seriously), besides teaching the novices (sāmaṇeras). He has been a bhikkhu only 2 years: ordination must come from a monk of at least 10 years standing. I have learned that this monk, of 11 years standing, who is the formal teacher lives at another arañña and comes here only once a year—a peculiar situation, and not very proper; this may account for the lack of buildings and endowments here.

There is also a temple room with a Buddha statue, an open-roofed area (commonly found in village temples, but the first I've seen in an arañña) and a small, young branch of the Bodhi tree growing near it. (The Bodhi tree is the tree the Buddha sat under when he attained enlightenment at Bodh Gaya, India. The southern branch of it was brought to Ceylon in the 3rd century B.C. and still grows at Anuradhapura—2300 years old, the oldest tree existing. Branches of the Anuradhapura tree are found in a number of places in Ceylon. 'Bodhi' means 'enlightenment'. The tree is of the species ficus religiosa.) One kuṭi has a huge rock as its back wall and is therefore very cool, but it is beginning to fall apart—the kuṭi, not the rock.

There are no paths within the araññā except leading to the few buildings: an uncared for path leads out the back, which I followed for ½ miles without reaching its end: perhaps it leads to a village somewhere; it's leech-infested and unused.

This evening another monk of one year's standing showed up. No one speak English.

There is, in addition to evening worship, also morning worship; about 6:00 AM, which is done in silence—how less razzmatazzy can it be?—which is also congenial and relaxed. The great advantage of the araññā is that it exists for as much the residents as for the lay supporters, but, since it lacks the benefit of a number of Western (white) monks as an attraction, it is not, apparently, well supported, or perhaps the austerity is intentional.

Dāna today was brought by dāyakās, but even so was not anything like what is found elsewhere. Curds and honey, yes, but small portions, and nothing that would be considered a luxury food, though, of course, sufficient: that's fine with me. My concern is only if it's healthy. Lots of unhealthy spices, but much better than the doughy meals I collect on alms when wandering. I was given some vitamin tablets—B complex and C—a few days before leaving Island Hermitage, and I take those daily. There is a month's supply of C's and 3 months of B-complex. The dividing line in food between luxury and non-luxury, by the way, seems to be Nestomalt, a malt-flavored powder which is offered in preference even to milk. There is none here: Island Hermitage has tons of the stuff, which has a sort of butterscotchy flavor. (Island Hermitage also has tinned cheese and other fancy foods in abundance.) A piece of coconut at the end of the meal is quite effective, by the way, in toning down the spice-burn of the food; lemon juice, if available, put on the food, will remove much of the curry-flavor and hot-chile-pepper taste, as well.

I also learned that leeches hate soap: the best way to remove them, once they've taken firm hold, is to work a sliver of soap under them; they will let go quickly. Well soaped legs will not pick up any.

The robes I wear while walking have become a very dark brown. This is odd. Perhaps perspiration reacts with the dye to produce the darkness. I suspect salt also works. They are darker where I sweat most and lightest where they are least in contact with me...

* * *

...Went to the dentist last week. He is in Galle, the nearest town, 9 miles south (an hour's traveling time), and he found that the filling that had been put in my lower right wisdom tooth (at Ein Gedi) had come out and the tooth was decayed beyond saving. It was extracted efficiently—far better than the butcher job that was done on the other wisdom tooth at Beit Oren—and no other work at all was needed. So in the last four years, except for the loss of the two right wisdom teeth (a loss of negligible value), I've had, I think, only one filling—a quite satisfactory record...

* * *

Last night, about 1:00, I awoke with a start when I realized something was nibbling my big toe on my left foot. I gave an involuntary kick, sat up, lighted the lamp, but saw nothing. My toe had a small piece of skin taken out of it, which I treated with antiseptic and went to sleep again. I was woken several more times by rustling sounds, movements, and finally lighted a candle. This was sufficient to keep the pitter-patter away from me, but I was too awake to get to sleep again. Slept several hours this afternoon as a result. I have no idea what it was. There is a kind of red and black striped cockroach which bites; perhaps a mouse. Do any kinds of lizards bite? I hope not, for I've always liked lizards and welcomed them into the room, since they eat mosquitos. I don't wish the mosquitos harm (though I do wish they would leave me alone); but if a lizard must eat them, he may as well eat the ones that would otherwise eat me. It would be unfortunate to learn that the lizard, too, will eat me. There would not be much hope left. Perhaps I will keep a pet frog

* * *

As for insects, the main insects at the Hermitage are ants (which get into everything and some of which bite something fierce, but otherwise are no problem), fireflies (which I like), and mosquitos (which I don't like—but we have screens on the windows, and any way the bite of the local variety does not produce a very long-lasting itch). There are almost no flies at all, though there are millions of them just across the lagoon. Perhaps flies are attracted to society. There are lots of spiders, but most of them are small and harmless. Termites produce construction problems, but otherwise are no bother. I had some once, going along the edge of the floor, but I sealed off their entrance with wax. The biggest animal problem is the dogs, who are totally untrained, extremely friendly (particularly when they are muddy), and fond of baying all night at the moon and howling at fishermen who come close to the island…

* * *

I have solved, I think, the mystery of a peculiar heehaw sound prevalent in the jungles. I didn't think donkeys lived hereabouts. Now I think the sound is that of hyenas. I've never heard one myself; but it's similar to descriptions I've heard of. But are there hyenas in Ceylon?

* * *

…As for music—yes, I sometimes miss it, but of course, one can't have everything (anything?). It may be of interest to you, by the way, that one of the more important reasons that led to my taking robes was my reaction to hearing a performance of the Detroit Symphony Orchestra, conducted by Walter Poole, playing Shostakovitch's Symphony #5. I didn't know its significance at the time, but the memory of it has never left me… As for your offer of insect spray—well… I have vows, both public and private, and in some ways of many years standing, against killing—and yes, included are insects as part of the monastic vows…

* * *

> December 15—There is a chameleon here that looks like a miniature pterodactyl: spiny-ridged back, fish face, pouch beneath its jaw, long tail. It's possible to get very close—2 or 3 inches—to its face before it moves, and I have grabbed hold of its tail. I have seen it exhibit the following colors: green (dominant body color); red (on its face when I get close with my robes); powder blue (only under its eyes, on a very scaly skin), yellow, brown, black, grey, orange, and white! Amazing creature!

* * *

I have spent several days in the hospital in Galle with a pain in my right side which the doctors said was probably an infection of either the kidneys or the urinary tract. I had been advised to go to the hospital in Colombo, but did not want to travel so far. After my stay in Galle (6 miles to the east), I see why the advice was good: facilities in Galle were so wretched that all the extra help and favoritism I was given did not compensate, and I returned to the Island several days ago with a severe cold and a slight fever—though apparently my kidney is now all right. Am taking aspirin, enteroviaform, cold tablets, and a native medicine which is rubbed on the skull (and which seems to be very effective against colds, headaches, and mosquito bites). Also drinking lots of orange juice. The oranges in Asia, by the way, are green, not orange, except when they are green, at which time they are yellow; and are very acid and require lots of sugar to be palatable.

I've been thinking for some time about taking my higher ordination, and, while I'm not decided that I'm fully prepared for it—there are a few difficulties in the way—I would like to be as prepared as possible. One of the requirements for the ordination is to have the permission of one's parents, and so I would like you to give me your permission so that that can be settled before proceeding further. Note that I do not require, nor do I ask for, your approval—that is hardly to be expected—but only your permission. (If you don't want to give me your permission then, of course, I will be obliged to continue with only my lower ordination, which may, eventually, make progress more difficult for me, but will not prevent me from progressing.)

Thinking back, it seems October is hospital month for me, isn't it? Last year it was hepatitis, before that Israel, before that Beirut. Oh well—finished for this year, at any rate…

* * *

December 20—On the 18th—my 'anniversary' in robes—the clouds gathered in the early afternoon, forcing the air downwards, heavily, and drowsily everyone weakened and at last fell asleep under the weight of the air mass. 3:00 I was wakened by knocks on the <u>kuṭi</u> door and told to look at the river. This river had been a refuge from the heat: running rapidly between rocks, clear and brilliant, it slipped between giant boulders into a smooth area of 50 yards, deep enough for swimming, shallow enough for bathing, reached by a flight of stone steps, before running into more rocks, and continuing its journey to the Indian Ocean amidst foam and splashes. Such had been this fine jungle river. Now, though, it was raining: air, its pressure released, rushed upwards, and water, replacing it, poured down, and the river was no longer a mountain stream but a muddy Mississippi; dangerous and rolling steeply above hidden dangers: it was about 20 feet above its normal level (of about 3 feet), wide and brown, and struggling to contain itself as more water poured down. The bridge going across the river, leading to the village—this bridge, which had formerly been a dozen feet above water—this bridge was nowhere to be seen, and we were stranded. It was reminiscent of the Deluge of Ein Gedi. Reminiscent only, however, and not climactic: after a few hours the rain stopped, the level dropped, the bridge, and other familiar landmarks reappeared, none the worse for the torrents—which may be common for all I know—and all was normal...

* * *

... 'It rained, and it rained, and it *rained*. Christopher Robin had never *seen* so much rain!' It's been raining very heavily, due to the N.E. monsoon (the S.W. monsoon being over), for the last 4 days (and nights too—only 36 more to go). The level of the lagoon waters rose and rose, and then the man in charge of the floodgates opened them up and the water ran out to the sea. It's a good thing he hasn't fallen asleep on the job, or we would have been washed away long ago. I don't actually understand the purpose of the floodgate which closes the channel leading to the sea. I had always thought a floodgate was something on a dam to *prevent* floods. The gate here, however, seems to serve the sole purpose of *causing* floods, and it is only when it's removed (or raised) that the danger, as well as the waters, subside, I recall Ray Bradbury's science-fiction novel, Fahrenheit 451 (471? 457?) in which firemen no longer serve the function of *putting out* fires, but of *starting* them, and the analogy has certain aspects which are quite alarming.

Something else I don't understand is why the lagoon is salty. (I know why the *sea* is salty, of course—many many years ago I was informed that it was due to a magic salt box at the bottom which continues turning out the stuff—but the *lagoon*?) The only source of water to the lagoon, as far as I can tell, is rain water. (There might be a small river on the other side, but that water would also be fresh.) And each time the floodgates are providentially raised, salt water runs out to the sea. Therefore the lagoon should become perpetually less salty. But it doesn't. Perhaps some engineer or divinity student can explain this...

* * *

Ñāṇasiha has not appeared; it seems, though, that he is not the one I know; for I have learned—possibly correctly—that there is a word in Sinhale which sounds like the word 'German' and has some possibly relevant meaning, but that the Ñāṇasiha whose arrival is imminent is not of German nationality: the one I know has lived for some years in a cave at a place called Wirawila; the one I don't know comes, apparently, not from Wirawila but from Witunawila which it turns out, is the headquarters of the leader of the sect to which this araññā belongs—it is the largest, by far, of the 3 sects in Ceylon, and also—except for the araññas, I suppose, it is the most lax, by far, in practice and discipline, disgustingly so, in fact: most of its monks are only laymen in monk robes...

* * *

... Yesterday I was presented with a copy of Heidegger's *Being and Time*—quite unexpected, unasked for, and extremely welcome—of all books, if I were given one choice presently, I probably would have picked that one as the most wanted. One of the local *dāyakas* gave it—wonder how he knew how to pick it?...

* * *

I had already planned to leave on the 19th, and to announce my plan. The day was hot and bright after yesterday's floods; the river is still a few inches above its normal level, however, and I left amidst a great deal of mud, my bags heavier by a flashlight and 2 spare batteries given to me at Dedivangala where I preferred to use candles, I have a flashlight which I purposely left at Island Hermitage, but I know by now that a gift, once offered, cannot be refused—it is just not possible, nor polite either (for refusal deprives the giver of the merit gained by giving). I have also learned that what I don't have I don't need: but if something is offered me, it will then become necessary—as with the umbrella, which in yesterday's heat was an indispensable sunshade (except in villages, where it cannot be used)—so I suppose the flashlight will be useful—was, in fact, useful that very night—i.e. yesterday, the 19th...

* * *

... As for mosquitos I have developed, and continue to develop, a product which is far superior, in terms of reducing their annoyance, than anything found in a can, bottle, or tube. It is useful, in fact, for every ailment known to man and beast. Unfortunately it can neither be sold nor given away (though it can be acquired), nor packaged and shipped anywhere (which is a pity, because there are many places that could use a great deal of it). Manufacture takes a long time, and individual needs require slight variations in the formula, though the basic ingredients are actually quite well known, even if their occurrence is not all that common. The name of the product is equanimity, and it is quite pleasant to make it as well as use it...

* * *

I returned to Akuressa—9 miles—along the same road of dull-witted villages, where I learned, after seeing the dead and bloody bodies of dogs lying by the road, that the government actually pays a man or men to go about shooting the animals—anti-rabies, I am told (they could justify shooting people on the same grounds)—and this from a government which styles itself 'Buddhist'—see the very first of the five precepts incumbent upon all who wish to style themselves as Buddhists, against the taking of life—and the villagers do themselves no good by permitting or even, perhaps, co-operating with such a project, which is carried out against dogs who are invariably timid—they are unbelievably mal-treated, quite causelessly as I have seen myself on many occasions—and finally I reached Akuressa, where I was summoned to the cop shop.

The top cop wanted to see me out of curiosity, apparently, not suspicion—though he did mention that there had been 2 murders in the last week I was not asked to account for my whereabouts. Then one of his other curious visitors lashed into an attack on the poor behavior of Ceylon's monks, as if he were giving me information I did not already have. I smiled to myself and continued on

* * *

... Now that the Vas—'rainy season retreat'—has ended, we move on to the '*kaṭhina* season'—*kaṭhina* being a special temporary relaxation of certain monastic rules concerning robes, which privilege is one of the benefits obtained by observing the Vas season. Traditionally it is, therefore, the time (for the laity) of giving—and (for the monks) of receiving-robes, and a ceremony—the *Kaṭhina pinkama*—is held.

The whole thing dates back to the days of the Buddha, when, of course, the ceremony served a definite purpose; at the end of the monsoon robes were frequently in bad condition, and a temporary relaxation of certain rules regarding them was something of practical importance. Gradually as the Sangha (the Order of monks) deteriorated—it reached its lowest point in India just before its virtual demise there in the 9th century A.D.—the ceremony became one of obtaining possessions, and the laity were encouraged to give for the sake of merit, thus taking a giant step towards the vulgarization of the Buddha's Teaching.

By now, except in a very few places which uphold the tradition, the whole thing has degenerated into a season of preaching and palaver, gobble and grab (they expect to be both fed *and* clothed in the best of style—although most of them don't even have an almsbowl, let alone use it)—and 95% of them don't observe the Vas anyway (though that is hardly the greatest of their faults).

I was able to get a glimpse of what goes on—shocking, indeed! tut! tut!, etc.—when five of us from the Island attended one of these affairs in the village of one of our (generous) supporters (he wanted to show the folks that there were many foreign monks, for there was not only myself and two of the German monks, but also—from other parts of Ceylon—Thai, Laotian, Burmese, and Vietnamese monks as well) who lives about 30 miles to the South and 20 more inland—the first time, incidentally, that I've been more than one mile from the ocean since arriving in Ceylon last January.

It was an affair meant, of course, for the local monks and laity and was geared to their level; and since the laity insist upon not only changing the Dhamma into a mystical—and therefore useless but emotional—doctrine but also in converting the monks into priests—and the difference is great—naturally this level was very low indeed—I expected as much but was nevertheless unprepared for what I saw, which could best be described as a cross between a camp-town meeting of Holy Rollers and a small-time carnival—yes, even with blinking lights! Amazing. The ceremony—which lasts for three days in that part of the country (we didn't attend the whole thing)—was, of course, a farce, except for the preacher who sounded like Sinhalese hell-fire and damnation but, as I later learned, was actually whipping the emotional pitch of the laity into a frenzy—very successfully too—of generosity. But enough. One word alone is too many, but volumes are not sufficient, to describe it all.

The day of the ceremony at the Island a great many lay people came—it's a day reserved for our principal supporters only—along with their families of course—and the parents, uncles, friends, business associates, idle curiosity seekers passersby and those who got on the wrong boat—and I feared the Island might actually do something similar. But there was a brief quiet ceremony of 3 minutes in accepting the robes, a 5 minute (also subdued, sans hell-fire) talk, and, for *bhikkhus* only, a ritual in the chapter house, lasting a short time. Also there was a fantastically opulent meal, which, unfortunately, we had to eat so fast we couldn't enjoy it at all, since everything was late, what with the vast crowds, and we had to finish before midday, after which time no food is eaten by monks (on this Island, at any rate). We were each given an extremely good quality outer robe—these robes measure about 100 inches by 80 inches—to go on the pile of robes—which-we-have-no-use-for-but-which-it-would-be-impolite-to-refuse. Actually they will be mostly used during the next year, largely in helping other worthwhile hermitages—of which there are a few—not so well supported as we are.

Naturally with the giving of robes it becomes appropriate to dye them, and this is, traditionally, the annual dyeing season as well. Since the robes are already dyed, though—contrary to tradition—it is now traditional to dye the robes that are older and in need of being dyed. So a few days ago, a huge cauldron of water and various tree-barks was boiled for 12 hours to make dye, and I have now spent some days dyeing old robes (2 upper and 2 inner along with a chest covering for chilly nights). The cloth takes very little color with each application and it must be dried thoroughly between applications, and so the process must be repeated many times before the proper russet color is obtained. Skin, however, takes this dye much more readily, and so you now have a russet son with only semi-russet robes. (Saffron, orange, and yellow, by the way, are not the prescribed colors and are worn only by city monks.) At one time I was struck by how much the bark dye smelled like shoe polish. Just now I was struck by how much it smelled like Jello. Do you think that Jello and shoe polish smell alike? (Depends on the flavor?)...

* * *

After going 2 miles along the southern road from Akuressa, I climbed a jungle path to a mountain top where I reached, exhaustedly, Kiyanduwa Araññā. I'd been told of the place by the people at Opate, and found some of what they told me to be true: the head monk was young—40 years old. (At Dedivagala, the oldest monk was 26 and the average age of the residents was surely less, which is, I think, a large part of the reason I found it so pleasant. The average age at Island Hermitage, on the other hand, I would guess to be about 45. He has 5 disciples, the youngest one being 32. There are no child-monks, or monklets—these are serious adults who have some ideas and want to practice them. Only one of them speaks a little English, so I could not decide whether their ideas are the Buddha's or not—I rather suspect not—but, they are, at any rate, not deluding themselves or playing games: children play the game of war, which, if played well, can reproduce every aspect of real war save one: the danger. So too, most people want their religious, ethical, spiritual—which word do you choose?—exercise safe, simple, and comfortable, and wind up doing no more than playing.

The people at Kiyanduwa have no temple for chanting: they have mud huts, few comforts, strict discipline which is wholly voluntary. They accept no food brought to them (as do all other araññas, including Island Hermitage, that I know of), but go daily for alms to the village, which involves descending and ascending a very steep and long path, the round trip taking a tiring 2 hours. Yet I have no doubt that the experience is good. One meal a day is all the head monk takes—though the others take a light breakfast at 5:00 AM. This one-meal-a-day business seems to prove to some people the saintliness of a person. To me, who can speak from experience, it is no such thing, of course, though it may indicate a seriousness which truly makes food and eating something bothersome, if not vaguely distasteful, a task to be gotten through as quickly as possible, repeated as seldom as possible. Or it may simply be a desire for recognition of ascetic practices—one must more or less hide the fact, if one practices it so. I suspect, in his case, though, it is the former. In mine there are a number of reasons; it is, in fact, a nuisance; also the Buddha has recommended restraint in this regard as good practice; so I'm willing to give it a try, and do find it, in fact, to be pleasant (a relief). I never feel hungry at all except about 10:00 AM each day—unfortunately most places don't eat till 11, which gives me one somewhat uncomfortable hour, unless I'm alone with alms, when I eat at my own convenience. Clearly, the only thing one can do at Kiyanduwa, for that is all there is to do, is practice. Nevertheless I think that I could not live there, for I felt a certain discomfort in the atmosphere—perhaps due to my own exhaustion from the trip and the climb—the road is unique rough and sharp.

In the evening a villager came up who knew quite a few words of English. He also knew how to arrange them into what generally struck me as a fantastic double-talk, not quite making sense, and so I tried to communicate through this distorting machine with the head monk, but I don't think much of what I said and asked got put properly and, unless the head monk was mad, certainly not much of what he said came through very clearly. He did, however, say that he would not accept me as a disciple—which I had certainly not asked for—unless/until I learned Sinhalese—which is unlikely—and that, since they were crowded and he could not help me or advise me I would best leave the next day, today.

The conversation, which involved several hours, required all of my effort and energy and concentration to learn that and very little more, and left me totally exhausted. I've never heard English words mixed up in such a fashion in my life. The monk who spoke the little English spoke to the head monk afterwards, explaining, I gathered, that nothing the villager had said had made any sense. The head monk then wrote a letter in Sinhalese which I have translated and says that he can't accept me as a disciple until I learn Sinhalese, etc., and makes sense. Perhaps, now that I think of it, my feelings about the place—that I couldn't stay there—are due in large part to that village distorting machine. He told me, by the way, that he was the town cop. Thank god, he's not the post-master...

* * *

... I've been investigating the weather condition in Ceylon—or, at least, the condition of the weather surveys in Ceylon (which is not quite the same), and have learned the following facts of interest or curiosity: It seems that the indigenous or native weather is 'clear cool nights, bright mornings, and afternoon or evening thunderstorms, particularly in the S.W.'. (Particularly *what*?) But we only have this weather when there is no outside interference, and 'Particularly in March and April and less so in October and November.' Other kinds of weather, it appears, then, are foreign imports, like American cars, penicillin, and English beer; and these effectively flood the market (literally!) and the local weather doesn't have a chance.

The SW monsoon apparently starts as SE trade winds, obeying Ferrel's Law (he must be someone connected with the Stock Exchange to be able to dictate laws to the trade winds) begin blowing from the SW as they cross the Equator. Then, because of 'increased thermal intensity'—i.e. heat—in India, or for some other undiscovered reason—the meteorologists are quarreling about it—it blows harder, becomes damper, and is called the Southwest Monsoon.

Northwest India, according to my geography, is some hundreds of miles away from the Indian—or any other—Ocean. Perhaps the National Geographic, in stating that the Somali current runs from East Africa to Northwest India, believes not only that it is a hundred miles wide and thousands of feet deep (is it fresh water or salt?), but also that it has the ability to flow uphill across half the subcontinent—indeed 'a phenomenon known nowhere else on earth in such magnitude and extent'...

* * *

December 20—left this morning: descending a high, jungle hill at 5:30. I saw the other hills spread out in peculiar shapes, mist rising from the valleys below and enveloping the lower part of the jungle in cottony shrouds while the upper jungle rose uncertainly in dark green. Above this were mounds of pink-cloud icings frosting the picture hanging in impossible suspension, while a single sun rose orange over the entire mass: the one candle above a wild yet possible birthday cake (in which, I may add, were half a dozen leeches). It augured a bright day with a hot sun and cool waters, finally splitting itself, not fragmenting but dividing into two: earth and sky, united at the horizon, at infinity. (I write between a rushing river and silent rice paddy fields: rushing, growth, chance, events, occasions for erecting monuments in the changes of a blade of grass, in a son's age, in a monk's age, in mankind's age.)

* * *

… As for writing, I do some, but not the kind of writing you mean. Mostly involved with the Dhamma. I'm occupied more with developing equanimity as a supplementary meditation subject (my primary one being the in-and-out breaths at the tip of the nose), and find it a far better use of my time. Of the 4 *Brahma-Viharā* (Divine Abidings—*mettā*/loving-kindness, *karunā*/compassion, *muditā*/sympathetic joy, and *upekkhā*/equanimity), the Buddha speaks highest of the last, although today—and, it seems from the texts, in the Buddha's day as well—*mettā* or 'loving-kindness' is the most popular. People even use the word as a salutation at the end of a letter. I wonder how they would react if I signed myself, instead of 'with *mettā*', 'with equanimity'? I would be delighted to receive such a letter, though I suppose most people would think it in poor taste or something.

Sometime early next month I expect to be leaving the Hermitage for an indefinite period in order to accept the invitation from another American monk—Ñāṇasumāna—whom I haven't seen since February—to visit him in his jungle seclusion and discuss some mutual matters…

* * *

I had to return a third time to, and through, Akuressa—wretched place. Worse than Colombo. Colombo, of course, has a great number of illusions and accompanying nonsense, Akuressa tries to imitate all of this ('cosmopolitanism' is one of the euphemisms for these illusions and nonsense; 'society' is another), but fails; thus they have here only the illusion of Colombo: that is, the illusion of an illusion; they doubly deceive themselves...

* * *

... Heidegger, I find, is superb, particularly in his analysis of what is involved in living authentically; in most that he discusses he is, I find, even better than Kierkegaard in his thought—but ohi! his language, It is as abstract as his thought is lucid, and extremely difficult, therefore, to follow. In his case translation can't help. Here's a random sample: 'Falling is not only existentially determinative for Being-in-the-world. At the same time turbulence makes manifest that the throwness which can obtrude itself upon Dasein in its state-of-mind, has the characteristic of throwing and of movement. Dasein's facticity is such that *as long as* it is what it is, Dasein remains in the throw, and is sucked into the turbulence of the 'they's' inauthenticity.' (I think in one of Guenter Grass' novels there's a parody of this—though it seems done already.) Kierkegaard, it seems, is much more quotable. I notice Heidegger quotes Schopenhauer, who once said that 'Life is a business that does not cover its costs.' H, it seems, does not agree. He says (roughly) that it may very well cover its costs, but that even so, it's still a business...

* * *

Finally found a road sign, upon which was perched a fine small eagle with an extraordinary beak: almost curves back upon itself. Yet definitely an eagle's beak; an eagle's eye. Everyone ignored it. I however went to the sign and looked up at the eagle. It looked down at me. I bade it good morning. No reply, only a terrible stare from such a small creature—only about 14 inches in body—and I continued on my way...

* * *

… I am trying, much as Stevie is trying to walk, to see what needs to be done and to be done with it. I, too, fall down quite a bit, but holding on to the Buddha's Teaching, I manage to make some progress on my own. Both Stevie and I, the monk, you remember, are of the same age, within 2 days. So I wish him, now, a happy first birthday, and his parents a happy wedding anniversary…

* * *

On the journey today—12 miles or so—I saw a fine lake, a very lovely area, and discovered an arañña I had not heard of and shall not hear of again—it was, I suspect, someone's idea of a joke—and finally reached a place which is a school like the one that was north of Akuressa, but larger and, therefore, if possible—it is possible, but only barely—actually worse than the other, especially in monk's conduct: not only are they laymen, but they're even poor laymen. Gawd! Head monk, principal, very worldly, wants me to study under him for a year—he'll teach me Pāli and Buddhist culture (whatever that is), all for free, of course, and I can teach him English and Science in his school and get a good salary and jam every other day (see Alice in Wonderland on that), etc. Maybe if he throws in an elephant I'll take it. I refused, of course; but he is not stupid and he knows what I'm after—that is, he knows what the Dhamma is for—but he's not interested. The other monks, who live under him, are all quite impossible nincompoops with radios and no brains.

Now it's afternoon; I'll stay the night here and leave in the morning. It would involve too much polemic to describe the place, physically, culturally, or on any other level—shall spare all of us the effort.

Night: this place has bed-bugs. First time I've encountered them since India. (In India bedbugs are a way of life.) Talked this evening with the head monk; revised my opinion, he is not not stupid (note the double negative): he is educated. He is the opposite of the Opate people. They asked very simple questions that were related to their lives; he gives only complex and high-toned answers that have nothing to do with life; he knows all about the Buddha's Teaching except how to use it. He has spent 25 years learning it much the same way certain people might spend 25 years solving crossword puzzles. He is, in short, a dope. And his school has bedbugs...

* * *

... The night before your letter arrived I had a dream about you, dear sister. I dreamt that either your birthday or wedding anniversary was approaching—I'm not certain which—and I wanted to give you a present, namely, a new pair of eyeglasses. The first problem was that being a monk, I do not handle money. There was, in the dream, some attempt to have someone else manage this for me: the details are uncertain, but it presumably worked out satisfactorily, since the rest of the dream did not refer to it at all. The second problem was that I did not have your prescription, and I remember an eye doctor to whom I was dramatically conversing with explaining in a tone of infinite regret that though he *could* make adjustable glasses, he could *not* make them adjust to all prescriptions: that it was a case of prescription first and adjustment afterwards. Then, of course, I woke up. The next day your letter arrived. I was very much mystified both by the coincidence and by the dream itself, since 'adjustable glasses' sounds like such a reasonable phrase, but, like the eye doctor, I can't imagine what it *means*. I was even more mystified the next day, however, for the night *after* your letter I had *another* dream, which consisted solely of me sitting in front of a typewriter (which I do not have) at a desk (which I do have) in a room which is on the Island but in which I do not live, writing a very regretful letter to you informing you of the many reasons why I was unable to give you a pair of prescription eyeglasses for either your birthday or wedding anniversary. I remember nothing else about that dream. At any rate, this letter is to inform you, very regretfully, that I will be unable to give you a pair of prescription eyeglasses for either your birthday or your wedding anniversary or any other occasion, and I'm very sorry about it, but that's the way it is. ESP? Retroactive precognition? Telepathy? Lunacy? At any rate, it has occurred to me, while writing this letter, that you wear contact lenses, not glasses, so the dream, it seems, is outdated.

I don't know if I'm glad or sorry to hear that apartment buildings don't have meditation rooms—and probably not only not in LA. I've been informed recently, however, that both the Beatles and Frank Sinatra's wife practice meditation under a Hindu yogi and have renounced several pleasures and LSD. This sounds even more fantastic than apartment buildings, and totally unbelievable; it is, therefore, probably true, but I hope you will be able to deny it for me.

One of the *dāyakas* (supporters) of the Island who was here the other day told me that he had seen me outside the Island. Not having left the Island in some time, I enquired further, and learned that he believed that he, while on a pilgrimage last month, saw me wearing a wrist-watch at the zoo. Most peculiar. I have no recollection at all of ever having been on a pilgrimage to the zoo with or without a wrist-watch. I didn't even know it was considered a pilgrimage site. I didn't even know, in fact, that there *is* a zoo; but if these things keep happening often enough, and convince me that everybody really *is* mad, then the zoo, or the jungle, will be the safest and sanest place, and I shall retreat to one of them forever...

* * *

December 21—night. This morning I left the school about 6:00 AM and went through some stretches of handsome rice fields, but nothing remarkable. Good alms today; ate well. Reached Kirinda village about 10:30—shortly after eating—and found it to be less unpleasant than most villages; arrived at Kirinda Arañña at 12:00. Short walk today; only 11 miles.

This arañña I find strictly traditional and traditionally strict. They belong to the small strict sect and their conduct is good. Their arañña, though, is peculiar: at Island Hermitage, as at most araññas, great care is taken so that no kuṭi is built in such a way that any other kuṭi can be seen from it, so there is a greater sense of aloneness. Here, they have built an arañña in the jungle, far from the village, but have carefully placed each kuṭi within sight—and sound—of as many of the other kuṭis as possible. Why do people do such things? Perhaps because of the tradition: things must be done just so, not because it's the best way, but because it has always been done so.

In some ways, I must be grateful for this, for it is this traditionalist that has preserved the Dhamma word for word through 2500 years, yet, grateful as I am that it was so preserved, I still consider those who preserved it fools, for they did not themselves use it. This traditional attitude, which is to be avoided like the plague, has not only not been eradicated here but has, in a few of its forms, been actually encouraged. My thesis is that any message which has survived 2500 years must be great; any great message must be misunderstood by most people; most people build a tradition around the message and then follow the tradition and not the message.

The monks here are serious; they, apparently, practice the teachings—to what extent I do not know—but their lives are strictly regulated. At a certain time each day they all do certain jobs: 4:00 sweeping, 6:00 chanting, etc., and when they sweep, or rake leaves, they don't do it any old way: they leave the sand with a definite pattern from the rake; no other pattern will do, and they do not hold the rake with left hand over right, but with right hand over left. (Their insistence on this point annoyed me no end, since it is simply not natural for me, a lefty.) Perhaps such extreme regulation of my time may actually be good for me—I've wondered about that before—and can't hurt me for a few days, at any rate. But I don't care for this _en masse_ attitude, which is more like enforcement than participation, abrogates the purpose of an _araññа_ (solitude), and I don't care for the idea of _having_ to do such and such at such and such a time simply because such and such has always been done so. There is too great a tendency for such a practice to become self-justifying.

My _kuṭi_ here is the only unoccupied one—there are 8 monks in residence. None speak English, but some boys from the village have come, unfortunately, as interpreters as well as interrogators, which has taken a lot of time. One of them asked me to help him with his problem: he wants to go to America, and needs someone to pay his fare. I pointed out that I neither had money nor dealt in it and so could not help, and asked why he wanted to go to America. He said he wanted to get rich. For all that I deplore his goal, I couldn't help admiring his honesty and surety of what he wanted: not many people are so forthright (or even can be—to themselves, in particular).

The jungle is old and large: very tall—unbelievably tall—and straight trees, with branches only at and near the tops, are filled with monkeys. The monkeys are small, silent, and not much fun at all. They have, clearly, never been in a barrel. There is a peculiar millipede, about 8 inches long, all black except for a vast number of white legs, so that it looks very formally-attired, as if in tuxedo, white gloves, and spats. In contrast, Island Hermitage centipedes are half the size, black on top and red on the sides: much more gay and lively, their legs move in a peculiarly fascinating pattern, sort of like waves. There is a fruit which falls off a tree onto my head as I walk in the walking area: hard—naturally—and dark green with a hare pit and seem to resemble olives except that they don't smell like olives (or smell at all) and fall from a tremendous tree. The leaf of the tree doesn't look like an olive leaf; though, perhaps, this is some long lost relative (black sheep of the family?). I'm told the fruit is inedible though many seem to be partly eaten by birds, so I'm tempted to taste one in the morning and see. In any case, it's difficult to reconcile this giant tree with the twisted, stunted trees one sees in Greece and Jerusalem...

* * *

... Full moon tonight: the full moon in the jungle will never be as good as in the desert, where, in the flat darkness, the moon's height over a vast visible area shows how it totally dominates the land: here there is too much else too close by for the moon's rays to spread out and grasp hold of everything firmly; it becomes a bright, intermittently visible (through drifting clouds and jungle canopy), surprisingly small ball (the desert full moon always surprised me by being so *large*); nevertheless it has its effects and adds a buoyancy, as if it were itself floating, something for us to grasp hold of, who are drowning in an ever-combustible sea of air, to grab hold of and pull ourselves out of it at last, and perhaps a less-than-full awareness of this makes one's steps lighter and higher, as if the inch difference will enable the fingertips to graze, scrape, perhaps rub sharply enough for a brief moment's pain, as it touches the bottom edge, calling for one *real* leap to be—on top...

You see? The moon *does* have its effect: when do I write this? It's not me that's writing, but the moon, Or is the air rarefied in the heights that a full moon pulls one to, creating a giddiness so that words rush out pell-mell...? I must stop now, or I shall never approach the subject for which I had intended this air-letter—but now there is no space left for that vast and weighty series of statements, ponderously bulky and immovable, possibly comprehensible, which I had intended to compose about the nature of communication. Ah, well...

* * *

December 22—Well, here it is, first day of winter. Not many snowballs in this neck of the woods. I feel, this evening, very amused at the monks here, who exhibit a vast concern over seeing to it that I have comforts about which I don't give a fig. They have prepared a special smokey fire in a pan and placed it in the kuṭi to drive away the few mosquitos that I have been totally ignoring. They break their own rules of etiquette to show me favoritism which I find embarrassing. I have been told, once, that the Japanese smile to show embarrassment. They are very kind though—they want me to stay here a month now (which I could hardly do)—when they assume my total ignorance of how to handle the most simple matters. They go to great lengths to show me how to turn the flame up and down on the lamp, how to fasten the window latch, how to put on my robes, how to clean my teeth (they're down on toothpaste); they caution me to wear sandals and take the lamp with me if I go out at night, and want me to always carry my traveling alarm clock with me if I go out of the kuṭi lest some brigands make off with it. And so it goes, every phase of daily life is assumed to be more than I can handle without help. This attitude, which I've encountered frequently in Asia, both as layman and monk, is explicable, I think, only in the view of the vast traditionalism inherent in the culture, which in a time of change creates great readjustment problems: the people can't conceive of anyone actually being comfortable in any but the most familiar surroundings. In other words, they have been taught to exist within a limited sphere—which works very fine as long as that sphere is intact—and assume that I must have the same limitations.

The traditionalism I find here is accounted for by the discovery, made today, that this is the oldest araññа in Ceylon; another proof of my theory. (It's over 100 years old.) There is an araññа about 4 miles away which I had intended visiting, but now learn that it is, more or less, an offshoot of this place and exactly the same; so I'll probably not go there.

The reason this kuṭi is so decrepit—the plaster is half gone, revealing crumbling mud and stones, the roof is of palm fronds, there are great gaps between walls and roof—is because a tree fell on it. I was visited by more villagers today, who hang around much too long, but gave me some beedis—native-style cigarettes—rather strong—which were nice—haven't smoked in a long time now, and a cigarette feels unfamiliar between my fingers. I can't think of any other stupendous events to record...

* * *

... December 18—One year in robes. Since leaving Wayne State U, this is the first time I have ever succeeded in doing any one thing for a full year—kibbutz was 11 months—and I find, at the end of a year, that I need not congratulate myself at all, for I have not 'stuck it out' but rather continuously chosen it: it is our ability to *choose* which *permits* our existence; only by continuous exercise of that will can we be aware of our present existence, and thus come to an understanding of it. It was in each of the moments in which I *chose* to remain in robes that I learned. I learned, at last, that I could not imagine any other rational choice for myself...

* * *

December 23—This morning I tried eating that fruit, which I found edible but not very tastey—slightly sour, not at all olive-like. I was told this afternoon that there is some meat inside the pit which is edible, but have not tasted that. Washed my robes today. Naturally I was shown the right way of doing it—my way was not at all good. The Kirinda way is correct. It takes out half the color as well as the dirt, but it is orderly. Also was given another raking lesson. It seems that the strokes I was making were too large. I don't mind raking in their pattern which is not a bad design, but I tried to produce some variations on it, just for the pleasure of seeing some variations. That was quickly corrected. There is, I am taught, only one proper pattern for sand to be raked in, and no other designs will do. Variants are heretical: they will tolerate no fake patterns in their sandbox.

I also met a newly-arrived monk who talked exactly like the translator at Kiyanduwa. It turned out that this monk was a former cop. Perhaps Ceylon police are all taught English like that? It turned out, also, that he received his novice-ordination at Kiyanduwa and also that I had met his mother, who spoke no English, when I was in Opate. He taught me how to sit when meditating (which, of course, I had been doing wrong. I just sat; he developed a five-minute ritual in going from standing to sitting position) and told me, I think, that I couldn't walk to Humbantota because the elephants would eat me and that therefore I must turn around and go the other way, by bus, with him to his arañña so that the nearby villagers could come and gape at me. I was taught how to pick flowers, how to pour water from a basin and how to dry my bowl after washing it (which I somehow or other had managed to do correctly). I was also given several further lessons in how to put on and wear my robes. While sweeping the sand clean I saw some monkeys having a fight overhead, during which both I and the just-cleaned ground were showered by large quantities of leaves, twigs, and monkey curses. I found that some monkeys are white-colored from their waist to their thighs, which gives the appearance of pants and solves the curious spectacle of the female monkey in trousers that I saw at Kottawa. I was also taught how to breathe correctly. (How could my upbringing have been so neglected as not to have been taught to breathe correctly? If I hadn't figured out something for myself I might have suffocated long ago.) I expect, at any minute, to be told to readjust my heartbeat.

I have also discovered that another American has taken the robes a few days ago. I met him once, in August, when I learned he wanted to be a missionary, to return to America, and preach to people dying in hospitals. What an ambition! How heroic, self-sacrificing, and absurd! How can a person who wants to preach in hospital sick-bays have an understanding of a teaching which says that we must strive individually for our own welfare?

* * *

... How do I not collect village butterflies? Sometimes with momentary difficulty; lapses of watching the senses, which will spin their alluring lies if not kept a constant eye on... Fortunately, there are also dogs, cows, pigs, etc... and one realizes that the butterfly now, in a blink, is a dog, cow, pig, etc. As you well-put it the erotic impulse is a very selective perception: selecting one's own immediate pleasure in a smell, a sight, a feeling, a thought, etc. If, along with this, however, one sees other things: for example, the dog-cow-pig-etc. in the butterfly; or a body slipped out of that impetuous organ—the skin—or a body decaying, dying, or dead; or being presented with a local dose of VD, being the cause of all the pain and suffering of child-bearing and child-rearing, or being beaten or killed by a jealous boyfriend, an outraged brother or father, or a pious scourge of dirty monks; if one also sees in those beautiful eyes the black hole of ignorance and misery, the hard life, the pains, the regrets, the false hopes, the real hopelessness—one can feel compassion, yes—but *passion*? And whence eroticism? (Gee, it was here just a second ago!) The flicker blown out in the fresh, cool breeze of another perception: mindfulness. Also definitely useful is the fine strait-jacket of the robes, vows I take seriously (or at least serio-comically): village butterflies don't flutter about monks—a greater relief by far.

V.

* * *

December 25—Merry Xmas. (Let's put the X back in Xmas.) Left Kirinda this morning, after declining an extremely pressing invitation from the Mahā Thera there to remain for a few months. He says—surprise—that he likes my manners. I think it might be to my advantage to return there some time for a more extended stay. It's rather artificial, of course, but it's like playing Czerny exercises on the piano. Before one can play Bach, one must master Czerny, no matter how artificial and non-musical it may be. So too with the strict regulated life of Kirinda. They spend 3 hours every morning getting their noon meal, and also time for morning meal; they recite suttas at 9, 12, and 6 o'clock daily, sweep twice daily—very different from the freedom of Island Hermitage, where each person is, within the confines of the island, free to do pretty much as he wants, whether to use his time well or to waste it.

Today—went 15 miles to Tangalla, reaching the seacoast road; it is 26 miles to Hambantota; but there is one more araññā, inland, which I will visit first. Alms was rather difficult today; the area being both poor and depopulated, but I finally managed to get a bowl full of bananas and biscuits, which sufficed. Nothing eventful, but hot and tiring; am staying the night at a temple outside Tangalla on the main road. This is the least Xmasy Xmas I've spent, even less Xmasy than last year in Calcutta (not Marienbad), or before that in Eilat or before that in Bin Gedi, Munich, and Iowa. For all I know there is not even a Christian (X-tian?) for miles and miles around.

Nature notes: Monkeys do not eat oranges. A crow's head, seen sideways, looks like a Marine. And I have found today, in addition to red, black, and white ants, that there is also a brown ant, actually sort of brown-grey, longish and looking decrepit, like it was made of old and dusty secondhand parts put together by an unskilled mechanic. Also there is a plant which has bracken-like leaves and a flower of a delicate purple tint looking like purple needles stuck into a tiny pincushion, forming a fine globe. The amazing property of this plant is that if the leaf is touched, it folds up like a pair of arms cowering against attack. The leaves function in pairs, on opposite sides of the stem, and apparently all leaves farther from the branch than the one struck also react to this process, which is very marked—the opposite leaves actually touch each other and give the plant the appearance of having shriveled up. It takes only 2 or 3 seconds for the plant to react, and about 5 or 10 minutes—related, I suppose, to the hardness with which the leaf is struck (a very light tap will only partly 'close' it)—for it to 'relax' again and assume its normal posture. Great fun to attack these plants and see all the leaves cower under the onslaught, and know that it's all a game. Then one glances over one's shoulder and wonders There are many flowers in the jungle but most are very inconspicuous. Some are very pretty, A large yellow flower grows on a tree and a bush alike. There is a fairly common small orchid, which frequently dwells on an old coconut shell; many tiny flowers; a rose-like flower on a thorny bush. There are also some colorful red and silver leaves, but all these are hidden in the masses of green that dominate the landscape, and one becomes aware of them only slowly.

* * *

… I have learned that the president of the Pāli Text Society is an old biddy named Miss I.B. Horner, which recalls your limerick, and brings about a new version.

Miss I.B. Horner
Sat in a corner
Translating a Pāli text.
While doing a *Sutta*
She misplaced a neuter
And discovered that she was unsexed…

* * *

December 27—Yesterday I left Tangalla and walked along the coastal road, but did not see the sea—there were rice paddy fields and a few hills in the way. The road does not come within sight of the ocean, as I recall from the trip I took down here last February to Hambantota. Received lots of rice for alms, both yesterday and today and on neither day was I offered any money, which was normal on other days—in fact on some days I almost despaired of getting food for people offered so much money, and then sometimes did not understand when it was refused. (Sometimes they did understand, so they know that money is not allowed for monks, but offer it anyway—and then complain that the monks are corrupted and don't know why that is so.)

I walked 19 miles, as far as Ambalontota, I had not intended to go so far, but there was a stretch of about 5 miles at the end where there were no temples. I wanted to stop at Nanagama, which is marked in large dark letters on the map, and which I assumed, therefore, to be a large dark town, but it turned out to be a few shops and tea stalls. Ambalontota, which is a large dark town beside a large dark river, is in light small letters on the map. The town, though, even has a museum, archeological, for, I am told, the history of the area goes back more than 2000 years. I did not go to the museum, but did spend the night at a large temple with an even larger _cetiya_ which, I was told, was 1500 years old. _Cetiyas_, by the way, are stone structures shaped like, but bigger than, wedding cakes (all edges rounded off) and are supposed to house the ashes of Great Monks. There are, though, an enormous number of _cetiyas_ and only a small number of Great Monks, so most of the _cetiyas_ serve more as a marker identifying the place as a temple.

Ambalontota temple housed not only monks but also cows, one of which had recently given birth to a calf over whom the monks showered pride and banana peels. The cows come into the main hall as they wish, and nobody seems to mind. I don't know if they are house-broken. In the evening the police came to see me and warned me not to go the last 3 miles to Madungala _arañña_ alone, that it was through thick jungle, very dangerous, with no people and full of wild animals. I refrained from pointing out that the towns were also full of wild animals and even the temples ware full of tame animals. A busload of pilgrims arrived, who had been to some ancient sites in the area, and spent the night there; noisy—almost as noisy as the monks. Wild animals would be a relief...

* * *

... The practice of mindfulness is cultivating the awareness of the ongoing process of sensations (pleasurable, painful, or indifferent), which give rise, by means of the attention given them, to perceptions, actions, behavior patterns; i.e. one's sense of self.

The practice of mindfulness is the practice of the Buddha's Teaching; meditation is merely a means of perfecting that practice; it should not end when meditation ends.

Only through the practice of mindfulness can the Path be perceived and entered upon...

* * *

Left Ambalontota about 6:30 this morning and took the road going inland beside the river. The road was decrepit and I was forced to wear sandals: I had the bad luck last night of stepping on a thorn ball, and dig as I could, at least one of the small thorns was still hidden in my right heel. It may have worked its way out by now, for I don't feel it now.

It was 9 miles to Maduragala <u>araññā</u>. The day was cloudy, and I took my time. (I don't like to arrive before noon, because of the possible problems with food.) Ate a pleasant meal beside the river. After 6 miles the asphalt ended and the road was dirt. My sandals broke, but I fixed them with string until I found a tea stall where someone ran off to get them fixed—2 nails were required. (At first the tea stall man wanted to give me his sandals, which, in fact, fitted, but I managed to refuse that.) The last 3 miles, of which I had been warned not to travel alone, turned out to be a broad track along which a jeep passed me, several kids on bicycles whizzed past, and cattle and water buffalo infested. Townspeople have a fantastically exaggerated idea of danger (except the dangers of a town). There wasn't even very much jungle, for houses and some farmland lined the road. The last half mile it began to rain and it has been raining ever since. I reached Maduragala about 11:30.

The arraññа is built on, under, and around a series of gigantic rocks. Some of the buildings use the rocks as their roofs, some as walls, some as floors. The place is much more impressive than Nugagala in this respect—though the jungle doesn't compare, of course—and besides it's well kept-up and not just mud huts with tin roofs. Because of the rain I have not explored, but there is a giant rock above the arañña in which is a fissure about 9 feet deep and 10 feet by 20 feet across, forming a pool in which I bathed; a dining hall about 50 feet by 30 feet of floor space with a ceiling of about 25 feet of rock, and a few other buildings: a fine temple room, quite large. I've been placed in a kuṭi very close to the dining hall and even closer to the water tap, in sight and sound of everything: most unfortunate, I will have to see, tomorrow, if there are any more isolated kuṭis available, for with 11 residents here, this kuṭi is untenable.

All residents are novices: 3 of them are elderly. There is one bhikkhu, I am told, who is away for 2 or 3 weeks. One of the old novices, and also a mason who works and lives here, speaks English. The umbrella given me at Nugagala, which was old, yellow (considered not quite proper for a monk's umbrella—reddish-brown and white being the 'proper' colors), and which had a broken piece (reparable easily) yesterday was taken from me and I was given a brand-new white umbrella of excellent quality. Very nice. I was also told that a German monk named Ñāṇasiha was here about a year ago. (This place is closely affiliated, also, with Dediyagala.) 'Gala', I am told, means 'stone', I don't know what 'Madura' means, but gala is quite appropriate. Nuga is a kind of tree whose bark is used to make the dye for the robes. 'Duwa' means island: Dodan=orange Island Hermitage is called in Sinhalese Polgasduwa, which means coconut island. There are coconuts at Polgasduwa, but no orange trees grow anywhere near Dodanduwa, which is not even an island, and sometimes oranges cannot even be bought there: not even the oranges which are green when they're ripe. I'm told that the head of the sect will be visiting on January 1, and am considering staying till then to meet him, depending on whether I get a different kuṭi

* * *

... Having emerged from a twelve-foot dry well, from which I rescued a fallen rabbit, I am now able to reply to you, who send ideas full of life, who live full of ideas, who preserve others, use yourselves, cherish relationships, and enjoy (enjoy!) existence: for, being none of these (and, nonetheless, still being), an act of identity must be committed each time I wish to communicate with those who talk of toads—real toads in imaginary gardens. In other words, before I went into the hole it did not exist for me; while I was in it, it existed in reality; now that I am out of it it exists in imagination.

Godawaya: forty days and fourteen miles from Karmagala, the surf shouts insistently across the beach, reminding my hut that it is only made of palm fronds, that I am only made of experience. Peace is allowable; as for apples I cannot say, but if Godawaya had been the Garden (with real toads) it would have been not possible for Cain to have struck his blow. Cactus and coconuts, soft soil and still softer sunrises, bananas and *bhāvana*: my day. Subtle sunset, night-time stars, sand, smoke a cigarette, smile, serene, sleep...

Doctrinal scoldings? Forgive: I miscommunicated. Don't forgive: I did not scold. How could I, when we do not, in fact, follow—either of us, I think—any doctrine at all? What I do follow is a set of texts written in the Pāli which contain a certain set of instructions along with descriptions of what will be found at the various stages of practice by one who follows those instructions. Anyone who imagines that the Pāli texts are a doctrine will find himself down a rabbithole, in a wonderland. It is because of this that your letters are welcome; it is because of this that I am *able* to disagree with you.

A few random comments on your letter:

1) Ho-Shan (whom you quote) says that 'the great knowledge is realized by 'abstaining from all reflection and discursive thinking'. The Pāli texts say (perhaps several hundred times and in many different ways) that the first *jhāna*, or stage of attainment, is a necessary condition for

the attainment of enlightenment, and that first *jhāna* is identified by five characteristics, two of them being: reflexive and discursive thought.

2) Ho-Shan also says that 'every being has the Buddha-nature within him'. How does he know what I have within me? (The Pāli texts neither state nor imply any such thing.)

3) You are quite right: Mahāyana does accept Theravada as true, while Theravada does reject Mahāyana (not so much as false—on my part, at least—as much as irrelevant). You find this, apparently, all the more reason to accept Mahāyana. Odd. I find it all the more reason to reject it. ('Two things only do I teach, monks: suffering—*dukkha*—and the Path leading to cessation of suffering.') If a solution to the problem of suffering—which is the problem of existence—*saṅhāradukkhā—is* to be found, two things are certain: (i) the solution is difficult to arrive at—else there would be no problem; and (ii) the solution is *specific* and not general—for it is *my* specific *dukkha*, *my* specific existence, which I am trying to put an end to, and therefore a *specific* practice must be followed rather than one which attempts to embrace many—or all—different disciplines.

4) You refer to an 'illusion of duality'. Neither I nor the Pāli texts make use of any such concept. Duality is real. Subjectivity (not to be confused with either *sakkāyadiṭṭhi*—personality-view—or *asmimāna*—the conceit 'I am') is dependent on the fact that there are objects—objects which are appropriated ('This is mine, I am this, this is my self')—which appropriation is what is meant by *upādāna* (holding): *upādāna paccayo bhavo*: dependent upon holding is being.

Finally we come to your statement: A is not-A. Here lies the crux of the matter. The Pāli texts are concerned with suffering, which *is* existence, which *is* experience. Therefore, they are existential in character, dealing with the structure of experience, but from *within*—for if I try to work outside the structure of my experience I leave my *dukkha*, my existence, from the account—i.e. delude myself about the very nature of my experience. Since that delusion, too, is structured, constructed, there must be a way of 'dismantling' it. The Buddha teaches that way.

There is no problem involved in changing our *mode* of being—we cannot help but do it—but the Buddha shows us the way in which we must direct that change in order to arrive at a position where we can eliminate the very essence of the delusion, *the reason to be*. But it must—can *only* be—done from *within*. Therefore anything which *cannot* be part of experience has no possible place within the Teaching. And I find that I am *not* able to imagine A being not-A: it is impossible for me, no matter how hard I try (and I have tried), for it is outside my experience: I have never *experienced* any thing being not-itself. Therefore 'A is not-A' cannot have any place in my practice. I know, however, that your experience is very different from mine: perhaps the structure of your experience is also very different from the structure of mine. Perhaps—if so, then we *ought* to follow different teachings for the Pāli texts contain within them the underlying assumption that A *is* A, and that A is *not* not-A.

Many Mahāyānists seem to believe that what constitutes enlightenment is the 'realization' that A is not-A. This is false. Enlightenment, as taught by the Pāli texts (*nibbāna*, more correctly translated as 'extinction') does not involve a change in the nature of our being or existence to *another* state of being or existence, or an alteration in our mode of thought or experience to *another* mode of thought or experience: it involves the *extinction of our reason to be*, whatever its nature may be. Once this is attained, *both* 'A is A' and 'A is not-A' become irrelevant, since when existence is this sense is no longer involved the word 'is' is no longer applicable.

So—if you find that you can, here and now, imagine A as being not-A (and if you are quite certain of precisely what you mean by it), get on with your work within that frame of thought. Fine. But if you recognize that you cannot imagine A as being not-A, and think that your goal is to so recognize it, you should recognize also that the Way taught by the Buddha—the Noble Eightfold Path—is *not* the way leading to knowledge of A being not-A; for the Dhamma leads to the cessation of suffering (*dukkhanirodha*). As for myself, being unable to imagine A being not-A, I shall continue within my dull non-mystical and rather unhappy frame of thought until—I hope—I succeed in doing away with it entirely, A, not-A, X, Y, Z, the whole works, and put an end to clinging to existence, experience and suffering (not to speak of lust, hatred, and delusion) altogether.

Nowhere in the Pāli texts does the Buddha teach dharmas, illusory dualities, or dogmas. What he does give us is a many-faceted diamond—and on any one of the facets of this diamond the careful eye can read the inscription:

*Sabbe saṅkhārā aniccā*: All determinations are impermanent.
*Sabbe saṅkhārā dukkhā*: All determinations are suffering.
*Sabbe saṅkhārā anattā*: All determinations are not-self.

Ride that for a while and see how far it takes you.

I shall probably leave here very soon (I've been saying that for the last month), and continue my eastward trek. Eventually I shall return to the Island Hermitage. Where else I shall return to I don't know. If you shall be returning to Japan, please send me a parcel of pleasantness from that island. As for me, Ceylon is too beautiful for just one lifetime. *Sukhi hontu upekhāya*: May you have the joy of equanimity—and of stringhoppers too.

V.

* * *

December 28—Last night was terrible—much noise until about 11:00 kept me awake till then, then the mosquitos kept me awake the rest of the night. I suggested this morning that my stay would be very short in such surroundings, and I was quickly given a new room. I am now living in a small cave, measuring about 12 feet by 9 feet, with the roof sloping into the back wall. The walls are made of several thousand tons of solid rock. There's another, larger, cave next door—so to speak—in which lives another, larger monk. There are several other <u>kuṭis</u> built into this rock, and there is room for more. There is also a cave unprepared but needing only a front wall to be complete. This <u>kuṭi</u> is quite comfortable.

This is certainly the most spectacular <u>araññā</u> I have seen, with huge outcroppings of rock, peculiar trees, thick jungle; one gigantic boulder on top of everything, high above the trees, on top of which there is a clear view everywhere but south. To the north and west I can see the mountains of central Ceylon in the far, far distance. Adam's Peak is visible on a clear day, but today is cloudy with rain threatening and only silhouettes are visible.

I'm told the monkeys here are not monkeys—so what are

they then, chimpanzees? They are light brown, about 2 feet high (with three feet tails), and a few of the larger ones will take food from my hand, rather politely. It's great fun feeding them. One of them, who looks like Art Carney, was willing to sit down next to me, and eat the bananas I gave him (including the peel), but not near the dogs, of whom they are afraid. I've been cautious and never leave anything outside or they will steal it.

I don't like the routine here—there is not the same spirit as at Dediyagala, and there is also more ritual. This ritual is fine for them: they have to have <u>something</u> to do all day, and if they won't practice meditation, then worship, flower gathering, raking, etc., are all harmless tasks. If one does practice meditation, however, then having to do other things at fixed times is merely a nuisance. Also they spend 3 hours every day collecting their food: there is a 20 minute walk (through soft mud) to the hall where it's given, and a 20 minute walk back with a heavy bowl; then busy work, etc., until we eat all together in the dining hall, which has a low rock ceiling, and is, therefore, hot.

One of the young monks and one of the servants arrived here several weeks ago from Kottawa <u>Arañña</u>. I did not remember them until reminded, but they remembered me. The young monk was, and is, apparently, very much taken by me, for it was he who wanted to give me his umbrella, and it was he who prepared hot water for me this morning for washing (!), and so on. What it is that I did, or didn't do, or tried to do, at Kottawa that has impressed him so I'm not certain.

This afternoon I slept for an hour, then rested, and finally went for a walk. There are waterholes in crevices in rocks; miniature frogs and tiny toads inhabit them; the biggest is as large as my baby toenail. There is a tree which has huge leaves and white flowers and whose branches are thick, white and rubbery; they can be bent into knots and will spring back to their original shape. I watched the monkeys—or, rather, what are not monkeys—non-monkeys—and found a small manila (a poisonous snake) who paid me no heed at all. There are paths and jungle trails for miles and it would take months to learn them all. The jungle here is on the edge of the SE dry zone of the island and is very different from the SW wet zone jungle—more trees (and different trees), not so much underbrush—the older a jungle gets the less underbrush it has—not many ferns or palm trees, nothing quite impenetrable. Quieter. No leeches.

December 30. I have, more or less, left Maduragala and am now living, in a way, at Karmagala Araññа, I have left a lot of my things at Maduragala, for I shall only be here a few days. Karmagala is a jungle hermitage about a mile from Maduragala; it is now abandoned—I don't know for how long there have been no monks here—and is beginning to fall apart. It is on top of the largest hill anywhere near here, which is not saying very much, for there are hardly any hills nearby. Nevertheless there is a magnificent view to the south where the sea appears as a thin line between sky and jungle, almost the same as the sky; to the north rise the hills of upcountry. Rough calculations seem to indicate that the biggest peak I see is 4100 feet at a distance of 30 miles. (Adam's Peak is 55 miles away, 7380 feet high, but is probably hidden—it would appear, if seen, to be slightly smaller than the largest peak. If I have a cloudless day I can probably see it: I can use my map as guide, since it has all the peaks noted.) I can see hundreds of square miles of jungle, which, from above, is rather dull: dull green and uninformative, but vast and somehow hiding something: we cannot know what, but we can know that its nature is dangerous.

There is a fine cetiya on the very top of this hill—really, there is only one other hill worthy of the name for several miles around—from which I can see the rocks—though not the kuṭis—of Maduragala. My map shows the sea as being about 8 miles away, and thus I calculate the height of the hill as being about 1000 feet. This seems incredible, though, for the climb is easy—over rocks and on a soft path which hides thorns—and it doesn't feel that high. Perhaps my calculations—and/or judgment—are off. There's a fine breeze up here, and a temple with a very nice Buddha (the small one, just next to the large gaudy one), and no monks. I cannot say, though, that there are no people: there are six laymen. Tonight is new moon, and on full and new moons it is customary for laymen to make religious observance. Apparently some villagers come up here on these days for the observance and spend the night. This is a very good practice: if is merely unfortunate that I came here on a new moon day. Half a moon would be better than no moon at all.

Nevertheless, I have been left more or less alone—they wanted me to conduct services, which I refused, and gave me tea and betel nut, which I accepted. They sleep in a large hall, of the sort every _araññа_ (except Island Hermitage) has for laymen to sleep in, while I am settled in a large cave in a good-sized hunk of rock.

The cave is about 50 feet long, but only about 20 feet deep, 10 feet in a few places—and 10 to 15 feet high. It's finished with front wall, windows, door, etc., and is stocked with a lantern, a Buddha image, and everything else required (the Buddha image, a poor one, I could well do without): even tea, sugar, and a kettle. I made some tea, which was good, though difficult, since I had to hunt for firewood, build a stove, make the fire, etc. I suppose these things are put here by the fortnightly laymen: at any rate, I assumed so and used them on trust. No one objected. I think the laymen will leave tomorrow.

For food I must go about 2 miles to the hall where the Maduragala monks are given food; I shall take it back here, however, and shall not go to Maduragala until I leave here. They know, of course, that I am here—they are faintly opposed to the idea. Their main objection was that I would have to go without afternoon tea if I lived here—I don't have to, as it turns out—and anyway why didn't I stay _there_, where I would not—horrors!—be _alone_? Since they know the answer to all objections they raise, they could not object very strongly (except by being _mauvaise foi_), and I left today after the meal.

The _araññа_ itself is much like Maduragala: spectacular rocks, though the _kuṭis_ in them are not nearly so elegant, except for the view, which is even better. Fine jungle. I share my cave with a family of chipmunks, who live under the drip ledge (a ledge so that water drips down rather than sliding into the kuṭi via the rock roof), and who do not appreciate my company but are very curious about me—lizards, and the usual creatures. The non-monkeys here are different than at Maduragala; at Maduragala they had a pouch under each cheek, while here they do not. In both places, though they have pink faces and black demonic ears.

There are at least a dozen kuṭis here; most of then are occupied by bats and stink to hell. The kuṭi on the other side of this rock is occupied by a bear: I could see the hollow in the bat dung where he sleeps and could see his footprint in the powdery dung. This is a big rock, though, and there is room for both (all) of us.

My plan now is to stay here tomorrow and leave on January 1, evening, to Maduragala, to see Ñāṇa Ānanda. He is the head of the sect which includes Maduragala, Kottawa, Dediyagala, and all the village priests thereabouts. He is also the preceptor of all the monks both at Dediyagala and Maduragala. He will, apparently, arrive on the 1st, and I am curious what sort of person he is. I shall sleep at Maduragala that night, and on the 2nd shall leave for Hambantota.

I have just recalculated the height of the hill and find that I am only 42 feet above sea level. This is an even more surprising figure than the previous one of 1170 feet. If I average them, however, I find that I am, above everybody else, on a hill 606 feet, and that's good enough for me.

December 31. Company—laymen—left this morning. I found, on the south edge of the topmost rock on the hill, a natural concavity in the stone which forms a perfect seat, complete with back, and just the right size for me, and spent the morning there, until about 8:30, when I prepared and then went to collect alms. It's a 40 minute walk, then another walk back up the hill, so there is plenty of exercise. Ate. Fed the chipmonks and non-monks. Went back to my seat. Rain threatened and finally forced me to evacuate and return to the cave, where I am now—about 3:30. Clouds all day. I'm very pleased with this place. In fact, I've decided to stay one more day, and so will not return to Maduragala until the 2nd.

On the way back from alms, I was twice attacked, and painfully wounded each time, by black ants. They look just like the harmless kind at Island Hermitage, but, boy, do they bite! Having been bitten by both red and half-red, half-black before, I can say that the black here are the worst. The bite is actually nothing; what hurts so much is that they flip their rear ends over their heads and <u>piss into the bite</u>! <u>That</u> hurts! (Talk about adding insult to injury!)

January 1. Alms this AM—from Tangalla people. One of them—a postmaster—told me he had seen me walking there and was impressed. He believes, it seems—not totally without justification—that monks are not generally capable of walking. He also threatened to visit me this afternoon, but was, perhaps, frightened off by the wild flowers or some such danger. (Do carnivorous plants grow in Ceylon?) I was visited, though, by 2 monks from Maduragala, who brought me candles, incense, matches, themselves, and a message that I should come back tonight, not tomorrow. The situation is still indeterminate: I shall go there at 4:00 (it is now 3:00) to meet the head of the sect, intending to return this evening. We shall see.

I found a wonderful cave, almost beneath my meditation seat, but it can be reached only through an intricate and fairly difficult labyrinth of rocks and climbs and drops, until it opens out onto a ledge with a few trees, a covered flat rock and the cave, with one mud wall built into it. It's impervious to elephants. I was also told that the cave I am in now has a history of 2000 years, and that <u>arahats</u> used to live in it. An <u>arahat</u> is a person who has attained <u>nibbāna</u>—a saint so to speak—and, while this may be perfectly true, it may also be perfectly false, for Ceylon's official history is, in fact, an official fairy tale, full of fantastic heros and villains, mythical creatures, demons, giants, defenders-of-the-faith, etc., and not quite to be believed. It was pointed out to me, though, that the ceiling of the cave still bears the remains of ancient art-work, and this is true: a few lines can still faintly be discerned: a hand, or possibly a monstrous foot, is visible, and some other indeterminate but definitely artistic lines can also be seen; so it is quite possible that the cave was inhabited 2000 years ago—probable I would say—possibly by monks, and even, who knows? by arahats. So much for history. As for the present, there are no arahats in this cave: of that I assure you. There are, however, two chipmonks and a butterfly.

For dāna I was given a plastic bag of curds and honey, which I ate part of and gave the rest to the non-monkey. It could smell the food, but, since, the curds were inside the bag, had great difficulty and much puzzlement in trying to lick the food. After considerable effort it finally found the opening, but still didn't get the idea—it licked the opening, and then went deeper and deeper—all the time trying to watch me, of whom it was suspicious, and another non-monkey, of whom it was even more suspicious. It took a couple deep breaths, stuck its red face in deep, took a sloppy greedy lick, and pulled the bag off to look about, its face white and yellow and very messy, its tongue going in circles. Non-monkey alms.

January 2. On the way to Maduragala, I managed to take a wrong turning and got quite lost for a while, finally finding the path again. It began to rain while I was lost, and by the time I reached Maduragala I had a headache and a slight fever. Ñāṇa Ānanda had not yet appeared. Therefore I spent the night there. When Ñāṇa Ānanda did appear I was awoken with a great noise and was taken to see him. He does not speak English, which surprised me, and so conversation was impossible. A few questions and answers were translated, some oil rubbed on my head, and then my head subjected to a squeezing process, which may have squeezed the fever out, for this morning I awoke feeling quite fine, after an uncomfortable night's sleep—uncomfortable because I had to share a room with one of Ñāṇa Ānanda's attendant bhikkhus, who made noise and kept his lamp—on late.

This morning, there being no purpose in my staying at Maduragala, I returned to Karmagala, in a light rain. There are some rocks to be crossed on the path leading to the almshouse, and in the rain it's extremely slippery and dangerous, and required 10 minutes of extreme care to cross a few hundred feet. Downhill was more difficult than uphill. Godawful spicey alms, almost inedible. Non-monkeys liked it well enough. I was visited by a large male with his harem of four females and an indeterminate number of assorted offsprings, these last remaining mostly amidst the trees, while the 5 adults sat around me and gobbled rice I threw them, grain by grain, picking it off the ground with both hands, occasionally squabbling and snarling and showing teeth. The babies came later to eat the few grains that were left. They were so ugly they were cute, with wide open eyes and nervous mouths, very uncertain of the world.

Tomorrow AM I shall leave here and set off, along a dirt tract which I hope will be a short cut, to Hambantota. If it is a short cut, I will save about 5 miles, having only 13 miles to do. If it is not, I won't reach Hambantota tomorrow.

January ?—Some days after 'arrival': that day I left Karmagala, descending via the D.S.R. (damned slippery rocks), I did not even find the short cut, and finally went down the road I went up. Alms superb: the best jackfruit I have ever had, good kidney beans, stringhoppers, etc. Ambalantota was dreadful. Finally, when there were 6 miles to Hambantota a man ran up and gave me a note from Ñāṇasumāna (at first I thought it was money and refused it) telling me where he was—about a mile away. If I had found the short cut I would have reached the main road beyond this point and would have had to go all the way to Hambantota to learn that he was staying on an estate 6 miles back, so the longest way is, once again, the quickest. Sometimes it's necessary to go a long distance out of your way in order to come back a short distance correctly.

* * *

... While moving slowly westward one morning I was attacked by a dog and my robe, if not my person, was torn. As I sat crosslegged (then as now) repairing the damage (as you say, my barber is my tailor) your letter was delivered, and I discovered that my robe was not all which required repairing.

In the last year, or so, the centrifuge of my mind has slowed down somewhat, spinning—by now—but little faster than a spider (or a string-hopper—mine), and a certain amount of sediment has been able to settle. The waters are, to be certain, clearer; but there is an ugly black sludge on the bottom which has to be hauled out and dumped. This sludge is not only ugly and black, but also sticky (though *not* a suitable construction material, for spiders or bakers) and gets all over *everything*. Sometimes it even gets into my pen, where it resembles the indigenous ink so closely that it can be used to write letters (This is the Voice of America…). You, undoubtedly, have found (upon receiving one of these) that your hands (not to mention your eyeballs) were coated with the muck. Distasteful. Scraping sidewalks. Won't come off. There is, however, one more quality which this material has: it is not only black, ugly, and sticky: it also means *no* harm. It just wants out. Dredging operations continue…

Since you are naturally somewhat repelled by the sludge, I would suggest this: when dredging is not carried on so furiously (and there is time, betimes, for washing as well) we can return to spinning moving (not rigid) substances.

Your communications are important to me; but your friendship more so; patience… please… and joy.

V.

* * *

So the walk is now finished.

It was not much fun at all, but I didn't really expect it would be. Its main features were an alternation between physical pain and boredom, combined with the intensely minor pleasures (looking at a hill, a tree, a sky, and suddenly <u>seeing</u> them) which, when so combined, are the teaching experience. It's pretty hard to say what I've learned otherwise. For certain something about relaxation. I don't think I'm really capable of <u>saying what</u> I've gained; only of saying that something was gained, I have no regrets for the experience (nor, in truth, for any experience, since arriving in Asia 4 years ago.) Perhaps one sentence will best sum up what I learned. It's not easy to understand, but it was not easy to learn: it took a month's walking; and the sentence (which cost many hours of thought) is more interrelated than at first appears. Here it is: I learned the best medicine in the jungle is Vick's VapoRub, and the structure of freedom, like the structure of a hurricane lamp, lies outside itself, not internally.

As to the rest, I'm not in much of a writing mood these days, and will let it pass by.

* * *

... Perhaps, someday one of the dogs here will dig up some bones, the island will shake, fires will issue forth and the Hermitage will go to the still lonelier depths at the bottom of the lagoon—in which case I shall wander off to be again *en route*. If I wander across the Siberian hinterlands, almsbowl in hand and robes held tight, across the frozen Straits, down Alaska and into the Rockies, I'll come a-begging at your door, brother...

# PART II

# Digging In, Digging Out

Godawaya, January 1968

… The ripples of the sand form lines of light and dark beneath a half moon, running uncertainly into the sea, which itself is lined, dark and jet black. These jet black lines move stealthily inwards, suddenly catching fire as cold green sparkles like a fluorescent tube, broken, reveals the wave in a glimmer of phosphorus an instant before whitecaps break looming towards shore, humming deeply, and break on the beach; the suds-covered water seeps into the pale sand with a hiss as the water rolls back. The moon is not merely half a circle: it is, clearly, a quarter of a globe. The brightest stars twinkle in a flux of color, never static: white, blue, green, red, orange, yellow…

I sit on the beach at night, a strong wind pulling at my robes, the stump of a coconut leaf stem stuck in the sand as a backrest.

By day I stay, mostly, in my hut, which is made of woven coconut leaves, open from belt to roof on three sides exposing the luxurious tame growth that provides the peacefulness of this primeval garden. Monkeys, large, black-faced, with silver-gray fur, peer from the cactus trees; a chorus of birds. Cows and water buffalo wander about freely. I am on an estate of about 100 acres on what is almost an island; about 80 acres are rice and the other 20 are undeveloped. On this island Ñāṇasumāna, myself, and an elderly American (late 60's) live. (The latter has been in Ceylon about 2 years and is practicing the teaching as an *upāsaka*—a layman—having built his own *kuṭi* here, at Godawaya, about 6 miles from Hambantota.) With mutual interests and outlooks, we get along well and don't bother one another. There is a coconut estate nearby where one can walk, as well as much open land; my grass hut, though, is quite comfortable. I sit outside soaking on sun, meditating, reading, resting by day, and go to the beach by night. The place is so idyllic and peaceful that there is a great tendency to forget that there is any world outside, and hence I have neglected, out off, and procrastinated writing for many days. The situation is not perfect for there is a constant attack by aerial creatures: gnats, flies, mosquitos; all have their prescribed times to plague one. I have learned the best way of avoiding them—the best places to frequent—and find this aspect tolerable. Attempts have been made to provide a net, so far unsuccessful—the servants too, I suppose, feel this resistance to doing anything involving the outside world. Ñāṇasumāna and I are guests, though, and here for limited stays.

You wrote once that the Heidegger quotation I sent you was incomprehensible, and, therefore, bad writing. You may recall that in the same letter I sent Kummer's Quartic Surface. This, I presume, was not more comprehensible to you than the Heidegger, yet you did not say that it was also bad. The reason, of course, is that the latter is mathematics, which is a language in which you have slight knowledge, while the former was in English, which you do—you suppose—understand. But you *do* understand *some* of the mathematician's language: arithmetic, algebra, etc. You recognize that that language is hierarchically structured, and that some concepts can best be expressed on one level of this structure, other concepts on another level. Thus, 2+2=4 is on the arithmetic level. It could *also* be expressed algebraically (X+X=2X—where X=2), but this, you recognize, is not so efficient as the arithmetical level of expression.

What is generally not recognized—or, at any rate, not made use of—is the fact that English, too, is hierarchically structured, though much more complexly than mathematics. Some of the levels of this structure have names: dialects, colloquialisms, 'business talk', 'shop talk', 'scientific jargon', regionalisms, formal, informal, and technical; and we have all learned a great many of these connected levels, which we can switch between without difficulty and often without awareness that we are doing so. But suppose we are faced with an *unfamiliar* level might we understand the words—or most of them—and still miss the sense? If we hear a rural black from the deep South talking we might find that, even understanding all the words, we still might not see what he is *getting at*, and of course he would not see what we were getting at when we spoke to him.

Within our lives we recognize this, and use language on the appropriate level. (The 3 major levels are formal, informal, and technical.) Some levels are more appropriate for communications of one type; other levels are best suited to other types. Heidegger, it seems, has something to communicate which is *not* an ordinary communication (he speaks of the nature of our being, and its consequences), and we could hardly expect him to be best able to communicate an unordinary—extraordinary—message using ordinary language. He was obliged, for the sake of accuracy of thought—indeed, for the sake of the possibility of communication—to write on a generally unfamiliar (but not totally unfamiliar) level of language, and if we wish to understand him, our first task is to learn his language. We have had to learn all the other levels we know—usually though this learning has been done in childhood, school, university, business, etc., and not independently, and it is the fact that the level of language is unfamiliar to you that makes him, naturally, incomprehensible. Yet how much of real estate would you understand if you didn't have a business-language for it? (If you are not aware of this language, I can only suggest you listen to yourself sometime when you 'talk business'—notice the phrase—and recognize what would be not understood by one who had no knowledge of business.) In brief: an extraordinary message *requires* an extraordinary use of language in order for it to be *possible* to communicate it.

Last night, since the full moon is approaching, the sea turtles crawl up on the beach to lay their eggs. These are the giant turtles who live for a few centuries or so and lay their eggs every night for a week or so around full moon time. They are *really* giants—one can get atop them (they're pacifists) and ride them. Their shells rise 3 to 4 feet, and they nuke a track like an amphibious vehicle. The natives wait and steal the eggs after they (the eggs, not the natives) are buried. Since they come in great hordes (the natives as well as the eggs) there will soon—within a few centuries—be no more giant sea turtles. Some of the turtles are killed, but the eggs, apparently, bring more monthly money at market than the meat, so the practice is, fortunately, not widespread.

I bathe in a river near a rock on which usually basks a very large and rather peculiar-looking iguana—about 8 feet long, but rather scaley. I have just learned that the reason it is so peculiar-looking is that it's not an iguana but a crocodile. It has caused no trouble at all—and we have been quite close together—even when I startled it in its sunbath and it slipped into the river where I was swimming and itself swam away. There is a gorgeous white bird, body about 6 inches, with a tail about 15 inches long trailing behind it like a cape, which often perches unharmed on the crocodile. I'm not the only one to bathe here also, and no one is bothered—maybe this *is* the Garden of Eden. Not quite: I have now learned there were once many crocodiles in this river; one ate a man a few years ago and it was shot; the other crocodiles have, it seems, taken the lesson to heart. A mosquito net has also been procured; it's pink and has given me both protection and a much rosier outlook on things.

As to what I learned on the walk, it might be put another way: Experience *is* existence. Does that help? And best ignore all the ill-will which was contained within the long account of the journey—an account longer, perhaps, than the journey itself.

* * *

(In the winter of 1968, I stood looking at the Daibutsu in Kamakura, Japan, then purchased in a nearby shop a similar chap in a walnut shell and sent him to Sri Lanka.—Hūm)

No plays provide No answer and play provides no lasting illusion; illumination whether from sunlight or snow-light will only serve those who open their eyes, think with their kidneys, and feel the substantiality of the ground under their butt, and not their but. Your eyes must have seen well of both strangeness and exquisiteness, for the Manjusri, perched in isolation atop the uppermost pinnacle of his enormous half-inch lotus blossom, reflects the illumination of Japan in the presumptive waters on which the lotus floats, plying equally substance and illusion: ivory comes from India, the Buddha comes from India, walnuts grow in Kashmir, and ivory Buddhas in walnut shells come only from Japan.

In case you don't know, one of the pieces of wrapping paper (all of which were printed with a delicate indelible blossom) was a map of the area around the store where you obtained Manjusri, the map showing not how to get to the store but how to go from the store to a beautiful park nearby. I hope you went. I did. I do.

You say nothing of your writing; perhaps your books will arrive here and speak for themselves. I say nothing of the Teaching; perhaps it may arrive there and speak for itself.

A bouquet of parentheses for you, brother: ((((((((((())))))))))).

V.

* * *

So Allan Okam is going to be a rabbi, is he? It seems that there's more religion in the family than I supposed. You say he was inspired by the rabbi who married him, but do not say what the nature of the inspiration is.

Is it a great respect for the rabbi as a person? Or a wish to serve God? Or does he conceive the duties of a rabbi to be directed towards his fellow men in the form of social work rather than directed toward God? Is he concerned for his welfare in this life or in another one? Or is the rabbinate, after all, just a good job, one with good pay (or is it poorly paid?), a respectable position within the Jewish community—a good profession? When he becomes a rabbi will he have accomplished what he wants to do with himself, or will he have put himself in a position where it will be possible for him to work towards what he wants to do with himself? What *does* he want to do with himself? It seems unlikely, from what you tell me of his corpulence, that he harbors any ideals of an ascetic—or even austere—nature. Will he go to Israel? It would be a good lesson—perhaps 'a rude awakening' might be a more accurate phrase—to see how the Orthodox live in Mea Shearim, their quarter of Jerusalem.

There is a copy of Thoreau's Walden here which I have been slowly re-reading, and find that by and large, I am still in deep agreement with nearly everything Thoreau says—and he says it so perfectly, with such evenness of style and wit that it is a great pleasure to read.

I have taken a walk to the other end of the island. A stream coming to the sea forks out into two branches, the eastern one where the hut is, being closed to the sea and the western one being open, the island is about 2.5 miles long but fairly narrow—perhaps half a mile. There is a fishing village at the other end, with a lot of long narrow outrigger fishing boats on the beach, I arrived there at sunset last night—it is so beautiful it puts this end of the island to shame. No use even trying to describe the luxurious growth by the river, on one hand, the sea, on the other, the village (which is small), and the river itself: it can only be seen and remembered. Certainly the most beautiful place I've seen in Ceylon (and that's saying a lot)—especially at sunset.

The cows here are so unworldly they run away when I try to approach them, or even walk by them at 50 feet. The mosquitos, on the other hand, are very brave. They stay in the bushes all day, apparently, and after sunset, I can hear them rising *en masse*, formidable in their collective hum, which sounds like a flying saucer noise in science-fiction movies (and you know how dangerous the flying saucers in science—fiction movies are!) for about half an hour before they become dispersed enough (or whatever it is that happens) to be bothered by them on an individual basis. A yellow-breasted bird with a long curved beak and a complicated cry flutters about my *kuṭi* and hangs sideways from the odd strips of leaf that hang from the roof; he's not afraid of me either.

In the next letter you send by envelope, could you perhaps enclose: (1) a package of Type-Erase, the pieces of white paper that obliterate errors and (2) some number 8 size *stainless* sewing needles (my attempts in the last year to get some sewing needles which don't rust within a week would make a long comedy!)?

This pen tells me it's tired of writing—as you can see by the work it's doing—so...

* * *

... Yes, leeches, mosquitos, etc. are loathsome creatures, and I have no particular desire to preserve them. The reason—the primary reason at any rate—for my unwillingness to kill them is quite simple: it is to my own disadvantage. When one engages in acts of violence the mind is not clear, as anyone who has ever lost his temper well knows. But in order to best be able to deal with ourselves and our world, it is necessary to understand what our nature and the nature of the world is; and if the mind is not clear it cannot do so. Therefore, the moment of pleasure at killing an annoying creature is paid for by the mind becoming less clear, less a useful tool for understanding itself; and refraining from killing has not only the opposite effect, but also the effect of calming one, so that these creatures become, in fact, less of an annoyance. That's what I was talking of, when I wrote you about equanimity, which is a side-effect of practicing the Buddha's Teaching. In fact, training a calmness of mind is half the practice: it is *samathā bhāvanā* (calm concentration); the other half is *vipassanā bhāvanā* (insight meditation, which, guided by instructions of the texts, works in direct accord with calm concentration, like two legs when walking). There is, as a secondary consideration, a desire to practice *ahiṃsa*—harmlessness—for the benefit of the creatures themselves—but this is purely a secondary motivation. I have observed through the past year or so, however, that as my practice increases and

I become calmer and more in control of myself, that this desire has, of its own accord, grown: there is, as the practice improves, not only a growth of equanimity but also of compassion.

There was a 15 foot long crocodile in the river, whom I used to see when I bathed. Sometimes he would swim by, only the top of his snout and his eyes visible at one end, and the end of his tail at the other; he came as close as 20 yards to me, but would not come any closer. Sometimes he would be sunbathing drowsily on a point of land about 30 yards off from where I bathed. He never did anything but mind his own business. (He could have killed me, I suppose, on a dozen occasions, but left me strictly alone.) Now I learn that he has been shot for his hide. I find this slightly upsetting, for I had a liking for that crocodile: there may be an occasional bad one, but, by and large, crocodiles, like snakes, would much rather not be bothered by one than to bother one. (A mapila snake—highly venomous—lives in a wall of the *kuṭi*, between two coconut fronds—I see him every few days, as he crawls away from me.)

Sometimes we get the 'fixins' for some Western food. We let some milk sit around a few days till it turned to clobber, and a portion of this has been sitting around for a week now, and we hope to get a Roquefort cheese from it, which we will use to make a salad dressing for our lettuce, tomato, and carrot salads. I tried my hand at some blinzes, using the clobber as the stuffing. The outside, however, was more like an omelet—still quite good, but not blinzes (what's the secret?). I also made some French toast one day; Ñāṇasumāna has turned out some good Boston baked beans. A Sinhalese garnish: simply flour mixed with coconut gratings and a very slight amount of water—steamed: the flour clings to the coconut in little balls and cooks that way. Simple and tasty.

February seems to be the month for sunsets—sunsets like you don't even see on picture postcards. I sit on a rock above the sea and watch the sunset, the sea, the river, and the fishing boats as they set out, each evening. In the morning I watch the sunrise, which is not as awesome as the sunsets, and then water the boats sail back into their small harbor: there are two natural rock jetties stretching out into the sea not far from my *kuṭi* and the harbor is near; on the beach a small fishing village has been raised in just the last 2 weeks, and the fishermen are hardworking, quiet, and keep the beach spotless. Their boats are about 15 feet long, but only about 2 feet wide; all outrigged on one side; some have sails; most seat two men. They sail out to the horizon, and at night their lanterns can be seen winking. Occasionally a steamship will pass along the horizon also, on its way to Indonesia or Japan or Australia, for this seems to be a main shipping route.

I sleep out now, on a plot of grass between two boulders—about 20 feet apart—near a cave (in case of rain), on the landwards tip of the big jetty, and so don't spend much time around the *kuṭi*, except in the morning, when I come in to eat (and, sometimes, to cook[1]), and afterwards, when I take care of a few odd matters, such as writing letters, I resort to my perch under a net. Sitting under it now, I note that gnats have, in the last few days, disappeared with the warmer weather's coming, and flies have taken their place. This is an improvement: gnats can go through the netting, whereas the flies can't. (Worst place I've ever been for gnats was Lapland, where they were a real torment.)

* * *

I've been in Bundala for a few days now, and find it a pleasant place. The walk from Godawaya, 16 miles by the beach (25 miles by the road) was rough, since loose sand is hard to walk on; but I broke it up into two days—an afternoon and a morning—of 5 hours each. A rather dull walk, with no houses or anything the last 8 or 9 miles—only sea on my right, scrub jungle on my left. Each day I go to a different house in the village—the date of the month determining which one—where I am given food and return to the *kuṭi* to eat it. In the evening the house which is scheduled to provide food the next day sends up some drink—tea, soda, limeade, etc.—and inquires if I need anything. They also bring a quart of lamp oil. (Since I use at most a quart a week, it will take only a simple calculation based on the volume of the room and the volume of a quart bottle to determine when I will be forced to move out.) Otherwise I am left alone to my work.

As to the purpose of meeting Ñāṇasumāna and Mark here, the main reason was because we have—all 3 of us—found the ideas of the late Ven. Ñāṇavīra Thera, an English monk who died (in this *kuṭi*) in 1965—to be very useful in our practice. Now all the material has been collected—manuscripts, letters, etc.,—and we want to make 3 copies of it. So we

1. While fully ordained monks (*bhikkhus*) are not allowed to cook, that doesn't apply to novices (*sāmaṇeras*).—Ed.

met to discuss how best to organize it, etc., for our individual needs, and to arrange everything (this is why a typewriter is necessary). That's the reason for *coming* here. The reason for *staying* was because we get on well together and being together was an aid to our practices, in as much as we are all doing the same thing. The reason for *leaving* was to digest all that had been accumulated in the 7 weeks at Godawaya.

This *kuṭi*, which was built in '57, is constructed on the standard design of Island Hermitage *kuṭis*—the room is a box, 12 feet by 8 feet, with a door leading out to the 'caṅkamana'—the ambulatory, which is 30 feet by 3 feet, and is a very important part of meditation. Usually the *kuṭis* have two small windows, with thick black vertical iron bars set in them (Sinhalese are terrified of theft), giving a 'prison' effect; the floors are hard cement. This has been improved by a 6 feet by 7 feet window (without bars) being placed in both the Northern and Eastern walls, allowing light and air; and by the cement floor covered with a mud floor, which is comfortable to walk on (and easy to keep clean), and by the ambulatory being remodeled so that one walks on a carpet under which is a sand base, which is far less tiring than walking on concrete. The bed (and seat) are raised two inches off the floor, and are simply mud with a straw mat over it. There is no movable furniture. The *kuṭi* is mud brick, with a corrugated asbestos roof and asbestos sheet ceiling. Tiles are not satisfactory because the monkeys, who jump on the roof at times, would break them.

A boy has just come (5:15 PM) with a big pitcher of limeade, some sugar, a cigarette (someone, perhaps, has informed the villagers that I smoke: this is the first cigarette I've been offered), and half a quart of kerosene. (It's no good refusing the kerosene: their job (as they see it) is to offer; my job is to accept.)

Odd: at Godawaya the mosquitos came out only at night; here they come only by day. Perhaps, it's the *same* mosquitos migrating to Bundala at sunrise and going back to Godawaya at sunset. Not very many here, though, except from 5:30 AM to 7:30 AM, when the sun shines in the *kuṭi*.

6:15 PM: I have just discovered one reason why there are so few mosquitos at night: a frog has just hopped in and plans, apparently, to spend the night. He is welcome.

A family of mice—2 babies and a mother—also live here. They've moved upstairs, though they were living in the bed when I arrived. The mother is very good and takes care of her babies: she is not the least bit afraid of me, either, though she objects to my coming near her babies.

Outside: chipmonks, black-faced monkeys, mongooses, many lizards 3 feet to 4 feet long, several wild hens. Elephants, bears, leopards, wild buffalo (very dangerous, I'm told) are about, but unseen—they avoid man if possible.

A poor quality typewriter is presently available; there are, apparently, no satisfactory typewriters for sale in Ceylon; so we'll have to hunt for one elsewhere.

Nickel-plated needles will *not* do. They may be rust-proof in the U.S., but having tried all different plates, I know that none of them last long here. (Neither do most locally manufactured products; e.g. the ball-point pen refill that is splotching and skipping over this letter is a *new* one.) I was given 2 needles in December, which I kept in a glass vial wrapped in cotton, and though I've been in dry weather all the time since then they are pitted, black, and dull. In any case, if no stainless steel needles are available, no need to bother.

J.-P. Sartre's novel *Nausea* is the best presentation I've seen in fictional form of the basic perception of the existentialist premise. The ending is phoney, but the rest of it—though not quite top-rate as literature—is top-rate as existentialism.

* * *

I last wrote my draft board in December 1966, when I informed them of my ordination, and asked for clerical status. So it finally came through, eh? My relations with the draft board have always been rather absurd, and this, I think, is the crowning glory, so to speak: 'minister of religion'. Technically true, of course, but in practice, nothing could be less likely.

I went down to the sea a few days ago to bathe, and found it so pleasant that I spent several noon-time hours there, which resulted in a very mild sunburn. The burn doesn't bother me at all, but it certainly bothers the villagers. They, being brown-skinned, have never heard of anything like 'sunburn' and when they saw my skin peeling thought that I had contracted some sort of skin disease and wanted me to see their native doctor. They were completely incredulous at my attempted explanation of what had happened to me, and did not understand why I refused to see the doctor. Nevertheless, I had no desire to undergo a treatment for something I didn't have, and refused, very firmly (to equally firm insistence) to do anything at all, except peel. They misinterpreted my refusal, of course, and assured me that the doctor was competent, that I was not leprous, etc., but disappointing as it was to them, to no avail.

It's not strictly true that I receive no newspapers. Sometimes I receive a parcel (of bananas, betel nut, curds, soap, etc,) wrapped in newspaper, and occasionally an English-language newspaper, I usually get the sports-page of the provincial English papers or else the Tea Board quotations of the Ceylonese Observer—a rather strange view of world affairs—but sometimes I get 'lucky': the other day I learned, via one of these scraps of paper, both that Harold Holt, the Prime Minister of Australia, had (presumably) drowned, and that some doctors in South Africa had succeeded in transplanting a human heart. The report seemed to indicate that it was not an *artificial* heart, but a real, live *human* heart that was transplanted. I recall, many years ago, Connie Francis had a hit song called 'If I give my heart to you', but I did not expect that it would be taken so literally. One question which the newspaper scrap did not answer was: what happens to the donor?

There is a Sinhalese grammar book here which I have been looking at. Did you know Sinhalese has four words for 'you'? The distinction is not singular/plural/male/female, but rather along caste lines: *thō*, *thā* are 'used in speaking when the speaker is angry, a discourteous form of address'; *umba* is used in speaking 'to an inferior'; *thumuse* is used 'to an equal'; and *thumunnūnsē*. is used 'to a superior or Buddhist priest'. There are also certain verbs which have the same four-fold division (come = *enawā*, *enta*, *enda*, *wuren*; sit, go, stand, eat, sleep, etc. are also fourfold; and please has two forms, as does yes, both having one form for all people and another which is used only when speaking to 'Buddhist priests'. All languages, of course, have such distinctions; but not many of them have the rules formally stated as part of a traditional heritage. Tradition rules in Ceylon, though: it's responsible for a good percentage of the stupidities which persist. (Odd: in the West the *newer* something is the better it is presumed to be; in the East it's the opposite—choice of stupidities?)

An elephant visited me about a week ago. It was night, so I couldn't see it, but I could sure hear it: great crashing of branches, accompanied by very solid nasal snorts. I shined my flashlight in its direction (there's a path running parallel to the *kuṭi*, separated from it by about 40 feet of medium—thick growth) and it went away: I've been told that they will always go away from a light at night. Also saw, early one morning, what I think is a pole-cat: it had a yellow belly, anyway. Do other cats have yellow bellies? Definitely a 'cat'ish thing, though not sleek like a tiger; about 2-3 feet long with a tail as long, sort of bushy; its tail and back were dull brown. It leaped from tree to tree at a distance of about 70 feet from the *kuṭi* and finally disappeared behind some foliage. If it saw me it paid me no heed. Also seen: an insect which is half bright red and half horizon pink—a very sporty combination (for an insect, anyway) a pure white insect; a mosquito with a body 1½ inches long!!! I could hear its whine in the daytime 50 feet away: I did not sample its bite, but a few of them could cause anemia; a whole herd of wild goats (near the sea); the chipmunks eat out of my hand; but the mongooses won't come near me.

Thanks for the blinz recipe. No other recipes needed. Ovens being non-existent in this neck of the jungle, mandel bread could not be made.

Do you know anything of a product which is sort of 'a zip-less zipper', consisting of two pieces of cloth which stick together and cannot be *pulled* apart, but are easily *peeled* apart?

* * *

After leaving Bundala I spent a few days at Godawaya, and then returned to the Island Hermitage, to digest all the material I had consumed during my four months in the jungle and by the sea. Digestion, though, is hard work, and results are coming in (going out?) slowly. Nor am I settled down yet: one of the German monks will disrobe soon, and when he leaves I will move to his *kuṭi*, which is far superior to my present one. There are not many people here now: the Mahā Thera, 2 Germans, 2 Sinhalese, and two laymen: an Indian and a Dane. The Indian will take the robes in a few months; the Dane is undecided. (Everyone is excited—everyone, that is, but me—about the Indian's ordination, for he is a high-caste Brahman from Benares. He seems to spend all his time in the library.)

I sent a telegram (the first, I think, that I have ever sent in my life) to the Island Hermitage to tell them I was coming. The telegram I sent said that I would arrive on the 3rd at 9 AM. The telegram which was received said that I would arrive on the 6th at 1 PM. The telegraph office has vastly underestimated my abilities. As a result, there was no boat waiting for me, and I had the alternative of either taking a fishing boat or waiting (as I later discovered) 3 days and 3 hours for the Island Hermitage boat. (I was a little late, but not so late as the telegraph office predicted. In this case, they are, it seems, much like the weather bureau—generally wrong.)

The fishing boat was a long narrow affair made of a coconut log with boards raising the sides, just wide enough for me to put my legs in, though not next to each other, but, rather, one before the other. I would have preferred straddling it, like a horse, but monks, apparently, do not do such things—at least not in Ceylon—and I was firmly told (in Sinhalese) to put my feet in the boat. As soon as we got a few feet away from shore we began taking on water at an alarming rate and were in the process of sinking, which was rather distressful. I can swim, but the box of papers, etc., I had with me—some of them irreplaceable—could not. We returned to shore, I and my boxes—a total of about 200 pounds—got out, and the fisherman went to the Island to tell them I was waiting. The servants came (at record speed) to get me, and I managed to get to the island at 11:00 AM, just in time for *dāna*. So my trip, unlike the world, ended with a bang, not a whimper.

No, I hadn't heard of LBJ's problems. At one time, the news would not have displeased me, but now I no longer care very much about it. Such matters no longer concern me, and—partly for that reason—seem somewhat unreal. (In fact, if by real is meant here—now and by unreal not-here or not-now, then the presidential situation is totally unreal, since I don't even think about it.)

Today is full moon day. It's also Sinhalese New Year day, and I write against an aural background of fireworks. It's also Good Friday. Tomorrow and the next day are also holidays. Maybe the day after a no-holiday will be declared.

Oh, yes—we made the blinzes again, according to the recipe you sent, and they turned out much better than the first batch. It's back to the chilies, now, though.

So ends another pen refill—almost before it started.

* * *

The box of books finally arrived; many thanks. Unfortunately, there seem to be many titles I don't recall at all and which are of no use to me whatsoever—and missing are a number of the books of greatest interest to me: e.g. Joyce's *Ulysses* (in a dark red cover with a black title page almost worn off and which is filled with my notes), Beckett, Dylan Thomas, Eliot, Kafka's *Great Wall of China*, Annotated Alice, *Faulkner Stories*, Brooks & Warren's *Understanding Fiction*, Snodgrass' *Heart's Needle*.

On June 24th I will take my higher ordination along with the Yugoslav, the Indian, and a Sinhalese[1]—very international.

I have still not yet moved—the German is forever postponing his departure and, with the waiting and unsettledness, I'm at a standstill in this *kuṭi* (and have run out of pen refills as well). He assures me, though, that he will leave before Vesak, which is May 12.

My razor-blade problem appears to be solved: I was given a new straight razor which I've learned to use and find it far superior in both speed and comfort to blades. The razor, which is made in China, is first quality steel—good enough so that I have yet to put it to a stone; just a strop is quite enough to keep it sharp.

* * *

At my higher ordination (June 24th) my name will be changed: I will thence-forth be called ÑĀṆASUCI BHIKKHU, so your addressing of envelopes can also be changed. It is not a deal of great importance, but, on the other hand, it is a deal of some importance. ÑĀṆA (Ñ is pronounced as in Spanish señot, Ṇ as a soft staccato n, Ā as ah, but twice as long as a—the whole pronounced NYAANA) means knowledge and SUCI (pronounced SOO-CHEE) means 'pure-clean' with an overtop of 'sweet'. BHIKKHU (pronounced bik-oo—the 'h's are pronounced, but very softly and cannot quite be compared to anything in English) is a title, usually translated as 'monk', but more literally 'almsman', and means one who has his higher ordination as opposed to SĀMAṆERA, or novice.

What 'irreplaceable paper'? It's largely material I use as a correlative to an aspect of meditation; it consists of a technical book *Notes on Dhamma*, a large manuscript collection of letters, and sundry shorter pieces, all by the late English monk, Ven. Ñāṇavīra Thera. We hope

1. Ven. Ñāṇajivako, unknown, Ven. Ñāṇānanda.—Ed.

to have it mimeographed, but details need to be worked out; such as a typewriter suitable for the work, and there is some uncertainty of getting the proper stencils. It will be easier to type one set of stencils and get all the copies we need than to type a set of 3 or 4 carbons and not have any copies to send to the few people who might be interested in the material. But—we shall see what develops.

The 5-colored flag on the postage stamp was designed at the turn of the century by the American Col. Olcott, who is a national hero in Ceylon, in statues, street names, etc., and is the 'Buddhist flag', if there can be such a thing.

* * *

I am glad to hear you are well and keeping cool. I am also well and keeping cool, though I don't have air-conditioning or air cooling. Nor, I imagine, does anyone in the village—you might ask, more appropriately, if anyone in the village has electricity—but yes, being on the coastal route, some of them do. But as for appliances of any sort more elaborate than radios and light bulbs, I doubt if there are any—perhaps the few wealthiest villagers might have a refrigerator. I get along quite well without such mechanical devices and find, when I encounter them (as in Colombo) that they raise for me more difficulties than they solve. There is a pump on the other island which is run for about an hour every few days to pump water into a storage tank, and when I was living on the other island, I found it to be a great disturbance. On this island, however, there is no pump and no disturbance.)

No, the customs people have not yet settled matters. They agreed—several weeks ago—to re-assess the duty on the mosquito netting, but I have not heard from them since. These things usually take 3-4 weeks, everything in the East being done slowly. Since I'm in no great hurry, however, I don't mind waiting. Sometimes—usually, in fact—it's better in the long run to proceed slowly than to rush about. Many reasons, not the least being that one has time to reflect upon one's actions, which develops both calmness and insight. Another difficulty with the customs people is that they have refused my application to import the typewriter that Mark is donating to our project. I'm in contact with Remington's agents in Colombo, and expect the customs people may reverse their decision, commerce *über alles*.

Remember the map of the Indian Ocean floor you sent last year? Well, I've framed it and hung it on the wall of the *kuṭi*, where it looks very nice. The frame is made of bamboo and I made it myself. The map is blue and yellow, the bamboo is yellow, the wall is white. The good thing about this map is that it is subjective. Most maps are objective, and so, while useful for measuring distances, are essentially *unreal*. This map, being subjective, has a point of view (located somewhere near the South Pole, about 1000 miles up), and a perspective which lends it both reality and interest.

* * *

The mosquito netting arrived—at last. The duty was reduced from 101 rupees to 23 rupees—still 75% duty, and quite high, but at least not absurd, and it was paid and the netting—of a rather unexpected, but quite satisfactory, weave—arrived. There is a sewing machine here (a 2 year old Singer, excellent quality), so I should have no trouble making the net, once I get some sort of ground material—I'll find out what is locally available for that.

'Vas', or the 'Rainy Season Retreat' starts with the full moon today—the 3 month period when monks stay in one residence and don't travel about. 'Rainy season', of course, refers to the season in the Ganges valley area east of Benares—Island Hermitage has rainy season all the time (particularly these last 2 weeks)—which starts about this time of the year. Looks like we'll have 10 monks here for Vas—2 Germans, an Indian, myself, and 6 Sinhalese—and there are also a Dane and an Australian, laymen, I don't think either of the latter will stay much longer (though they've been here for quite a few months already). In any case, that's a pretty full house; a very full hermitage…

* * *

So Talmudic scholars count angels on pins, do they? I always thought it was the Catholic scholars who did that, and that the Talmudists counted the shekels on the Catholic scholars. There are Buddhist scholars as well, but I'm not sure what they count. The Buddha's Teaching, at any rate, has nothing to do with scholarship whatsoever in any form. Here's Kierkegaard on scholars:

> 'Let the enquiring scholar labor with incessant zeal, even to the extent of shortening his life in the enthusiastic service of science; let the speculative philosopher be sparing neither of time nor of diligence, they are none the less not interested infinitely, personally, and passionately, nor could they wish to be. On the contrary, they will seek to cultivate an attitude of objectivity and disinterestedness. And as for the relation of the subject to the truth when he comes to know it, the assumption is that if only the truth is brought to light, its appropriation is a relatively unimportant matter, something that follows as a matter of course. And, in any case, what happens to the individual is in the last analysis a matter of indifference. Herein lies the lofty equanimity of the scholar and the comic thoughtlessness of his parrot-like echo.' (*Concluding Unscientific Postscript*, pp. 23-24).

The only proper application of the Buddha's Teaching (or anything else, for that matter), then, is for one's own personal welfare. But—the scholars (and others) would not agree...

* * *

As there's no news at all here—which, I suppose, is good news—because I don't do anything and nothing has happened to me, perhaps I'll fill up the aerogram a with a few comments on your comments on the comments of the TV panelists on Yoga and Buddhism—though, not having seen the show, I will doubtlessly do them an injustice in my rash assumptions of what they said. Yoga, however, is a discipline with different emphases and goals as practiced by various Hindu sects. It can have for its purpose anything from bodily health (for which it is probably as good a therapy as anything else) to 'unification with the Divine Being', or other such mysticism. It has no part at all in the Buddha's Teaching: so if the panelists were discussing these two subjects as a unit anything they might have said would be founded on a false assumption—vis. that they are related. If they were confusing *hatha* yoga (which is a set of *bodily exercises*) with meditation (which is the practice of *mental concentration*), then too they were making an identification so basically false as to obviate whatever conclusions they might have reached. Besides, the Lotus Sutra and the phrases you quoted are all from a Japanese sect and does not at all represent the Buddha's Teaching—the Japanese themselves admit this—but rather the (mis-)interpretations of the 27 Japanese Patriarchs (some of whose teachings are in direct contradiction with the original texts—and in direct contradiction, as well, with experience).

As to the conclusion they draw, I can only say that meditation is inwardness, activity is outwardness; and whichever one is chosen as the ideal the other will drag it in the opposite direction. (I went to Galle last week to see the dentist—no cavities—and even the little activity in 'going to Galle' produced a very marked effect on my practice—as does writing letters.) But—these people have no real practice (else they could never have cone to the conclusions you say they did in fact come to) and therefore cannot speak from experience. That being so, they have done no more than add their voices to the babble of confusion which surrounds the public image of the Buddha's Teaching. Most people, if they knew what the Buddha actually taught, would be totally surprised (and that includes most Sinhalese). Besides, how could Dennis Weaver know anything of meditation? How can he sit in the 'Lotus' posture? How does he cross his legs, when he can't bend his knee? Hey, wait fuh me, Mistah Dillon—hey, Mistah Dillon—WAIT FUH MEEEE!

* * *

Though it's possible some Sartre, Beauvoir, Camus, etc., has not been translated into English, I would think it unlikely. You can check on this very easily by consulting the large catalogue of books in print, which is certainly in the library. Then you can let me know if any of the books are still untranslated in which case I will have to write only to the French publishers asking permission to quote and provide translations—for the relevant passages. Then, if you can get copies from the Library of Congress of the books which are translated but not in the Detroit Public Library or the Wayne State library, that would be all that is needed. Even if you can't get the books from the Library of Congress, though, you can get the publisher's data from the catalogue. I have copies of the French books, so there is no need to obtain these.

The typewriter we have now is an ancient Royal which is very difficult to use and which I use only for things that must be typed (besides which any typing is most unwelcome; hence the handwritten letter).

The dentist is one of the regular *dāyakās* of the Island, and does his work on us for free. He is the one who extracted my wisdom tooth last year and who gave me the lift to Galle last December when I went out walking.

Four sheets of plywood—one of them seven-ply-were delivered today, with which I will build a desk, which will meet my needs. It will be 12 inches high, no legs, so I can sit crosslegged at it. (I find high furniture affects my thinking, and much prefer staying at ground level.) The desk will fit into a corner of the *kuṭi*. I made a cardboard model, 1/6 scale, which is quite satisfactory. Probably, though, it will take a long time to get built. The plywood will be attached to a frame and the 7-ply piece will be large enough for the top and for the bottom of a storage box. (The sheets are 4'×4'.) Eventually, I expect, there will be some remodeling of the *kuṭi*, as well. Perhaps, by it falling down.

* * *

Now I am nearing the completion of the frame of the desk—just a few more uprights, several additional braces and runners for the drawers, and the frame will be complete. The additional braces may not be really necessary, since the frame stands solid now, without shaking or wobbling in the least. No screws or nails are in it—all the joints—dozens of them!—are dovetailed. Though I intend to cement them with a tube of EPOXY which has been given me, the frame is quite solid without it. What a lot of work is involved in it, however! The frame, when completed, will have approximately 50 separate pieces, all of which are dovetailed, so that means about 100 dovetails. The 45° angles proved a difficult technical problem, but I think it's solved satisfactorily. I changed the design slightly, moving both drawers over to the left side and leaving the right side open for leg room.

Recently read Tolkein's *Lord of the Rings*—a marvelous work. One of the finest pieces of imaginative fiction that I've come across.

The constant threat of rain the last few days seems to aggravate the mosquitos (and some of the monks as well).

I was told the following story: A monastery once opened up a fish-and-chips shop on the side. One day a customer knocked on the door and one of the residents answered. 'Are you the fish friar?' asked the man. 'No,' replied the resident, 'I'm the chip monk.'

* * *

The desk, at one time, was kind of fun to build, spending a few hours on it in the afternoon; but now it's becoming a burden and I'd rather be done with it. But the epoxy is insufficient to glue it together, and locally made carpentry glue is altogether unsatisfactory—besides being very smelly, it doesn't have much stickum in it. I want to finish up these projects—desk, book, *kuṭi*, etc.—by the end of the year and leave next year free for my practice without all this objective work, which is a real brake on the subjective work.

No, no wild baseball celebrations to report here. Just—if it's Reportable—calmness—gradually (subjectively) developing, purely an internal affair, having little to do with the surroundings—and with it an increasingly clear perception that other affairs serve only the purpose of *preventing* this calmness and subsequent clarity. Once a certain degree of the latter is achieved, such 'celebrations' would be seen as self-anesthetizing, and would, in being seen, hardly be 'celebrated'. But most of us love our stimulations, excitements, intensities (which are inflations of *ourselves*) too much to allow such clarity to occur—so, a wild to-do for any reason at all, and, if no reason comes along, we will manufacture a reason (baseball, rioting over racial injustices, campus rioting over a change of season), keep the blinkers firmly in place. But—such things concern me not at all, and what I write about them now is more with the intent of filling up a letter when there's nothing to say than it is with criticizing them (after all, it's what most people want—let them have it—so long as I'm not forced to participate), and I find I no longer have very much capacity for complaining about anything at all, let alone about the normal state of the world. And that, I think, is not for the worst.

* * *

As for the book I'm working on, it's only an incident in my work and not its sole purpose—which your 'after the book, what then?' question implies. After it is done I shall have the use of the book in my work and shall not have the distractions of preparing the book to interfere with that work, which I have been engaged in for almost 2 years now. Since it is the *only* work which has ever had a satisfaction in it, I don't see much sense in giving it up for something which actually repels me. Do you? So I don't expect to return to the States. I was unhappy there: here I am developing the way I want to. But explanations are useless, tiresome things. Whatever my reasons, they are sufficiently strong for me not to hedge about my future: I'm doing what I have to do here and what I can't do in the States. (This, of course, does not rule out the possibility of a visit—with a return here. Or have you considered a visit here—most welcome?)

Received a parcel of poetry—no customs, no declarations at all. Poetry (Snodgrass, etc.) must be in a very privileged position in Ceylon (or, perhaps, in such a low position that the customs people don't even want to look at the titles).

* * *

About the epoxy, I didn't think you could send it in a letter—actually I imagined you would send it in a reinforced toothpaste box or something of the sort. But please do send some, since without it there is little more I can do towards finishing the desk. If you would send two sets in separate packages on different days, there will be twice as good a chance of one of them getting through without the usual month-long delay at the customs house. All pieces of plywood for the covering are cut and many of them are in place, though not all of them are glued in place yet. I don't want to use nails because it would ruin the appearance of what will otherwise be a quite professional job—the main difference between a professional job and the one I've done being in the time it took to do it rather than in the appearance of the desk itself. I'm actually quite pleased that it's turning out better than I had hoped. The tools I have—since you asked—are quite limited: a large saw, a small saw, chisel and mallet, hammer, ruler, files (one large, one small), screwdriver (for the screws in the hinges), drill (ditto), pliers, and jack-plane. Most of the dovetails are very close fits—some of them can only be hammered into place—but a few loose ones took some correcting. The desk is absolutely solid now—strong enough to stand on without any signs of stress. But—it's not yet finished, and I'll be glad to have it done. The most difficult part was not the dove-tails—which turned out to be easier to make than I had been led to believe—but the 4 corners which are 45°. It took a lot of thought and experimentation to get them right.

I learned from a scrap of paper just a few weeks ago that Nixon and Humphrey were the candidates for the election—apparently the V.P. candidates are Muskie (who, for some reason, I seem to recall as the governor of South Dakota or some such forgotten place) and Wallace (which Wallace I'm not sure). But no further news has filtered down to me, and I don't know who won. (Nor would I, I expect, even if it had filtered down to me.)

I was invaded, about that time, by the creepie-crawlies, which—in case you don't know—are insects ½ inch long, brown, which wriggle about very rapidly on rather intoxicated courses. They came in thousands at sundown—never earlier—and lasted for about four hours, by which time they had all mysteriously vanished away. I had them four nights in a row and then they went away. No idea how they got in. They're totally harmless—quite helpless, in fact—but it's quite distracting, when I'm trying to meditate, to have them falling from the ceiling—which is, perhaps, their means of entry—and crawling up my back. Perhaps they're adolescent ants being evicted from the nest (there are some ant nests in the roof). In the day there's not the slightest trace of them. I think—to judge from the lizards and other small creatures—that this must be the mating season in Ceylon.

Ants in my robes, so to speak.

* * *

There are still three 'references' needed which perhaps you could check on. First, there is a work by McTaggert called *The Nature of Existence* in two volumes. Only Vol. 1 is available locally. In Vol. 2 could you—if it's available at the library—copy paragraphs 353-4 and send them to me. (The book has bold-face paragraph section numbers, though I don't know what page numbers are equivalent to 353-4, only that it's not in Vol. 1). Secondly, can you find out who is the publisher of the British translation of Wittgenstein's *Tractatus Logico-Philosophicus* and when it was published, etc. Thirdly, there is a work called *Dictionary of Religion* edited by a person named Kern or Fern—I can't find out which is the correct name. Could you find this out?

Part of the work I've been preparing of Ven. Ñāṇavīra Thera's writings consists of letters he has written to various people and serves as a good introduction to his thinking. I know of no better way to give you some idea of what it is that I am actually doing—and what my own attitudes are—than to show you these letters and say, simply: 'I agree.' Therefore I'm going to begin sending them to you, a section or two at a time (via air mail—to send it all at once would be beyond the capacities of our postage fund) at intervals of a week or so—there are 10 'sections'.

Perhaps you will not make anything at all of it—it is by no means easy, but there is much that does not require any technical knowledge—simply good will (a desire to understand rather than to find fault) and an effort of the intellect (the *mode* of thought will be, at first, very difficult for you since it is not familiar). My reason for sending it is not to 'convert' you by any means, nor to argue at all, but rather to give you the opportunity—if you want it—to arrive at some understanding of my own views. How much understanding you obtain will depend on how much good will and effort you care to put into your reading of the letters. I certainly don't expect you to agree with it, but I do rather hope you might, to some extent at least, simply understand it. At any rate, you can expect the first two sections fairly soon. If you don't want to even see them, tell me. If you find them of interest then keep them as long as you wish—forever if you wish. But if you find that you don't want them (or no longer want them) then please return them, as there are others here who would like to use them. So—keep them, return them, or refuse them, read them or not as you like. But don't misunderstand my reasons for sending them or for asking you to return them if and when you are finished with them.

We were served a new food a few days ago—chocolate-covered cheese. Sounds peculiar at first, no? But—there is chocolate milk, chocolate ice cream, etc. So why not chocolate-covered cheese? And, in fact, it turned out to be one of the best combinations I've ever had. (We had yellow cheese. I imagine a white cheese would be best with the chocolate mixed in rather than as a covering.

So Humphrey lost, did he?

> Humphrey Dumphrey was dumped from the boat.
> Humphrey Dumphrey alone could not float.
> All of America and half of the vote,
> Were gathered by Nixon and lost by the bloat.

And Nixon won, did he?

Nixon's stones may break my bones, but Spiro Agnew will never hurt me.

And Nixon, Humphrey and Wallace were all running, were they? Three blind mice, three blind mice, see how they run, etc… Or, better, yet:

> Rubadubdub
> Three men in a tub.
> And who do you think they be?
> They're candidates, lawyers, Washington voyeurs—
> Turn 'em out, knaves all three!

Humphrey, though, had a real yearning to be president:

> Humphrey, Humphrey, candidate,
> Had a yen he couldn't sate.
> He put it to the voter's test,
> But they have sent him West, man, West.
>
> I imagine the voter's attitude, however, to be:
> to poll booth, to poll booth, to throw some rascal in.
> Home again, home again: where is the gin?

Oh well, the elections provided me with the malicious pleasure of writing these lines, so all those millions weren't wasted after all.

* * *

The epoxy had to go through customs (something one would expect to get stuck there), but finally arrived safely with a duty of RS. 1.50 (25¢) and yesterday I finally finished the desk, putting on the last coating of French polish. The graining—which is matched and very handsome—stands out nicely in the wood, which is the color of dark honey with a low gloss. But I've certainly had enough carpentry now to last me for a good long while.

I imagine you find the Letters somewhat disquieting and not at all 'healthy' I would not dispute this, but I would again emphasize that they represent my own view, and were sent not to evoke any emotion whatsoever but simply to afford an avenue of understanding—if you wish it—of the way I am. If you don't want them, by the way, *don't* return them—let me know and I'll send you an address to mail them to: there is one person (Eric[1]—remember him?—who is now in Canada) who might fine them of use and I'd like him to see them. At any rate, you'll receive (if you want it) a copy of the complete work when it's published. (I've had a letter only a few days ago from a complete stranger in Colombo, who has offered to pay all publishing costs and says he will be coming here on the 24th to discuss the matter further. But there is no shortage of people anxious to be the publisher of the book.)

Anyway, perhaps the Letters will help you to understand why I can't accept your conditional offer of round trip transportation. If not, all I can add is that it seems to me that your stipulation that I doff my robes for the occasion shows that you are more interested in seeing me-as-you'd-like-me-to-be than in seeing me-as-I-am. But me-as-you'd-like-me-to-be—alas!—does not exist. I think I've already told you that I can feel affection for you without missing you, and that if I did visit it would be primarily (though not entirely) at your desire. That I would return here is beyond question and discussion. Therefore even if I did agree to go in Western clothes it hardly seems likely that the visit could be a success, since your stipulation shows that you would try—directly or indirectly—to induce me to remain and then there would be tension conflict, anxiety, and unhappiness. And if my going to the States would cause that then it seems that the only reasonable thing is not to go. If and when the conditions which would be responsible for the tension, etc., are eliminated there would no longer be any need for any stipulations or conditions, and then it might be possible to plan a successful visit.

I gave the lunar photos you sent to the Mahā Thera; he appreciates that sort of thing. My explorations are in an entirely different direction. Speaking of the sky, though, Venus (or could it be Sirius?) has been so bright of late that it actually casts a distinct shadow at night for the few hours it's still visible after dark. Now, of course, we're getting a new moon, which is also up before the sun has set, so it's no longer visible: but in another few weeks, perhaps the star will be visible again, after the full moon. I've never seen a star so bright before.

Eric returned to Canada (his wife is Canadian; he is American) via Japan (from Australia), from which he sent me a lovely little Japanese Buddha seated cross-legged on a lotus blossom which rests on a pedestal supported by a cat (or perhaps some other animal—I don't know its

---

1. E=H—H

significance, since the Japanese teachings—which are multitudinous—are far removed from the work I am doing here; though Japanese Zen seems to be the big thing among some of the California set), the whole of this structure is carved out of a piece of ivory about ¾ of an inch high mounted in a polished walnut shell which rests on a wooden base. Some very fine details in the Buddha (if it is in fact a Buddha—it might be some Japanese deity or patriarch for all I know).

* * *

Well, what an attractive aerogramme the U.S. P.O. seems to be putting out now, during 'Human Rights Year', with the globes and birds (what do the birds symbolize? or do they symbolize nothing? 'free flight?' 'bars-do-(or do-not) a-prison-make?'), and arranged in a much more convenient and usable form on a much nicer color paper than this dull grey which tends to obscure what is written on it, which tends to be obscure enough.

Big population explosion here at Island Hermitage—7 Western laymen now—4 Americans and 3 English—are here now, although 3 (1 American + 2 English) will be leaving in a week—the 3 whose absence will be least regretted. The 2 Americans from California, who have been here 6 months, will remain, as will a friend of theirs who showed up a few weeks ago—though he's so turned on that I don't know if he'll be able to stick around long enough to come down. Also arrived is an English friend, Graham, who I knew some time ago and who will certainly stay for a long while and almost as certainly be ordained here in the near future. He's been wandering around India and Nepal for some time—and that's where the departing boys are running away to: running away from having to face their own existence—which is all there is to face at Island Hermitage, since there are few external stimulants/irritants/distractions to allow them to forget about their own existence—although they don't know it. He says about 90% of all Westerners—not only backpackers but everybody—in India are busy being part of the drug scene—this is about a 10% increase over when I was there a few years ago—and 75% of the people on the West Coast are also so involved according to our California correspondents. I imagine Detroit has a lower percentage, but hallucinogens seem to be the coming—coming? come!—device for euphoria and general forgetfulness. I'm certainly glad to be far removed from that society.

The main difference between 'them' and me (at least now) is simply that I have something that I see is 'to be done'—i.e. meditation and all that goes with it—while they do not have—have not found—or refuse to recognize/accept that their existence itself requires of them a task to be done—that, in one sense, it is not purposeless (although what that purpose is is not an easy thing to accept)—and so continue *seeking outside* of themselves (via more and more intense stimulants, drugs, etc.) to find out what task there is; however, that can only be learned by seeking inside of oneself, and they, going in the wrong direction, naturally do not find what they (don't know they) are looking for. Occasionally a few individuals come to understand—largely through despair and anxiety—that they've been going the wrong way and reverse their direction, and only those who do understand this are the sort who will/can stay here. Hence, the departures for India and the rest (or no rest, rather).

Well, how's that for filling an aerogramme with nothing to say?

* * *

Today is Sinhalese New Year and the place is very noisy with fireworks going off almost every second, and a great mass of *dāyakās* (their children run about the islands shouting at each other—and the adults are no quieter: the whole affair is a yearly picnic to them, but to us it's our *food*).

An elderly German concert violinist named Neumann has arrived on the Island—his sixth visit, I believe—and intends to be ordained and still another German seeking ordination is expected to arrive within the next week or so. In the meantime the Mahā Thera is having a good deal of fun being very secretive about the ordination plans—he won't say when it will be or even who will be ordained. Maybe he's no more certain than they.

I expect to go down to Bundala sometime this month, and may (or may not) stay for the month of May. I may stay elsewhere for May. At any rate, I feel that a month away from the Hermitage will be to my benefit: a slight shift of viewpoint may bring to light things which I'm now in a position—as a result of the last year here—to see but can't quite make out through the particular obstructing foliage indigenous to the Island.

* * *

Well, we've finally exhausted the supply of old grey aerogrammes ('the old grey aerogramme, it ain't what it used to be), and I can write on a much more legible blue.

I left Island Hermitage about a month ago and I've been at Ñāṇasumāna's *kuṭi* in Bundala ever since. We spent some days talking over what needed to be talked over, then he left for Godawaya, and I've been here alone ever since, which is exactly why I came here: what a relief from the bustle and rush of such a major metropolitan center as Island Hermitage. But, alas, in a few weeks, I'll have to return there to attend to final details on the book—i.e. getting a complete printer's typescript prepared (a beginning has been made already), after which we will be prepared to go to press. There will be no trouble at all with support: a number of people have offered/requested to finance it (one of them is willing to go as high as 100,000 Rs.), and it is only a question of choosing the most suitable—or, possibly, least unsuitable—person (who can also attend to various details with the printer). No—finances are not the hang-up at all, but rather coping with the amount of work involved (the book will be in excess of 400,000 words, which is a pretty big book).

So here I sit in a comfortable net chair—the only piece of furniture in the *kuṭi*—watching the chipmonks hurry to gobble up what they can of the leftover rice I put out for them before the mongooses, monkeys, hens, and other jungle wildlife come along to gobble it up themselves. Even had a glass of milk today, which is a rare treat here (and an impossibility at Island Hermitage, where the shelves are filled with tinned dried condensed and virtually useless Nestomalt), which I poured all over the rice and had milk rice. There's been some *very* out of season rain here this month, so everything is nice and green and the cisterns are full and the bathing area is fresh (and, also, the cows are giving milk—they're usually dried up by now).

The weather—when it's not raining—is sunny and even a shade (if that's the word) on the hot side, and the wind is constantly from the east, so I get the sound of the surf very clear even at the *kuṭi*, which is a half mile from the sea (by the rather circuitous jungle path—certainly a bit less for the crows). Some days I go out for long walks in the afternoon, but the ground is too hot in the early afternoon to walk on (with bare feet), and later on I have to return by about 5:00, at which time one of the villagers brings me a flask of tea—and it's not polite to make him wait too long. Now, though, we're entering the bright half of the month—the moon is waxing and does not set until—tonight—about 10:00 (and later by 50 minutes each night), so it will soon be possible to go out for walks at night: during the hot season (which this is here) that seems to be the only time at which it's comfortable to move about. Otherwise—whether at the *kuṭi* or in some part of the jungle—during most of the day one just stays put. Which is also fine.

In the year since I've last been here a few changes have been made in the *kuṭi* itself—primarily that one whole wall has been removed so that there is now no barrier (except a bamboo curtain which rolls up) between the *kuṭi* itself and the ambulatory, and the place is much lighter and more open. I don't know how well that works out in the season of heavy mosquitos (March/April), but in May it's quite nice: the few mosquitos that do show up are tolerable.

So: there you sit reading this, among your tulips, with the days growing longer and longer (not much difference—only about an hour's total daylight—between even the extremes of December and June this close to the equator—6 N.), warmer and warmer, and greener and greener (Never much shortage of greenery in this part of the world—also many jungle flowers of very fine and exquisite pattern and color, but they are usually a bit hidden and one has to learn *how* to see them; on occasion I've espied some lovely tiny orchids growing near my *kuṭi* at Island Hermitage).

Anyway this month is turning out to be a very welcome break allowing me to do a lot of sorting out and seeing new perspectives. I should be well prepared to return to Island Hermitage and get back to the other perspectives. How's your perspectives?

* * *

You are right—occultism is certainly not the right word to describe what I am doing—but neither is your second guess (mysticism), as you should be finding out from the Letters. Actually, I have never had the slightest interest in the occult (if by that you mean secret messages from the Dead about the Nature of the Beyond and such things), nor in mysticism: whenever I come across such books I find them intolerably boring, and don't recall ever having managed more than a few pages of any such book. Rather, I am, as you suggest I should be, facing the world and its problems—but, instead of trying to start with everybody else, I'm trying to begin with myself. (Where else *can* one begin—or end?) Where I can do some good at least: but all of this business of whether to start with oneself or with others is only a matter of one's basic attitude, for which *at best* no more than explanation is possible. Here is Kierkegaard's explanation:

> 'An immediate enthusiast assails the world's ears with his twaddle early and late, always on his feet and arrayed in buskins, he plagues people with his enthusiasms, and he does not notice that what he says does not inspire them, unless they begin to beat him. He is well informed, and the orders are to effect a complete transformation-of the world; but there he has heard wrong, for the orders are to effect a complete transformation of himself.'—*Concluding Unscientific Postscript*, p. 45.

Perhaps the search for the answer to what life is will go on eternally—although I don't by any means admit that it *must* go on eternally—but that does not mean that *everybody* is *always* in some way seeking a re-solution, in some way or other. And better, then, to do so with full awareness of what one is doing—rather than try to hide the fact of one's search amidst the diversions of the world. Yes, I'm sure you do understand me better than I think. But did this ever occur to you? Perhaps I understand me better than *you* think.

Yes, I've been getting sporadic news about the astronauts. But what is of greater interest to me was a long article I came across about the boat 'Ra' which Heyerdhal is sailing to Central America from Egypt, and I should very much like to hear any reports you have about that. Heyerdhal sounds like a fine man, and I'm sorry that I never read his earlier books (Kon-tiki and Aku-Aku).

Speaking of books—would you care to send another shipment? (Strictly up to your own inclinations, and, while welcome, not of major importance.) If you feel like buying anything, next time you go to Hudson's, I understand that some of Heidegger's books are now available in paperback. The only book of his I have is Being and Time, and I should very much like to see anything else he has written.

One old filling (lower right molar) had partially chipped off and had to be repaired, so I'm now going around with clenched jaws trying to wear the repair job down to a comfortable fit: it feels like a bead of food stuck in the tooth.

You will have noticed that I have an ink pen now, acquired rather accidentally, but which is actually very pleasant to write with—after all those years of ball-point pens. Perhaps it's because of the pen that I've written such a wordy letter.

* * *

While in Colombo—yes!—I heard the radio broadcast of the moon walk and learned all the details. I might point out, however, that if one does not ignore the vast body of evidence existing in India, this was not man's first visit to the moon. When one's meditation practice reaches an advanced stage, the Buddha informs us, it is possible not only to visit the moon, but to hold he sun and moon in one's hand. From the development of my own (slight) meditational abilities I can see (not altogether clearly) the principles involved in doing this and find this statement perfectly credible. Some, however, might be disinclined to accept it. (Or, for that matter, need to make the trip.)

As I slowly recover from the shock of Colombo (which was very shocking indeed), and recover equilibrium and peace, I send you the same.

* * *

When I said that Colombo was shocking I did not mean it morally, spiritually, or aesthetically, but literally: just as a ride in an old car over a dirt road is shocking, so the unevenness, the drive, the rush, the *movement* of Colombo is shocking after the calmness of an unhurried contemplative life. To judge from recent reports life in the West must be even more shocking these days. Most people, of course, want and even seek out such activity: it is an excellent way of avoiding the necessity of facing one's existence, since activity and reflexion are antithetical.

One of the things I got rid of in Colombo was most of my connexion with the book publishing—that, too, has simply become too great a disturbance to my real work and goal, and although it might have been nice to publish, it is actually not only peripheral but even unnecessary. And the work involved, of course, as I can see clearly, would have been detrimental to my meditation—which comes first because I want it to come first: it's the only thing I've ever done in this life that has provided me, independent of everyone else, with actual satisfaction. Nevertheless Ñāṇasumāna is still holding to it, and he may (or may not) eventually get the manuscript into print.

As you've had the Letters for more than half a year now and have said nothing about them, I assume you haven't found them enlightening or even relevant. If this is so, or you're done with them, in any case, could you please send them to my friend Eric in British Columbia? You might find a book called *Anti-Semite and Jew* by J.P. Sartre (Schocken Paperbacks, New York) more to your taste (except the last few pages, which bit of propaganda may be ignored as irrelevant to the excellent portraitures of the rest of the book).

Sorry to hear of the Ra's failure. Where exactly is Barbados? I mean how much of their journey did they complete? But the moon-walk, I suppose, would impress the majority of people far more than the Ra ever could, which is an extremely paradoxical fact: the thing I felt about it was that although it was a 'triumph of science' (actually it was a triumph of technology, which is not at all the same thing as science; in this regard I'm now reading Jacques Barzun's *Science*, which clarifies the issues of a 'scientific culture' and is beautifully written as well; I was very impressed by another book of his *The House of Intellect* and all the other cant phrases) there was a sense of disappointment in that *everything happened on schedule*: theme was so much planning that the feat itself was not and could not possibly be considered as a 'triumph of *man*', who, after all, is truly a non-rational creature who chooses to live in a planned society (which is one of the great causes of the anxiety so much more prevalent in the West than the East). I do not condemn planning, of course, but merely observe that you have to pay the price for everything, and the price for planning (actually 'pre-planning by *Others*': what is removed here is the individual's *own present* choice when he allows his actions to be dictated by a distant organization in regards to which he reduces himself voluntarily to a fraction, thus sacrificing—again, not without benefit or justification or loss—his individual identity) seems to be the loss of certain human values the absence of which creates (or arouses) a feeling of malaise and insufficiency.

How much more *human* the Ra expedition is! (or, alas! was). It is unfortunate that the Ra expedition *did* fail, but its real attraction—an attraction I did *not* feel towards the moon trip—was that it *could* fail.

After all, it is only possible to succeed to the exact same extent that it is possible to fail, and, in that sense, the moon trip was not such a success. But, perhaps, at this point, you will feel that I am overreaching my point. Physically, of course, the moon trip could fail, but emotively it could not—there was a feeling—in Ceylon, anyway, I can't say about the U.S.—that there was a certain *omnipotence* at work: but this opens up a discussion of social values East and West beyond the scope of a letter.

(After re-reading this I think what I want to say is simply that the Ra had in it more of a sense of *adventure*. In the moon shot, technology was the middle-man between man and the elements: the encounter was not so direct and man dealt more with the machine than with the moon—and his own mind.)

* * *

I was presented a few days ago with an enormous bag of peanuts, so right now I'm stuffed full of nuts—I've been eating them all morning—and a bit lethargic. And—soon now the lunch bell will ring—I've been so stuffed on peanuts that at the past few regular meals I've been a bit off ma feed, paw.

An Indonesian monk arrived here a few weeks ago—young—but left a few days ago. Seemed afraid of the life here, always carrying a tremendous club about with him to protect himself, he said, from snakes. (In the 2½ years I've been here I've seen—on the island—only 3 or 4 poisonous snakes altogether—I frequently see a 6 feet long non-poisonous and non-aggressive rat snake—and I don't think anyone's ever been bitten by a snake here.) Very strange that Asians, who live so much closer to the jungle, are so much less able to adapt to it than Westerners.

Also a day or two ago someone dumped an unwanted and partly tamed monkey on the island (the island is a convenient dumping ground for the village's unwanted animals: cats and dogs are constantly being dumped; but so far as I know this is the first monkey)—black faces with silver grey fur—apparently still young—who accepts an occasional banana and occasionally allows himself to be handled, but is also a bit too wild and will probably be removed (most of the animals dumped here are dumped right back on the mainland, else we would be overrun with them; and this is a hermitage, not a menagerie) before it takes to bounding into the *kuṭis* and breaking up the tile roofs.

Some nights I take the rowboat out into the lagoon and drift about for a few hours. Other nights I stay in my little park. Daytime, however, my park has become more of an arena: the mongoose sometimes catches one of the beautiful noisy white birds that are nesting hereabouts and drags its body I don't know how far up to the park where he putters about with it. Iguanas who happen along the path smell the body and come trundling after the scent, whirring their throats in a strange mechanical gurgle-growl, rolling from side to side slightly as they walk like some mechanical toy, their incredibly long blue forked tongue flicking in and out constantly. They have what appears to be a seam along the side of their hide and, altogether, seem to be contrivances rather than living beasts. But they follow the scent up past the *kuṭi* to the park, where there generally ensues a cold war of threat/counter-threat for possession of the field and the bird. Eventually, a second iguana may show up by which time the struggle will turn into a free-for-all. The park is strewn with loose feathers. I shall have to discourage the mongoose from bringing his lunches up here.

* * *

As regards the book publishing, I have more or less cut myself off from any further editorial work (one purpose of my Colombo trip was to cut those strings); it's simply not very important to me since the whole project has nothing to do with my reason for being in Ceylon (although the *contents* of the work have a great deal to do with my being here). Anyway, there is no reason to regret having dropped another project (another hang-up), since it is another step forward in my project of dropping projects (which project itself will necessarily be the last project to be dropped).

Our monkey—a young black-faced (silver-furred) male which was dumped on the island several weeks ago by an unknown party—is tied to a post now, since he became rather aggressive: alone and apart from his tribe among strangers this was understandable, but, as he attacked several people, he had to be tied-up. (I was sitting down, minding my own business, when he came up behind me and jumped on my back. He didn't bite, but his claws tore my robe. He has bitten a few people, though never seriously and seemingly more from nervousness than from anger, more from fear than aggression.) Anyway, tied-up now, he is very peaceful, and will allow himself to be scratched and fed bits of food—but is *very* fussy about what he eats. He will eat the light part of bread if it has been dipped in milk-tea, but will not eat the crust; he will not eat some fruits, nor rice (and I know that his wild brothers *love* rice)—all in all a still rather neurotic monkey who would probably be better off if he were taken back to the mainland and left to rejoin his own people—but that is not within my province to do anything about.

* * *

Our monkey has been removed to the mainland—just as he was getting used to his surroundings here—and, I hear, has had to go through the whole business of readjustment once again. Anyway, he won't be back here again, even though he was finally a pleasant fellow to have around. But I expect I'll be seeing quite a few monkeys again, since I am planning on taking a bit of a trip out around Ceylon—which, after all, I have yet to see—starting from Kandy.

Well, Werner, a German seeking ordination, came in for a chat. He is very unhappy and makes himself unhappier by worrying about his unhappiness. Perhaps that's what he wants—strangely enough, people do tend to act in ways that hurt themselves—in a sense, perhaps we're all secret masochists—but since I don't let Werner's unhappiness make me unhappy I don't mind him stopping by. Finally, he left just before the bell rang for evening chanting. I expect—as I began to write you some hours ago—to be going first up to the Kandy area and then going wherever the wind doth blow fair. But I shall not be leaving until the second half of November, in order to be here for the *Kaṭhina* ceremony, which is held shortly after the end of *Vas*, and is the annual giving of robes, and will be on the 17th of November this year—not because I particularly need a new robe, but because it would simply be politie.

I don't know quite what to say about your 'lecture' that might be of use. Of course, from your point of view you are quite right, but everyone has his own viewpoint, and it would be foolish for any of us to assume that the viewpoint of anyone else must be the same as ours. Naturally, I would like to do what would please you; but if the price be to give up the only way of life I have ever found acceptable and to adopt a way of life which makes me miserable, then I would be doing the same as Werner, wouldn't I? Of course, I am not seeking a utopia—a perfect society—which we know is impossible (and I had any dregs of the possibility knocked out of me in Israel). I'm simply trying to get rid of various hang-ups that I've picked up which are a source of dissatisfaction. You speak of the arts of music, painting, literature, etc., which are all fine; I am practicing the art of living. I try to shape my life so that it is ethically and aesthetically pleasing by molding a blend of such factors as graciousness, softness, equanimity, compassion, honesty, and the like. Anyone who wishes to do or create anything will naturally seek conditions which are best suited to his work and to avoid as much as possible any unnecessary distractions. So too with me. I don't reject the world, or curse society, or blame anybody: I am simply not interested. My work, the work I consider worth doing, lies elsewhere. If I gave it up and adopted a way of life that would make me miserable, then, like Werner, I would inevitably communicate my misery to others—to you—and that would likely make you miserable as well; so what good has been achieved?

Probably I've said nothing much that would help you, and if I were to go on restating the same thing in still other terms, it would be unlikely to be of further help. But I am not arguing with you: I am willing to accept you whatever you are, or wear, or do, or say, because I love you and above all else you are to me my parents, who did more for my welfare than can be comprehended at a sitting. But to act contrary to my own most basic needs and goals would be nothing more than a betrayal of the care and love you have given, and would not in fact be a good thing and would not, in the end, make anyone happy, better, or wiser. What more can I say?

* * *

As the sun sets slowly in the west... Over the hills of Kandy, sweet and clear, a constant medley of chirps, whirrs, and other insect cries—Ven. Ñāṇaponika's place, several miles outside the city, warm days and chill nights—a panorama of weirdly shaped hills—trees: jok, coconut, teak, mahogany—a dazzling train ride up from Colombo—cliffs, valleys, boulders, orange clouds, brisk air, autumnal. Walks in the forest (when dry; leechy when wet) around ponds. The city still retains a vestige of its former culture, but is very English-imbued.

The Temple of the Tooth: a great building, formerly the palace of the Kandyan Kings—stone floor, sense of massiveness, drum and clarinet-like music—piercing runs and trills against a thunderous rhythm—also very solid and compelling so that one doesn't think just follows—over a bridge across a moat—up turnings of stairs—into the heart of the sounds—again through an ornate door opened by a guard—up a narrow staircase—with no idea where I was going, all very mysterious, adventurous—suddenly in the center of the building, conducted through numerous doors and rooms, each with walls and ceiling covered with the Buddhist-Hindu admixture that forms the popular Sinhalese religion—to a gold lame curtain—people bustling about me with strange tasks—jugs, silver, beaten and wrought, of water, trays of white flower petals, a strange unmonklike monk—impossible to describe the whole thing because from first to last the entire atmosphere left me fascinated, exhausted, and above all bewildered. Finally led into a small room where, behind a cage of solid gold was a casket, dazzlingly bejeweled, of gold—housing another casket, 7 caskets, and inside it the tooth of the Buddha, preserved (perhaps all the water, I couldn't help thinking, was for brushing it?). Everything very traditional — piety and reverence with the collection plate inconspicuously (but unavoidably) close by (though I was not expected to make any offering).

A gentle old Cambodian monk I knew in Calcutta had summed it all up for me 3 years ago when he said, in a very kind, wistful voice, 'Very joyous and good—but two thousand five hundred years—dat pretty old for a tooth. I don't know. And he very gently shook his head, very quietly, and just a little bit doubtfully.

Both much more and no more than I expected to find. I'm glad I went.

To be more (or less?) prosaic, I left the Hermitage on the 17th, the day after the *Kaṭhina* ceremony, for Colombo, spent the night at Vajirārāma and the next day took the evening train to Kandy, where I am briefly the guest of Ven. Ñāṇaponika, an elderly German (ex-Orthodox Jewish) who has a small bungalow which he calls the Forest Hermitage where he engages himself in propaganda activities as head of the Buddhist Publication Society), and dreams sad dreams. When I leave Kandy, whenever that may happen to be, I shall head toward Matale District to visit Ñāṇasiha, a young German monk who engages in no propaganda at all and who dreams happy dreams and who is living on a coconut estate with an elderly Yugoslavian monk, an ex-professor of philosophy, the nature of whose dreams I don't know, and after that I shall probably continue northwards toward Anuradhapura and Polonuruwa, possibly with Ñāṇasiha, possibly not. There, I'm told, is the test weather in Ceylon at this time of year. If either the weather or the time if year change before I get that far then I shall head for wherever the climate is best at the next time of year. I refuse to commit myself even to the extent of carrying a map. Like the smoke of burning incense, I shall drift the way of the breeze. (Howzat for writin', huh?)

* * *

There is a discourse where the Buddha says that it is not by going that one reaches an end. An end is reached by stopping. Activity is a means without an end, and therefore purposeless and empty. Reflexion at least might (and in fact does) reach an end—although you will have to take that statement on trust until you see for yourself—and is therefore purposeful. (In one sense, the purpose of reflexion is to understand what activity is all about, and in this sense they do in fact combine—one can reflect upon activity—in order to reach an end, to fulfill a purpose... If they are combined in the opposite way—by acting upon reflexion—then, as said above, there will be nothing achieved.)

Are thoughts about death necessarily morbid? Or can they be simply realistic? Is it not one's attitude *towards* death which can be either morbid or realistic—morbid if one takes it as being something other than what it is—an inevitable and frightening event awaiting each of us—and tries to sugar-coat it (eternal bliss in heaven) or to ignore it by means of distractions (i.e. activity), and realistic if one decides that however frightening the event may be one will face it squarely and try to understand it (an absolutely necessary step on the Buddhist path) for what it is—i.e. a real event we will not avoid simply by calling any concern about it 'morbid'. To one so concerned, of course, this is absurd and therefore humorous. Is it a morbid mind which sees the humor inherent in every situation? Or is it not true a truly morbid person is incapable of laughing, let alone at himself?

* * *

Your welcome letters have been arriving in this jungle of wild improbabilities like drops of syrup falling into a bowl of clear water. Now that winter of your content is approaching, you will be snowed by a large manuscript (Ñāṇavīra Letters) which I'm having sent to you. It is, in its own way, the jungle fabric of choice: rip-stop, though you will have to see for yourself whether or not it's double-stitched.

I've been doing something like your diet for the past few years: mostly fruit, vegetables, and grains; plain as possible. But I found that any rigid 'I will's' and 'I won't's' only lead to trouble, so—after recovering from a massive protein deficiency earlier this year—I remain flexible and healthy without hang-ups and still manage to get along well with the simplest fare, and therefore no need for flu shots, vaccines, etc. But—there is always natural tree syrups (and a fine sort of syrup here made from the coconut-blossom pollen) which is, I am informed, full of all the *undiscovered* vitamins. This is an irresistible recommendation, and therefore I lap up syrups as they fall, dropwise, info my alms bowl of clear water, with all the joy with which waves lap a phosphorescent beach.

Long ago you once remarked that *nibbāna* could not be 'simply annihilation'. After having drunk the syrup of the fruitfulness of that remark, I reply: indeed, *nibbāna* can *not* be 'simply' annihilation—or, rather, it is not annihilation *at all*, for there can only be annihilation if there is something to be annihilated, and it is precisely our delusion to assume, or conceive, the existence of a 'self' to whom annihilation (as well as birth, suffering, and death) might apply. A delusion, of course, is no illusion. But an insidious reality.

Your basket of preserved plums, generous windows, healing walls—my goodness yes. That time may come. That time may come.

The face in the borscht bowl
sends greetings to the spoon
that leaves no ripple.

V.

* * *

Your *Bones*[1] arrived last night and found a resting place—no longer need they stalk the musty corridors leading to the offices and minds of musty publishers in search of a reader (not quite blinded by the must, although it makes him sneeze a lot). I was glad to find, again, sweet Carmen V. Paka,[2] though I haven't yet found any reference to that famous Mexican bandit, Pancho Sila.[3] Did I steal Carmen from you, or did you steal her from me? She also occurs, rather obliquely, in *A Foreign Retreat*, the old piece I was having across Asia. Since then, by the way, I have finished several other books, but since there is no more room on my skin to tattoo them they have had to remain part of my oral tradition. Except, of course, for the collection of Letters which I hope you have received by now.

Well, if your diet is keeping you healthy what more can it do? Anyway, it's certainly good to avoid, as much as possible, the stimulation-soporific cycle of Sinhalese food. I don't know what amino acids and B complex contents are, never having been introduced, but they sound valuable, and I'll no longer allow anyone to rape my white rice and white sugar of them if I can help it. But can I help it? Is it my fault? Obviously not—monks are not rapists—we take what we get, virgin dark rice or a whore of a Nestomalt tin, or else we fast (weekly or monthly, as much or as little as we like). In other words, I envy the purity of your diet, but regret that in Ceylon even the lettuce comes both cooked and curried, which is better than a poke in the eye with a blunt stick. How *does* one get out of this confounded rabbithole? The next stringhopper will be dedicated to you.

Betimes, here's something to tide you over, Mr. Wuthy Intalocketer:

All night I lay entwined in gold
so tenuous it seemed unreal
embracing what I could not hold
caressing what I could not feel.

---

1. *Worthy Bones*—what became *our* novel—Hūm. It has never been published.—Ed.
2. WB's Jewish St. Joan—a pun on the Pāli *kamma vipāka*: 'ripening of karma'.—Hūm.
3. A pun on the Pāli *pañcha sīla*: the Five Precepts of Buddhist morality.—Hūm.

All frail she kept in sleep a lone
and chartless dream while what she held
held me in keep. I might have flown
apart were I not grounded, celled,

Solidified. Yet when I tried
to free my pale schemed heart she kept
me bound and flightless by her side.
Reality, I found, was debt.

All frail she slept, and undefined,
but in the night I lay entwined.

And sumpin' else:

The goose that laid the golden egg
died looking up its crotch
to find out how its sphincter worked.
Would you lay well? Don't watch.

V.

* * *

Ñāṇasiha, the German monk, and I have come to his place at Cetiyagiri, about 30 miles north of Kandy. It's about half way up a small two-peaked mountain, green and rust, which is occasionally decapitated by a sharp cloud. To the south are the rocky massifs of upcountry, below are the long terraced rice fields in the valley before the Eastern hills rise, dusky in coconut groves. The rice fields have just been transplanted. Every field has its own shape, its own internal pattern and its own shade of green, and sometimes its own reflection when the several inches of water in them catches something worth reflecting. The ribbons of dark earth which separate the fields like a scrawl and the workers' bright clothing makes a fine painting with no need for oils, brushes, or canvas. Although this is supposed to be the NE monsoon season we've had only 2 rainy days here in 2 weeks and today is even hot. There is a large rock next to a small path, and when the sun drops lower I often sit on it and watch without reacting.

There are 2 Sinhalese monks living in some caves above the hut where I'm Staying—actually the hut of Ñāṇajivako, the Yugoslav, who, you may recall, took his higher ordination at the same time I did. He's gone to Nuwara Eliya (the 'summer resort' town of Ceylon, high in the hills) for December—what a time to go! Do Floridians go to Maine for December?

Outside his hut is all in flower-bright orange spots, pale purple spheres, dark purple ovals, a kind of flower which, although a very simple 4-sided monochrome, comes in clusters, and each flower is a different color. The whole scene, in short, is romantic as hell, but also pleasantly simple. I go down the hill in the morning and, after walking along one of the rice paddy field dikes, I wander along the footpaths of the village, away from the asphalt street, from house to house, collecting my alms—beneath coconut trees (which are very cool) and close to the rubber trees (all austerely leaning in the same direction, with mottled trunk and sparce leaves—not at all cool).

Ñāṇasiha has a mud hut about half way up the hill, or mountain, very solitary and quiet and a lung-clearing climb, which he has largely built himself—a fine job. A paste made out of the dirt of termite hills makes an excellent plaster for the walls; mud-and-wattle floor, roof of woven coconut fronds.

I sure wish I could accept your pessimistic evaluation of the possibility of doing anything to alter some unfortunate facts, for then I could sit back and say, "There's no use my trying to achieve anything of real value, because it can't be done." Unfortunately I'm not able to have the necessary confidence that there's nothing I can do about it (the 'it' refers to whatever you please), so I'm not able to sit back.

| | |
|---|---|
| *Aciraṃ vat'ayaṃ kāyo* | Soon, soon will this body |
| *paṭhaviṃ adhisessati* | lie stretched upon the earth |
| *chuddho apeta-viññāṇo* | unheeded, uncognizant, |
| *niratthaṃ vakaliṅgaraṃ.* | like a useless stick of wood. |

(Dhammapada, 41)

* * *

Being the most important tourist/pilgrimage site in Ceylon, Anuradhapura overflows with many things, many strange people fulfilling—or not fulfilling—strange destinies. And being the rainy season, Anuradhapura overflows also with flood waters. Even the most ordinary citizens, in the currents and whirlpools of enthusiasm they have worked up in order to convince themselves of their religious certitudes, manages to cover his ordinary plain surface until all that is visible of him are his peaks, a few humps of personality protruding, like Mt. Ararat, above the floodtide of his ebullience, seeking doves with leaves in their bills.

The available leaves are all from the species *ficus religiosa*, or bo-tree for the main attraction, in the moistest center of the arena, is Sri Mahā Bodhi, a tree of aforesaid species which according to legend—and legend is probably correct in this case—entered into the world as a branch of the tree under which the Buddha sat on the night of his enlightenment, which branch, having taken root, was brought to Ceylon by the daughter of King Asoka (whom H.G. Wells called the greatest king in the history of mankind) some 2200 years ago, making it the oldest tree in the world still living.

The Sinhalese make a very big to-do about it. Such a big to-do, in fact, that it is impossible to get close enough to have a decent look at it—surrounded as it is, by a gold-plated fence, not of barbed wire but of pickets—and then an ordinary wall on a lower level and finally a third wall through which one can glimpse the branches of the tree—which are thin and supported by iron posts—and the leaves, which are of a peculiar reddish sheen unlike the normal green of the species—more like the color of poinsettia leaves, I'd say—and certainly there's no way anybody's going to sit down under it (which, of course, is the only reasonable thing to do with the tree). Therefore Ñāṇasuci was disappointed.

Because I had the foresight to put up in a resthouse close to the river running through town, I was able to become a refugee. The weather has been abominably wet (until a few days ago when it cleared up—sunshine today) and one day the police came and told the resthousers that the water in the irrigation lakes had risen to the danger point and we had to leave because that night they would open the floodgates to release the flood and the waters would engulf the place. So I found refuge elsewhere in a derelict school-house smelling of cleaning solutions and mildew, where they fed me eggs until I was ready to burst open with the new supply of protein vitality and am stimulated protein-wise almost as much as the Sinhalese tourists (who insist upon calling themselves and me as well as 'pilgrims') are stimulated by their holiday-making orgies of faith (which, as Maugham correctly notes, is the most powerful intoxicant the world has ever known).

Perhaps the most interesting of those I've met so far is the 66 year old gentleman who, beginning at Mahārama (near Hambantota) has bicycled here and intends to continue up to Calcutta, across Burma, and as far as Singapore before taking a ship to Japan. He has a shock of black hair, partly braided, and a double-wedged beard of white, baby smooth skin, burning eyes, a bicycle with no brakes, a T-shirt carrying slogans of the Family Planning Association in green and a wealth of self-contradictory ideas culled from various Eastern teachers. He speaks perfect English and says he has at various times been a tea planter, a teacher, a businessman, and a hermit (for some years) in the jungle living on roots, leaves, berries, and jungle fruits.

In the Anuradhapura area are many fine forests—not jungles, but nearly parks, with tall trees (jungle trees are usually scrub) amidst lawns kept closely cropped by cattle and waterbuffalo and also some hills with caves in them in very beautiful surroundings. Several hermitages are here also, but I wouldn't be happy with the weather, which, I'm told, is either intolerably wet or intolerably hot, and although my mosquito net is proving invaluable I'd rather be in a place where it was not so useful.

Would you like a leaf from the Sri Mahā Bodhi? (These leaves are not easy to get, and are available to me only on the basis of my white skin and brown robes—if everyone who came here got one the tree would be stripped bare in a few days.) But this may have a religious significance for you that would be objectionable (although it has no religious significance at all for me—its value is more as a symbol or reminder of my own work).

Wandering is hard, comfortless, and free. But freedom is a comfort. A state of mind rather: the ability to give up what one would keep. Therefore wandering is hard, comfortable, and free. But what is comfortable is not hard, therefore wandering is soft, comfortable, and free.

In the two years since I last went out wandering I've acquired the strength to be able to appreciate—i.e. understand—freedom in a greater degree. Therefore I am progressing.

* * *

Nuwara Eliya is perched atop a 6200 feet peak which seems to be made mostly of tea bushes, waterfalls, and dark boulders, with a few towns and villages on the way 30 miles from Gampola, where it begins its climb from 1600 feet. Tea estates look like green quilt-work with thin black borders around each patch—almost the same dark green as coconut trees—with widely spaced tall silvery trees (to hold the soil?) on hills which are usually at least 45°. Past Gampola (which is 12 miles south of Kandy) there are no other kinds of crops growing. About Nuwara Eliya are wide lawns, bright pastel buildings, and a few buildings with gingerbread including a charming post-office with a clock-tower. It's the summer resort of Ceylon, but January is no month to be there, for at night it is freezing cold—into the 50's. (Actually it feels much colder than that because of a moist wind.) Even a heavy blanket and all my robes were not enough to keep me warm at night. The thin air warms up in the daytime and in the sunlight, which sends wisps of steam up from the ground, it can be quite pleasant. Some people wear long winter overcoats, others walk around in short sleeves and trousers.

On the way up, approaching one village, I came upon a big procession of children carrying papayas on sticks, the fruit decorated with various devices, and a couple elephants with a small boy atop each. The villagers told me that the two boys on the elephants—each about 10 years old and dressed in matador-style clothing with tin-foil-and-sequined crowns—were to be 'given to the Sangha by their parents' the next day—i.e. they would be ordained as novice monks at their parents' wishes, not their own—and that the parents had arranged the celebration of the event. The boys were solemn, wide-eyed, and frightened (whether of the elephant, the ordination, or both, I can't say), though everyone else was enjoying themselves (except perhaps the elephants for whom it was just another day's work). By the way, I found out that elephants can be rented by the day for between 50 and 100 rupees/day (depending, presumably, on whether it is an old elephant or a late model one), which at the tourist rate is $5-$10, or about what it costs to rent a car. Of course with an elephant there is no mileage charge or gas to pay (unless in another sense) and while it may not be as fast as a car, an elephant is certainly more versatile. The drummers in the procession were doing a peculiar sort of dance reminiscent of the Soupy Shuffle.

After coming down from Anuradhapura—an eventless trip—I spent a while with two Americans at their house before going on to Nuwara

Eliya. They want to be Buddhist missionaries to the States—although one of them is seriously reconsidering now whether it might not be better for him to find out first what the Buddha's Teaching is all about before giving it to the world. Also at the house was an Englishman, who had been ordained in Burma and after 8 years as a monk disrobed, since now he has a situation in England (to which he is returning) where he will be supported by some interested people and can continue his meditations under conditions which may be better for him than what he can find in the East—i.e. a familiar culture, etc.—but for which life as a monk would be difficult. It could be an advantage, but it could also be a disadvantage, particularly if the interest of his supporters flags. While I've met few people with whom I could discuss the Buddha's Teaching more freely, he tends toward the mystical view that (because everything is always changing, nothing really exists, whereas I do not accept the presumption that things are always changing—they change sometimes and sometimes they remain the same for a while, and they certainly do exist), so I think we both only clarified our ideas for our own benefit.

You ask about the cyclist to Calcutta—there is a ferry boat crossing the narrow Falk Straits which separate Ceylon from India (about 10 or 15 miles, I think and the fare cannot be very much for that journey. There are some Hindus who begin from someplace in India—perhaps Benares or Rishikesh—and *roll* to Katuragari in SE Ceylon, where there is a Hindu goddess living (so I'm told), and where there is a big ceremony every year, with fire-walking and all the other things (firewalkers, of course, are well-authenticated—I've met many people who have seen it and a few who have participated. I've also met a fellow who, in a frenzy of religious (Hindu) fervor, puts nails through his arms, legs, and tongues, and neither bleeds nor feels pain)—anyway there are people who roll to Kataragama (whether sideways or head-over-heels I've not learned), and while on the ferry boat they roll up and down the deck. So cycling isn't such a feat as all that.

Did I mention that Anuradhapura is the only city in Asia where I've seen corn-on-the-cob? To shock Cornbelt Buddhists? In any case, it's extremely popular—sold cooked (sans butter or salt) on the street.

I meant to say, by the way, that the bo-leaf was a symbol of my *work*, not worth.

* * *

I once had a little black box inside of which dwelt a genie. The rear two thirds of the top of the box was hinged and could open up-the hinge was on the back side, not the side side. On the front third of the boxtop was a silver lever jutting up and forwards. Beneath it a plate indicated that it was OFF and if it were pushed backwards it would be ON. I turned it to ON, and, at once, from the entrails of the box, came a chirring, rumbling, groaning sound. Slowly, the box rocked from side to side while the clattering continued. And then, slowly, slowly, the lid of the box rose and a little green hand reached out of the box, grasped hold of the lever, and pushed it back to OFF. Then the hand retreated, the lid closed, the rocking ceased, the groaning was silenced, and all was normal once more... If a machine can be made to turn itself off why not a man? Although the hand never left the box, the rabbit may not only leave its pit but fill it in as well. Because an act of will is itself insufficient to renounce (or to see) *sakkāyadiṭṭhi*[1] it does not follow that no conditions attainable are adequate. A bubble can burst from the inside. Strangely—and wonderfully—enough the ground is real: it is the abyss that is illusory, whether or not one strives (for Freedom or Bondage), the cleavage—or what one takes to be such—is the real problem.

I'm out wandering now—about halfway at the moment between Kandy and Pollonuruwa—and your words, panting and out of breath (or, perhaps, that was me), caught up with me and delivered themselves. As to the letters, you are perfectly free to make use of them without any time limit and to share them. But, when you are finished, the next designee is the designer. My own copy was lent to an individual who now will not return it—talk about misappropriation of the Dhamma!—and so I should like to make use of the copy now with you. As I'm out for a while, and since you will doubtlessly send it by air, there's certainly not even a near-future need of it, though there will be, perhaps, in a few months, by which time, I suppose, the need in B.C. will have been partially assuaged.

As for sending you a copy of *Notes on Dhamma* (I'm sorry to inform you that it's not a great hoax), as I say I'm out now and have no copies available—in fact I've had to put my spare copy away in order to protect it from aforesaid individual and it is now unavailable to me. As soon as I return to the Hermitage it will become available and then I shall

1. *sakkāyadiṭṭhi*: (Pāli) personality view.

be happy to send it to you. In the meantime you can have a rest of no-reading for a few months to prepare you for the shockwaves of *Notes*.

I'm perched on the side of a small mountain where, sitting on the top of a rock beneath which is a fine cave, I can look down on the paddy fields in the valley, which have just been transplanted, and every field, separated from the others by small dikes, has its own shape, internal pattern, and distinct shade of green through which can be seen the reflections of the sky and the coconut groves on the hill across from me. To my right are some jagged barren mountains, all around me are a profusion of wild flowers. I can wander through the village, along narrow dirt paths winding about: re-crossing the paddy fields, and collect my alms food, and then climb back up my mountain and sit on the rock, under it, or beside it (or even nowhere near it), and enjoy my stringhoppers, bananas, mangoes, sweets, etc. Then I can lie back, light up a *beedie* or shrootie—I usually get some native smoke on my alms round—and rest contented. Most of the day I just sit on the rock and watch the trees, fields, sky, etc., perhaps not entirely unmindfully.

There is a *vihara* higher up on the hill (I'm only about 200 feet up), and at evening they ring their bell. Then shortly afterwards the villagers will emerge from the dark shadows of the coconut trees surrounding their houses and walk, singly and in files, along the dikes of the paddy fields, a silent drift of calmness as they go to vespers. Watching them, with my robes around me against the wind, which rises at evening, in the last red light of the clouds which sometimes blanket the top of this mountain after a day of causing as little harm to creatures—myself included—as I could manage, I feel a real quietness.

> To prayer, to prayer I go… I think I go.
> I go to prayer. Along a corridor of woe
> And down a stair, in every step of which
> I am abased. A cowl I wear.
> I wear a halter rope about my waist.
> I bear a candle end put out with haste.
> I go to prayer.

V.

* * *

With the same post as this letter will go a request to an individual to unearth a copy of *Notes on Dhamma* for your consumption. He will presumably send you—if he sends you anything at all—one of the original copies, i.e. without, the many later additions including translation of various texts. This may be a disadvantage—I'm not sure if your Pāli is good enough to manage the more difficult passages without a crib—and if so, my apologies. If you are really taken by the book—and I must say that of all books this one most requires the reader to 'live with it' for some months or years--no doubt arrangements can be made to supply you with some or all of the missing sections and later additions.

The views of your two friends on the Letters was of some interest. They were both obviously very shocked by such a direct presentation of Buddhadhamma ("The world, for the most part, Kaccana, upon hearing this Teaching, quakes and fear and trembles") and try to account for it on the one hand (by P) by thinking that the shock was due to Ven. Ñāṇavīra's discussions of suicide and on the other (by D) by perhaps a more healthy but nonetheless still fearful cynicism. After all the Dhamma *can* be frightening—it may be—will be—(wrongly) apprehended by most of us as an attack on our most precious possession, our 'self', and it takes a considerable amount of strength developed through calmness (*samatha*) to be able to look down into that chasm without contracting vertigo.

One other point that P raises is worthy of comment, namely the acceptance of the texts and the age. As you say, Ānanda didn't have a tape-recorder (though he did have, apparently, a remarkable memory, having memorized *all* the Buddha's discourses). But even if it were shown that the texts were not 25 hundred years old but 25 years old this would demonstrate nothing whatsoever except that historical scholarship is a farce, which is already known. The sole criterion for accepting the texts is whether they are *useful*. (I know I needn't tell you this, but your friend P seems to feel that how old a text is is somehow relevant to how useful it is and also to either be unaware of or to ignore Ven. Ñāṇavīra's attainment of *sotāpanna*, and, of course, as a *sotāpanna* he is using the texts as a formulation of his own direct knowledge. Anyway, the whole question is complicated—too complicated for a letter—but both points are dealt with very well in K's Concluding Unscientific Postscript (among other works), a reading of which might be profitable for your friend P.

Odd, is it not, that P, after a thoroughgoing attack on acceptance of the Pāli texts as a guide to exploration of one's own experience, should then proceed to describe himself as a 'good Madhyamikist'? As to the Note on Suicide (whose is this? yours or D's?), I would only remark that if we did not enjoy life considerably we would not *need* to contemplate death, and that the only true way to commit suicide is to *nibbāna*. In a sense, this is the essence of the Dhamma.

Thanks very much for your poems. In exchange I offer my latest haiku.

> I knew a man who
> though he could not name the stars
> yet could see them.

> V.

* * *

My walk ended some time ago with visits to Bandarawela, which I didn't find nearly so lovely as the tourist booklets claim. Buttala, where I stayed with a 104 year-old monk who lives in an open cave in the jungle all alone—a fine old man—and a few days visiting Mark at Godawaya. Things have not yet worked out suitably for me to stay at the house in Kandy[1] which I mentioned earlier, so I'm temporarily staying with Ven. Piyadassi in a forest reserve adjacent to Kandy town—from parts of it one can overlook the entire town—yet it is very quiet and secluded. My residence here, however, is temporary. Most likely possibility is to get a mud hut built somewhere in the reserve, which much appeals to me. But here too some possibilities are less than others, and so nothing is definite.

We interrupt this letter for a Special News Bulletin. Since the preceding paragraph was written I have a) found a suitable location, about 200 yards behind the house, for a hut, and b) found someone willing to arrange for construction of a hut. This will take me one or two weeks to do, unless there are unforeseen delays. The place is on a grassy hill accessible by a charming footpath. Jungle all around, but a patch of a few acres are bare of trees and afford a splendid view of Kandy's hills—village nearby (1.5 mile) for food, well already there, needs cleaning only. I will be a 'squatter' on government land (Crown Forest), but am not likely

1. Forest Hermitage.—Ed.

to be evicted since the D.R.O. (District Revenue Officer) would have to be the one to evict me, and part of the cost of the *kuṭi* is being paid for by the D.R.O.'s wife. As soon as further details become known the News Service will interrupt this letter with further Bulletins. We now return you to our regular letter.

Here the weather is in the high 70's in the day, middle 60's at night, sunny with showers every few days (leeches are only a problem for 24 hours after a rain; after that the ground becomes too dry for them and they disappear—I don't know where to—and even for the day after a rain if I remember to soap my feet well they'll keep clear of me), usually in the evening—typical February weather hereabouts. Also, typically, there may be a postal strike, in which case a foreseen delay will hold up this letter.

* * *

Arthur C. Clarke (who wrote the screenplay of 2001,[1] which seems to have been a film) was one of my favorite science-fiction writers in the days when I read SF. I was aware that he lived in Ceylon, and in fact the house on Sanghamitta Mawatha is rented by a friend of his who co-authored at least one book with him.

Behind it (the house) my hut is now finished to the point where I am living in it comfortably—most of the remaining work is just 'winterizing'—i.e. getting ready for the rains, which begin here about early May.

Some lumber mill donated enough wood to eliminate the need for mud walls, but mud, in this climate, is by no means to be berated as a building material. Certainly in an area where there is snow it is quite impractical requiring far too much maintenance, but in the tropics it is a fine structural material—cheap, sturdy, strong, and *cool*. When plastered over with the mud of termite piles it is not only long lasting but also attractive both in color (tan) and texture (which can be anything you want depending on how finely the termite pile is ground up and how it is applied). Bricks, after all, are only baked earth. In the tropics the earth gets baked naturally. There is a product called 'swishcrete' (love the name) made of 1 part cement to 14 parts earth, which lasts 20 years or more.

---

1. *2001: A Space Odyssey*—Ed.

The walls, however, are wood, since for mud walls—which I rate as superior to wood—there would have been problems transporting the quantities of water needed. (Water is the most serious 'problem' here—there is a small river with pools running at no more than a gallon a minute at the very bottom of the hill, but that's quite a climb—especially back up, by which time I would need a bath again—so I go to a grotto about 1/3 mile away where there is a well in picturesque surroundings, bathe there and carry back the gallon of water I need daily—usually from the village, which has tap water, saving me the need to boil or filter the water—but also usually people bring the water for me, so that the water problem is not 'serious'.)

The roof is of cadjan (coconut leaves woven together), which, being porous, is extremely cool. The land is about four acres of hillside (descending farther the hill becomes almost precipitous) with jungle on three sides, but the 4 acres are almost treeless and, being atop a hill, afford a rather spectacular view—mountain peaks, coconut plantations, and the whole works—yet is protected by the jungle from most of the weather and noises of Kandy (which is within walking distance—a 2 mile walk through the forest reserve will bring one suddenly into the very heart of town). Pacing west I can enjoy some fine sunsets. Bushes are (so far) in perpetual bloom, and all in all the land in a similar location in the U.S.—say a few minutes drive from the heart of L.A. yet still almost entirely natural, quiet, secluded—would doubtless be much sought after property. In the distance, at dusk, I hear the *muezzin* calling his chants from the Moslem mosque in town, and watch the endless stream of bats flying across the skyline. In the day time it's monkeys, parrots, occasional water buffalo through trees that must have come from a Japanese garden-so I'm quite content here for now even without a color TV.

Lamb me tell ewe some otter gnus. Right off the bat, first morning in the gnu home, just after having eaten breakfast (which included an onions-and-chilie-pepper sandwich—*pugh*!—which apeset me so horibully that verminit I thought, 'Iguana be eel! I've been pythoned! Where's a dogtoe?'—perhaps, though it'll put heron mynah chest) a parrot mastiff elephants lumbered by my newt haress on their way to work, which was carrion off the huge coconut-tree logs lion about the place. The two antelopes (who were racoonpanied by their drivers) thrashed their trunks hunter their staggering binders, pigged them up, and weaselly boar them byena hare. (They are for ocelot too heavy to lift even when cut insectshuns.) Wallaby damned, I thought. Monkey around with them animules and weasel be in a fine cattle of fish. I wouldn't want them for anemone. But of horse sow capabull creatures we shell rarely meat. It did my hart good. The frog lifted and the morning was pleasantly wormed bison, and to snake my thirst I drake a long swallow of water. I cassowary ibis one log after a few inches terrier of a roof support—deer deer, I quailed—and oxed the driver if the elephant colt be eggstra careful hen his awkward fitchewation. 'Serpently,' he replied. The elephant steered the log with his trunk, turning it carefully eaglempt it in his jaws, and gently brute away from mouse. I watched them aphidly owl morning. At noon they went away. (Lemur know if ewe want furother gnus and alligator round to it. When read several times this paragraph may become intelligible. Tiger beast ewe kine, hmm? And if heifer ewe asp wether amphibian or just kitten, owl condorly adder least llama gnat lion.) Whelp, I goose that'll rabbit up for now. Any moa this stuff chinchilla guy.

* * *

I'm getting settled down here now, although with typical Ceylon inefficiency I've not yet finished all the work on the *kuṭi*, I wonder if I ever will? For always there seems to be some little thing that can be done to make the place more... complete? For instance, there is a supply of fine granite rocks close by, and, as sand is brought up, I'm gradually making stone walls to replace the wooden ones, which will make the place more natural in its surroundings, and eliminate problems such as termites (which, in all tropical areas, are very much of a problem—at Island Hermitage I've seen them build their tunnel in and out of the pores of a cement post to reach the wooden ceiling). This is not such a big job, actually (except for bringing the sand), since my walls are only two feet high.

Between the roof and the walls I have placed a number of straw mats sewn together, which can be rolled up in nice weather and rolled down and fastened tightly in windy weather or for complete privacy (though without any walls at all the location is already as private as can be). This has worked out very nicely so far, and we've already had some very heavy wind and rain. Also the mats are good looking. They probably won't last a year, but they are altogether only about 20 rupees—2 dollars—and easily available, so replacing them should be no problem.

The roof will need replacement every year or so, since it is cadjan, and since the pitch is not great enough for cadjan alone to be leak proof, it has been covered with a brown-colored tar paper, which works quite well. Corrugated asbestos, and tiles are both too expensive, and shingles (which are also coated tar paper, aren't they?) are unknown here. The roof is single-pitched except for a bit with its own pitch over a small storage area, which almost runs into the rise of the hill.

The posts are independent of the walls, and two supporting the roof are of a green species of bamboo that is about 6 inches in diameter and very strong, set into the ground at an angle of about 30° sloping back, so that no pillar obstructs the view and to match the slope of the mountain (Pujiyami?) in the distance and blend the place as much as possible into its niche in the jungle.

Hut enough?

Yes, leeches are a nuisance, but if you're going to live in the jungle then they must be endured. They only come out with the heavy rains, when it's very wet, otherwise the paths are free of them and their bite is no more irritating than a mosquito's, but you tend to bleed a few drops if they actually do bite, which stains my robes (how *do* you remove blood stains?)—often I don't know I've been bitten until I feel the blood trickling—and they are tenacious and a bit difficult to pry off (they're not slimy or anything)—on the other hand, they don't fly, so given the choice I'd rather put up with leeches than mosquitos (though I've got a few of them too). A nuisance, not a problem. They rarely get inside the *kuṭi*.

I have an outhut hidden away behind some bushes, though, of course, any place equipped with running water will have a flush system. For my water I must bring back a bucket from the village every few days, when I can't collect rain water (though we've had a lot of rain this past week and I've collected it).

On the many paths and in the open spaces grows a coarse, thick-bladed grass that never gets more than an inch high and is extremely pleasant to walk on (when dry and leech-free).

Today is Sinhalese New Year—last night and tonight I've been watching many skyrockets over the hills of Kandy (have you seen the comet lying low in the east about 5 AM?), and enjoying the holiday fare that is given me in abundance at each house on my alms rounds—bags full of sweets, stacks of milk-rice cakes, bottles of fresh milk, and so on. Also very little spicy foods. Sinhalese (and even more so Tamil—i.e. South Indian) chili peppers are much much hotter than the hottest Mexican varieties. The Sinhalese truly don't believe I can stay healthy on a diet in which I avoid them as much as possible. I don't see how they can...

Yes, I've heard about the World Fair in Japan. In fact, I've been planning for a long time not to attend. Having lost my interest in sports, I've decided to give up not attending Olympic Games, and switch to not attending World Fairs.

* * *

I've built a small hut on the edge of the jungle here, not far from the Forest Hermitage (if you went there when you were in Kandy you'll know which jungle I mean) and have been here a month now—fantastic scenery and all that jazz.

I've also had time to re-read *Worthy Bones*, which gives me quite a bit to gnaw on, though I might wish I felt more sympathy, or indeed any sympathy, or even any empathy for any of the characters. My relationship to them seems to be lacking. Whose fault is this? Mine? Yours? Theirs?

Hope by now *Notes on Dhamma* will have reached you (you may find yourself in the same relationship to Notes as I found myself in with Bones)—it was sent sometime ago.

So it looks like it's maybe all over with the Island Hermitage and me—again, lack of empathy for the characters, I suppose.

The hut is perched atop a small mountain overlooking the Odeon Theatre, Mt. Fujiyami, and some granite cliffs reminiscent of those in the interior of Crete. Then there are the gentle dusky green and rust-brown hills which roll away beyond the clearing, lowbushed, surrounding my site, with closer and heavier jungle on three sides. I am, presumably, not far from a lunatic asylum to judge from the number of madmen who visit me or pass by on strange quests.

Tucked away at the bottom of the mountain, out of sight—like the outhut—is the village where I collect my food and mail each morning—a rather mixed bag which would not meet with the full approval of your dietician. Tucked away at the top of the mountain, consuming string-hopper hearts after carefully unraveling the string, I wish you a happy

(Sinhalese) New Year (April 14), a Merry Vesak (May ?), and continue trying to undo what is to be undone.

(Your letter arrived after sealing this. Shall be happy to receive a new set of Bones—shall donate the old set to the local museum of Natural History—they will closet them. Does your Notes have English translation?)

V.

* * *

Yes, creativity is important to me—which is one of my reasons for meditating, since meditation is a creative art using the 'artist' himself as the medium. But it is a very difficult art form.

Right now the monkeys have just finished eating the remains of my breakfast, and about half a dozen of them are perched on my new stone walls—one looking over my shoulder, several on the floor—in the hope that there might still be a stray banana peel (which there ain't). Now, with the stone walls (about 2-2½ feet high), a new sand-and-mud floor, and a wall portion made of large green bamboos vertically placed, the room looks clean and right—at last. There are still things to be done (e.g. construction of a cistern to store rainwater, cementing over the mud which was used between the stones, etc.)—I suppose there always will be something more that could be done—but it can not be done too.

The monkeys have gone away now and I can see them jumping from tree to tree. One of the females gave birth last night and showed up this morning with her baby, the umbilical cord still attached to the baby. It is quite an education—and now always a genteel one—to observe the monkeys. By now I can recognize them as individuals. Some of them have distinct personalities. The Big Chief, for instance, is fearless and sits himself down in front of me at feeding time with a grunt, expecting at least half of everything going as his natural right. His queen (who is, in my opinion, the ugliest monkey in the troop) reminds me of Snow White's stepmother. Some are bold, some afraid, some friendly (one of them lets me pet him), some gentle, some aloof, some unsure of themselves, etc. There is a very definite power structure in their society. One small monkey will climb up onto my lap and pry open my fist to get at the piece of bread; but when the Big Chief is around he won't even pick up food when I throw it at his feet. (Whether he is simply a 'good subject' or whether he's particularly afraid of the top brass I haven't yet learned. Certain monkeys tend to hang out together, forming sub-clans within the larger community. They have definite sounds for warnings, etc. Arguments—almost always over food-are settled by force (back-biting) only when there is no doubt who will win; otherwise there is a fairly elaborate series of sounds and gestures conveying anger, threat, conciliation, etc., which they will go through, coming to blows (or, rather, teeth) only in a rare last resort. Even then, no quarrel ever takes more than a few seconds to decide and only a few more seconds to be forgotten (though perhaps the overtones linger longer, creating the social structure and changing it, constantly needing to be renewed and the balance of power reweighed).

I've also been observing the butterflies (of which there are numerous varieties hereabouts) and find that they seem to have a primitive social structure too, and seem to be surprisingly aggressive for such beautiful and flimsy appearing creatures. Lightning bugs, on the other hand, seem to get along with each other without difficulties.

So much for nature studies. (Says the creeper to the vine.)

* * *

The description of my *kuṭi* is now outmoded. I was offered—and accepted—an asbestos roof, which has now been constructed and so all problems—whoops! I'm writing this at night, by candlelight, and just felt a mysterious creature pushing against my robes which, upon investigation, turned out to be a frog who, friendly but shy, hopped off—and so all problems with repairs, etc., seem to be ended. (The straw mats which previously formed a movable—they could be rolled up and down—part of the stone wall have now been made into a ceiling and replaced with jute—good looking also). As for other natural resources, there's a small stream at the bottom of the hill, a well about 150 yards away, and less than a mile is a movie theatre that serves Kandy and is equipped with 70mm projectors, stereo, etc.

Yes, I remember the 'Golden Book Encyclopedia', and also remember the trouble I had choosing between it and the 'Golden Book Bible' when, one day at Shirley Jaffee's clothing store, you said I could have one of them. The encyclopedia, I recall, was two pages longer than the bible. Do you remember that?

Yes, the political climate has changed. Although the new government calls itself 'socialist', it strikes me (as an outsider) as being rabidly nationalistic and will attempt to promote the welfare of the Sinhalese majority by attacking the Tamil and Moslem minorities. (As in most every country I've seen, the minority groups in Ceylon are simply 'better people'—more cultured, economically more successful, harder workers, etc.—than the majority. Perhaps this is, in most cases, necessarily so, else the minority groups would simply not survive as coherent groups. Anyway, if the government survives for long, which is by no means certain, it's likely that they will breed a great deal of unrest if they carry out some of the oppressive—rather shocking—measures which they are now talking about carrying out. But in Ceylon—as everywhere else—most political talk never amounts to more than just talk.)

* * *

The difference between August and September is greater than that between any other two consecutive months. August 31 is still summer and September 1 is already looking towards another winter—an attitude which persists even here in the tropics, where it doesn't hold true. The rainy season ended in early August (well water after a rain is both ice cold and muddy making washing more difficult—and I'd used up all my firewood and no more could be collected that wasn't wet—though I could heat a bit of water on a small kerosene stove) and we've had three weeks of fine balmy weather, but the last week has been again cloudy with frequent rain and some fog. The rain was not entirely unwelcome, for it allowed me to collect water (off the roof) into some barrels, so I've a fresh supply of water now and need not go to the village to bring it up. I can collect enough now for about a month, though would increase my storage capacity with some more barrels. At any rate, we've not gone so long as a month between rains since I've come to Kandy.

A few weeks ago I took a walk to the top of the mountain which I look at from my *kuṭi*. It seems to be about 1500 feet above Kandy (Kandy is 1600 feet above sea level), and is often shrouded in clouds. The weather was fine the day of the walk, though, and the climb was very pleasant except for the last 150 feet or so, which was very steep, rocky, and difficult, requiring a lot of caution and effort. At the top there was a grand view of Kandy town and valley and also several of the other valleys which I hadn't seen before. I could just make out the *kuṭi* in the distance, a small white dot which I could identify only by location in relation to roads and landmarks. A 12 hour round trip. If I ever go again I'll try to borrow some binoculars. The climb seems to be popular—I met 3 other parties when at the top, mostly students from Peredeniya, about 6 miles outside Kandy (the main campus in Ceylon), which was fortunate, since they had brought water with them, and I hadn't.

The Mahāweli Ganga, the largest river in Ceylon, is only about a mile or so from my *kuṭi* at its nearest approach. It begins in western upcountry and flows down in a big loop around Kandy, going south and finally turns NE and flows to the sea. So another day I went for a walk down river some miles, but found the entire bank on both sides was already occupied by hundreds of people swimming, washing, doing laundry, gossiping, etc., so if I go for another walk along the river it will have to involve either a bus ride out of the inhabited area around Kandy or else a trip of several days.

Some time ago a telegram arrived from Bundala announcing that Ñāṇasumāna was dead. It took some days to find out what had happened—he seems to have been bitten by a viper (vipers are prevalent in the dry area) and for some reason—I still don't know the whole story and have heard conflicting details—there was a long delay in getting to a doctor (vipers are not all that poisonous, and if promptly treated are not normally fatal to a healthy adult). Strange and sad news. You may recall that the goal of my first *carika*—or wandering—in Ceylon was to visit him in his jungle seclusion. He was an American, as I think I've mentioned, and a friend. A good man; earnest in his endeavors. His death also appears to be the death of the project to publish Ven. Ñāṇavīra Thera's writings.

* * *

Since I was presented with my horoscope (unasked for), I presented it to you (unasked for), merely for your amusement—not for what you'd make of it (if anything). While horoscopes may be in the same category as reading cards or tea leaves—i.e. that the reader is more important than the system with which he is shackled—and it *might* be conceit to think that the great stars influence (*not* 'determine') one's life, it might also be conceit to imagine that one is free from all such influences. A good case can be made for astrology. A good case can be made against astrology also. For myself, I have no particular interest in systems of any sort. A system is necessarily a complete view, and it is impossible for an *existing* individual to have an outside, or complete, picture of his own existence, since as an existing individual he is enclosed within and part of his world). Still, I did find it amusing—and possibly even useful. Whether or not there's anything 'to it' is totally irrelevant. The only important question is not 'is it true?' but 'is my relationship to it a true relationship?', and if it is then *its* truth or falsity doesn't even arise. Can I not only apply statements in the reading to myself but also *do* something about it?

What Yoga book are you using, mother? And which exercises are you doing? I find that I've dropped many of the exercises I was doing and now concentrate on just a few, doing them for longer periods of time. It's a matter of experimenting to find which exercises make you feel better; but it's always a good idea to include at least a few of the exercises that tone the glands (which are usually the stimulating exercises, and one feels invigorated afterwards). Iyengar's 'Light on Yoga' is the best book I've seen: Schocken Books, New York. Since we're on books, I've just read Berne's 'Games People Play', and found it one of the best non-fiction books I've read in a long while: Black Cat Paperback (Grove Press).

The few acres of clearing I'm in abound in fruit (as well as flowers), and guava are now ripening on the tree and there's enough around for the monkeys, the village children, and even myself. Also a kind of fruit like a large pink grape, slightly tart, but rather refreshing. Jack fruit grows year around, as do papayas. No bananas here, but there are several different kinds of berries which might be nice if cultivated but wild tend to be small and not too flavorful.

* * *

While astrology continues to not fascinate me, I do, on the other hand, have an interest, of sorts, in breathing, and am glad to know that while doing your yoga you do a great deal of breathing. So do I. Actually, my fundamental meditation practice is mindfulness of breathing, whereby one simply sits down, continues to breathe normally, but 'watches' (mentally) the breath—i.e. one is aware of the breath as it touches the tip of the nose. This practice results in a feeling of great calm and ease (which becomes greater as one becomes more experienced), and also in a certain clarity of perception. Due to the calmness the breathing (as well as other bodily processes) slows down; but the emphasis is not on the breath as much as on the paying-attention-to-the-breath.

So you can sit in the lotus position, can you? Perhaps I inherited my own ability to do so (in spite of an otherwise rather unsupple body)—and perhaps the corresponding ascetic inclinations—not entirely out of the blue.

Do I want a tape-recorder? Well, I don't want the possibility of involvement with the customs people—and also I don't want a tape-recorder. Gradually I'm coming to understand that the way to find a solidly-based happiness is not by acquisition but by renunciation. If it is better to give than to receive, it is better yet to give up.

No, I have no objection at all to seeing other people, along a river bank, or anywhere else, nor any particular interest in seeing other people. Also I have neither objection nor interest in their seeing me. What I do try to avoid is fusses, which are seldom if ever worth the trouble; and I've learned that if I ever sit down to meditate (or sometimes merely sit down to rest) when other people around me a fuss is very likely to be made over me—'What country are you from?' etc. etc., cups of tea, and endless quantities of socializing, all of which I find simply not worth the effort of being involved in—and therefore I have a preference for solitude, where there is nobody to fuss over me and nobody for me to fuss over. It is possible, of course, to simply ignore people, but 1) this requires at least some effort which might otherwise be more profitably directed elsewhere, and 2) sometimes they can intrude themselves in a very positive and aggressive manner. (Their conversation—with rare exceptions—consists of a series of questions all of which are totally predictable since I've heard them so many times before and which are also, therefore, of no interest at all even if they had any intrinsic interest to begin with, which they didn't, and generally concern subjects which I find no pleasure in thinking about and are not really even my concern; finally, often enough I really don't know how to answer the question without arousing hostility. For example, when wandering about if I am asked 'where are you going to?' often enough I'm not 'going' anywhere at all, but simply wandering about; but not only would people be totally dissatisfied by a reply 'Nowhere, I'm just wandering about'—for they want positive content, something they can *know* and *cling* to: 'I'm going to Colombo': that they can repeat with assurance that they have understood—but, being dissatisfied, they would either plague me with further equally-difficult-to-answer-and-equally-dissatisfying-for-them questions or otherwise try to pass off some of their dissatisfaction onto me. In short, then, I avoid people because—with certain exceptions, of course—it is usually well worth doing so.)

Now that this diatribe (explanation? you asked, after all) is over, I find that so is this aerogramme.

* * *

Well, it's a good thing I didn't wait a day before posting my last letter, for the next day the government, having made foreign postage rates uniform, which is a good socialist measure towards uniformity, then proceeded to the next good socialist measure, which was to increase the rates. (The rates for book-post were increased 400%—a message there?)

As I predicted in that letter, I am now wandering—for the last 3 weeks. This trip is far and away superior to all the wandering I've ever done before—at last my meditation, I find, is sufficiently developed that I need no diversions. I stay off the bus routes, preferring to walk on the tea-estate roads, footpaths, and jungle tracks. I walk for a bit, then find a friendly tree to sit under for a bit, then walk for a bit more, and thus pass each day without discomfort, weariness, or anxiety. Since I don't need diversions from this, I don't have to carry all the paraphernalia I required before. One small Dhamma book is quite sufficient: otherwise my requisite of three robes, the mosquito net, and a few small things (soap, toothbrush, bandages, sitting cloth, etc.) make up my whole burden, which I manage with ease. So I've been having an exceptionally fine time so far, putting in 8 or 9 miles a day, some days less, on circuitous routes which so far—so I'm told—have brought me about 45 miles from Kandy.

I spent a few days in a Hermitage to have a few things sent to me by Mahinda, the American monk now staying in the Kandy *kuṭi*; in fact, he took a bus to where I was and delivered them personally. He seemed so pleased to stay in the *kuṭi* that I gave it to him. If I should again want to settle somewhere, I may find another place. If Mahinda wishes, he may let me stay in the Kandy *kuṭi*, or, possibly I can go to either Bundala or Godawaya, both of which are presently vacant. In any case, it matters not at all to me. My home is mindfulness.

> The mindful exert themselves
> To no abode are they attached.
> Like swans that quit their pools,
> Home after home they abandon.
>
> Dhammapada (v. 91)

You ask why I'm interested in giving up. The answer is that I find that by doing so I am happier for it and also more understanding of my situation. The Dhammapada—as well as all the other texts—states the idea frequently in verse, which I translate a bit freely, and unpoetically:

> "The distracted man, whose delight is in the abundance of family and flocks, whose mind is set upon his holdings, is seized and carried off by death as a sleeping village by a great flood." (v. 287)
>
> "It is not a strong shackle, the wise say, that's made of iron, wood, or rope. Far stronger is the longing for wealth, diversions, sons and wife. That bind, the wise say, is resilient, supple, and hard to break. This too they cut off and, giving up sensuality, without any longing, they renounce." (vv. 345-6)

> From attachment springs grief.
> From attachment springs fear.
> For one wholly freed of attachment,
> Whence grief? Whence fear? (v. 214)

This is such a satisfying state to achieve, and the path toward it is so satisfying, I can't see why I should think to do anything else. (Case in point: When I gave Mahinda the *kuṭi*: I was gladdened not merely by making a gift, but by the relief of knowing I no longer *needed* the place. It was pleasant to live there, certainly, but to need it is not at all pleasant, and I just find my life became better, more pleasant to live, when I no longer had any reason to care for something as unimportant as a *kuṭi*; as bound up with both its *idea* and substance.

Does this answer your question? No? Well, sorry. As far as music, art, and literature, it was not so much a matter of giving up anything that mattered to me as much as it was a matter of watching my interest fade away in the face of a much more interesting occupation: meditation. As you have not cultivated this ability, you can know nothing of the subtle, non-sensual pleasures it offers, compared to which the pleasures offered by the world to the senses are akin to creating artificial itches and then providing the means to scratch them. My own slight experience confirms the report of *all* the intent meditators—of all religions—that it is the superior pleasure. This, of course, you can only accept—or reject—on hearsay evidence, which is not the case with me. Meditation and renunciation, you may see, go hand in hand.

* * *

Godawaya. Going for walks in the afternoon, sometimes I pass the fishing Village—about 15 huts on the beach. The huts are made of cadjan in an arch shape, held in place by a framework of sticks and vines and tied with jungle creeper. The huts are about 10 feet by 20 feet on average-long and narrow—but one hut is somewhat larger and serves as the native equivalent to the American drug-store—tea, biscuits, tobacco, social life, can all be obtained there. A few mongrels sleep on the sand in front of this hut, waiting for a windfall. The village is still going up—the fishermen have just moved to Godawaya for the half year when the wind comes from the NE. When it turns they take their houses down and sail off to another part of the island for the other half year.

In front of the huts are the boats—each made from a hollowed-out coconut tree with clapboard sides built up, a mast in the center of the boat—but many of the fishermen now have outboard motors—Evinrude, Johnson, etc.—and do not use their sails. The boat would capsize at once if it didn't have an elaborate outrigging on one side. Three men to a boat, they sit on narrow seats which leave no room at all for shifting weight, let alone moving about. Like fishing on a tight-rope. In the evening they push the boats into the sea, row some distance out from shore and then either start their engines or set their sails. At night their lights—lanterns on each boat—can be seen blinking on the horizon.

At night I've seen a curious phenomenon on the beach. While walking—only when the moon is up and nearly full—where one has stepped, the sand glows green, and one can see his footprints phosphorescent for some minutes, as well as specks of sand that were kicked up while walking. Drawing pictures with a stick and watching the green lines appear (and disappear) is great fun (art is short, life is short).

Near midnight on a full moon night—or nearly full—the giant sea turtles come to land sometimes to lay their eggs. These turtles are about 4 feet across and 6 feet long—i.e. their shells—and they are very slow and stolid. Some distance above the high-tide mark the turtle will dig a hole with its front paws (claws? hands? feet?), shoving the sand about until there is a rather deep hole. Then it will ponderously crawl into the hole, clearing more sand as it does so, thus making the start of a trench, lay its eggs, and cover up the hole.

Now all along the beach people own 'turtle rights', and on appropriate nights they keep the turtle-vigil: if any turtle lays its eggs on 'their' land (though they do not own the land—only the turtle-rights—obtained from the turtles, I doubt) they will wait until the turtle (which takes absolutely no notice of anyone at all—it is quite possible to ride on its back, and it will continue about its business as if it had no passenger) has finished laying its eggs, then remove the sand and collect them. One turtle can lay enough eggs—each the size of a ping-pong ball—to fill a bushel basket, and the eggs will fetch five (Ceylon) cents each in the market. As a result the giant sea turtle is—like the elephant and the *bhikkhu*—a dying race, and has all my sympathy. They will live, I'm told, for several centuries, so perhaps, will be able to wait for better times. The turtles themselves are never harmed, I'm told—by a person who owns no turtle-rights—that the turtle is considered an excellent creature (he pronounced anathema on the owners of turtle-rights) and related several stories of turtles doing good deeds, such as rescuing drowning sailors. I have never eaten turtle eggs (which are soft-shelled and look gooey), so can't say if they're any good.

In any case, I can see no good in eating them, and prefer peanuts. Sometimes I amuse myself by translating some Pāli verses (from the Dhammapada) into English verse, and find it's rather like eating peanuts: as soon as I've done one I want another.

The Truth having heard,
the sage does become
like a lake that's unstirred,
sedate and unplumbed.
(v. 82)

Although a throng a million strong
one might defeat on fighting field,
by far the best is that conquest
that over self one wields.
(v. 103)

* * *

I've returned to Kandy. The monk to whom the *kuṭi* was given has disrobed and gone home, and upon learning of this I thought it best to return, rather than leave the place vacant and untended, since it was originally built for me. I find, though, that it's been much altered in my absence. So it goes.

To answer your question, why 'everybody' doesn't meditate: I don't know. Why doesn't everybody become a real—estate dealer? Or a shoe salesman? Is the store worth watching anyway? Let those who think so watch it, and those who think not may ignore it. I don't feel that I'm returning anything as 'payment' for the food etc. I'm given (although, obviously, the people who feed me feel that they're gaining something by doing so, else they wouldn't do so—but whether their gain is from me or from the act of giving itself is another matter). Nor have I any interest in providing a return—commerce is not my game. (I suppose that were I actually starving I might find some interest—but then again I might not: I reckon that I could live off the jungle's fruits, nuts, herbs, berries, leaves, and roots.

A few evenings ago I heard—but could not see—a fight in the tall grass in front of the *kuṭi*: between, to judge from the sounds, a mongoose and a viper. The mongoose's sounds were recognizable, but the opponent did not hiss, but rather hummed in a peculiar—though obviously aggressive-manner. Cobras, I think, don't hum—they hiss—so I suspect a viper.

The monkeys come by only very occasionally nowadays, largely because a village dog comes around to eat up the leftovers. An elephant (and its keeper) happen along once in a while to feed (the elephant feeds: the keeper just chews betel).

* * *

You have, presumably, read something about the political flare-up here—in fact you probably have more information about the general picture than I do, since there was a clamp-down on communications and, with no newspapers, the only information I could pick up was second-hand reports and 'official announcements' (which, of course, are hardly reliable).

In the areas of the major towns, such as Kandy, there was little fighting, and Udawattakelle itself is particularly safe (it's only a few hundred acres, and with its steep hills the only exits are roads into populated areas: any insurgency forces that were foolish enough to enter would be effectively tramped). However, at night I could hear sporadic gunfire from a distance, out Matale way (to the north): never anything like a battle; rather, I would suppose, sniper action against the military patrols. The curfew, of course, did not affect me, since I had no need to leave the jungle anyway, and could walk within the jungle without hindrance: but after the first few uncertain days (when curfews were noon to 6 AM and, for one day, 24 hours), the curfew now seems to be 4 PM to 7 AM. Between 7 and 4 all is quite normal and everyone goes about their business unconcerned, then there are some quiet hours, and after nightfall occasional gunfire is heard—the noisiest night I heard perhaps 5 dozen rounds fired over a period of about 6 hours—4 or 5 shots, then nothing, for maybe another hour; last night there were a lot of firecrackers going off (it was New Year's Eve, and though fireworks have, of course, been banned—there was none of the extravaganza of skyrockets that I saw last year—obviously, with the tension now largely dissipated (even in the trouble spots, such as Matale, full-day curfew has now been lifted) people wanted to make something of the most important national holiday of the year.

Since the insurgents are a bloodthirsty anti-American lot, they probably have the backing of the Chinese equivalent of the CIA. I've known about their plans, their views, etc, for some time now: they don't hate Americans, but rather America, and are—or, at least, were, perfectly friendly, conducting themselves toward monks as is expected of them in a Buddhist country—actually some of the university monks are members of their group ('university monks' are a special breed of malcontents who have nothing to do with the Buddha's Teaching)—however, in spite of 4 or 5 scattered incidents in the last few months, I was surprised that they should have taken up arms so soon. Probably their hand was forced by the discovery of a large hoard of explosives and the accidental detonation of two of their munition 'factories': they could hardly pretend to be a secret organization any more (though, of course, even before, everyone but the government knew, and ignored, their activities in the lackadaisical attitude of Southeast Asia: why *should* anyone inform the government?)

The future will probably involve continued flare-ups from time to time—it is most unlikely that the insurgents will actually be wiped out—as sporadic strikes are launched against the army and police. The immediate future will be quiet as the insurgents reorganize and lick their wounds; the middle future will see more such incidents; and, unless the government can make the necessary cultural (not merely economic or political) changes so that the populace will be able to see a non-violent way of bridging the gap between where they are and where they want to be—and the policies they are now pursuing (isolationist nationalism) are not going to help people readjust their basic patterns of thinking (a narrow-based, rigidly traditional semi-fatalistic non-responsible et cetera)—the distant future will see the sort of forced revolutionary change of thought pattern which is, in fact, what is making China a major influence. I don't know. Maybe that really *is* the best way—or only way—or most likely way—that Southeast Asia is going to avoid the fate of the dinosaur. Certainly no other system (Singapore or Hong Kong cut-throat capitalism wouldn't work in this climate)—can claim much success.

I've been discussing with two friends—'Putta and Vimalo—the possibility of spending the summer in the Himalayas with a view to going to see a particular teacher in Thailand in the fall. Nothing is settled yet, but it's possible that we may actually go, in which case it will be sometime during the first half of May.

* * *

The situation here is, as you say, messy. There are two completely different wars going on in Ceylon. One of them, as reported by the government, is daily on the verge of ending (weeks ago we were 'warned' not to become 'complacent') with the complete collapse of the rebellion: the few remaining 'pockets' of active insurgents are being 'flushed out' (the government's phrase) as the rebels, their food and war supplies running out, futilely flee while patriotic villagers cheer and aid the army and police in glorious pursuit. In this war there are a few thousand young people who have been misled by sinister (i.e. unpatriotic) forces. Many of these youths are surrendering and their leaders kill one another and themselves as they see their plans collapsing about their ears; but a few 'hard-core' insurgents still cause a bit of trouble. The main task of the country is the rehabilitation of the surrendered and captured rebels and the reconstruction of damaged areas (which are ever being revealed to us as more extensive than we thought yesterday).

The other war—the real war—is not so easy to find out about. Everyone has his own version of what has happened and continues to happen: the isolated farmers, the impoverished villagers, do not have the same experience and background as the Colombo socialites who hold nightly 'curfew parties'. But, from my own observations, from first-and-second-hand reports, the space between the lines of the government's tales, and from snippets from the foreign—mostly Indian—press (which the government tries to keep from the hands—and eyes—of its citizens), the following version seems likely.

Because the insurgents assigned to the Wellawaya area (at the south-east base of the central highland tea country) opened their attack a day too soon—whether by error or necessity is uncertain—the uprising of April 5 fell short of its goal of immediate victory. The government had time to secure the major towns, and to defend some of its positions. An attack on the Prime Minister, Mrs. Bandaranaike, never came off. Forewarned, the police of Polonnaruwa post hid in the trees and wiped out a bane of 70 insurgents who found themselves unexpectedly trapped in the deserted police station they had planned to seize. A large cache of explosives was discovered on the University of Ceylon campus, near Kandy, shortly before the uprising, along with thousands of blue uniforms (hidden in the girls' dorms) and battle plans, and the projected attack on Kandy never came off.

Attacks on Colombo were sporadic, unorganized, and doomed.

Nevertheless, large areas of the country came into rebel control in the first days of the uprising. Although the rebels numbered only 10,000 to 20,000 at first, and had not the strength to hold ground against sustained attack, in the next two days their numbers swelled to between 75,000 and 100,000 as large numbers of youths—a few of them pre-teens—joined up and surged into rebel territory. Weaponless, untrained, and unorganized, these boys—and girls—lacked the resources and the heart for fighting and quickly fell back—or just fell—wherever the government counter-attacked. Vast numbers of them quit the movement as readily—but not as vociferously—as they had joined it; those that did not quit made up the bulk of the 30,000 to 50,000 death toll of the first month of battle. But many towns (there are no 'cities' in Ceylon in the American sense: even the capital has only a few hundred thousand people)—any towns continued to be held by rebels for weeks until they were driven out (along with everyone else) by bombing raids and heavy artillery: many of the towns 'liberated' by the government were reduced to ashes and rubble: it is widely believed that much of the destruction came *after* the police-army forces recaptured towns and villages known to have produced many insurgents. My Lai? Shhh! 'Rumor-mongering' is a crime under the Emergency Regulations, and more than one newsman has been thrown out of the country for telling the truth; more—many more—than one citizen has been arrested. Perhaps the comparison is not apt—after all, in most of the world police and military brutality is not an issue, but an accepted fact—but still, the government has been most reluctant to acknowledge that many of the battles were won from the helicopters which the U.S. supplied (via Britain): after all, Saigon is not so far from Colombo.

As foreign supplies poured in, the army and police (about 25,000 men, backed up by reserves) were able to get the upper hand on the rebels, and by the end of the month the last towns were retaken—although many villages are still under insurgent influence. A four day amnesty at the beginning of the month further weakened the insurgent forces: about 4,000 of them surrendered. These, however, were mostly the late-comers; the original cadre has yet to be broken, and may even be stronger today than when they first set out, their strength emanating from concentration and experience. They have retreated into a number of densely jungled areas where, apparently, they stored massive supplies before the troubles began. With the monsoon expected to begin any day—rendering heavy equipment ineffectual—they will not be easy to dislodge. They can be expected to wage continued battle for a long time to come, specializing in guerrilla tactics.

Ceylon, however, is not Vietnam: since it is an island there is no possibility of establishing an equivalent of the Ho Chi Minh Trail; the people are used to peace and may not react to a long siege with the same—what? equanimity? stoicism? restrained grief?—that the Vietnamese seem to show. Nor do the combatants have any long murderous tradition of combat to maintain and to maintain them. And, in spite of its ineffectiveness, Mrs. B's government won a sweeping election victory less than a year ago and still retains much of its popularity (though much of this is being dissipated by widely believed—and probably true—stories of atrocities, primarily perpetrated by the police). The rebels are a politically rag-tag band of sophisticated (by Ceylonese standards) students and graduates, and simple semi-urban semi-rural dispossessed, and they have put forth a plethora of schemes and programs—the government has allowed only the most outrageous of these plans to be made known (the rebels lack all facilities—perhaps interest as well—to communicate with the populace except by word of mouth, which means, again, that it has no unified program) such as the plan to solve unemployment by killing everyone over 55 years old, and to solve the food shortage by killing everyone under 8 years old. While it is not likely that these sort of programs represent the views of the leaders, the leadership seems to exist only on a very limited and tenuous basis (there are a number of groups of rebels in different parts of the country: communication between them must be a difficult proposition), but the bulk of the populace seem, oddly, to have believed these tales, although they don't seem at all impressed by the so predictable atrocity tales of the government press—tales which don't sound very atrocious, particularly when compared to the tales one hears of the police. The police in Ceylon, of course, are no more concerned about the poor than are the police anywhere else, but their excesses of the past month—often revenge killings—would be a major public issue even in Ceylon except that under the Emergency Regulations public issues—and even private issues—are illegal if they are critical of anything the government supports, and you can get 20 *years*! for breaking that law.

So much for the revolution.

* * *

Katunayake airport—in place of the bus stand which it resembled when I flew in to Colombo in '67 was now a small but tastefully-constructed modern building. While I was sitting in the lounge waiting to board, a purser walked by carrying a small box with a large label reading 'HUMAN EYES'. Rather startling. Even eye-opening. Once on board we barely had time to take off—smoothly—rise above the turbulence of the clouds, have a cup of tea, and fill out landing forms, before we were circling over the Madras airport.

Madras airport, of course, has not changed: India has an atmosphere of non-change, and the red soil—a pale reddish brown—looks as old from the air as it does from the ground. Riding into Madras on the airport bus I felt, again, the turbulence and dynamic undercurrents of India and already Ceylon began to seem a quiet provincial backwater. Symbolic was the billboard sign ('The right bank in the right place') posted just outside an old ruined building. Although the ruin was not, in fact, the bank, the impression that it *might be* lingered. Outside a Hindu temple—one of those very solid decapitated-pyramid style South Indian fantasies with figures cascading down all the sides in a mythological unifying embrace of all extremes—was a sign advertising 'The Greatest Show on Earth'. It might have been advertising all of India. And I had forgotten the sacred cows that roam the streets trying to nip vegetables from the market stalls. Madras has a baked (100°F. by late morning) colonial air to it still, mingled with the South Indian culture—the North appeals more to me, where the cultural development has been more through accretion than refinement, yielding more diversity than subtlety—but the native culture is probably felt more fully in some of the other places—Tanjore, Madurai, etc.—that I've not seen, so perhaps my feelings about it are not well-based.

The train trip—of two nights and a day—to Calcutta was uneventful except for the peculiar fact that on the morning after we started the sun rose in the west. There is no doubt about this: we were traveling north-west, and facing the direction the train was traveling the sun clearly rose on our left, and continues to rise higher in the sky, all morning, on our left. 'Putta and I noticed this independently of each other, and mulled over various explanations, pondered possibilities, considered probabilities, and mused many a musing for about three hours, when we turned from contemplating the bright patch of sunlight pouring in the western windows, and discussed what possible—or impossible—phenomena might account for this. Apparently only the two Buddhist monks on the train had noticed this—or if anyone else had noticed it they had not noticed anything odd about it—or if they had noticed anything odd they had had the good sense to keep it to themselves—and the only explanation we could come up with which did not call for immediate rejection was that 'This is India, man.' At noon the sun reached its zenith and slowly descended as it had risen—in the west.

Oh yes, one other thing happened in the afternoon of the same day. Two well-dressed Indians boarded the train and sat down near me. One of then asked me where I was from, and we began talking. The other Indian said nothing at all, so I conversed with the first Indian and found him quite alert, interesting, and open-minded. He, like some other Indians whom I've met, seem to be very interested in the 'Krishna Consciousness' movement, which they all insist is 'very big in the States'. (Is it? What is it?) But I rather enjoyed our talk and was glad to meet a fairly intelligent man. At the next stop, however, our talk was cut short when the fellow abruptly rose from his seat and marched off the train, leaving all his magazines and newspapers behind him. The second Indian gathered up these papers and picked up his valise, preparing to leave also. Just before going he turned to me and said, 'The person you were just talking to is mentally disturbed. I'm his warden, and I'm taking him to the insane asylum nearby', whereupon, he too, got off the train, leaving me feeling somewhat disconcerted. After all, one hardly expects to hear such things of a person one has just been pleasantly talking to. The obvious explanation, of course, is that he was the last sane man in India, and had to be locked up before he did any damage.

In any case, I find the spirit of India very much a refreshing coolness after the hot and tight attitude of the Sinhalese for almost 5 years. An initial release of energy (which may account for this long monologue) may be nurtured and developed in India, where the entire culture is much closer to the days of the Buddha than Ceylon ever was. Everyone can do their own 'thing' without evoking any surprise, without arousing other people's hangups (except, perhaps, the fellow who was being taken off to the asylum—but I don't know his story: maybe he wants what he's getting—presumably so, since he went through whatever one has to go through to get it), or, indeed, without even being taken seriously, and all through North India the culture is set up to accommodate people who want a life without social bonds and ties--the society is organized to support those who haven't the slightest interest in supporting the society (whereas in Ceylon the Sangha exists largely as a pillar of society rather than—as it was originally intended to be—as an association of people who have given up the lay life), and as a result is more fluid in its own way.

Such is life inside a pinball machine.

* * *

Going north out of Almora there is a steep climb along a paved road for about 1.5 miles, until coming to Chota Bazaar ('Little Market'), which lies at the foot of Crank's Ridge. Turning off the paved road one enters upon the Ridge, a horse-shoe-shaped protuberance (visible from Almora and blocking the north and view) perhaps 6 miles long. The dirt road-jeepable in good weather—then makes a huge arc along the top of the Ridge, and it is sometimes possible to look down both sides at once—steeply sloping hills (often more vertical than horizontal) of pine forests (which are tapped for turpentine) and deodars (a tree similar to the pine) with grassy fields and long-trod footpaths, during the rainy season (now) brooks well up out of the upper slopes and cascade down to the valleys thousands of feet below, where minute villages are nestled among the terraced rice-paddy fields that slope upwards to the forest line. Since there are few thorns, bushes, and other obstacles I can wander among the slopes freely clambering over stone walls which separate fields, wading (and bathing in) icy streams, sitting on rocky outcroppings or at the root of a tree. Except for an occasional boy tending his herd of cows, buffalo or goats, and for the prematurely yellowed and wrinkled village woman who passes by carrying a basket on her head laden with pine needles, straw, or vegetables, there is no one about.

Although there's a lot of farming in the valleys, these high foothills of the Himalayas are still wild: in the day I can watch eagles soaring above, their wings quivering for balance only rarely, and at night I sometimes hear the yelping howl of packs of jackals or a solitary wolf. And on the topmost peak of Crank's Ridge—perhaps 7500 feet (Almora is 5600 feet)—is the Kasr Devi temple, an ancient complex of low stone structures where I can sit, in sunny weather, soaking it all in. And, of course, when the skies are unusually clear for the rainy season, I can look north, to the snow-peaked mountains 50 miles away, and be always astonished at how much higher, and more massive, and icier blue white they are than I remember them being the last time I saw them: the most prominent peak, Nanda Devi, is over 25,000 feet high, and although over 50 miles away it is easily capable of sending icy blasts of wind (and, perhaps, more subtle emanations not only far beyond Almora, but even, in the southwest, to Rishikesh, the Hindu holy of holies, a hundred miles off. The details—the minutiae of life—here are always surprising; a wonderland. The mountains, the hills, valleys, flowers, birds, clouds, fogs, and sunsets all strongly and strangely affect the people who choose to live at this height (altitude an attitude?).

The road also has its influence. Beginning at Chota Bazaar it continues far, beyond the Ridge, and the knowledge that it carries on into Tibet already gives it a certain mystique: On clear mornings the massive fortress-like mountain called Trisul (in Tibetan: I don't know the Hindi or English names) is visible in the far northwest, pure white with peaks at each of its four corners, nearly 100 miles away, but still dominating its quarter of the horizon, and Trisul is in Tibet itself, the forbidden (and forbidding) land.

The road, running along the top of the Ridge, sometimes seems like the Razor's Edge, worn blunt, but also—since daily there is a certain amount of going up and down the road—being nearly circular I find myself in a position reminiscent of an ant that runs endlessly along the rim of a cup, ever retracing its own steps, and—since everyone else on the Ridge does the same thing—I always meet people on the road and we stop to wave our tentacles at each other over a cup of tea, or to just talk briefly before hurrying on to circle the rim of the cup once again.

There are many Westerners here doing various Things—Hindu Things, Buddhist Things, Tantric Things, Freak Things, or simply quiet things—and many very cool heads among the Indians as well, and also some very peculiar congruencies and incongruencies: perhaps in another missive I can describe the local fauna who live north of Chota Bazaar, and you will understand why the area is called Crank's Ridge.

A cottage has been rented for three months; a three-room affair with a patio with a fine view to the north; it's on one of the hills atop the Ridge, but off the 'main' road, so all is quiet with few visitors. (I call it 'the Mole Hill' because I want to make a mountain of it.) It has a stone floor and a slate roof and is a rustic mixture of colonial and native styles. Our landlord, Major B. Thomas Chodhury, is a well-off wog—i.e. a native who has tried to get into the (former) colonial power-structure by adopting English ways: he vacations in a big house just above the cottage; but since he's usually in Delhi—as he will be for the next two months—we have the use of his fine large unkempt gardens, as well as the rest of the (non-commercial) estate for Rs. 40-/month—a bit less than $6. With a few bits of furnishing—a large rug in the main room (where we mostly live, and which is about 14 feet by 12 feet), straw mats, etc.—it's quite cozy, particularly with a roaring log fire in the fireplace. Water is not much of a problem in the rainy season—we have 4 gallon tins brought up from a tank not far below now—but when the rain stops we'll have to have it brought from a mile away, the nearest spring, where it is enriched with minute particles of mica (a lot of the stone hereabouts is mica, which glitters beautifully in the sun, but is ugly for the guts) which have to be carefully filtered out: the water shortage is what keeps the population sparse in this area: aside from a few other Westerners living on another part of the estate, our nearest neighbor in any direction is a 20 minute walk—that's over to Snowview Estate.

It's afternoon now, and I'm sitting on the porch. The day's light sprinkle is over; the sun shines on the hedges and deodars, and I can look out onto the far end of the Ridge and the patchwork slopes leading down to the valley—a few bits of houses, sprinklings of trees, a few fields, pasturage, light green, dark green, dusky and russet, and onto the next few ranges of hills, deeply etched with shadow and stippled by forests and fields, and then mountains of white and grey cumulus clouds mass high to obscure the sight of white and blue Himalayan crags which, perhaps this evening, will become visible again, One of the semi-wild dogs hereabouts wandered up, sniffed around, and wandered off again—they live on gleanings from houses and shops on the Ridge—and somewhere distant is the sound of a wood-chopper, and in another direction, also distant, some children are shouting and laughing. A farmer came a while ago and sold me a kilo of peaches for 75 paise (about 10¢). Soon apples will be in season. Two eagles soar over the valley now, one at eye level, and everything sparkles in the thin air of nearly 1,5 miles high. Time passes very slowly in the mountains, and the scent of the pine cones linger in the day, the coals of the fire linger in the evening, wisps of valley-riding fog linger in the morning. Perhaps I shall linger here a while longer.

* * *

As it's a 20 minute walk from Snowview—the next estate going into Almora (and, apparently, the end of the line for the postman)—the postman will sometimes come out here to deliver mail, sometimes he will drop the mail off at a tea stall to be brought up (hopefully) by anyone coming up this way, and sometimes especially in bad weather—he will simply throw our letters away, and then, not having anything to deliver, save himself the 40-minute round trip. He will also open letters and steal anything worth stealing. He is quite open about all of this apparently he doesn't even consider it improper conduct—a sort of bakshish for his trouble, I suspect—and this being India, there is, of course, nothing to be done. Taking this creative postal service into account, we should, perhaps, design our correspondence accordingly—if that's possible. Perhaps, we can come up with our own Enigma Code or something.

Right now it's about 8 AM and I've just finished my usual breakfast—two chapaties—made in the fireplace—with home-made jam (plums in season) and tea and am sitting on the verandah looking to the NE, where about 100 miles away rises the snow peak of Anapurna in Nepal, the third or fourth highest mountain in the world. The Kumaon hills where I am are atleast 30 miles south of any of the great Himalayan peaks, but the north wind brings the sharp taste of snow and glacier past us down to the plains, another 50 miles. Clouds from the valley below (about 2000 feet down, at more than a 45° angle: the base of the valley is still nearly a mile high) sweep westward, sometimes obscuring the sweep of the ridge opposite; but the clear blue sky—almost as deep blue as the purple knife-sharp shadows of the mountains—remains clear, and the mountains themselves are never quite obscured by these vagrant clouds. Shafts of sunlight through a haze some miles away break onto a huge silent cloud sitting like a sea in a valley several hills off, and the top of this sea-cloud is blindingly white, while the hills around it sparkle with a preternatural green: the pine forests cover the higher reaches of the hills, while the lower halves are sculpted with brown-and-green rice-field terraces broken by dots of white houses and ribbons of silver-brown rivers.

In the mornings I do whatever tasks need to be done—washing, sewing, cleaning, cooking, etc.—or sit quietly. I try to work slowly, with awareness of the present, so everything takes longer (but the great lesson of India is patience) and thus gives me more satisfaction. I'll probably go for a walk soon—through the hills, in the forests, or find a rock to sit on or a tree to sit under for the rest of the day. Towards evening I'll make my way back to the road—a glorified footpath really—that runs along the ridge on which sits the hill on which sits the cottage in which sit I—and will usually meet one or two other Cranks of the Ridge, who have, probably, been doing the same thing, spending their day in their own quiet way, developing their own amity and inner peace, and we may just smile and pass each other, or talk for a bit, drink tea at one of the shops that sprout (like a leaf on a vine) along the side of the twisting footpath. We watch the sunset. Sometimes we watch each other. Always the mountains giving an extra dimension. (How would a two-dimensional person living in a picture feel if he could look out and see the three-dimensional picture frame?) Perhaps Kumaon is like a picture—it is certainly like a fairy land, or perhaps Alice's Wonderland—in three dimensions and looking at the mountains that frame this picture is like looking into a fourth dimensional perspective. That may not seem rational or sensible; but neither do the Himalayas.

Today seems to be a peculiar mixture of clouds and sunshine, giving the air a vibrant luminescent quality and making the surroundings appear (when they appear) as if they were painted with DayGlo colors. Not a breeze; unearthly still—hardly kite-flying weather (though I have a small kite ready for a windy day; it's a big sport in the East—though for me it's just a means to soar). The monkeys made one of their rare visits here this morning; they seldom come so close to the leopard run, which crosses the Ridge about ½ mile south of here. A leopard took a cow from Snowview a few days ago in broad daylight; they are usually only about at dawn and dusk. They won't go near a person if he has a light.

In the evenings, I sit quietly smoking a hookah—the coolest possible way to take tobacco—and read, or study Hindi, or watch the stars.

Conditions are rough here, and comforts are few, conveniences non-existent; but, by making each moment as graceful as I can, I try to make each day an act of grace. If I can succeed in that I shall be content to accomplish nothing else at all.

* * *

No, my handwriting is not a strain on my eyes. I didn't even think it particularly small. I've a little book of texts, etc. that I've collected over the years. Intended for use while traveling, I wrote as small as possible to get in as much as I could, and that's *really* small. I used a Parker 21 fountain pen and it took a lot of care to write, especially since much of it was in Pāli. Anyway, that's how I learned to write small and legible. Perhaps, I'll next take up thumb-nail sketches.

Perhaps it is the rarer atmosphere that makes kite-flying difficult. I'd ascribed it to my lack of skill. Two nights ago the mountains were visible at sunset for the first time since the rains began; then at dusk huge fires were lit everywhere in the valley, and on the Ridge, and on the distant hills, celebrating—I think—the Hindu New Year (at Autumn Equinox?), and yesterday, for the first time since Nepal in '66, it was possible for me to see the mountains all day long, and this morning—about 10 AM—there's still not a cloud in the sky. Not a breeze, which makes me suspect that I can now retire my kite (a large diamond shape, which I made myself).

No, I have no interest in writing books. At present I'm concerned with another art-form, one admittedly less salable, but much more satisfying, which is called meditation, and might be looked at as turning oneself into 'a work of art'—i.e. making oneself more pleasing to be in the presence of—and this takes up most of my time. I sometimes pick up a paint-brush, however, and see if I can coax the color and line into something resembling a *thanka*, a Tibetan religious painting. This requires delicate work and fine concentration.

As for the Cranks of the Ridge, there seems to be little space left on this aerogramme, but, perhaps, special mention should be made of Buddhananda, who I stayed with briefly when I first arrived. He's a fat old Englishman ordained earlier this year after his retirement from the Intelligence and Security branch of the British High Commission, whose mind is still warped by his past: he's always pulling off little 'coup d'etats' to 'keep in practice', such as picking the lock of a door when he has the key in his pocket, and he knows the intimate life of 250,000,000 of India's 500,000,000 population. He tells, in the strictest confidence, the same stories to everyone he meets, even casual strangers. He has a black heart of gold. He's lived on Crank's Ridge longer than most of the Cranks.

* * *

I'm convinced now that the magnificently sculpted mountains have strongly influenced the people here, so that their minds become better sculpted. Everyone out here—the Indians, the freaks, the lamas, Tibetans, and other oddities—seems to be on well-directed trips (of different velocities and varying rates of cycles per second) trying to find a level at high altitude. The openness of the Himalayas is an open invitation to spread one's wings, drop one's burdens, and join the eagles in the sky. So for the three months of Vas (rainy season) retreat I'll be living on Crank's Ridge, where I feel very much at home. The mountains—let alone the rest of the fairyland trip—may help me to live in peace, to be as straight as I can, and to cool my head. That, at any rate, is what's on the menu for this Vas. We shall see how well I fill my plate.

Lama Govinda will be leaving shortly for a year or so, lecturing at, I believe, Southern Methodist University (he's been invited by the Methodist Church), and Suññata Bahaji is in Denmark at present, visiting his ailing elder sister (he's somewhere about 85 years old), so we're a bit short on Big Names at the mo, but Baba Ram Das (Richard Alpert) is down the footpath at Kausani—about 8 miles toward Bageshwar—and, locally, we have the Ven. Buddhananda (Ronald Boughan), a recently ordained former Intelligence officer for the British Foreign Service, who, says, with a sinister and confidential grin, that he still keeps a hand in the game. (Did you meet him when you were out this way? He lives in Snowview.) Then we have Win Chamberlain, the producer-director of a film called 'Brand X'. (I've never heard of him or his film before, but apparently it got good reviews and a bit of attention in some of the more ethereal segments of North American culture: have you heard of/seen it?) and an intimate of Timothy Leary. We also have Leary's ex-wife, a lanky Swede married to a Harvard grad student doing studies in Tibetology (he'd been a Tibetan monk for four years in—yup—New Jersey), so it's not surprising that rumors maintain that Leary Himself has fled from Algeria (where, I'm told, he was being held prisoner by the Black Panthers—politics makes incredible bedfellows) and is hiding out either in the Kumaon hills or in Scandinavia. (Neither of us, of course, will believe a word of it, will we?) And then... but enough: you are now aware that the spiritual-pharmaceutical fringe is very biz in these parts (at the mo).

I've been to see Lama Govinda several times, and shall see him a few more times before he splits. He's a fine old man, alert, friendly, with a good head, fine vibes, and lots of undiscovered vitamins. He came from Germany together with Ven. Ñāṇaponika (of the Forest Hermitage and Buddhist Publication Society fame) and Swami Garibalda, who holes up near Jaffna. All three, at one time, were Theravada monks at the Island Hermitage. It's interesting to see, after thirty years, what each of them has done with his life. Certainly Lama Govinda—scholarship and other diversions aside—has been making some good use of his time, and has profited by it. He manages, nonetheless, to enshroud himself in a few romantic veils (stitched in secret by his wife?).

If I can keep the body together (which will require reasonably good health) and shitting at the proper rate (which will require some funds), there will be nothing to stop the mind from holding together and shitting at the proper rate. 'Monks, whoever eats and drinks needs to shit and piss' And again: 'There are, monks, these four foods: solid food, whether coarse or fine, contact second, thirdly mental-intention (*mano sañcetanā*) and consciousness as fourth'. Your tract on defecation was good. What about the void in the bowels after the movement? If it all comes out in the end, when does the end come out? As for contact (consider the sensory-deprivation experiments), mental-intention (i.e. time-structuring) and consciousness, what they produce (i.e. shit) is worthy of consideration. So too is it worthwhile to consider what they are, which, in the present terminology, is that they're itches produced by the mosquito bites of the mind. Shit is what happens when we scratch them. Thanks for pointing that out. Dhamma is a spiritual calamine lotion. It is also a mental flit bomb. It's for eliminating the cause of the itch, and not for finding a better way to scratch. There are no mosquitos on Crank's Ridge—except the ones we bring with us.

Om Hūm,

V.

* * *

Actually I've got it all figured out now—it's simply the altitude making me a bit giddy. But *also* (for nothing is really just 'simply') the sap is great up here, flows freely providing much *viriya*,[1] and is leaving me with a lot of time to do a lot of work on myself. I find the various scenes amusing, not presumptuous, when viewed from the proper distance (2.628' 4½", to be exact), just as I find the mountains presumptuous, not amusing,

1. *viriya*: (Pāli) energy.

when viewed from an improper distance (anything less than 25 miles), and besides there's a big difference between being against things and being up against them. I'm against *lobha*, *dosa*, and *moha*,[1] trying to *not* be up against them, and nothing else. But I've lost interest in the pharmacy of enlightenment long ago, and have failed to renew my subscription. (I used to sell Life, but I *never* sold Time.)

Your piece of ultimate reality arrived, my blessings to an honest postman (like what could he *do* with it, anyway?), and I'm closer to Thailand, not Ceylon, every day now, but there's coconuts there too, never fear, never fear. Still, even when I get there, I'm just gonna try to find me a nice mountain, 'cause the lowlands just ain't for me. Whether to pass through, around, under or over, but neither down nor up. Perhaps just 'on'?

Lama Govinda, by the way—will be in Vancouver, apparently, some time around the end of the year, or maybe after. Since you sang for your tea—in Pāli—when you saw him in Almora—maybe you'd like to try again?

*Recycle* wastes??! Lawdy, ain't goin' 'round once 'nuff?! We always do end up going around twice, to say the least, but let's not make a virtue of non-necessity. Water's fine for fighting fire, if you *got* water (Oh! Is *that* what Vas is for?), but one thing you can be *sure* you've got if you're fighting fire, and that's fire, and as far as I know I've never met a man who had water (which, I believe, is the essence of the *sotāpanna*[2]—viz. Ven. Ñāṇavīra Thera—and not of the *puthujjana*.[3] This suggests a different, non-recyclable, use for wastes, does it is not? Or doesn't it?

(Look, my friend. First I hold it up at the ends of my fingers, balanced there like the egg the magician makes appear out of nowhere, and exhibits. Look, this piece of space I hold for us to examine. Now I set it down, and see how quickly it is absorbed into this table and runs out to saturate everything.)

Ho hūm,

V.

* * *

---

1. *lobha, dosa, moha*: (Pāli) greet, hatred, and delusion.
2. *sotāpanna*: (Pāli) stream-attainer.
3. *puthujjana*: (Pāli) commoner; unenlightened person.

The last time I saw Buddhananda he confided to me, with the air of divulging a state secret, that he was going off to Sarnath for a while. (Sarnath, a few miles outside Benares, is where the Buddha first taught his Teaching; consequently there's a large Buddhist settlement there with numerous temples from various countries.) So, my mail drop's now at Mary Opplinger's place: she's an elderly Quaker from New England who has been here for 16 years. Her husband—a Swiss working for some Swiss Church-sponsored foreign-aid group—being off in Africa for the past few months, she has recently discovered a Hindu recluse who she is very taken with and whose teaching she now follows without being any less a Quaker for it. She's an expert in homeopathic medicine and treats all and sundry—natives, hippies, freaks, cranks—who call at her door. (In fact, her medicine cured some sores on my legs, caused by insect bites, that I'd not been able to rid myself of even using antibiotics and other Western potions.) She is, I suppose, the den mother up here.

I'm told that at Tibetan altitudes (over 10,000 feet) it's possible to fall asleep in shadow and wake up with both sunburn and frost-bite. These cooler clear days seen like a portent, though it never gets that extreme here—but, for sure, winter's icumen in, and my thoughts run to thick woolen and fluffy down. Yet Time if not the seasons has a different character upon the hills—it changes only as a cloud changes, simply shifting about imperceptibly while never seeming to change at all—and it's easy to forget that in other parts it moves with the steady rhythm of an army on the march. But the clock and calendar of Kumaon—the sun, the clouds, the trees—are still timely.

* * *

Mountain villages, unlike plains villages, are spread out with fields between the houses, so there are no houses 'next door'—the nearest is several fields away, and not on the same level either. Plains villages, on the other hand, often have the narrowest passages between houses, and sometimes share common walls like apartment buildings. (The plains villages are also sometimes enclosed by defense walls.) In Ceylon the opposite pattern is found: in the plains the houses are spread out with fields between them (Ceylon never had the invasions, etc., that require defensive village works), but in the hills the villages are built by the tea estate owners for the tea pickers, and are as close as possible to each other to allow for more tea bushes. (No tea is grown in Kumaon, which is the dry side of the Himalayas, but Darjeeling tea is highly valued.)

You'll notice that refugee relief taxes now apply to postage, as well as a lot of other things. When I was in Delhi recently there were several mock air raids—mock in every sense, since they were looked upon generally as a nuisance to be cooperated with as little as possible. The Delhi papers are full of Bangladesh Freedom Fighter Victory Reports—which have an air of vague plausibility and cars have bumper and windshield stickers: LIBERATE BANGLADESH; PUNISH YAHYA; CRUSH PAKISTAN. The only concern we have in Almora is that if a war does start (no one really knows if it will) they may try to evacuate us, since we're close to restricted border territory, as I'm told happened in '65, when they got everyone into evacuation centers ready to ship them out of the country, but the war ended before anyone got sent out (as it almost certainly would again), and so everyone was released again. War in these parts has something to be said for it. My only brush with belligerents so far was in Delhi: a troop of Hare Krishna freaks from California besieged the city, trying to convert the blase Indians to the True Faith—talk about selling ice-boxes to the Eskimos!—I was first mistaken for one (a Krishna freak not an Eskimo), then spiritually propositioned by one (a Krishna Eskimo for all I know)—and would have—preferred, I think, a Moslem invasion by the Pakistan Army.

Far from that madness, the fields are green with winter wheat. The cherry trees are in blossom (yes, I know it's late November; nevertheless the cherry trees are in blossom); leaves glisten in the bright sunlight, which each morning illuminates the dew gathered in thousands of spider webs. The nine forests waver green and silver through wafting fog.

* * *

I'm happy to know my small paintings arrived safely and have afforded you some pleasure. Yes, they took many hours each, the detail work—one of the distinctive features of *thankas*—being a very slow and careful job. The original designs were taken from a series of prints from which I selected figures I liked and copied them onto blank paper in outline, then painted the outlines, restoring the original detail as much as I could. I used water-color, a very fine brush, and concentration. I began with a box of schoolchildren's type water-colors, but eventually wound up with bottles and tubes of all sorts.

The war seems to be over—so I'm told. Probably you were better informed on what was going on than I was (or am). Still, it affected me more seriously than I'd expected, since it created a kerosene shortage and for a while it looked like we would have to use candles at night (a more expensive proposition). But then we scored a 4-gallon tin, which is a month's supply. Also, I've had a one-year extension of my visa, so there's no concern—there never was—of being evacuated. (Even evacuation would be alright with me: it would probably mean a free trip to Nepal.) However, since the government will not evacuate me due to the heat of the war, I'm now obliged to evacuate myself due to the cold of winter and in about a week I'll be leaving for Bodh Gaya, the place (in the plains, to the east of Benares), where the Buddha attained enlightenment.

Already departed from the scene are an elderly American, Henry, formerly a Vedantic monk for five years and a psychiatrist, who is trying to buy an estate up here to settle on (Henry has given up his practice, having, presumably, made a bundle); Jennifer, a plump young Canadian girl (her father was an American who fled to Canada during the Korean war to evade the draft) who, having been nurtured on LSD ('acid baby' is, I think, the term used), no longer has much interest in freak scenes and has a cool collected head—she's joining her brother in an ashram near Bombay; Gary, an American, who has a hashish-smuggling racket, and his girlfriend Judy, English, formerly a Tibetan nun, both to take a meditation course from an elderly Burmese gentleman in Bombay; Sally and Win Chamberlain, who are under-(or over)-ground New York film-makers; Tensing, a Harvard graduate student on a foreign study fellowship doing Tibetan studies (he's the former monk from the New Jersey Tibetan monastery) and his Swedish wife, who was formerly the wife of Richard Leary (Timothy Alpert?)—with whom(s?) both Henry and Win also had connections—and various hippies, heads, and other types too probable and improbable to describe.

Still around are such people as Nick and his Swedish wife Eva, who have just returned from a three month trip to Tibet (a small part of which, nearly inaccessible is held by the Nepal government—they tell of 21,000 feet passes, seeing people washed away crossing rivers, etc., and have some excellent photographs of the journey—Nick speaks fluent Tibetan); Sunnyata, an 84 year old Danish Hindu *sadhu*; and Pat, a middle-aged American following Hindu ascetic practices (she vas formerly a successful artist, and gave me some basic advice on the *thankas*); Carol, an English girl who practices witchcraft; and a host of others. Names keep changing, but the typos don't.

It's been an amusing 6 months, watching it from the outside. But I couldn't imagine being more than a spectator, and so Bodh Gaya seems the inevitable conclusion to Almora.

* * *

(On the day I finished a 40 day fast by Elk Lake, on southern Vancouver Island, I received the last aerogramme from Almora. On the inside of it was painted in water-color-*thanka*-style—an emaciated *sadhu* reminiscent of Siddharta Gautama sitting cross-legged at the root of the bo tree on the verge of becoming the Buddha; only he, with green halo, was seated on a green lotus in a black void—Hūm)

How's dis for mountains, hey?

Will I arrive at Mahāsamuddra and cross over, by possibly monsoon, to find out about Siamese rain and other such romances? Or will it be back to the land of coconuts, and all those undiscovered vitamins, stringhoppers, rabbit holes, mad tea parties, and whatnot?

What's going on? Something coming off?

V.

* * *

In two days there will begin a meditation retreat at the Burmese temple here in Bodh Gaya, which I expect to join. Listening to some of the Burmese monks chanting Pāli, the lilt and cadence struck me as oddly familiar. Finally it dawned on me: the abbot of the Buddhist temple in Calcutta, Ven. Dhammapala, who ordained me, and taught me my first Pāli chants, was originally from a village near Cox's Bazaar, not far from the Burmese border, and his teacher, the monk who ordained him, was a much-revered Burmese *bhikkhu* who lived alone in the jungle near his village. Ergo, I guess I have a bit of a Burmese accent—in Pāli.

As for the persons joining the retreat—which lasts ten days—most appear to be young Westerners: some are earnest, others are looking simply for what they think of as 'far out', others are curious, a few, monks and laymen, have extensive previous practice. A very mixed bag—but all quite friendly, and—even though many of those involved have strong Hindu leanings—there is a very different atmosphere to the whole thing than I've met in the Hindu groups—somehow it seems less frivolous. The freaky gesture, the wild eyes, the zennish talk ('everything is one; nothing really exists; it's all the same,' etc.)—when these are seen they stand out as something foreign to the atmosphere, rather than part of it, as in the Hindu sessions, and there seems a clearer sense of direction—and calmness—here. Even the Hindu-oriented have noted this. One, a follower of Baba Ram Das (Alpert), who wears his hair in a topknot, was, he said, amazed to find a place where people actually mean what they say and do.

Bodh Gaya itself helps. None of the English-country-estate lawns and gardens of Sarnath. The mud huts of the village extend everywhere, almost up to the doorsteps of the pilgrimage places, but the area is dominated not by the village with its fields of rice, and bustle of life from people, dogs, wild (or atleast loose) pigs, sheep, goats, cows, and buffalo, but by the Mahā Bodhi temple, a very high and unusual temple behind the tree under which the Buddha sat at the time he attained Enlightenment. (The original tree is no longer there: it was *accidentally*? destroyed by the British when they were doing excavations, and has been replaced with a shoot from the tree at Anuradhapura, which is itself a shoot from the original tree.) The temple is a gorgeous structure unlike any I've ever seen; a sort of synthesis of architectural styles of all the Buddhist countries and the ancient Buddhist *stupas* or monuments of India (such as at Sanchi); very elegant: a bell-shaped dome is topped by what resembles a Papal cross of stone—with three crossbars—surrounded by three smaller domes; every inch of the building is sculpted with ornate designs, and, perhaps, more than any single features its many meditative niches and corners give it its distinctive character.

Life centers around this temple for the devotees, especially the Tibetans, many of whom measure the circumference of the area surrounding the temple with their bodies, prostrating themselves endlessly as they slowly work their way around the grounds. Inside the temple one room echoes constantly to the chanting of the pious as they read from their sacred books—books made of sheets of paper unbound, about two and a half feet long and perhaps six inches high, with Tibetan script (but, they say, Sanskrit language)—about seven lines to the page. The sound struck me as not unlike that heard inside an orthodox shul, but the Tibetans, in their purple and yellow dresses, dark faces with sharply pronounced features and high cheekbones and long hair, often in braids or topknot, hardly look like East European Jews. (My impression—just passing—is that probably 25% of the Westerners here are of Jewish background. I remember reading somewhere that something of the same percentage of Jews were involved in the San Francisco scenes of the 60's.) The large contingent of Tibetans about is due partly to the presence of the Dalai Lama, who is staying (for the winter, I think, before returning to his usual home, Dharamsala, about 100 miles west of Almora) at the beautiful Tibetan Rest House.

It's cold still—though I've enough warm robes—in the mornings even colder than Almora. Here the air is heavy and the sun rises and sets as a dull cold orange ball giving off insufficient heat to penetrate the heavy air. But once warm it stays warm for a while after sunset, and shadows are not cold. In a quiet, unadorned way the place is rather enchanting.

I look forward to the retreat.

* * *

While the usefulness of the sessions was limited—the limitations of a large group of uneven and different practice (the teacher knew what he was doing, but it was not what I was doing)—at the very least I got in some days of intensive meditation, which did me good; practice tends to degenerate under the traveling conditions of the last two months.

After the sessions, I took a four hour bus trip north to Rajgir, ancient Rajagaha—south of Patna (you won't find any of the Buddhist pilgrimage places on any map but a historical map): here is found the cave where the First Council met a few months after the Buddha's death to decide what to do with the Teaching; also are found many places where the Buddha lived, and they all have stories behind them, told in the Suttas. Rajagaha was the ancient capital of the Kosala Kingdom, and is surrounded by hills which provide a natural fortification, atop which huge walls, about 40 miles in length still stand today in partial ruins. There are many tales of the kingdom to be gleaned by scattered references in the Suttas. As there were 2500 years ago, there are natural hot springs, and public bathing tanks have been built. I found one item not mentioned in the tourist guide books: while searching for a particular place I made some wrong turn and got into some heavy bush atop a hill. As the cowtrack began petering out I stopped to look around and thought of turning back, when I smelt a penetrating, rather noxious odor, which was vaguely reminiscent of something. I looked around for the source and saw nothing, and then looked down—almost at my feet was a rotting human corpse. Actually, to be accurate, it was only the top third of a corpse, from the chest up, without arms. It was probably one to two months old—half the flesh on the skull still remained; but I'll spare you the details. I went back to an old Jain temple where some Indians were sitting and told them of what I'd found. They were curious to see it, so I took them back to it. They examined the corpse, and I was eventually able to learn that they knew who it was, and who had murdered him, but they had no intention of doing anything about it. As a matter of fact, neither did I, and for all I know it's still there. It's the first time I've seen a really ripe body—seen? I nearly stepped on him. Although the Buddha suggested the contemplation of such things as a little exercise in reality—the glorious future of every one of us—it certainly put me off my lunch.

From Rajgir it's only a few miles to Nalanda, the site of one of the greatest ancient universities, where 10,000 students attended classes at its peak—it was about 700 years old when it was destroyed in the Moghul invasion of the 13th century. A new university has been established close by the ruins, primarily devoted to 'Buddhist studies', and I stayed there with a Laotian monk I'd met in Bodh Gaya. In a spell of very wet weather, I trekked up to Vasali, headquarters of the ancient Vajjian Kingdom: little had been done in the way of excavation there, although there are two *stupas* where small quantities of ash from the cremated body of the Buddha were unearthed, as well as one of Asoka's pillars unfortunately defaced at the base by tourists who had chiselled their names into the stone ('E.F. Simon, 1831', 'J.S. Stevenson 1790', etc.)

Kusinagar, where the cremation actually occurred, was next, a pleasant enough place, but aside from the death and cremation of the Buddha not much happened there, so a day of radiant sunshine later I went on to Savatthi, where the Buddha spent 25 years, and saw extensive ruins—a large city existed there at one time, perhaps even bigger than Rajagaha—amidst sparse jungle. By this time my capacity to absorb was getting pretty clogged, and I realized I wouldn't he able to get much out of Savatthi beyond surface impressions: too much happened there. So, after a couple days of wandering around, I called it quits, and went on to Lumbini, just across the Nepal border, where the Buddha was born. The site is marked by an old Asokan pillar, now cracked up the stem and with its capital in fragments. But a beautiful temple was there—looked after by a fine old Nepalese monk—full of ornately-carved woodwork of traditional Nepalese handicraft, Tibetan-style wall paintings, and many other fine touches. From Lumbini I had to re-enter India to get to Katmandu, there being no Nepal road, and it took an exhausting three days on narrow-guage trains and a rattletrap truck to reach Kathmandu.

When the truck conked out at a pass of about 8200 feet (Kathmandu's in a valley; only about 4500 feet) I got out and had the pleasure of making a snowball. I felt it was the least I could do, and—since I did no more—apparently the most I could do too…

* * *

Perhaps you should read this letter sitting down. To begin with—an event that should make you happy—I've disrobed. Yesterday I went out to Ananda *kuṭi*, the local Theravada Buddhist temple, and announced my intention. 'That's perfectly alright,' Ven. Amritananda, the chief monk of the temple, told me. 'There's no obligation for anyone to be a monk longer than he wants. ' He's a very fine person who made the whole business very simple, amiable, and light, when with others it could have been much more difficult, and I'm quite grateful to him. So, it took only a few minutes to change into some clothes I'd borrowed—I'm having some things made for me, Nepali trousers and a Tibetan shirt—and I walked out a layman again.

It's ironical, I guess, that this should happen in the same place where, almost 6 years ago, I more or less decided on ordination: Nepal is a strange and magical place for me, and—although I dislike mystical explanations—I'd be unwilling to say that the valleys and snow-covered mountains played no part in the decision to disrobe. Certainly, though, other factors are also involved. Perhaps it wouldn't be possible to explain them all (perhaps I don't even know them all), and, perhaps, too, you are satisfied simply to know that what you've wanted has happened, without caring about why, but still something might be said.

After having written that last sentence I thought for some minutes about what might, in fact, he said. How can I summarize these years of inner development? So much has happened that even a bare outline would be a major effort; yet an outline, bereft of the significance of detail, would be meaningless. Perhaps, though, the central themes would revolve around the ideas of understanding my own capacities and limitations, and of finding that things must be done in the proper order: I didn't know, when I was ordained, that one must be a good layman before one can be a good monk, and that some qualities are better cultivated in the city and not the forest.

Naturally, there have been some immediate influences which helped bring me to a position where I could accept these things—influences, that is, other than the eternal Himalayan snows. (One day a bunch of friends climbed into a landrover—incredible vehicle!—and we went up to a hill near the Tibetan border, camped overnight, and watched the sunrise over the mountains. Everest, far to the East, was a very minor peak on the horizon. Annapurna was brilliant. There was a frisbee; a campfire; a guitar. Very windy and cold. Very beautiful! But how to enumerate then, weigh them, or evaluate them? of what value to do so? But even without explanations, I know you will be happy to know I've disrobed, and that the years as a monk have been valuable, useful, and peaceful: they were not wasted.

I've been in the hospital. The trouble itself turned out to be not very serious—an infection; but because it was located in the urinary tract it was very painful, and I had to be taken to the hospital and was kept doped up for a day and a half. Also at first it was thought to be appendicitis (the pain was general rather than localized) and I was prepared for surgery before the doctors found out what was wrong. However, I've now been released and need only some mild antibiotic (ampicillin) for a few days. The hospital was very good—a Western missionary affair with British and Canadian doctors—but also expensive: the bill was over $30. (My sense of the expensive is no doubt in for a shock.)

I am accepting your offer of a ticket to the States. I have some ideas of what I might do there—especially what I might not do there—but right now these are just ideas, not plans.

I would, presently, even like to avoid the preconceptions which are the prerequisite of pre-plans.

By the way, the rhinoceros (which is on the Indian aerogramme) is found in some of the valleys of Nepal. I don't know if they're found in the Indian Himalayas, but they're certainly not exclusively African, any more than the lion, elephant, camel, or ibex.

I feel rather like one roaming back to America.

# PART III

# Getting There

The Negev, 1965

## The Negev

Bound between the reaches of two mountain ranges,
born within the heart of anger,
left beneath the stench of sulfur dust
precipitating slowly on the ruins of that birth,
the Negev's first uncertain days—when strata buckled
between phases of a crazed and frantic ride
and deranged chasms' crumbling sands first bore the brunt
of the decimated yet unblunted boulders' fall—
Those first uncertain days were meant
not as creation but as death. Destruction
was the purpose of that force which thrust against the land,
and surely, in the tumble and the rise,
was too improbable to ever have been planned.

The Israelites were first to know the product of creation's wrath
and named it as the Negev: their Desert of the South.
And terrified they fled at its birth, or tried to;
tiny figures climbing slowly from the death below
along precipitous and jagged salt-stone cliffs.
Though it could be owned by no one it had worth,
and first was used by Jews for patient centuries.
And then the others came from unknown races,
wanderers and settlers in search of any place
that could be half a home; and they competed for it
with the sun, aridity and rocks which

were they soil still could not be farmed
and only barely grazed. These others left their signature, a scratch,
upon enduring surfaces. The Jews left nothing more.

Successive waves of conquerors were conquered,
driven off from what they strove to own
by newer nations or by something else,
and not the desert, this, for rock and stone
have many times before been domineered by man.
That thing which drove man back cannot be known,
is greater even than the land:
the pattern and the interplay
of force and need which feed the desert
are what make the lack of life
so plausible. The energy derived
is much too varied to be held
and far too great to be controlled.
On what kills man, the desert thrives.

Assyrian, Roman, Greek, and Turk,
the hundred other great, the thousands, lesser
lurk briefly behind weak shadow-lines
or tread cautious lives
beneath the weight of too much sky
until they're driven off by
rushing floods of heat.
Leaving behind their signs:

The coins, all green and
weathered,
scattered,
lie in distances apart
from those that can be
measured,
distances of mind, not only
miles and time.
The potsherds, reconstructed
now by man,

lie broken with the shattered bones
within which minor tales of minor
shames and battles
lie muted beneath the Negev's
other claims.
And stones which were once walls,
spaced and salted with evaporated sweat
of strife against a witless force
too great to know and therefore called by man
in plural as 'the elements',
lie in broken and half-broken mounds,
reclaimed and half-reclaimed by the
surrounding wasted span
of sandless half-spent half-certainty
of Negev's rocky grounds.
These signs, and more, lie dormant and unseen
along the shifting scheme of hill and plain
that calls itself by no name that we know
but which we call the Negev.

And of these signs that man has left behind
(and often, unplanned, stayed behind himself)
no one is mark of mandate nor of claim
to having held the will, volition—state it as you will—
of elements or strengths or surfaces or depths,
not so much as the least stone part of that
untamed rim within his hand.
For if the Negev can have masters they are these:
the energies and elements which, so long before—
when Lot's vain wife first beheld the fires of destruction—
almost as an accident created from that strife
(by destruction of the Cities of the Plain);
the desert which depends yet on these for its—
let's not call it life, but surely it is something more
than mere existence; instead let's call it
continuity;
the Great Sahara, South and to the West
a wasteland as you'd think a desert ought to be—

sweeps its sands across the Sinai shelf,
and keeps the Negev separate from itself
by northwest-running granite hills,
a vastness which can spill those unknown forces that maintain it
out across the breach into the Negev's lands
in a final flickering of blurred strained strength
beyond whose power the Sahara is spent
so that the essence of the desert is transferred
but character is lost and no imprint is lent,
no genetic pattern is impressed. The Negev stands
dependent but irrevocably alone.

The granite hills define its western reach.
The northern Negev has no border.
Here the combinations, tempers, of the air,
undefined, disordered, wavering as mist before a wind,
hold back expansion, but two things there are
that can draw a line through and then say:
'the desert ends right here'. Though really,
though the Negev's not the world its end
is as uncertain as a fading whimper.
We draw our line across a hundred miles
(we must lest we allow a nether land
which, as we cross it, might extend
its lack of certainty, exactness, onto us
so that we find ourselves as vague
and ill-defined, abstract).

We gaze then on the surface of the world's deepest rift,
where oily waters, salted far beyond
the limits any life can tolerate
keep chained in secret far below its shores
those still lost Cities of a near-forgotten,
buried, once sweet fruitful Plain.
The Dead Sea still seeps sulfur fumes
where Sodom once reigned royal and Gomorrah
grazed her herds of sheep and goats.
Now drifting muted waters sweep those shores

where some dreary and gnarled trees before
the mountains loom like moonscape, leaping
from the bottom of that stained defeated stand of strife,
of raped and dread depleted land.

Midway between the Dead Sea and the Mediterranean
appears the one tired mark where man's slight spark of fire
has endured within hostile terrain. Beer Sheva bears the signature
not merely of an Arab settlement, lost beside some wells,
which grew too quickly after far too many mired years
of service to the struggling camel trains
that single-file, slowly, cross the southern hills.

It grew too tame too fast when Israel's men
reclaimed the desert they'd deserted at its birth
and massed new matter to the flawed and crumbling edge
of Arab's baked adobe, Bedouin tent, and raw unshaded sun
until one has almost to sift beneath the new facade
of frontier toughness and technology,
the khaki-clad and weaponed pioneer,
whose strides are swift and forward,
to find the dark-eyed boy, the deep-eyed one,
    suspicious and bewildered,
kaffiyeh headdress hiding cunning of a kind
    we cannot know,
robes to ankle-length disguising
the curved glint of a silver-sheathed blade;
the deep-eyed youth of a culture aged too quickly
    with no place left to go.

Beer Sheva bears the marks not just of man's,
but of the desert's sons.
Too far beneath the northern rich green fields
the Negev's dust stalks the streets and wields
the power ancient prophets sought to yield
from wilderness: the roll of distant drums
beaten by a drummer yet unknown.

And as escaping heat waves speed in from the distant Sinai hills
and spill their strife across the torn and sunken Negev floor,
they lap against the Jordan mountains which retain
and hold that quintessence on which the Negev feeds.
The Jordan mountains grant the desert life
and something more: a mold, a shape, by which to be
contained. Structured. Defined. Entrapped and real.

And to the South the desert narrows
like some insane inverted pyramid,
a shell that pours its vital marrows
splashing, spent, into the unplumbed slash
of depths that are the Red Sea's floor.

And where, at the tidal line, the Negev's plain is buried
and confined, the Red Sea carries on the chore
of being that which drums apart the Jordan height
from the Sinai hills, separating them
with timeless unrepentant unforgiving might.

If the Negev can have masters they are these
the elements that gave it birth, the energy
and interplay that give it continuity,
the deserts, mountains, that surround it,
    and the seas.

* * *

Ein Gedi, 1965

The wadi is flooded. The wadi is the watercourse which collects water during the rains in the desert and carries them off in great flash floods. The wadi which separates the kibbutz from the fields on one side and everything else on the other originates in Jerusalem: we're on a mesa. When it rains a lot in Jerusalem the waters pour off the hills there into our wadi, course through the Wilderness of Judea (we're actually right on the edge between the Wilderness and the Negev), and finally muddy brown and roaring, plunge down 1300 feet of rapids to the Dead Sea.

Yesterday about a 6 inch wide stream of clear water was trickling through the wadi. It rained all last night here and, presumably, in Jerusalem, and this morning the water was about 10 feet across and 3 or 4 feet deep. The wadi itself is about 25 feet across so it's not a total flood. When it's a total flood it is impossible for anything to pass by and all our food and supplies must be flown in by helicopter. This happens almost every year. The floods are late this year, however, so it might not happen.

The best thing about the wadis being flooded is that it is not possible to get to the fields to work, so we have today off. The worst thing is the wind and rain preceding it. We have sheets of plastic covering most of the crops to protect them from bad weather and cold, and Saturday the gales became so strong they tore some of the plastic strips off and everybody had to rush down to the fields and work like crazy for about 2 hours to put the plastics back and protect the crops. We have, just last week, transplanted 80,000 tomato seedlings into a field 15 acres big. I planted about l.5 miles of plants myself, every 16 inches apart. This plastic had torn loose and was a devil of a time getting back in place. Some people are calling me to go down the mountain (we're about 300 feet above Dead Sea level) and have a closer look at the wadi.

11:00 AM

The above was written at 9:00. By 10:00 it had begun raining hard, we were by the wadi, and it had reached its full expanse of 25 feet, It's narrower, deeper, and faster farther up the mountains. We walked up the pathways along the wadi for about an hour, crossing into Jordan by the way, and finally found shelter under an overhang. As we sat there resting (very rugged terrain, hard walking) just ahead came a huge crash which might have been a cannon until we saw huge boulders cascading into the wadi, hundreds of feet to fall by now. At this point we decided we'd had enough. Graham, an experienced rock climber, decided it was too dangerous. More boulders came crashing down opposite us on the other side of the wadi. We ran along as pebbles and small stones rolled down. There were occasional great crashes as something big fell somewhere. Eventually we got back to where the mountain sheers off instead of sloping. Here there's a broad expanse. On our right, when we had left there had been no water. Now it was already flooded several feet making the expanse an island. Even as we stood in the center we saw a trickle of water flowing down threatening to divide the island in half. So we ran to the shallowest point and forded the right side of the wadi. The great Italian boots I got last May kept me dry, everyone else had soaked feet.

We climbed back up the path to the kibbutz, As we looked back one half of the island had disappeared. A waterfall had broken through the path leading to the fields leaving a sheer 8 foot cliff—impossible to anything except our bulldozer, which will be busy when the waters subside.

In the distance we can see 300 foot waterfalls cascading down sheer cliffs of huge mountains bathed in clouds; and even as I write this in my room I can hear the roar of the wadi's waters far away.

The roads are quite impassable now, and I expect if the waters don't subside by tomorrow we'll have food flown in and the pregnant women will be flown out.

8:30 PM

The kibbutz, we found out at lunchtime, has been trying to reach Jerusalem all morning. The only connection is by radio-telephone and atmospheric conditions were so bad they couldn't get through. (Jerusalem, on a map, is actually very close to us. It's only the border that makes it such a long way round.) Finally the weather broke about noon and the sky cleared up a bit. About 1:45 the helicopter came. I know they didn't take anyone back with them, but couldn't see if they landed anything. It certainly wasn't mail if they did, and probably not food judging from dinner tonight. It went away shortly and no other helicopters came to-day.

Not only is the road impassable because of the water, but huge boulders and rockslides have obliterated sections of the road. It will take at least a day with full work teams to clear what's there now. And about 5:00 it began raining again and is still raining. The best weather report we can get indicates rain in Jerusalem, so there's very little chance of the flood receding tomorrow.

Wednesday.

Yesterday a big helicopter came—one that could hold 9 people—and unloaded vast supplies of bread, milk, eggs, cheese, etc. We were almost on the point of running out of everything but chocolate bars, so it was very welcome indeed. The helicopter took some people back with it.

Today it rained a little but the waters have receded to only a trickle, leaving tons of soil on the road. A truck went out this morning (or perhaps the Jeep) and made it to En Bakek and back with more supplies. The roads might be cleared by the end of the week. There's been no mail in or out for 3 days now—I don't know why the truck (or Jeep) couldn't have taken mail or brought it back, but it didn't. Perhaps En Bakek is also cut off, but I don't think so—it's half way to Beersheva, and the floods shouldn't be as bad there.

Tuesday.

The wadi is flooded again! This is the first time it has ever flooded twice in one year. Rains in Jerusalem melted the unusually heavy snowfall in the hills and made their way down here.

This morning we went out to work in tremendous winds and uncertain rain, preparing a new tomato field by laying out plastic strips over each furrow to protect the plants we'll put in from the winter weather. We wanted to finish today, so we worked through to the end, about 12:45. Just as we finished the truck came to the fields to take us back, tearing along like hell. They'd heard from Jerusalem that floods were imminent. We piled on and crossed the dry wadi. It's about a two minute ride from the wadi to the kibbutz. As soon as we got there we ran to the edge of the mesa and saw a wall of water tumbling down the wadi. If the truck had been three minutes later we would have either been trapped on the other side or washed into the Dead Sea!

This is the view of the cultivated area from the kibbutz on the mesa: across the north bank of the wadi is a large field of egg plants, onions, peppers, and new dates; in the wadi itself we have five smaller fields (two empty, one cucumber, and two tomato), which are separated by five walls—these fields are bounded by a sixth wall with windbreaks (at the east and west corners), by an unpaved road to the south, by the main paved road to the east, and Wall l to the west.

We watched the water rise quickly. The water piled up against Wall 1 finally pounding it down and pouring in. Wall 2 never had a chance and crumbled immediately. If Wall 3 went the road will have dropped low enough for the water to flow around Walls 4 & 5, wiping out 20,000 cucumbers and 80,000 tomato plants—the ones we put in just a few weeks ago with so much effort and work.

The roar of the water was tremendous. In the distance huge waterfalls fell hundreds of feet, feeding the wadi with more floodwater strength. Water poured through Wall 2, ripping it to pieces, rushing against Wall

3, which held, and held, and, finally, slowly, began to leak water under its foundations and, as we all watched in silence, it collapsed.

The protective plastics, which had shimmered in the sun, were swept away instantly, uselessly, and the fields were covered and drowned. The work that was lost!

The water flooded over the road and washed to the sea.

We went down to the road later and found a swift river flowing across it, which Sol and I decided to ford. The water was bitterly cold, and running very fast. It rose no higher than my knees, but the splash as it hit me rose to my thighs. We held on and moved across it, finally reaching Wall 6. There was, of course, no question of crossing the wadi. Huge boulders, 200-300 pounds, were leaping through the air like frogs, crashing against each other with great thudding clashes constantly, so swiftly did the water flow. It crept up over the bank on the other side and carved a path through the peppers and the young date palm plantation. It began to undercut the wall just beyond where we were standing. Whole trees bobbed to the surface, were pulled under, and reappeared five seconds later 100 yards farther on. We took photos, then turned back as the water cut deeper under the wall. Returning we had to go against the current. We had to walk on the road, where it was swiftest, because everywhere else it was too deep.

Finally we felt it was too dangerous to cross the main flow. It had picked up much force in just the last few minutes. We stood there, wet to our thighs in freezing water, unable to go further, when, after about 5 minutes, the tractor came down with Franco driving it. He cut through the water and pulled us in. On the way out the wheels of the tractor were slipping slightly. And this current was nothing, nothing whatsoever, compared with the speed of the water in the wadi!

So we got out safely. About 30 minutes later Wall 6 gave way, flooding the entire area where we were and finishing the few tomatoes that had survived the previous deluge.

Once again, of course, there was no traffic, no mail, only a mile wide circle of muddy water in the Dead Sea, very clearly defined, shaving the range of the flooded wadi's force, and, miles to the south, a second ring showing the impassibility of that other wadi. I've washed the mud off of me and am lying here in bed, still listening to the roar, penetrating even here, of the wadi far below.

Saturday.

Late Tuesday night we saw car headlights to the south. Somebody was trapped just south of the lower wadi, between it and the En Bakek wadi. He'd probably been there since the wadis flooded, about 1:00. They got him out about 12:30 at night, I don't know how, but we saw the Jeep he was in the next day. It was a total wreck.

By Wednesday the waters were low. Thursday they were gone and a huge mud flat surrounded the areas where the windbreaks were, which is just beginning to dry. We've been working long and hard hours since then to repair the damage and we're almost caught up now.

Early Friday morning Moshe's wife had twins and last night the kibbutz had a celebration for its first multiple birth. So life goes forth—and multiplies.

* * *

The third flood of the wadi was very minor. Friday night, about 5:30, it filled up to a level and speed slightly less than that of the first flood. By Saturday AM it was virtually gone, with only a slight brook, about 3 feet across, 3 inches deep, and clear and drinkable, left. This brook has persisted and flows even today. The rest of the wadi is dry, hard, slippery-no-longer mud, beginning to show cracks from the sun's usage, and rocks, stones, and pebbles are imbedded in it like cheap jewelry.

We've gone onto a fairly steady 6 AM to 5 PM shift now, 6 to 1 on Saturday. (Sunday, of course, is a weekday.)

The Peace Corps rejected me. I got a letter stating that I was medically unqualified, because of my sinus. They said that while my condition may not hinder me here, when I got overseas it might. I wrote back informing them that I already was overseas, as overseas as one can get, and that if working to reclaim the desert 70 hours a week didn't affect me it wasn't bloody likely that teaching English would. To no avail.

Sunday and Monday we had a huge dust storm here which blotted out the mountains even the near ones, made a specter, pale and evanescent, of the sun, and crept under the doors, through the screens, into our mouths, into pores of our skin. The entire world turned powdery white. Not yellow, as I'd always imagined dust storms—I suppose because the Negev isn't a sand desert—but white. High winds kept the dust circulating for two days. What a mess to clean up after!

I've been verging on a decision to stay here—to become a member of the kibbutz and remain permanently in Israel. I love the life here—the work is the only I've found substantial and meaningful. The socialistic way of life suits me—the faults in the system are few, and those that bother me, in fact, are usually because they are undesirable reversions to capitalism. (Down with revisionism!) I get along well with most of the people, and the Negev, of course, is wonderful. I haven't made a final decision yet and keep wavering between several alternatives. At the moment, though, I think I had better wait for three reasons. One: I think it would be impossible to escape the Israeli army until I'm beyond the age of draftability (30?). Second: I have only been on the one kibbutz and I should see others to have a basis for comparison. Third: I still want to see more of the world and I'm afraid that if I don't the desire will get stronger and stronger while I become more and more committed to the soil here. Perhaps I better get the wanderlust out of my system first. So, at the moment, my plans are to leave here next month for Eilat, where I'll work for a few months (work's easy to come by, I'm told, about 20 times better paying than the kibbutz, and probably 20 times less satisfying, but I can camp on the beach for free, and so save a lot), then head off either south to Africa or east to Asia... we shall see...

The most important of many things I've learned in my seven month stay here is why I left the U.S. and what I am looking for. When I left I knew that I had to, that there was a dissatisfaction so basic and profound that no amount of social reform could change it, no amount of withdrawal less than total would allow me to escape it. Even now, knowing what it is, I find it difficult to plainly state my case. It has to do, though, with a sense of values that has become not only distorted but artificial. It is distorted, for instance, to want a new car every year—and I mention this not as a major complaint, but only a minor but common symptom of a far more important illness from which I am attempting to recover—because the reasons are ones of pride of possession rather than pride of accomplishment, a desire to be ahead (and above) others rather than equal with them, a certain exertion of authority and power that I find wholly repugnant. But it is also artificial because the desire does not spring naturally from the complex of forces within a dynamic culture but is placed there through advertising, propaganda, and example to induce the consumption, acquisition, and waste necessary to prevent the society from collapsing upon itself.

I'm not expressing myself well. My own collections of many things were the personal symptoms of a wide-spread American disease that places emphasis upon Most; Fastest; Biggest; Newest; etc. and equates these quantitative things with the very different qualitative thing: Best. That's wrong to the point of immorality. But even this, I think is a symptom of a larger, more dangerous thing I've tried to escape from. Perhaps you can see what I'm driving at—at the basic sickness of mind, a perverted and distorted sense of values that makes it moral to kill your neighbor if he tries to break into your fallout shelter—or even allows that such a thing needs to be discussed; at a society that can murder to maintain a dictatorial, unpopular puppet regime in Saigon, or refuse the Dominicans the right to a freely elected and popular president, and then, after these murders, rapes, and tyrannies, frown and tut-tut and shake its head disparagingly because someone reads Joyce. Or Miller. Or Balzac. A society where a woman can die in screaming agony on the streets from an insane man's knife and not turn on a light or make a phone call—surely such a society can be no more sane and no more innocent than the crazed murderer.

And the cure is so basic, so deep-rooted, that it will never be affected. You know the things—relatively minor things—that happened to me personally right up to the moment of departure, when the government tried to stop me from leaving the country. These have affected me, as have all the impersonal, or distant, things, and I have been seeking a society free of this. I may have found it on the kibbutz—if not in Israel. And I may not have. I'm not certain yet. The reasons I'm leaving Ein Gedi are related to all of what I've written, in an obtuse way. There's not space left to go into it here, nor have I the energy, for I'm rather exhausted mentally right now, as another episode—the Desert Months?—of my life is ending, but be patient and in time I'll try to explain more about what has happened here—and in myself.

* * *

Eilat, late '65

My estate is beachfront. The Queen of Sheba hotel is halfway around the bend of the gulf, Aqaba, in Jordan and opposite me is the red mountain range which was at Ein Gedi and extends south behind Aqaba. Farther south I can see the tiny white cubes of native houses and the cliffs of Sandia Arabia, and, if I walked about 6 miles south on the Israeli side,

I'd reach the coral beach and, just beyond it the border with Gaza. The water is very blue, a mirror of the sky, not red, nor has it parted yet, though if it does, I shall cross over.

My mansion is my tent with reinforced walls of pieces of plywood, which I'm told is from artillery shell boxes, and seem to be plentiful among the flotsam of war and peace washed onto the beach.

Like us.

There's actually quite a little squatters colony here—most of the abodes are temporary, go up and down like the tides, but not all; a few fisherman's huts are more permanent. I've found that most of the community are people like myself—travelers, just stopping on the way, to do some work, get something behind them, or just be quiet, have time to think, watch the world go by.

I'm working as a handyman at a hospital—part time and sometimes more—and, as my expenses are minimal, am managing to save most of it for my ongoing trip—probably East—though when it will go on again I don't know. Right now I'm content to watch the stars, listen to the surf, swim in the moonlight, and even scratch the sand fleas.

As a hospital handyman shouldn't look too much like, er, a beachnik, I've made a convenient discovery: an abandoned kibbutz about ½ mile away, which still has running water, etc., and even the showers and toilet work!

I'm getting so I can half converse in Hebrew on the job, but reading and writing is something else! With no vowels, and some consonants that can be pronounced various ways (like different letters in English), I can read something and get some strange meanings or none at all. In short, if you don't already know the word you can't know how to pronounce it: Catch 22! I'm content to speak a little and be illiterate. (Registered Jewish—so I can't swim over to Jordan—only sink.)

* * *

The election here is over and so is the faction that favored leaving the beach colony alone—not out of kindness, but as a source of cheap labor. Rumors are rife they're going to bulldoze us under (though that would be a bit of a public spectacle, and maybe some immigrants don't have short memories of such actions) or burn us out (easy as felafel: just slip a few shekels to unemployed sephardim).

I doubt the climate with the bureaucracy can get much worse, in any case—they're about as mean-spirited a bunch as I've ever had the misfortune to encounter.

You could say my sympathies for the country (except for the kibbutz and the desert) are at a low ebb. Any day now I could open my mouth and out could slip the words 'Occupied Palestine', and *then* they'd know what to do with me (unless I know first).

* * *

Remember the Newsweek article about the 'hippie haven' in Eilat? Well, probably some pressure was put on the Eilat police and Sunday three friends, Ben, Pia, and Gina were going to the hospital to visit Dieter, who was there with a torn muscle, when the police picked them up and took them to the station where they held Ben 'for investigation' while releasing the two women. They wouldn't let anyone see Ben that day, so Monday I went with Pia and Gina to the station to find out if Ben had been charged with anything and if we could see him. The cops told us to wait and we did, I stood quietly by the desk while the women sat down. We waited for about an hour, when, for reasons unknown—since I hadn't done anything but stand quietly by the desk waiting for information—two of the cops began shouting at me in Hebrew, which I couldn't understand, when suddenly a third cop barged into the room and grabbed my arm, shouting in my face, 'Let's go:' I began to reach for my bag of groceries on the floor when he suddenly pulled my arm and pushed me up against the edge of a door. While I was still off balance he shoved me out onto a flight of steps, which I fell down. When I went to the hospital later X-rays showed that I had a broken rib and a dislocated arm.

I've contacted a lawyer, who is preparing a case and seems to think it's pretty airtight—I've got witnesses and a medical report—for assault and battery and a civil suit for damages. I can get about with some difficulty (the hospital gave me pain pills) but am, of course, unable to work, I've also written the embassy, though from previous experience with them, I gather I'm not the sort of 'American abroad' to elicit much sympathy.

In the meantime, Ben has disappeared. We know he's no longer in jail, but no one's been allowed to see him and no one will tell us where he is. He's almost certainly not in Eilat. Maybe with a little inducement he confessed that the colony preys on the purity of Israeli youth and masterminds the drug-smuggling in the Middle-East.

Yesterday three more friends were picked up and it's from what they shouted through the bars of the jail that we know Ben has disappeared. None of us even dare to walk down the street alone any longer, but I can hardly leave at this point with a cracked rib, wrenched arm, and funds depleted by medical expenses.

So that's the situation as of now—a matter of concern, but not a matter to become frantic about—my lawyer seems on top of it.

* * *

On Tuesday, my lawyer, Mr. Levi, told me I had to get the name of the cop who broke my rib and hurt my arm. I said I was afraid to go back to the station, but he (and others) told me not to be silly, so back I went. To make the story short—I'm so sick of it by now—the cops refused to tell me the name of my attacker, and did so so obnoxiously and insultingly that I finally said, 'Oh, go to hell', and walked out. They arrested me, beat me up, and threw me in jail. I needed a doctor very much, and, as I found out later, some people found out I was in jail and tried to get a doctor for me, but the police wouldn't let him see me.

That was Wednesday and I was charged with disturbing the peace and resisting arrest. (I may have 'disturbed' their 'peace'—as they disturbed mine—but I *didn't* resist arrest.) The next day I went to Beersheva—I was taken there in a paddy wagon, that is—and was remanded for 8 days and refused bail on the grounds that I might 'intimidate the witnesses'. The only witnesses against me, of course, were the police, and it was a kangaroo court. Saturday—surprise—the consul came to see me, got the police to guarantee to let me see a doctor, a lawyer, and have visitors; and—surprise—they didn't let me see a doctor or lawyer. I did get to see my girlfriend, Tove, for two minutes, however, because one cop disobeyed his boss's orders—so he told me—by letting me see her. Jail conditions I won't describe. Call it the Palestinian suite.

Finally on Tuesday I went to court for a preliminary hearing and was released on 2000 pounds bail, which friends brought up from Eilat out of their own very thin pockets. The charge has been changed to; 1) trespassing 2) insulting the police 3) disturbing the peace. Nothing at all is being done about the beating (the first). I still don't even know the cop's name. (The second beating I had coming: for getting the first beating.) But I'm free until tomorrow, Friday, when I go back to court for trial. I expect to be found guilty even though I'm not. The maximum sentence is 3 years 7 months and/or 13,500 pounds.

Yesterday I went into hysterics for a while because of this and other things that have been building up and I'm afraid to go into town—for fear of the police—if they get me again... maybe they'll finish their work. And I can't leave because of the bail and they have my passport.

I don't know what else to say—I'm sure I've forgotten something important, but I don't know what yet. If you don't hear from me for some time it will probably be because I'll be in jail and can't get any letters out.

* * *

The trial was yesterday. Today I'm a free man. It was very much a farce after all. The witnesses told so many conflicting stories that before they had all been called the judge adjourned the session and called me and the prosecutor into his chambers where he worked out a deal. If I didn't agree to it I would be found guilty on all counts with stiff penalties. So I had to agree to plead guilty to the disturbing the peace and insulting a cop charges and they dropped the trespass charge, which was by far the most serious (3 years, 10,000 pounds). (Trespass against *what*? Walking into a police station? Breathing their air?) I was sentenced to the days in jail I'd already served, 30 days suspended sentence, and a fine of 500 pounds, which, after all the other expenses, pretty much cleaned me out. But it's all over now, and all I want to do is get out of this country, and forget the whole thing. There's no chance, after all, to do anything about the beatings because they'll cover their own tracks and can make it so long and hard and costly for me that it's not worth it.

There's a boat to Istanbul on the 14th of March and I think I'll be on it. I shall be traveling alone for Tove would not stand by me, which was a good part of all the emotions that led me to the state of hysteria last Wednesday. I'm very hurt by it, because I had hoped it would be something lasting between us, and now I can't even bear to think about it. From Istanbul I don't know where I'll go; maybe back to Europe; maybe overland to India, It's something I can't know yet, because I'm still very lost, but I need some time to be alone, lick my wounds, and think things through.

So much for the Promised Land.

* * *

Istanbul-Tehran, '66

Thunder Over Troy

Carriage horses clop along the cobbled streets of Chanakoy.
The hotel window, varnished by the rain, is two-toned: lights
    and black.
Electric blur of lights are broken rhythms to the lightning, envoy
of a past beneath my feet. I never felt my past would lack

a future till today I walked among the discovered stones of Troy
and cold and wet I searched but could not find a coin to take away
with me, and then I saw I really hadn't even past. Alloy
must be forged with care and circumspection to avoid decay.

I'll sleep beneath the thunder, huddled small. The words I speak
    destroy
as much, I'd like to think, and vainly seek confirming evidence
in poems but, in this room, cold beneath my depths, I have neither joy
nor home nor Homer, for my tale is one based on impermanence.

* * *

(At the Iran-Afghanistan border crossing, I first met Bob—although, as he said, he didn't remember seeing me in Israel, he did remember being seen by me.[1] The Customs man peered at my passport *upsidedown*, then observing my awry—though not upside-down—appearance, asked me—perhaps, mixing up his English phrase-book phrases: 'Who is your

1. In a letter to his father from Afghanistan Bob mentions 'an American writer, a serious avant-garde type whose plot and style are a wild and rushing means of dealing with themes that strike me as unfortunately banal—questions of existence and reality'—mea culpa—Hūm

barber?' With the proper deference all petty officials demand, I replied, 'My barber is my tailor.' Not a crack appeared in his solemnity though he did right my passport, and, evidently, was no more convinced by the photo. Bob, however, next in line, cracked up, and then I couldn't hold it anymore, and, for some moments, our gales of amusement held up the traffic at the border. Perhaps to stop—or atleast get behind him—our laughter, he shooed us past.

At sunset the bus stopped in Kandahar. The muezzin's last cry of the day and a peculiar fine smog hung over the blue mosque; apparently, after the last prayer everybody in town lights up a pipe of hashish. We walked into a tea house with funny smiles. Seated down the table from me, Bob rolled an eye at me and nudged some head next to him, 'What's that guy on?' 'Pencils,' I chirped. 'You could die of lead poisoning,' he commented. 'I chew but don't swallow.' We broke up.

So we bummed to Kabul together. My first impressions of the man: an uncommon gentleness; a thoughtful suffering; a wry humor; a literary bent. Maybe what attracted me most I can't explain—karma? kismet? who knows? But I knew I sensed one thing about him that I found very appealing; a kind of muted astonishment tinged with aghast incredulity at not only being who he was, where he was, but being at all.

In Kabul we dropped our rucksacks at a Sikh Gurudwara or temple, which allowed the modest traveler to doss down in a big carpeted room for free. My first sight of Bob there was him snoozing on his unrolled sleeping bag in a corner. Beside him was a kind of mosquito coil for flies, I guess, because around it was a pile of dead flies. Between ourselves—me and another new traveling companion a Ukrainian-Canadian woman named Mirotchka (who would marry me a few years later and divorce me a few years later)—we called 'Mikhail' (as he called himself) 'Flies'. I remember being impressed about how 'out of this world' he appeared in sleep. Later I had other occasion to remark how soundly he slept; plumbing the depths of Morpheus' realm.[1] Perhaps his experience of sleep suggested his facility to meditate. I remember he sometimes could drop off rather unexpectedly. He once mused aloud about the possibility

1. His father's mother escaped from Czarist Russia: with a baby, she was smuggled out of the country in a group with a guide; marching at night, sleeping, hiding in the woods during the day, putting morphine in the babies' bottles so they wouldn't cry—Hūm.

of having a touch of narcolepsy—some chemical imbalance. At the time, some chemical imbalance was self-induced: a troubled time; his quest for relief getting a desperate edge—the perennial recipe for radical decision.

After leaving Israel until he took the monk's vows in Calcutta—for about a year—he experimented with drugs. 'Experiment' is the operand word here—I remember seeing him gently stoned, but no more, and I doubt he harbored any romanticism about being a junky; besides, it had already dawned on him that everybody was *already* a junky, a junky of their delusions, and he, with or without drugs, was trying to find a way to get, in the deepest sense, 'straight'.

Still I sensed the well of sadness he carried with him—from Israel and, no doubt, before—and its chemicals atleast were telling on him—so when he took the robe and renounced dope of all persuasions, my relief was only second to his—Hūm)

* * *

(The ruins of ancient Taxila in Pakistan planted in Bob's mind—and my own—the seed of *Worthy Bones'* Mesopotamian Buddhist kingdom of King Agba that was sacked by the White Hun-like Anu, the evacuees of which established their faith on the island of Samadhi in the mouth of the Red Sea where the novel unfolds—Hūm)

Taxila, '66

Taxila was a commercial center of antiquity dating as far back as 5th century B.C., which was finally sacked and ruined by the White Huns in 5th century A.D. There are several interesting sites to the ruins, including remains of Buddhist temples and monasteries. The architecture has a Greco-Indian style to it: robust, yet austere. One site south of the Suhap mound was called the Stupa of Kural. High on a hill it was built by King Asoka of India for his son, Kural. Kural's stepmother had forged a royal dispatch ordering that his eyes be put out. Though the ministers didn't want to carry out the order Kural, stationed in Taxila as his father's viceroy, insisted it be complied with. After being blinded he begged his way back home to India where his father recognized him, had the queen killed, and a Buddhist saint restored Kural's eyesight. Near here I found an old small tea cup, perhaps 4000 years old. North of the Sirkys city-site I also found a Buddha head showing heavy Greek influence, which was of importance here around 2nd century B.C., though Buddhism itself didn't become important here till about 200 years later. It's probably one of the earliest heads, because Scythian and Parthian influences soon dominated—but I've seen similar heads in the museum so I think my hunch is right. Anyway, these ruins are something—not that they themselves are so extraordinary—more like they remind me of something extraordinary...

* * *

Delhi, India—'66

When I first entered India everywhere I looked on the ground I saw these red splotches of spit and was wondering if everyone in the country was tubercular or had some other gruesome disease. Actually, they're just addicted to chewing betel nut, which turns their spit and teeth red. When they smile at you they don't look like vegetarians.

India's a tough country. It reminds me of Israel in a way. Both countries are so varied, ancient and modern, with so many different people, religions, climates, madnesses.

Every Indian seems to have a 'thing' and I've begun to find out some of these 'things'. The first was when, seeking a temple, I walked, rucksack on my back, down a street and was stopped by an Indian who demanded to know how much my pack weighed, 'I don't know,' I told him. 'Don't know? But how is that possible? Take it off and I'll tell you. I can tell you within a pound.' 'I don't care to take it off,' 'What's that? But don't you understand? Free! The weight! You must know how much your pack weighs!' 'Why?' 'Why? Here, take this.' He produced a large sack from beneath his robes and told me to estimate its weight. I declined. He told me it weighed 17 pounds. He changed its weight every day. He could tell to within one pound how much anything weighed, merely by lifting it. He would tell me, free, how much my pack weighed, I didn't care to take it off, though. I wanted to find the temple. 'But you must know how much it weighs,' he insisted. 'Why?' 'Because...because everyone has a burden, and they must know the weight of their burden.'

He was hooked on weights. That was his 'thing' and he felt that everyone must be fascinated with how much things weighed. His life was based on this idea and when he finally left, perplexed at my resistance to his philosophy, I watched him attack other people with his demands.

They usually let him tell how much their packages weighed, and he wandered erratically down the street, a human balance—accurate to within one pound.

I met another Indian whose thing was collecting either—I'm not sure which—photos of large animals or large photos of animals. Perhaps large photos of large animals. He had over 10,000. He couldn't believe that I didn't have any. He wanted to take me to his home and show them to me. All 10,000 of them. And he assured me that everyone in India—nearly everyone in the world—was interested in collecting either photos of large animals or large photos of animals.

Other people—many—have a thing about money. Get-Rich-Quick schemes. They all dream of amazing wealth without work or responsibility. One man wanted to go to every palm reader in Delhi, get their readings and advice, collate them, average them, analyze them, compare them, and, at last, have certain advice on how to become rich. After that the rest would be easy. He wanted to know if I was also interested in having my palm read.

There are a lot of palm readers in Delhi, but even more beggars. Some are dressed in only a cloth a few inches wide and a few feet long. Some never wear clothes. A few of the beggars are quite well-dressed, though. I suppose that even begging has its successes and failures. The most successful beggars in Israel, by the way, were the Jewish beggars. On one corner I saw a group of ten women begging, their copper bowls in front of them, seated in a line and gossiping so much they hardly had time to bless you or Allah when money dropped in their bowl. Any Westerner who contributes so much as a *paise* will be descended upon by a swarm of hundreds of beggars—mostly children—or the most lame and inane—all screaming 'Baksheesh!'—gift!—at the top of their voices and trailing after you for miles. Some of the most pathetic cripples are hired by entrepreneurs in the begging business; they get their cut for making all the marketing arrangements (such as securing the best spots) and see to it that their clients look pitiful but are kept alive in less torment.

The beggars aren't everywhere. You can walk two or three blocks empty of them, then find ten or so working one intersection. They're always in clusters like the shops. Clusters of shops all selling the same products. Walking down a street I might pass 8 bakeries, followed by 17 household goods stores, a dozen fruit sellers, 5 or 6 druggists, 20 shirt stores, 11 shoe stores, 8 tobacco shops, etc., each group of stores in a cluster. Feast or famine. Specialty items can usually be found in only one part of the city, and if you don't know where you're out of luck.

New Delhi is very beautiful—in Victorian architecture and English-planned parks. Old Delhi is dusty, crowded, and shaking. There are so many contrasts, so many madmen, so many strange things—it will be a long time before I can begin to understand it better. But somehow there is, in the Hindus, a collection of attitudes—hopelessness, greed, corruption, stupidity, intolerance, manias, etc.—which makes me think Pakistan may be a place of promise, a country succeeding, while India merely bumbles onward in a circle.

* * *

Srinagar, Kashmir—'66

The houseboat, which is called the Bluebird, is close to Dal Lake on one of the canals leading to the Jhelum River, by a golf-course. In the morning I sit on the deck eating my English breakfast and watch the pukka-sahibs driving, chipping, and putting. The boat rocks slowly, slightly, as shikaras (Kashmiri gondolas) pass by on the green water, and I look from the golf course to an island, steaming in the mist, or across the road to the tourist shops—Cheap John, who makes papier maché and not inexpensive toilets; Cheerful Charlie the woodcarver's store, Suffering Moses, purveyors of all tourist items; Worst's, the worsted cloth man—the names Indians and Pakistanis choose for their businesses always seem to be parody rather than serious. I suppose Cheerful Charlie thinks his store's name to be in the best English tradition and all through Pakistan and India there are Cheap John stores not one of which is a plumber's shop. Signs also amuse me. One in Karachi read 'Public Thoroughfare. Trespassers Will Be Prosecuted' and another on the road I will never understand though I've puzzled over it for some time. It read: 'Preserve trees. Prevent goats. They are your friends. Help Pakistan grow.'

* * *

It seems that I'll be in Kashmir a bit longer than I bargained for, since I've come down with jaundice. I've been to the hospital and had all the tests made. The disease seems to be serious but not at all dangerous, and since there is no medication that can cure it the only cure is rest—at least 3 weeks in bed. That, the doctor said, does not mean 3 weeks mostly in bed, but 3 weeks flat on your back, 24 hours a day.

I went on a camping trip—when? I've lost track of time—west of Srinagar. I walked about 6 miles to lovely small wooded valley, Swiss-alpine almost, enjoyed wandering around, but apparently the strain brought out the jaundice which had been enervating me for weeks with what I thought was a bad cold. I see now it was the incipient jaundice knocking me out—I'd stay in bed a few days, feel better, go out one day, feel bad, and bang!—two more days in bed. So the strain of the camping trip finally brought it out and I barely made it back to Srinagar—very weak, feverish as I've been ever since, until yesterday. I had a bowl of porridge this morning—I've eaten hardly a thing for days—and feel a bit stronger though any exertion exhausts me, so I guess I'll have to stay bedridden as the doctor ordered. Thinking about him makes me feel better though. He's English from the Christian hospital. His name is Donald Duck. Doctor Donald Duck. At last—someone with a more embarrassing name than Bob Smith.

Yesterday I saw a quite spectacular meteor—I wondered if I was just seeing things—but today it made the front page of the Indian newspapers nudging from the headlines the usual riots, government corruption, unbelievable barbarism, and natural cataclysms. They'll be back tomorrow.

* * *

I could stay here for a long long time. In my book only Istanbul ranks with it. The quality is very hard to get at that creates a great city. What are some things Katmandu and Istanbul have in common? Certainly the vast number of mosques, temples, pagodas, churches, shrines, stupas, and secular public buildings as fantastically designed. Just to walk past them is a trip. Also people leave you alone. They don't poke their nose in your conversations or simply stare at you all the time like in so many other countries where white skin announces you in no way I appreciate. If I can't expect anonymity here, atleast I'm allowed to proceed with my affairs freely—as in Istanbul. And—as in Istanbul—there are central areas where most everybody lives with everything available. Also wandering around you're always stumbling on some surprising and beautiful spot. Add to that—here—the incredible backdrop of the Himalayas. But, really, I can't say just what it is that's so good about Katmandu. It just has the right atmosphere for me.

Bloody cold at night, though, and it doesn't warm up until late morning. The water's so cold it's painful to wash and washing clothes is nearly hopeless—they don't get clean and take forever to dry—also the water's so polluted that even the backpack crowd at the Globe and Blue Tibetan won't drink it (even in Kabul, where U.N. doctors warned me that the water was unsafe, I drank it with no problem, so I take this hitcher's injunction to heart).

The U.S. Embassy is—surprise!—extremely unfriendly and nobody not prepared to be shipped off to Vietnam to be killed can use their toilet.

When I came into Nepal, a rickshaw driver—a sturdy, smiling Tibetan refugee—actually tried to help me without wanting money, which amazed me. Unheard of in India. Then I hitched up here without difficulty. Got my first view of the Everest range, 50 miles away and 26,000 to 29,000 feet high. Vast mountains, snow and cloud covered, rearing into the sky almost unearthly; certainly the most gigantic thing I've ever seen from that distance—and one of the most awesome.

Nepal's two English-language dailies both carried several long pro-Israel articles yesterday, obviously reflecting the King's position. The King, Mahendra looks like Peter Sellers with 5-o'clock shadow and large rimless glasses. Very un-king-like.

So, that's about all I can say—just that I like it here but don't know why, that I could get hung up here very very easily, but don't want to, atleast this time around.

* * *

One morning I set out in glimmering lifting mist for the Monkey Temple, The cold night gave way to a warm, sunny day as I walked across the sacred river which flows through the valley. Buffalo were cooling themselves in the water. Ancient wooden houses, with overhanging second floors, decorated and painted, lined the banks on one side, pagodas and temples were amidst the trees on the other shore. In the farthest distance, as always, the amazing mountains loomed above everything. Even clouds seldom rose to obscure them but huddled lower, sometimes as low as the valley itself. Hard lines and deep shadows hid parts of the peaks.

I passed a beautiful rooster and a man weaving; shuttles, feet, and hands working and moving in fast complex patterns. The rooster watched sternly, now and then pecking at himself. No sidewalks. Few cars. Little unnatural noise. Past a statue of the god Kali, where the Ghurkas hold their annual cow-chopping rites, beheading cows with one blow of their swords. Finally reached a huge hill forest. Steps went way way up, steep but perhaps 1000 feet long with a double railing down the center. Monkeys were everywhere, doing everything: Fighting, eating, staring, scratching; showing very human emotions. They enjoyed sliding down the railing and the ride did look like fun: a bannister a 1/5 mile long is certainly tempting. Monkeys helped defend this temple against invaders, and so earned perpetual rights.

I attended the afternoon services, where monks chanted texts in rhythmic accord; strong, deep voices in a vertiginous wave; and played drums, cymbals, conch shells, trumpets, and a fantastic clarinet-like instrument, and altogether the music and chanting produced a striking impression, the weird wailing overpowering everything until I became weak and slid to the floor only to find myself on the ceiling. It was the sort of sound that can be neither recorded nor replayed, only felt, intuitively, like a vivid dream.

A couple days later I got a trekking permit and set out for Namche Bazaar, near Everest and the Tibet border. Walked 2½ days out—it's a 10 day trek—and 2 days back. It got too much for me. The leeches, mosquitos, dysentery, cold all contributed, and finally 10 miles from the towering 24,000 feet range, 14,000 feet above me, I gave up and turned back. But the sight of those mountains made it all worth while, even fording the icy rivers, and they'll loom large in memory for a long long time.

Today is Saturday: the 'Shabbat' hereabouts. Nepali numbers look like Hebrew script. *Another* Lost Tribe? (I've lost count.) I'm recovering from my trek with apple-pie. Although some might consider this just the sort of anti-American calumny they'd expect from me, I must declare: the best apple-pie is made in Nepal. Yep, it's as Nepali as apple-pie.

* * *

(From Kabul Mikhail, Mirotchka, and I took a rickety bus over a hair-raising mountain road to the valley of Bamiyan; a half day's ride from the city. In a rose-colored cliff there is carved the largest Buddha image in the world. Bamiyan was once a great center of Buddhist culture and learning; then Genghis Khan came to study. Mikhail was particularly awe-struck. That night back in the Gurudwara, I was cutting my toenails, which, in Mikhail's eyes, were apparently flying around the room like a fragmentation bomb. 'You have the most ferocious toenails I've ever seen!' he ducked. Next morning he explained he'd dropped his first tab of LSD for the Bamiyan trip.

Our paths diverged from there—he to Taxila, Srinagar, Katmandu, among other places; Mirotchka and I ending up in Shantiniketan, Bengal (once Rabindranath Tagore's ashram; now the site of a fine arts college), where I got down to work on the first draft of *Worthy Bones*. We lodged with the Datta family, Mr. Datta was a retired civil servant who had worked with both Tagore and Gandhi. Mikhail came from Katmandu to visit us there, staying a few days, before going to Calcutta, where he was ordained as a novice Buddhist monk. At Shantiniketan he spent a good deal of his time playing chess with Mr. Datta. Mr. Datta had become very good at the game while serving a jail term with Gandhi. He was very surprised that Mikhail was his match. Maybe, it was his Russian blood, but Mikhail was a superb player, who probably could have been a master had he devoted himself to it. He once told me that the best computer will never beat even a good chessplayer, because the computer 'can't make use of mistakes, get inspiration from accidents'. As a man born with legs as stiff as they come in the West, I envied how he could sit in lotus position for hours at ease over the chessboard.

One day after he left we got a note from him inviting us to visit him in Calcutta—he had a few things he'd like to give us (at the time we were quite open to receiving anything that might be converted into, say, food)—with the note were two train tickets. We noted the address—the Bengal Buddhist Association, Buddhist Temple Street—but thought no more about it (We all stayed in all sorts of temples—free digs, for one thing).

When we got to the temple, we asked to see 'Bob Smith', and got a curious smile from the abbot, then we were ushered into a room full of monks sitting around on the floor. We just saw a small sea of bald heads and orange robes, not a Russian black beard in the lot, and turned to leave, when a picaninny voice at our elbow, piped, 'Is me, boss!' Before we jumped out of our sandals with surprise and delight, I coughed up, 'But is you is or is you ain't?'

That became the traditional one-liner I'd post to Sri Lanka or wherever over the years, when I didn't hear from Bob for several months. He never did answer it, when he answered. Until he, sadly, didn't answer it and didn't answer.—Hūm)

* * *

(In the fall of 1973 I received a postcard on the front of which was a Buddha image composed of the sharp shadow and white light reminiscent of a statue in full-moon light.—Hūm)

Boulder, Colorado

I'm back in Boulder, but not yet in Bouldest: where is it? As the French say, Bould est.

The aspen are turning: the hills are green and gold and gorgeous: sometimes I think autumn is even better than spring.

Tonight: the smell of snow in the air. Tomorrow: the last plums and apples on the trees will freeze and wither—winter pickings for the birds.

I ride my bike down trails to places where only the wind follows me and spend weekends in a tent.

I trust Ñāṇavīra's words have arrived and that he still has one or two left to say to you. I have one or two myself, which may be arriving there soon, or may not. Depends on how ambitious I get, depends on the whether.

V.

* * *

(During the three years that Bob was home, or not at home but a-roam like the Nepali rhino in America, we saw each other three times. The first time I went to see him in Boulder, Colorado. I don't remember much we said, just taking in each other bemusedly, a few 'rhino' hugs, and the usual banter between sit-down comics. He'd been occupying himself with camping in the Rockies, a girlfriend, a book about his monk years called *Getting Off*,[1] and a job mixing chemicals in a chemical factory which poisoned him—giving new meaning to being a working *stiff*. Our

1. Published by Path Press Publications, 2011.—Ed.

visit ended with a bout of jaundice that landed him in the hospital. As he nodded out of sedation he asked me to read to him from a draft of *Worthy Bones* I'd brought along. I stopped reading when he appeared to have dropped off. But, eyes closed, not a flicker of waking on his face, he said softly, but very clearly: 'Don't stop.'—Hūm)

* * *

(In the winter of 1974 I received a sheet of onion paper taped to which was a newspaper photo of Norman Rockwell with his arm around Colonel Sanders and two clippings that read, respectively: FARAWAY PLACES COME HOME and National Foundation for Sudden Infant Death, Inc.—Hūm)

Boulder, Colorado

The snow and I send Thanksgiving greetings and give thanks for what is. Life is so settled for the winter: my world, not being sanforized, has shrunk to the proportions of a job, bike riding, and, soon, some skiing. Dabbling into this that and tither.

A climb up the rabbit hole every once in a while and a peek into the real world, then a scuttle down to the underground warmth. Huddled together at the edge of a mountain, burning a candle and cursing the wind. Why not let the candle be and so forget the wind? I don't know. What would I do then? Curse the darkness, I suppose.

Go gentle into that good night.

V.

* * *

(The next year Bob rode his motorcycle through the Rockies to see me in Sooke, on Vancouver Island, in British Columbia. At the time I had a room in a ramshackle old rooming house. One day I opened my door and saw Bob in my bed with bemused smile. How was the trip, man? Learned something about bikes. Nothing about Zen. Yeah. No real problems—only going through a bridge. Wha?! Somewhere in Washington his front wheel went through a rotten plank of a wooden bridge and the bike flipped. But you're OK?! Some parts more than others. He poked his foot from beneath the covers: it was in a cast. Wha?!!

A busted ankle. My twinge of shocked sympathy burst into hilarious laughter till tears ran down my face.

Bob *could* tell a joke—like slowly, slowly setting a mousetrap —a mellow-toned, most excellent teller of tales—not even the glint in his eye telegraphed the punch-line. Me, I always just wanted to blurt it out, but Bob made getting there the best part.

Foot-cast humming in the wind, we rode into Victoria and that evening saw a movie: *Sleuth* with Lawrence Olivier and Michael Caine. Some buddy picture. His review: Who did it ain't who done it. Hmm? We all do it—and did it—only a Buddha done it.

When he left Sooke—with his dark, unruly hair and beard, shades, and leather jacket—some heavenly Hell's Angel with a plaster foot—he was heading for Mexico.—Hūm)

* * *

(Fragments from a Mexican Diary—Hūm)

November '75—El Llano

Dumped bike twice today. Popping out of gear. Clutch-plate or what? Once it just slowly came to a stop and tipped over. Don't know why I can't handle it. Overloaded, overtired, maybe.

Pass commemorative monument at 28th parallel (commemorating, apparently, the 28th parallel). Without a doubt the ugliest monument I have ever seen; all angular, ending nowhere, and making no sense at all, like a staircase without a house.

Crest a hill to feast eyes on Gulf of California: fantastic. Descending to sea level: birds of prey, some hovering motionless, barely moving their wingtips, others by the side of road lunching on some creatures that didn't look both ways before crossing the road. Wayside chapels, two feet high adobe with crosses and fading wreaths. All Hallow's Days the wreath's put out. Forest of stately tall green cactus; beyond them clean beaches, white frothy surf, pale green waters of a lagoon, the deep dark waters of the gulf, white-capped. Some miles out a large island, barren red-brown, sharp jagged mountains jutting out with grey-white cliffs; a little village barely visible nestled in a cove of the island; and in the far far distance vague shadowy shapes of mainland Mexico.

Camp near the sea in the shade of a date palm grove; only natural sounds, no human signs. Lovely, lonely beach: volcanic stones, colored shells, fish skeletons. Desert cacti meeting pure sea and sparkling lagoons.

Pass a monster on the road—it was going maybe 40 MPH, probably as fast as it could go: a half-ton truck with a big camper on it pulling a long trailer with a large boat on top of it and two trail bikes mounted to the front of the truck. Guy must have every toy going. Reminds me of someone who goes through a cafeteria line and takes one of everything there is, until his tray is so piled up he can hardly walk without spilling things. Monster passes me as I siesta. Later, on a steep downgrade, I see a truck missed a sharp turn and went over the side into the bay of La Paz. The toy truck?

Under the stars, power failure: I was watching the lights reflected on the ocean, when they all went out (except the stars of course)—when that happened it reminded me of the solitude and peace of Godawaya, in Ceylon.

Morning: bit to hell by something, maybe everything—notice lumpy spots in my arms smaller: competition? a case of self-arrest?

A glimpse of the future: had a flash, while working on *Getting Off* that its completion will *require* me to live up to its viewpoint by taking the robe again. There are several layers of irony in this fact, which makes it seem both extravagant and compelling.

* * *

Panajachel, Gautemala—December '75

I ran into a big legal hassle in Mexico over possession of a roach, and the upshot of it all is that I left the country and have now found a place in Guatemala. Since that place fits well I'm not too perturbed over the situation, though it would have been nice to have continued my swing through Mexico. There's just more uptightness in this part of the world than in Asia, and so it's necessary to be careful.

Anyway, I've got an adobe hut in the barrio of Panajachel, which is the main town on Lake Atitlan, so I'm close to water, but pretty high up—about a mile, like Colorado, and, like Colorado, in very hilly, even mountainous country. Unlike Colorado, however, there is no snow at all, and the highest peaks are volcanic. There are three volcanos around the lake, in fact, and it makes for a primeval scene.

My life here is organized along lines similar to my Mexican days (how few of them there were!): meditation, writing (I'm getting near the end of Chapter III of *Getting Off*, playing the recorder, going for walks (but no swimming: this lake would freeze your fipple!), just being quiet and peaceful. By the way, I'm finding the letters I wrote you (which you returned to me a while ago) a good source of ideas in reconstructing my attitudes and concerns in those days. Thanks, man. Give my love to Mirotchka, wherever she roams, and keep some for yourself: there's plenty for both of you.

* * *

Met a fella the other day, a poet of sorts, sez he's putting together a book. 'Oh?' sez I, 'Yeah, it's an anthology,' sez he, 'Oh?' sez I, a bit more 'nerested this time 'cause it sounds like there's some action in it that's still loose. 'Yeah,' sez he, 'it's gonna be both prose and poetry, shorter pieces mostly, and mostly directed towards Eastern themes.' 'Eastern?' sez I, 'cause when I say 'Eastern' I mean India and the like, but I've talked to people who, when *they* say 'Eastern' mean like New York, or Boston, or someplace like that. Maybe even Cleveland. 'Yeah,' sez he. 'You know, Hindu, Buddhist, that whole thing.' 'Oh,' sez I seizing opportunity by the balls, 'Are you looking for contributions?' And then I tell him about myself, and so he gives me his name and address, sez he's mucho 'nerested and will seriously consider whatever I send him. He's a published poet who's spent the past summer with the other published poets who seem to flock each summer to the Naropa thing in Boulder. He's doing the book with another dude, the name escapes me at the mo. So anyway, I tell him too that I got this friend up in B.C. who lives in a stump and does prose poetry of a very unique nature but with an Eastern angle and mebbe he'd like a look at what my friend is doing too? And he sez, 'Why, sure thing. Just tell him to send three or four things, don't let any individual piece get much over 1000 words. Tell him that if I have to edit anything I'll send him an edited copy for approval. Then he writes down his name and address. We talk some more, and then before leaving he sez, 'Oh yeah, tell your friend to include a note so I'll know who he is and all that,' And he splits. About five minutes later I'm telling all this to someone else, and he asks me, 'Does he pay?' and gol'durn it to tarnation, I knew all along that there was an important question I wanted to ask him, but I couldn't remember in time what it was. Don't that beat all?

V.

* * *

Rivers do more than gurgle, betimes. Sometimes, like people, they rage and destroy. The river here has never had much claim to banks—a rather impoverished affair, it's always seemed, in a bed a hundred times its size, like an ill-fitting suit on a hobo—and it's meandered down to the lake uncertain which way to go but choosing, for convenience, the path that led downhill. It was easily gone over with the help of a log for a footbridge. [...]

Rumors were rife. On the evening of the third day a friend made his way back to the village from Guatemala City and confirmed reports of vast destruction and high death tolls. It was also learned that the nearby village of Tecpan was completely destroyed and so those in Panajachel collected food, clothing, and medicine and made their way to the village.)

I've just returned from Tecpan. I went up there with no idea of what destruction looks like. Tecpan simply doesn't exist anymore.

There are streets of thick choking dust surrounding blocks of rubble and tin roofs sheltering ruins. And there a door stands, holding onto bits of wall, still standing, opening up onto fields of rubble.

People seem totally dazed, we wear kerchiefs on our faces against the dust. An emergency hospital has been set up in the school yard because little rubble is there. I've come up here in a van with some other people, including a doctor—a young German woman.

We try to help at the hospital; people are screaming. The smell of decay is in the air. We treat a woman whose head has been cracked open, exposing her brains. A girl's hand is crushed and broken open, the wound filled with dirt, stones, and pus.

People wear the meanest of rags—all that's left to them.

(Bob and his friends learned that in fields outside Tecpan a tent hospital had been set up and so they proceeded there.)

On the way, we see a man who has put his injured wife in a chair and is carrying her on his back. We stop and give the woman something for pain and then take her to the hospital.

(The 'hospital' was two tents with hundreds of people milling among armed soldiers 'doing nothing'.)

I helped pitch a third tent... brought water from a nearby well, dirty, and brackish. We began trying to treat people. I help the German doctor for a while, then find a Guatemalan who doesn't seem to know significantly more about medicine than I do. Except for the German, the doctors don't seem to know what to do. Casts are put on wrong. People who have huge bruises and probably internal injuries are given a painkiller and sent away without proper examinations.

(All the help he saw was from civilian volunteers with no government aid except in the form of the military which was there strictly to keep order—or, as he also saw, occasionally to pilfer. He wondered about the plight of the other towns, Patsun and Chimulterengo, which at that time had not been heard from.—Hūm)

If Tecpan is typical, this government is doing nothing for the countryside except sending its most inexperienced doctors reserving all benefits for Guatemala City itself.

This is due to the split in the culture between the European-born Latino minority which controls the country and the native Indians, by far the majority, who have no power at all. The Latinos have a long history of ignoring the needs of the Indians, and this is an example of it.

There are signs posted everywhere that we foreigners are using up precious food supplies and therefore should leave... that enough help is available.

But these are base government lies. Until I see convincing evidence to the contrary I have doubts as to whether the Indian population is receiving any significant help at all from any source other than the volunteers. I plan to stay until I'm forced out... We just had another jolt...

* * *

Panajachel—February '76

To let you know I'm alright, i.e. unharmed physically, I'm working in the refugee camps and stricken villages. Towns consist of streets six inches deep with dust, surrounding neat squares of rubble, two or three feet high, covered by a sprinkling of rooftops, some at crazy angles. Here and there a door frame stands, connected to wall fragments, jammed shut, the only way one cannot enter upon these huge adobe-shattered courtyards. Refugee camps consist of endless twisting lines of people waiting, waiting for food, medical attention, used clothing, shelter against the cold winds, against the continuing tremors, against the fear of their own mortality. Villages consist of uncomprehending Indians standing about in piles of rubble too stunned to do anything more than that, or too hungry, or too hurt...

I've not disposed of your novels: they're stored in L.A. at my sister's place. Hope I don't have the world's only copy and that if you need to refer to yourself you'll be capable of doing so through other carbon papers, or perhaps even through none at all.

I finished Chapter IV of *Getting Off* the day before the quake and shall begin Chapter V after things settle down and return to complacent normalcy. These days there are more important things to do than to talk for hundreds of pages of my attempts—*my* attempts, mine, mine, MINE!—to become egoless, and crack a few jokes of doubtful humor.

Anyway, I have no intention of leaving Guatemala voluntarily (although there are rumors that they're going to clear the country of tourists because of food shortages, health dangers, the P.M.'s astrology chart, or whatever other reasons they wish to find), so my address remains unchanged (although I can't say the same for myself: the quake has left me changed, for how long, and whether for better or worse, remains to be seen).

V.

* * *

The earth continues trembling, following Kierkegaard's advice: 'The most that anybody can do for another in that sphere wherein each has to do solely with himself is to inspire him with concern and unrest.'

The earth fills me with a certain unrest as aftershocks remind me that the outer shell of the world is thin as a hen's egg, and has been incubating a long long time.

A dark-eyed gringa yoga teacher fills me with a certain concern as she gently reminds me, 'See this? This is. See that? That is.' Amazing what one doesn't see, no?

And sandwiched in there somewhere is a slice of time when I manage to scribble messages to the outside world: I AM TRAPPED INSIDE A GUATEMAIAN FORTUNE COOKIE. DON'T HELP.

Monsoon approacheth. Very mild: sunny bright mornings, clouds at mid-afternoon building up, thundering but not yet strong enough for daily showers—give that another week or so—then clearing up after dark into starlit nights. May be the mildest tropical monsoon I've been through, yet it washes all the tourists right out, and Panajachel is entering its quiet part of the year.

Yes, if you want your books back you can get them from my sister, but I am bound to say that I would feel a personal reluctance to return them: they have, even unread, some value to me, and unless you truly need them I would ask you to let them stay where they are.

My own book, having creaked past the half-way point, is coming slowly to rest, perhaps for a bit, while I take a rest from such labors, plan an Easter trip to the Caribbean side, renewing inner wells of creativeness, now somewhat dry. Work out of the way, maybe they'll fill up.

V.

* * *

(Few months later I got a postcard of a semi-abstract water-color evoking a Gautemala-like landscape across which floated the words THERE IS ALWAYS IN YOUR CENTER A WARM LOVE CENTER—OPEN—ENTER with translation in a familiar hand *Local Dirty Postcard*.-Hūm)

Movement afoot! Shall return to California before crossing the Pacific to Thailand. Some possibility I may get farther north first. Shall let you know as developments develop, possibilities possibilize, opportunities opportune, unless spared them myself. There's no doubt about it—either I will or I won't. There's no doubt about it—I wander what is.

How 'bout you? I'm less a writer these days than a musician, less a musician than a bum. I'm not even a bum.

Watch out or you might not be too.

V.

* * *

(When Bob hitched into Sooke for the last time, I just bumped into him walking down the street. Over a cup of coffee in a cafe he studied me thoughtfully, 'You don't look a lot older than when we first met.' 'When you saw me or were seen by me?' He smiled, a little tired, maybe—'You find a short cut from Kabul to Sooke?' 'I just went straight ahead,' 'I just went straight around.'

This trip, my 'stump' had sprouted in the hills and to it we repaired. He pitched his pup tent in the hillside clearing and we had a pot of rice and bean and talked. He told me about Guatemala; beautiful country and people—the Indians; rotten politics, and the 'dark-eyed gringa yoga teacher', who 'helped me see—then see that she was going one way and I was going another.' So how was the uncelibate life lately? He smiled, 'Too late,' I found that the old adage 'what you don't use you lose' seemed to be working out pretty good for me. He said it seemed to work differently for him: 'Even using it I can't lose it.'

Not that it had anything to do with the subject, but he was somewhat intrigued presently about the notion of 'black holes'. We came to the conclusion that although the Buddha's Teaching pointed out our main problem and what to do about it—this was probably just the light edge of an ontological black hole.

I mentioned my work on the sequel to *Worthy Bones*—Mohel in America—more or less the same story: only instead of a plot to pinch the Buddha bones it was the Declaration of Interdependence. 'So what is it?' he lifted an eyebrow at me and his recorder to his lips. 'An accusation,' I said.

With a ghost of a smile, he nodded, then blew—quite beautifully—a Bach bourrée.

Through my stump window I watched him in the autumn twilight sitting cross-legged by his tent watching the gulls wheel over the salmon-spawning river in the gorge below—he seemed a natural part of the scene, with not a breath of pretension. (As I look out my stump window—12 years later—I still see the rocks—in the same place, just bearded with moss and lichen—that he placed there as tent pegs.)

After a few months back in LA, where he finished *Getting Off*, with little satisfaction, and even less satisfaction trying to find an agent, get it read, etc., etc., with a sigh of relief that even brushed by me in the Sooke hills, he flew the American coop once more—and for the last time. In Asia again, he slipped into his Mexican premonition, his monk's robe again; it seemed to fit better this time around; anyhow, it fit for good.—Hūm)

* * *

Legian Kelod, Bali—'78

For coastal island-type living Bali is as good as I've found. It's a very easy life, though, and it's rewards, the real, are not earned—unlike in the Himalayas, where I felt (wrong-headedly, no doubt) that every wonder had been earned and was therefore (somehow) worthier, or perhaps it was I who was worthier, I don't know.

Your offer to give me *Worthy Bones* is incredibly generous. Before I accept, however, I'd like to see what I can do with it. *That* I gratefully accept. I quite agree that you should retain final approval—after all, it's your story—or rather, it seems, stories. How many versions have there been now? Perhaps you could send me both an 'ancient first edition' and the last re-write so I can see how your jungle has been growing. I don't expect to run any roads through it—more a matter of trimming back some of the overgrown undergrowth, leaving the trees free to reach sunwards. I want *Bones* to be something publishable, and something to be read. It's a great story, which impressed me when I read it. I would like to see it stand primarily as a story, revealing its meaning in its movement, rather than as a series of images succeeding each other, each beautifully portrayed but each basically static. I say this now so that should you not agree with this concept you can tell me so now instead of later. In any case, wait till I'm settled into my rabbit-hole in Thailand before sending Zem Bones for me to nibble on.

What is the difference between 'ceasing of activity' and 'ceasing of the activity of greed, hatred, and delusion'? True, the Buddha was active. The Buddha was an *arahat.* Not only are *only* arahats capable of non-karmic action (if by non-karmic you mean 'activity not involved with greed, hatred, and delusion') but that's the *only* sort of activity the *arahat is* capable of, or involved in. (This leaves out of account the *sekha,*[1] whose position is in-between. In fact, anyone who succeeds in acting non-karmically is by that fact an *arahat.* The rest of us just keep scratching our itches. Activity without scratching is non-karmic. (The *sekha* doesn't always scratch, but he still itches.)

---

1. *Sekha*: (Pāli) 'one in training', noble being: he stands half way between the *puthujjana*, who has no realization of the Dhamma and the *arahat* (or *asekha* 'one finished the training') who has full realization of the Dhamma.

Balinese Buddhas, by the way, are rather unsettling, having breasts and very shapely bodies. Scratch, scratch.

V.

* * *

Legian, Bali—'78

Since you ask 'how far outside Bali' I am, I'd suggest you look at a map: Bali is an island, and if I were outside it I would be doing even more swimming than I do.

I have a room in a *losman*, or small family holding where rooms are rented, in the little village of Legian. It's a five minute walk from the Indian Ocean where the surf, I have learned, is up, but though I've already tried to ride it I have not yet been up, and see that there's a lot to learn about it. It will probably be my morning occupation for a while.

Legian has no P.O., the nearest one being the beach village of Kuta, a mile away. I rent what they call in these parts a 'pushbike' for a few cents a day and that gets me around the neighborhood. Denpasar, the capital of Bali, is about 5 miles off, and none too close for me: it's a cauldron of noise, traffic, oil fumes, and other pestilential emanations of the modern world.

Morning on the verandah and I'm writing this as I sit in a comfortable bamboo chair, bare feet propped on an ottoman, the remains of a fruit salad and a thermos of tea on the table. No power here. But the sunrise provided plenty of electricity. I watch the family life around me. The patriarch is the uncle—in his 80's—spry, with a sly, almost toothless smile. There are several other old relatives, a few children, and a charming young woman who with grace combines the roles of waitress, maid, and servant. In front of me is a well-kept arbor with purple hyacinth flowers. The girl is shaking the dead leaves out. Beyond her is a vegetable garden with papaya trees, then a coconut grove. A cow pasture. Many exotic plants and flowers.

Last night was full moon and I went to a fire dance—a quite spectacular affair with costumes, music, and fire—at a local temple. There are nearly as many temples as coconut trees in the village. I've been to another dance—the Legong, which ends with men in trances holding swords against themselves and pressing the points in, but somehow remaining uncut. The swords are very sharp, as I learned by examining them. Afterward, to come out of the trance, they drink the blood of a freshly decapitated chicken. The dance—like all traditional Balinese dances—required a great deal of technical proficiency and was done to the music of a gamelan orchestra—an otherworldly cacophony of sounds. The gamelans are a sort of xylophone, which are accompanied by gongs, drums and flutes. I was reminded of the music at the Monkey Temple in Katmandu; though this seemed music of 'the spirits' rather than 'the spirit'.

I biked up to Singaraja, on the north side of the island, and stayed a few days on the beach. Singaraja has calm waters, no surf, and there are patches of coral with colorful tropical fish, though not so brilliant as the coral reefs off of Eilat or Belize, nor so clear as the water of the Caribbean. Both oil and shipping have contributed their filth. Still I enjoyed myself in snorkel and mask floating motionless over the reefs—also I tied a rope behind a native trimirand, and, with snorkel, had it pull me around—past a small shark, which caused me no trouble, as well as a beautiful iridescent blue starfish. Walking on the black lava sand beach is a quite different feeling than on a white sand beach; perhaps it's the memory of volcanos between one's toes.

Back in Legian, the rains—of the rainy season—seemed to have started early; the water is much cooler, so no more moon-lit surfing, but in the evenings I make music with friends at a local restaurant—me on recorder, somebody else on guitar, sometimes a mouthharp or drums.

At first I wondered if I was hearing rightly, and it struck me as rather comical, but now I understand that all Balinese have one of 4 names, denoting their order of birth: #1 child is named Wyan, #2 is Madé, #3 Nyomin, #4 is Ketut, #5 starts again with Wyan—there is no difference in names according to sex. I'm not sure if this makes learning names four times easier or four times harder.

Bali is such a fine place not because it has beautiful beaches and a tropical climate—those are common enough—but because it has, on top of this, a gentle and enduring culture which values most highly the creative arts—not only music, dance, and painting, but also architecture (especially temple architecture), sculpting, carving, etc., as well as an appreciation for the natural beauty that is rare in Asia. But Bali is only one small island in Indonesia, and though its culture is Hindu (derived long ago from India, but long since gone its own way) the rest of the country is Moslem with its usual strictures and oppressions.

Sadly, my usual visa hassles will soon expel me from the island. But that's always the way with paradise isn't it?

* * *

Jogjakarta—Singapore—'78

I was several weeks in Jogjakarta, in central Java, taking a batik course from a fine old man, who looks like a fisherman in a Chinese painting, and is a master of the art famed throughout Indonesia. I don't know where he stashes his gold though, because he lives like a fisherman too, and is a man of few words even if I could catch them. I've made three batiks and have the basic knowledge now to carry on on my own—given the right situation—that is, becoming like my teacher—I might.

Jogja is not a bad town, small enough to be tolerable for a while, with some history to it—several ancient temples, and of course the ruins of Borobudur about 25 miles away—one of the Buddhist wonders of antiquity—a 1200 year old monument of carved rocks and statuary covering a small hill. The plan of the site was a fantastic attempt to depict in sculpture the whole hierarchy of existence. On the lower levels are depicted the animal, the demonic, the vulgar human occupations; as one ascends the hill the sculpture becomes finer, more intricate, depicting the higher callings of service, healing, the arts and sciences; then the realms of the muses, graces, and fates, so to speak; until one reaches the plain and unadorned summit and within a bell-shaped stone niche sits a serene Buddha almost abstract in its austere lines. Unfortunately, the monument's being extensively renovated, and much of it was closed off when I was there.

Transportation around Jogja is by bicycle rickshaw. Streets are potholed; some cobbled. Buildings are old, tile-roofed; the paths in some places are too narrow for traffic. Beggars (the first I'd seen in Indonesia—I saw none in Bali) wait outside the tourist-catering restaurants on Malioboro, the main street, named for the Duke of Marlborough (or the Marlborough Man? this brand of American cigarettes is a coveted black market item)—only a few, not like Calcutta, and more ragged than thin, or even that serious about begging. Handicraft shops abound—batik, silks, leather, buffalo-skin lampshades, elaborate fans, smoking pipes, puppets of the stylized traditional ilk, ivory and wood carving, and so on. The Central Market is a huge place with vendors selling everything there is to sell in Indonesia, and in the fantastic food section fantastically huge rats mosey about, unmolested and unafraid.

One better not show a whisker in Singapore: I'd expected to find unhappy people living under a strict authoritarian regime, and instead found a reasonably content and relatively prosperous people living under a strict authoritarian regime. It's a city-state that's crowded for space, and there's construction everywhere to further the plan (already well under way) to turn the city into a high-rise jungle. The streets are clean (it's $250 fine to litter), the water is safe to drink, the traffic hazardous, prices 3-4 times Indonesia's, goods are plentiful, food abundant, there are high-rise shopping centers with supermarkets selling U.S. brands at slightly more than U.S. prices, and people poor enough that they sleep on the sidewalks, wrapped in a bit of cotton, but there are no beggars, for begging like littering and spitting and jaywalking and longhair is forbidden by a strict authoritarian regime. The city is 80% Chinese, but it still has an area that is known as Chinatown no different than any other part of the city I've seen. That says something. I'm not sure what.

* * *

Penang, Malaysia—'78

Penang, and its town of Georgetown, is Somerset Maugham country. He used to write short stories at the E & O Hotel. I stayed in less prestigious surrounding in Batu Feranghi, a fishing village about 10 miles outside of Georgetown, and wrote no short stories. A Holiday Inn is a-building on the beach. I didn't build anything but didn't tear down anything either.

Loosest border I've ever crossed (atleast for this train; maybe it was carrying some midnight ramblers?). They didn't look at anybody's bags, and gave us our passports back in bunches to sort out for ourselves. The southern isthmus of Thailand has some very huge rocks, 50 and even 100 feet high, rising out of flat ground, rice fields; trees cling to the top of the rocks and the sides are barren granite. Caves in some of them. They looked like they just dropped out of the clouds. Might linger here a while when I come back this way—as I will, since I have to renew my visa in a few months in Malaysia. The wretched cold I had in Singapore promptly disappeared (to my surprise) when, in Penang, I had a spicy curry meal. From my alms-collecting days in Ceylon, where chilies were a definite occupational hazard, I've viewed with rueful humor the

Indian—and Ceylonese—claim that chilies are necessary for health in the tropics. Perhaps no pain's in vain.

* * *

Kaeng Pan Dao, Thailand—'78

Though the days are warm, just short of being hot, it must drop to the low 40's at night, and a cold fog rolls in, which doesn't burn off until about 9 in the morning, and sets the trees dripping and is sharp enough to cut through cloth. Consequently, I need a few blankets at night. December, I'm told, is the coldest month here. In Ceylon, as I recall, January was the coldest. It's surprising how cold the tropics can be in winter. And this will be my third winter this year, for it was wintertime in LA, and when I arrived in Bali (south of the equator) it was winter there also. Though it wasn't cold in Bali—far from it—it got dark early and light late. Now it gets light shortly after 6 AM and dark by 6 PM. The thing I enjoy about Northern summers is the long summer days. I've had more than my share of short days this year.

Still, the north of Thailand seems to be the right place in the cold season (which ends in 2 months), for in the south it's still raining (they have two rainy seasons, as was the case in Ceylon at Dodanduwa), and in the east it is also cold, but without the hill tribes and the color and beauty of the hill country of the Golden Triangle. (There's gold in them thar hills: opium.)

The country hereabouts is mostly heavy jungle with clearings in the valleys. Some tea is grown, and some coffee, as well as more infamous crops. Houses are made of bamboo and are on stilts, raised about 2 feet off the ground. Beneath the house I stay in there are dozens of little indentations, the work of hermit spiders set to trap ants. One never sees the spider—at most a leg flicks out and throws some more dirt out to steepen and deepen the inverted conical walls of their traps, and make it harder for ants to escape, etc. I remember these spiders also from Bin Gedi. (I doubt if they remember me.)

While not expecting to meet any more ghosts of Bin Gedi, I did. In a tea house I met a guy I'd met briefly at the kibbutz in '65, He was, at the time, on his way back to the States after 2 years in the Peace Corps in Thailand. Now he's made his home here (10 years ago). He didn't remember me, and I didn't remember him, until Bin Gedi just happened to pop into our conversation. He's a lawyer now with less idealistic interests.

In a few days I'm going up to Chiang Rai and Chiang Saen, right on the Mekong, where Thailand, Laos, and Burma meet—the heart of the Triangle—to see what there is to see, then move south again (there being no other direction to go from there), perhaps reaching Bangkok again in a few weeks from now.

* * *

After breakfast, last Thursday, I walked out to the road, and before I could set down my rucksack I picked up a ride north to Thaton, the end of the road, north of Pang. At Thaton the river Kok flows east past Chiang Rai, and into the Mekong. I took a river boat to Chiang Rai, through some swift rapids, past jungle with small tribal villages here and there—3 to 10 houses make up a village—for a 3.5 hour trip.

Chiang Rai, the 3rd largest city in Thailand, is not much more than an overgrown village pumped up with a few government facilities and offices. The main streets are not clogged with cars and motorbikes. A quiet and comfortable provincial place by all appearances. In the morning I took a bus east to Chiang Saen, a 40 mile 2 hour ride to the end of that road.

Chiang Saen is an ancient capital, but today it's just a town at the end of the road at the Mekong River with a few ruins. From there a dirt road parallels the Mekong and I went along it another 7 dusty miles to a village where the Mae Sai River joins the Mekong. Across the Mekong is Laos and across the Mae Sai is Burma—both of them jungly hilly country. In Laos I could see a village. At night drums summoned the villagers to their nightly indoctrination meeting.

A party of trekkers arrived, with guide, at the same time as I did, to a collection of bamboo shacks that calls itself the Golden Village—the only place to put up. The trekkers had been out 4 days going cross country to various remote villages. The usual intrepid band of odd travelers one encounters around unlikely bends of the world. That afternoon I joined them in a trek to a Laotian refugee village about 4 miles off, where we met the villagers and had a look around. The people of Chiang Rai, I'd thought, were the most attractive I'd seen in Thailand, but the Laotians were simply beautiful, fine, simple people. We were invited to stop for water at one of the houses, all very spontaneous, and with the guide translating there was a chance to ask them about conditions in Laos, what they've found in Thailand, etc. How they escaped, who they left behind—it reminded me in many ways of the Tibetan refugees of Nepal, another very beautiful people.

I'm full of disorganized impressions, information, and tales of what is actually going on around here, and it's all quite astounding just how basic and difficult and dangerous a life they lead. (There's quite a bit of guerrilla activity in this area, not to mention out-and-out banditry by heavily armed bandits—it's not rare for trekking parties to get held up, and once in a while people are killed or disappear.)

We lingered until we had to hurry back to return before dark, for in this neck of the jungle don't go about after dark—there are not only guerrillas and bandits but also government patrols, Thai, Laotian, and Burmese, and one doesn't want to meet any of them. So after a bath in the Mekong—at this point ¼ mile wide, muddy, and shallow—we sat around a fire in the evening and swapped tales.

The next day I returned directly to Chiang Mai and then went out to U Mong, an artist colony/temple, where to sit myself for a bit. Galleries of paintings on Buddhist themes, some fine forest walks, and a gibbon who is very friendly and whose best friend is a puppy dog.

* * *

In Thailand, I've noticed, dust pans have long handles on them (unlike in the States) so that one doesn't have to bend down when sweeping up the dust. The brooms, however, all seem to have short handles on them (unlike in the States) so that one does, after all, have to bend down when sweeping up the dust (just like in the States).

The Immigration Department no doubt sees the wisdom of it all, for they have said that they will consider my application for an extended visa and to report back to them in 30 days. In the meantime they committed me to a firm address (even a P.O. box wouldn't do, which, in any case, costs and doesn't leave much leg room). That'll be the hermitage in Kaeng Pan Dow, a place that pleases me, and since I expect someone will be checking up on me (though they haven't yet, not that I know of), it's probably a good place to be.

* * *

A few days ago I was only out for a couple hours and came back to find I'd been robbed. They wiped me out of any items they could fence (cassette recorder, camera, and electronic calculator-alarm clock) and that I intended to sell, when I was finished playing with them. Now, it seems, I've, indeed, finished playing with them. Fortunately, I had my money and passport on me. I reported it to the police, of course, who made some show they were doing something (although it was I who was doing something: filling out useless reports) but really had no intention of actually catching a thief, finding and returning my stuff, or anything of that nature. I thought maybe because I lived at the Wat (temple) they might atleast put on a good show.

Since then the thieves haven't stolen anything more from me (though given their taste for substantial item, I don't know what I have left). One resident sage suggested one should always give the thieves more than they expect, so they'll be satisfied and won't return. Sage advice, indeed, if you haven't been robbed, or have something left to give (allow to take?). Just what do thieves *expect*, anyway? Whatever it my be, I doubt it promotes satisfaction, or they wouldn't be thieves (i.e. not return). Obviously, I didn't understand the sage advice.

Perhaps, the thieves wouldn't either, as they've been around the Wat atleast 4 times since my robbery. Once they tried to break into the kitchen through the front door (they cut a hole in the screen) and once through the back window (paint chips from the locked shutter could be seen the following morning), but failed both times. Simony doesn't appear to be a motive, further evidence they don't appear to be religious thieves. (I use the plural because there seems to be more than one of them; perhaps a small gang.)

I went back to the police to ask both what had been done towards following up the leads they had on my case, and what was going to be done towards ending these continuing burglary attempts, and, as I wouldn't fill out any more useless reports, they seemed slightly offended and definitely disinterested, so the next day I went to the US Consulate in Chiang Mai. The Consul told me right out that she'd been in Thailand 3 years and could offer no help. (Such a response from a U.S. Consul was atleast refreshingly honest.) The Thai government was generally corrupt, she said, but the police were the most corrupt of all. If I wanted them to protect me (and the others at the Wat) against the continuing harassment of the burglars I could get them to do it for about 100 baht (ṭ5) a night, but otherwise they'd prefer to sleep on their desks. But she did send one of her Thai employes with me to the Provincial Cop HQ and we spoke with the chief, who said he'd speak with the Chiang Dao chief, etc., etc.

My last night in Kaeng Pan Dao I heard a lot of stones, or sticks, or something striking the roof of my hut, and I'm sure they were thrown from the path above, but didn't go out to investigate. The next day one of the monks (not the sage one) said he'd seen two men on the path at night, who ran at the sight of him. Were they cronies of the crooks trying to lure me outside to seek revenge? Village kids playing a prank? Whatever, I've decided it's over and done with, and to forget it.

The political situation here hasn't affected me as yet. The Vietnamese, who don't seem able to stop fighting, still haven't a complete hold on Cambodia. (Though after Pol Pot and the Khmer Rouge one wonders what there's *left* to hold.) There are various insurgents (Communist and Whatnot, especially the latter) in Thailand, but Vietnam is so far, it seems, not in a position to aid any of them. The Thai government is so corrupt that many people will welcome a change. (This is the real reason why Vietnam, Laos, and Cambodia fell—corruption, not ideology.) But I don't see this as becoming a problem here for the immediate future, and by then it's possible other factors will come to dominate considerations—China, famines, who knows.

So it goes.

* * *

(Between Wat Suan Moke and the Sooke hills Bob and I winged our dispatches about *Worthy Bones*, after he started to see if he could get the head bone atleast *not* connected to the butt-bone—though perhaps it ended up that way on purpose, and consequently most of the correspondence would be incomprehensible to anybody who hadn't read half a dozen drafts over 15 years of an unpublished novel—among whom was, perhaps, *neither* of the co-authors. Nonetheless some of the shop talk is amusing, even if incomprehensible, so I've included snippets of it for my own perverse pleasure.—Hūm)

Thailand feels like the end of a long trek from Indonesia: no more borders to cross for a while. There's a very deja vu feeling to the whole trip, since it touches in so many ways upon that trip in '66. Yossarian was also involved in going around twice. Bangkok, however, offers a totally different contrast than Calcutta: *there* the overriding factor was the contrast between the wealthy few—the old elite and the nouveau riche—with their highrises and edifices—and the utter poverty and squalidness of millions of lives, and the inescapable awareness of the wretchedness that could be, that was… *here* the contrast is between the quietness of the forest places and the feeling of the city temples (noisy, but always a relief from the wretched traffic noises and fumes of these clogged streets) and on the other hand the utter accessibility of means of gratifying any of the sensual pleasures. Abstinence and indulgence. Abstinence—a withered and sere old crone. Indulgence—a seductive young wench if ever there was one. Why do I keep entertaining this notion for the ugly one? There must be something perverse in my nature.

Meanwhile, I guess I'll wander over the P.O. and see if there are any *Bones* there for me. If there be and they don't slap me with death duties or bust me for grave robbing, I intend to spirit 'em someplace I can set for a spell to gnaw on 'em. I've just noticed my handwriting. If it keeps getting smaller as I near the end of the page it will eventually become illegible, but that won't matter for I would never get to the bottom of the page, where this letter will end.

THEREFORE:

Consider the extraordinary implications of this statement, made by one of the world's foremost authorities on schizophrenia:

> 'The ability to pretend, or to lie, is a good prognostic sign. Delusional life is reality for a patient, not pretension. When he is questioned about his delusions, he cannot deny them or lie about their existence, even when he knows that admitting them will have an unfavorable result, such as the rejection of his demand for discharge from the hospital. He cannot lie or pretend because he cannot shift to an imaginary assumption. (Schizophrenics treated even with moderate amounts of tranquilizers often reacquire the ability to lie.) The denial of delusions, which are so real to him, reacquire a power to abstract or to shift to a set of facts that from his point of view are unreal. At times, when he knows that admitting his truth would mean being kept in the hospital, he will try to be as evasive and defensive as possible, but he will not actually lie. When the patient is able to lie about his

delusions, he is in the process of recovery. He will not have to lie for a long time, because the delusions will soon disappear...'

V.

* * *

The postal system, inscrewtably, has coughed up (with much clearing of the throat) your *Bones*, and I sit in my *kuṭi* sucking on the marrow, even after midday. It's a big book and with all the fat on it, it goes well with the lean diet of my morning meal. The book—like much of Joyce—is unreadable without the help of a dictionary, a Britannica, several Who's Who, a What's What, a set of almanacks, and primers for Greek, Sanskrit, Hebrew, Arabic, etc.

I remember when my agent (who may be, like yours, dead, for all I hear from him) told me that *Getting Off* was badly overwritten and had to be cut, my reaction was—How could I *possibly* cut *any* of those sweat-drenched words, all so... so... so *expressive* of the very being of my soul... And I took the knife (Occam's razor) and carefully sliced a word—and it hurt, and I bled, but when the wound healed (I heal fast) I saw that maybe there was, well, just a *slight* superfluity—maybe this sentence here wasn't *truly* essential. Another lop.... And after a few days I was going at it tooth and nail, slash and burn, rip, rend, and reduce, cutting away all those joyful words that, beautifully organized as they were, had nothing to do, actually, with the story I was trying to tell....

I've still got many of them, in an envelope in my sister's garage. (My mother saved my baby hair, baby shoes, etc.—the habit comes to me honestly.) About 25%-30%, in my case; I lost a lot of words, a lot of pages, and in the end *Getting Off* was a lot lighter and a lot healthier for it. It doesn't need to include every witticism, every verbal cleverness, every show of dexterity of which I'm capable. It can't. It need only be a spare, sparse and straight story. (No doubt there's still some veins of marbling through it, but that's another matter.)

What I remember about *Bones*—from the 1st time I read it, back in Ceylon—was not all the verbal play (which is mostly unintelligible to me, lacking the erudition which you acquired—how?—in the Canadian woods) and association-through-sound (which is soon wearying), but the *story* of the search for dem bones, and a large (but definitely unstated) body of implications which grows (in my mind, not on paper) from that story, and, which, 10 years later, is still remembered, and that's what I intend to rediscover from your mss. (which, thick as it is, also makes a nice desk on which to write this letter) and that's what you'll get back from me… *Alaṃ.*

The Schizo Expert, by the way, is Silvano Arieti; the book is 'Interpreting Schizophrenia', You might find it worthwhile. Elsewhere he writes: '…There was nothing for her to look forward to. It was the end of her time; if by time we mean dimension in which we wish and will.

As for myself, Thailand is long and narrow, not straight and so I seem to imitate a yoyo (like Yoyosarian) or a vertical ping-pong ball bouncing about between the *wats* of the North and South, caroming cross-legged from *kuṭi* to *kuṭi*, and shedding a certain amount of superfluous weight with the exercise.

V.

* * *

To my paper bed of dormant intentions, I add your generous letter. In NY the bums use the Sunday NY Times for keeping warm. In Thailand, I've got words to heat my brain, if not my body, that neither they nor I (but you) have ever heard of.

Last month I was robbed, while chanting the evening chanting. The thieves took the costly goodies, the cheap goodies, the useless stuff, the indispensable stuff. But, among the few things they left behind was your manuscript, *Bones*. Talk about devastating literary criticism!

This month I paid a visit to Ajahn Chah, the meditation master of NE Thailand. Most impressive dude. No time, no place, for scribbledehobble (as you call it), save on the sly or on the run. Day starts 3 AM—much group work, not my bag, but, they say, put aside your ego, your wishes. Do it this way and see, so I do but don't see. If you feel like doing it, he says (about meditation), do it. If you don't feel like doing it, he says, still do it. Put aside this ego—'I want *my* Dhamma *this* way—I like *my* Dhamma hard-boiled / soft-boiled / sunny-side-up / all of the above / none of the above / etc. etc.' First *see* Dhamma, he says. *Then* decide how you like it. What a way to spend a February! From 9 PM to 3 AM I can do as I like, except on the full, new, and 2 half-moons, when we stay up all night, chanting and meditating (and drinking a lot of tea). The Western followers of Ajahn Chah include some of the most impressive of the Western monks I've met in the East. Too bad. If it weren't so I could dismiss his way as so much self-abnegation as to be unworthwhile. But he is not so easily dismissed, this Ajahn Chah... What will I do *next* month? (Hmm, dormant intentions?)

Don't see any universal truths I wouldn't see.

V.

* * *

I'm still in the Northeast at Wat Boong Wai. The Northeast is very different from Bangkok and the North—the people are of Laotian descent and are much like the Laotians I met in the refugee village in the North—the finest people I've met in Thailand, though I believe they're scorned in the city as ignorant village peasants. Not to say there isn't banditry etc. around here (though I've not been bothered), but the people seen naturally friendly and helpful, not reserved. They have ways different from Bangkok and foods also. For instance, their staple is a heavy sticky brown rice that I quite like—the light white rice will seem insubstantial after this. We get one meal a day here, but the food is good, and vegetarian for those (like me) who wish it—fresh green leaves of many strange sorts (including the touch-me-not plant that closes its leaves when touched—I never knew they were edible before, but now I know why they close their leaves), some of which take some getting used to, are steamed and eaten spinach-like. One villager brings a pot of soy milk every morning, and we each have a glassful. Eggplant made into a kind of spicy paste is common. Fried crickets are considered a special delicacy (I'll try one when they come up with a vegetable variety). Also a sort of olive that, pickled, is quite tasty—sharp, a bit musty. Only after I ate some did I learn that they're pickled in urine. And then, there are other delicacies that not only will I not even consider trying, I wouldn't even consider describing to you. Fortunately, I can depend on plenty of less exotic fare for my meals-bamboo shoots, yams, boiled pickles, fried cucumbers, boiled peanuts, raw ears of baby corn, about 2-3 inches long and eaten cob and all—all quite satisfying.

Bits and pieces of fact and rumor about the trouble in Vietnam filter through the jungle, but it doesn't affect us here though we're closer to Saigon than to Bangkok—not only in terms of miles, but in terms of culture too, perhaps.

* * *

Wat Pah Baan Taad[1]

A rough one hour flight in a sputtering 2-engine prop over heavy cloud cover up north to Udorn Thani—spent more time on the ground going through formalities than in the air—glad to land, 'cause I was getting tired of paddling.

Now it's noon. I'm sitting underneath the hut (in Thailand houses are almost always built on stilts: this one rests about 5 feet off the ground on 9 substantial concrete pillars) in a chair whose legs each sit in a cup of old engine oil, to keep the ants off. It's about 105°F, down here, and a lot hotter upstairs. A breeze is like sitting next to a giant 1000 watt hair dryer. About 1:30 we'll gather for a cold drink (assuming the ice that's been ordered has been delivered as ice, not cold water) to manage the peak of the heat. Mornings are crisp, evenings pleasantly cool, nights edging toward chilly. Lizards don't mind the heat—they scuttle about in the sunshine, then pop down holes or chase each other about, seemingly not in play. They have green markings with an orange band on each side. Strange swift movements, then long pauses. Pineapple plants and mango trees (with fruit still too green) surround this hut—others have bananas, coconut, papaya. Oddly, there are few birds, perhaps it's the off-season. But the continual squawking of a couple of tame parakeets fills in. The sand here, too, is bored with hermit spider traps. The spiders live hidden below their traps, waiting for an unwary ant to slip in. There are plenty of ants, though I've yet to see one get caught. The other day I left out a square of chocolate laxative. Within a few hours the ants had eaten a large portion of it. For the next two days there was ant shit *everywhere*.

This place is more intensively directed towards meditation than any wat I've seen yet. There's no routine other than morning meal and late afternoon leaf-sweeping and water hauling. No chanting or other group activities. But the sun is fierce, and so too is the teacher here. I'll sit a while longer here then likely go to the South, although I've just received an invitation to go to a place near Chiang Rai beside a waterfall on a cool hillside, and this offer is presently rather tempting.

* * *

1. A forest monastery of Ajahn Mahā Boowa.—Ed.

(While caroming cross-legged between *wats*, Bob was not only gnawing on *Bones*, but had picked up his verse translation of the Dhammapada again, which he eventually completed and called *The Track of Truth*.—Hūm)

102. However many verses one might say,
set, to no set purpose, side by side,
far better is one line about the Way
which, having heard, one's pacified.

171. Come, behold this world; 'tis as
the well-wrought carriage of a king.
Where fools are lost the wise man has
no desire for anything.

172. He who was heedless before,
but is heedless no more,
illumines this world,
once dark and in shrouds,
like the moon freed from clouds.

212. Sorrow is born from what's dear.
From attraction springs fear.
When from that liking one's fled,
there's no more sorrow. Whence dread?

174. This world is blind; there's few with sight.
As birds, escaped from nets, take flight,
those few go to realms of light.

179. His victory no one can alter or change.
No part of his conquest partakes of this plane.
That wakened one is beyond measure or range.
How trace a trackless one?
Where's that domain?

* * *

(Sometimes news of the world took its time to get to the Sooke hills, so I was always glad when Bob included a few newspaper clippings with his missives. The two enclosed with this one informed me that an eight-year old elephant named Jumbo, who had perhaps the world's biggest sinus problem, died of a heart attack during tusk surgery; and that to mark the occasion of Karen Ann Quinlan's 25th birthday a mass was celebrated at her bedside where she'd lain in a coma for some years. 'We have so much to be thankful for,' her mother, Julia Quinlan, said. She never thought Karen would celebrate her 25th birthday.—Hūm)

Wat Suan Moke—'79

Yes! I've always (!) thought that if Ajahn Chah ever went to India he would promptly be re-named Achan Acha.[1] Even his name goes around twice! He too goes around twice: having been once to the West, he goes again, at the end of the month. And, possibly in late June, he *may* be in or around Vancouver. If you can drag your hill over there (will the ferry take it? would it float? are there city ordinances about hills walking the streets?), it might be worthwhile to meet him. (He also brings his hill.)

I'm at Ven. Buddhadasa's place in the South. He has no plans to go anywhere. Neither do I. It's flat, nearly sea-level, and muggy, but it has a distinction only shared by Kandy, in Ceylon and Almora, in India, both in hill country, among all the Asian jungle I've been in: *no mosquitos*, I haven't figured out why. (Maybe the mosquitos are still figuring me out.) Gnawing on *Bones*, I also haven't figured out how the hip bone's connected to the thigh bone, or any other, for that matter. Where's dat ol' heart bone? Amazing how bones can be fleshed out.

On this long narrow isthmus if I go long either east or west I'll soon be in the sea. Up or down—the yoyo bit again (again!)—is the only way, I can only be lost in half as many ways. Lost? Isthmus be de place. Merry isthmus!

V.

(Dr. Johnson met Descartes: I stink, therefore, I am.)

* * *

1. *ah cha*: (Hindi) Yep! OK! Right-on! etc.

I've finished *Bones* now. I must be in very select company, having read it twice—once in Ceylon. It's the only book of yours I've been able to read through. The density of your prose requires an effort that few will care to make, even if assured in advance of the value of the effort. For myself, I could only make such an effort when in very suitable surroundings, such as the monastery I'm now at -- Buddhadasa's (you may have heard of him).

When I read an earlier draft of *Bones* in Ceylon I recall a much stronger plot line than I seem to find in this version. Indeed, on reading this version quite carefully, and spending some time considering it, there are still some points of importance that are not at all clear to me. Now, no doubt I could sit dawn and invent what needs to be invented to fill in these gaps (and no doubt in some cases I will), but still this book has been with you for many years now, and I'm sure you've got it figured out in your mind, even if not on paper, to the point where all action and motivation (apart from language) are clear. (I remember in Afghanistan you told me the whole plot, quite coherently, in about 5 minutes. Something like that would be useful to me in writing.) Therefore, I pose to you the following questions and ask that you reply in as mundane a vocabulary as possible, being as specific as possible. Your collaboration in removing these uncertainties (or, atleast, raising them to a higher level than the mundane level of plot and motivation) can best be affected by replying in this manner...

Why does Mohel have to go through all this holy man shit, or even talk with Premier Takataka, as part of his effort to get the Buddha's bones? His doing so is *great*, but it must be believable; i.e. we must feel he is acting sensibly, with suitable motivation to reach the goal set for him, in the most efficient way. If we can be made to believe that the holy-man-cum-politics is the only way the bones can be had, we'll *love* it; but first we're not made to believe this and second, Ven. Tanha's *offer*, with no *apparent* motive, completely undermines all these efforts, making them seem pointless posing or lunatic activities which, somehow—how?—manage not to destroy the purpose, but waste our time in trying to get to the point of the book, which, whatever it is, has to do, surely, with obtaining the bones...

I could also use more about the political involvement of the various characters. Like a chronological account of the Samadhi political events, as if it were a magazine account, say—identifying the various factions, their main interests, strengths, and weaknesses, etc., and what they do-with/to each other.

If the story hangs together in a coherent context, it's beautiful. If it doesn't, it's just a lot of beautiful words floating past in the gutter.

Consider these questions and comments no put-down of your work on *Bones*, but a real interest on my part to find a way to retell what I remember to be a good story (good stories are always worth a retelling). You've got much of your story in your head, and the book is for yourself. I'd like to share the story around and need to have some answers to do so—your answers if I can get them; otherwise I'll have to find my own.

Love to you, brother,

V.

* * *

Your encyclopedia arrives and arrives and arrives. Helps in many ways, of course. For instance, to my question of why Mohel didn't fly to Samadhi, your reply that he *likes* 'boat lag' explains everything, and no further explanation is necessary. On the other hand, the explanation that you once saw a bomb-scare at a U.S. consulate explains nothing, for the question here, as elsewhere, is not the question of 'is it possible?', nor is it the question, 'is it in accordance with the philosophy of the book'? ditto for your 'holy-man-bullshit' explanation. It may very well be the *point* of the story, but is it the *story*? If the story isn't a coherent story, its point isn't a coherent point. How does the holy-man-bullshit routine help Mohel *get* the bones? Regardless of the point of the story. (I can invent reasons, of course, or else change the story; but I'd like to have your reasons, either on the level of 'he did it because it accomplished—he hoped—this and that…' *or* the 'he *likes* boat lag' level. But to say that it's philosophically correct is merely philosophically correct. What you say about the 'nursery-school notion' of cause-and-effect is perfectly true, and also beside the story. Perhaps to the point, but beside the story, which at least creates—or tries to create—the illusion of reason, connection, one action following another not merely sequentially but with some logic, moving with reason and economy towards a definite stated and promised goal. More gristle, please! More, more, more…

Your 'overloaded oakie in his old Model T' simile was excellent—I had visions of you breaking down yourself when seeing all the paraphernalia I've unloaded from the story to lighten the load on the axles so it'll go somewhere—that's what happened to me when I unloaded *Getting Off*, and it was me doing the unloading, not some stranger sleeping with my book—and am now glad that you'll be glad to sec it lighter.

what fun it is to rummage through the pile, seeing what can be used here, what there, as I lighten the load and head that ol' Tin Lizzie into the westering sun...

V.

* * *

Part of the Xerox machine—the human part—seems to be non-functioning these days. Since that means nothing is getting sent to either friend or publisher, I'm trying a remote repair, like with space satellites (except that it's the satellite that's sending out repair-instructions to ground control); but it may be all the thought and typing I've put into marketing may be for naught. A pretty depressing thought after a year's work. So I won't think about it for both of us.

I'm about 100 pages ahead of you having a hard time working out a plausible sequence for the Big Scene—i.e. when Khalid and the army and everybody confront each other just before the cremation. It's complicated. Motivations—both the characters' and mine—seem a bit forced. Fortunately, I can soon start killing then off wholesale (if they don't get me first) and thereby simplify all future action. Your min-autobiography of Mohel—M by M ($M^2$)—received, which marvellous piece seems to have just tripped off your fingers in one sitting. I don't even see you chewing the end of a pencil . How do you do it?

(Thanks, too, for *Freedom at Midnight*—loved it, especially the raja with the toy trains that ran amok. I think anyone who has read this would be saddened at the killing of Lord Mountbatten. Shed a tear for your Sufi saint, too. Khalid just killed Bab Khatmo.)

V.

* * *

BEAD[1]

Your miscellaneous variety (or various miscellanies) received with thanks. Bits of transparent obscuration through which I get glimpses of...what? Style? Fact? Poetry? Truth? Why did you quit the local rag? Feeling too secure? Forced to take a raise or go? Or just tired of inky thumbs? Anyway, glad your Passovers are regular. Saves the need to swallow Pax Lax. There is no coprolite at the end of the tunnel. You'll see. Or you won't.

Khomeini would hate Bab Khatmo.

Bab Khatmo would love Khomeini.

Bani Sadr would try to work with both.

A few of your good solid clues as to what it's all about have been useful, but nothing more gossamer, please, as there are plenty of cobwebs here already. Aside from the odd good line (which I will steal), what's it all about? I'm beginning to wonder the same about *Bones* Redux. Pity...

The troglodytes are in bloom again. Pterodactyls sing their rhymic songs. Secretary birds take dictation. Sumerians cum in.

V.

* * *

Forty years old today. Stocktaking. Thinking of what I'm glad for, what not. One of my most glad things is your friendship.

That said, everything else seems trivial: reports on the condition of the jungle today.

By now you should have the first 200 pages or so of *Worthy Bones*. Probably, the most intensive stretch of writing I've done: a pace I'm already unable to maintain. But while it happened it was exhilarating to see it coalesce -- perhaps as it was, in the beginning? I feel pretty good about it so far, but of course don't know whether that's anything more than throwing myself a bone for the trick. Does it in fact seem to be 'taking shape' instead of just being a pile of shapeless old clothes thrown into a forgotten corner? Have I dropped any stitches? Probably be a peculiar hump-backed critter who'll wind up fleshing out the stitchery,

1. In *Worthy Bones*, Sir Makepeace Gravenhenge, the English collector, who hires Mohel to pinch the Buddha's bones, dated his letters BEAD—Before Enlightenment After Death. My letters to Bob were dated likewise: good luck to any chronicler of them.—Hūm

but can he walk, does he have bad breath, dirty toenails and warts, or is he just a slab of meat cooling itself in the butcher's display case, on its way to becoming shit? Maybe I should go back to poetry.

V.

* * *

I think you're right: our virtues and vices complement each other, at least in the realm of what you call scribbledehobble (I haven't yet decided what I call it, but it won't be nice). Well, I've done my half, and since you said you were starting at the other end and working forward, you will presumably be meeting me very soon in some dark volcanic tunnel somewhere. So I'd better stop and let you get on with it. But that, of course, is making a virtue of writer's block, which may not be necessary but what else can a poor lad do when he comes to feel that it's all vanity, all a useless exercise in manipulating, and all so obvious? And so poorly spelled? Even with characters killed off, *Worthy Bones* is overstaffed. In fact that's the problem, or part of it. Too many characters spending too much time explaining to each other a plot that's too involved and doesn't spend enough time happening, what with all the talking about it that goes on. You and me are the only ones who like the book, and I'm not so sure about me. The few others who've seen it try to find something nice to say about it. It's a good title. That Bourree Jizi plays is groovy, too. Good use of the semi-colon. Keep it up and it'll be just the right length. Not that praise would eliminate the blockage. Maybe a plunger is needed, or a roto-rooter. (Actually, though, it's not a blockage at all; it's emptiness. There's just nothing left to squeeze out except words, and there's already so many of them... Think I'll take up painting. Particularly since I ain't got no paints. Just brushes.)

Oh, I'm going on with it, atleast for a bit, but it feels flat now and dry. The dryness can be solved by soaking the mss. thoroughly in a bucket of water; but what about the flatness? Yeast? Maybe, I'll save it for Chanukah. It would go great with bitter herbs. And how can I concentrate with all those people meditating out there?

What I *really* need's a stringhopper.

V.

(What's it all about, huh?
What's it *all* about?
*What's* it all about?
What's *it* all about?
What's it all?
What's it?
What?
*huh*?)

* * *

The electricity is out tonight, for reasons I've been unable to discern, so this is a candlelight letter, flickering somewhat, but not yet guttering out.

This is a really big *wat*. (A big *wat*? sorry, the flickering). I haven't yet explored in any direction (except the front) to the point of finding its end. I'm told that in the back it includes a small mountain from the top of which one can see Chaiya (4 miles away) and the sea (? miles away). The *wat*'s also a famous place and every day cars and buses of tourists (Thais) arrive to look about—they usually stay in the front areas, and don't bother the residents, who live in the back (maybe 50 people; 35 monks and assorted creatures). In front are many sculptures (copies mostly of famous ancient Indian artwork), and a museum (original paintings on Buddhist themes, a sound/light show, and other 'Buddhism-in-art' type endeavors), for the place is the center of the 'Buddhism-can-be-creative', or 'ethics-through-aesthetics' school of thought, founded by the chief monk here, Buddhadasa. Perhaps a good atmosphere for my own creative efforts. Certainly not a bad one, though some of what passes for creativity is a bit ludicrous. But, then, imitation rather than originality was always the focal point of much of Asian culture. Innovation for the sake of seeing-what-will-happen is not often smiled upon and, indeed, this place had some hard times in its earlier days as a result of that sort of thinking—thinking which it is hardly free from.

Still, I'm left alone to my own devices, except one day a week when we all participate in group work (putting up a 2-story brick building these days, since now brick is cheaper than wood—in fact, the building, intended as a dorm for overnight guests—Bangkok students by the busload, etc.—has no windows; is this innovative, or just forgetful?), and also though I've not been invited to share in the food here (unlike all the other *wats* I've stayed at) there's a restaurant just outside where the owner cooks not just the same tired old fried rice with an onion and a tomato, but a nice variety of vegetarian dishes (for me only, apparently—everybody else expects meat, chicken, or fish, and gets it), and Buddhadasa speaks English, which helps a lot, as do quite a number of the other monks, also unlike most other places I've stayed at.

So my inclination is to stay here, though, of course, it also has its defects, mainly along the lines of the people pouring through here. But I want to park myself for a while so that I can arrange my situation to be the most productive—re *Worthy Bones*.

Unfortunately, there's the visa hassle, and I can only stay if I can get a letter of sponsorship. I've not asked for it yet, preferring to make myself known first, but I'm told it's not likely I'd get one, since Buddhadasa as a general policy doesn't do that (I'm not the first Westerner to pass through here); but I'll probably ask anyway. If he says no, I'll have to consider my next move—it may take a bit of juggling.

Thais, like Chinese, have, in their language, a sound between our 'L' and 'R', which makes it difficult for them to distinguish the two sounds (just as we have trouble distinguishing between the various tones of Thai and Chinese languages). I wasn't aware until lately that this problem extends to writing as well. But how else is one to understand a shirt with a picture of a pair of cute and cuddly little cats, underneath of which is the legend ANGOLA KITTENS. Or is this some new breed?

* * *

Contemplating a clearing around the hut which was slowly growing back to the jungle, I glanced at my thumb and noticed it was turning *green* (Ein Gedi disease?); in jig time I had it cut back, transplanted a few jungle flowers and plants, and put in some flower and vegetable seeds. The seeds are from Bangkok—so far, of the flowers, only the azaleas have even sprouted, nothing at all heard from the zinnia, phlox, pansy, or sunflower. There's not much available in the way of flower seed, and what is available seems, mostly, dead. Of the vegetables, the plum tomatos are promising, and there's hope for the carrot. The cauliflower sprouted up quickly, but is now threatening to die, as most of the onions have. The eggplant may be a slow starter—it's just beginning to show—as are a few of the regular tomatos. The corn is coming up like nobody's business, just the way the watermelon and honeydew began, but the melons seem to be going, now, the way of the onions. The squash seeds are trying hard; in 3 or 4 months I may get a few squash. And that's the whole garden. Some seeds remain for a second try, and I'll probably see if I can't find some beans and things when next I go to Bangkok, which will be in a few weeks to apply for a new visa.

In season now are mangoes, which I love, messy as they are to eat. Some pineapples, but very few bananas in this area, for some reason. There are several fruits I've not seen before and don't know the name of: a fruit with a thick purple skin (inedible) and a sweet juicy white interior of segments; a fruit like a lychee nut but with a red/green bristly skin, juicy translucent meat around a single seed; a small brown fruit with orange custardy pulp around two longish seeds, like a miniature zapote, a Guatemalan fruit, but better. Durian, called the 'king of fruits'—I know someone who should be named Durian—but which is a bit strong for my taste: as a flavoring it's not bad, but by itself it's rich in oil, very odorous (cheesy—like, perhaps, limburger), and overwhelming in flavor. It can be smelled a block away. Some people are fanatics about them.

On a clear day (it's been raining much of the time lately), I like to climb to the top of the hill in the back of the *wat*) where I can see the roads and fields, and, about a mile away, the Gulf of Siam, with some small islands looming darkly above the haze which rests on the water. There are hundreds, or thousands, of islands in the Gulf. The coastline is under heavy guard these days, both to prevent the 'boat-people' from landing (stories circulate of the coastguard deliberately sinking boats and letting the boat-people drown) and to try (with little likelihood of success) to capture the pirate boats which have come to the coast to prey on the boat-people (mostly middle-class/upper-class ethnic Chinese who would rather flee Vietnam than go to work on the new collective farms—a desperate choice).

* * *

(More news of the world reached the Sooke hills from Suan Moke. Some of the clippings read: 'If you get unemployment down too quickly to full employment of, say, 6 percent, you will have wasted this recession,' Mother Teresa, of Calcutta, when asked if she doesn't become discouraged in her work with the destitute and dying; 'God has not called me to be successful. He has called me to be faithful.' 'What we want to achieve is a balance between gross national product and gross national happiness.' 'Calling Hussein a "schizo", Sadat expressed confidence the Jordanian monarch would join the peace process.' 'When you have a hammer in your hand everything looks like a nail. That may be the gloomiest prognosis of all.'—Hūm)

Oh? Do you really think most of my letters are questions? Am I anything but a quest-ion? Anyway, since you're a garbage collector (or didn't you get the job? overqualified?), here's another piece of garbage for your collection. I've tried to get you a really decent collection—a hundred pages or so of *Worthy Bones*—but, it seems, without success. Too bad. It would be suitable as toilet paper, or may be suitable as part of those rolls of old paper used in India to make tubes in which to place a dose of salted peanuts (to go with the monkey that didn't come with your spitting hurdygurdy). Or...

Ever thought of writing a comic book? That might be more on my level. As for me—ain't writ nothin' nigh unto these 3 months now, and aside from some flavorsome feelings of guilt, couldn't care less. *Worthy Bones* 's within a hundred pages or so of the end, and slowly losing ground. The characters seem to no longer have dialogues: their talks are parallel monologues.

May not be around here too much longer. The old bureaucratic boot. You may have heard of Thailand's efforts to 'repatriate' the Khmer—it was less than successful and so now since they've *got* to get rid of *somebody*... Accordingly, my visa is being given a hassle, and then they try to get *me* involved in it too. We shall see... I might just ordain again and teach the bastards a lesson.

V.

* * *

Sometimes after reading your flights of fancy, all very clever and whatnot I feel like a dung beetle busy rolling my little piece of shit in an unimaginative and mundane manner, just trying to get to wherever it is I'm trying to get to. Plodding. But those clouds that you swoop in and out of, and roll up into balls, and push them to wherever it is you're trying to get to—they're too light and airy for a stolid down-to-earth (in-the-ground?) type like me, who, though not unimaginative, prefers to imagine things with lots of gristle, and whose imagination is constrained, perhaps—'flightless'?

I've read *Even Cowgirls Get the Blues*, and liked it mucho, but now must—with a bit of anxiety—not read *Another Roadside Attraction* lest I find myself using up energy in going around non-existent obstacles. Or do they exist? Like waking up in the morning to find an elephant in your room…good grief… Just the other day someone asked me if I'd read so-and-so's account of when he was a Buddhist monk.

There's been talk of Ajahn Chah going to Vancouver, but I guess not. Yes, Groucho would have had a terrible time if he wasn't there. And when a wealthy dowager looked down 6 yards of nose at Stan Laurel to tell him how delighted she was to meet him, he replied, 'I'm not either'. Ah well. If I get the energy I may send you an unpublished short talk of his (A.C. not S.L.), which will at least help keep the P.O. solvent. I'm not pushing him like I was Ñāṇavīra, mind you, but… well, I liked the old gaffer, and he seemed to be pretty sharp. You won't find any Big Macism in him.

*Bones* still nedds to get hold of the right piece of gristle here and there. Trouble is, cloud-gristle is so hard to get a hook into.

But you got a hook—a *nail*—in a package of dates? Were you charged extra? A special Khomeini Suppositories?

When I was in Guatemala there was a S.F. fag type who claimed to be Tom Robbins, and who did a very effective impersonation, but who was probably a fake. Perhaps *Another Roadside Attraction* is also a fake? This fake T.R. said that his next book would be called 'Divorces'. Sounds like Siamese twins are only half as Siamese as once believed, I haven't heard from my agent in nearly a year. Maybe he died? Maybe I can help? Maybe I did?

Abrazon,

V.

* * *

For your various missives and hitives, too, as well as hard-to-come-by 9×12 envelopes, in one of which I'm posting another installment to be Xeroxed and thence dropped (by carrying crow) on your stump—for these and thou, salaam… And they say that serialized fiction is out of style. Gosh, I had a list of points on which I wanted your opinion and info, and now, of course, I can't find it. I even emptied out the top half of my overflowing wastepaper bag. Not there. Well, poor old Mia Memory isn't much given to total recall, never has been, poor dear, but one of them was about the 'King Oliver on Trumpet' quote: where *did* it come from? It's beautiful, and if I see a chance I'll work it in, but, is it your own original, or, as it sounds, is it from Shakespeare or the Bible or James Branch Cabal or something? Also, I don't know if there is any meaning to some of your names that I could have (easily) missed. Such as: Jizi (other than 'thief' in Swahili, is it involved with 'righteous'?)

Of course, if you see a place where a character isn't drawn in well, where motivation is misdirected, confusion reigns (and rains), or whatever, give me a tweak; and if you have a handle on how to set things right, give 'er a crank. Or two. Yes, actually the only major characters of your version I've killed off is the entire diplomatic corps. In this regard I may be outdoing Joyce himself, who avenged himself on an outrageous British diplomat in Switzerland by portraying him as a drunken sailor (in Ulysses). Anyway, too many characters spoil the book.

Your piece about Mohel's Spanish scam brought back memories... that I don't even have yet. Certainly a place for them in a prequel: Falangista Mohel. Mohel meets Gidgit? Mohel and Gidget Get it On with Godzilla?

V.

* * *

(Enclosed with this letter was a copy of Bob's formal come-on to the mean offices of NY publishing.—Hūm)

A breather, it was. Having caught my breath, I'm back at work. Not on the book, mind. But the publisher's mind. No need for you to do anything, since this effort is intended to be decisive. If I get no more than nibbles, you can finish it, fiddle with it, or flick it aside.

From W.W. Norton comes these encouraging discouraging words:

> '... We have decided against an offer of publication. This is a witty, well-told, and extremely inventive story. But it is also unbelievable. Mohel, Jizi, and Carmen are reminiscent of Batman, Robin, and Bat-

> girl, as they wheel and deal in the power politics of Samadhi. They are all cartoons of real people. The plot is a fantasy. One is not sure it's tongue in cheek or for real. With no apparent purpose other than entertainment, the novel cannot succeed, for its lack of credibility alienates the reader.'

You should have by now, or soon, my contribution to this fantastic purposeless incredible alien entertaining failure.

A metaphysical bricklayer, Thomas Mann? Who said that? You? Him? My hope is that *Worthy Bones* is not just some metaphysical bricks. Anyone can shit metaphysical bricks all day long, pile them up, and call it a novel, but it's just a pile of shit. I tried to include not just the shit, which is certainly needed to create *whole* characters, but also the flesh, blood and gristle and bone that are needed to support a brain and an alimentary track.

And to do *that*... well... my problem's not with the Editor in me (who's often overambitious but can be controlled) but with the Creator, who's a lazy little fellow who has to be practically beaten or cajoled before he'll do fuck-all. Or else just wait patiently until he's in the mood. Or?

V.

* * *

(Sometimes running around the margins of Bob's letters were postscript bugs, which seemed to be chasing one another, or perhaps were bugged to keep circling the square edges of their paper world. 'SLOGAN OF THE MONTH: A GAPING CHEST WOUND IS NATURE'S WAY OF TELLING YOU YOU'VE BEEN SHOT'. After reading a book on St. Francis by Chesterton: 'Francis is the greatest Hindu Italy ever produced.' And... 'If the Buddha were alive today he'd probably get arrested for insighting the people to quiet.'—Hūm)

Okay, I'll try again. The complete incomplete *Worthy Bones* has, I gather, not settled well in LA, so maybe it can be coughed up if my feather keeps tickling that distant throat. Beyond that I've got notes and scribblings which I'll send to you if you ever decide to do anything further with it. For my part, unless some publisher takes a definite interest in it I doubt that I'll find the enthusiasm to go back to it. This isn't because of the story, but because of my telling of it, which I feel has gone downhill more and more precipitously as the story got along. Not bad, perhaps, for half of it, but then somehow it lost energy, picked up a lot of heavy weight and lost a certain essence of human interaction which had been its motivating power earlier on. It got too plotty. Ponderous. Some good moments, perhaps, but essentially *static* moments: the book doesn't seem to be moving along, and that's why it got to be such a burden. I had to *push* it along, whereas in the early part it had its own momentum.

I think any reader would sense this, and find the reading as tough going as I've found the writing. If you are going to do anything with it, strive for dynamism. Sure, motion is illusion, but that's what people are after, after all: illusion. Nobody's gonna pay hard-earned money for reality. Who needs to? Reality's free. It's everywhere. We've got more of it than we know what to do with. If you can slip a little *uneasiness* into the illusion, make them feel not quite so sure of themselves, that's about all that can be hoped for.

I think *Worthy Bones*—for both of us—has not been remiss in the uneasiness department. I think it needs to be more illusory, and that means more believable. The plot is absurd, of course, and I've known this from the start, but then I know of some very successful books with very absurd plots. (*Slaughterhouse-5*, for example, going from WW2 to another star, and all that.) But I think in order to make a plot believable you gotta skim over it lightly, not pay so much attention to it, and what I've been doing is delving into the details of the how's and wherefore's of it, trying to establish its reality through accretion instead of suggestion. Some good accretions in there, but that's all they is, accretions, and they don't really succeed in making anything more believable, do they?

On the other hand, of course, it's entirely possible (though, I think, unlikely) that I'll wake up one day full of enthusiasm and see clearly what needs to be done to correct what's been done poorly (I don't see this now; perhaps you will: you have a much lighter touch than me) and set to work. But barring that, or unexpected publisher interest (in which case I would finish it even if I knew it to be a flawed finish) I'll likely be finished with *Worthy Bones*. It was fun for a long while, though. Thanks for letting me play with your toys.

I leave in a few days for Malaysia, where I'll get a 60 day tourist visa and—hopefully—be allowed to re-enter Thailand for that time, I figure I'll probably do that twice—once now, and once again early in November—and then I'll make some sort of decision. The logistics of various things seem to make it preferable for me to delay such a decision until November, Bureaucracy Willing. Until the November trip I'll stay at Suan Moke. Then I'll move up to Bangkok to settle my hash.

I have no choice but to make some sort of change in my life now. It's been a rather good life, quite suiting me, so far, and I wouldn't want to do anything too different. Considering the options available to me, the least different thing I can think of is ordaining again. Perhaps I'll think of something less different in the next 2 months, or perhaps I'll decide to try something more different anyway. But that seems to cover the range of my choices. It's enough to make my teeth itch.

* * *

I've had a bad case of visa-itis, which required emergency treatment at the Thai Consulate in Penang. My file received an I.V. solution of 5% black ink and 3% red tape and is now recuperating. I've managed to get back to Suan Moke with an interrupted past and an uncertain future. Not a great deal to say for the present either. (Although one thing about the present, you can't fault it for endurance.)

Could your 'gift' of *Bones* (if such a gift can be made), besides being graciously magnanimous and possibly saving complications (I've got an excellent collection of complications which I must show you some time—I save them, like bits of string), also have been inspired by the suspicion that by the time I'd finished with it it would be too removed from your intents and attempts to want anything more to do with it? (When either of us whistles now, what comes?) I have, I see, made it a rather different book. Or, atleast, more like a book I remember… once upon a time, I've not put a highway through your jungle, but I've cut out everything that looked to me like undergrowth, trimmed what was left, and did a bit of planting myself. Perhaps everyone needs his own jungle. Your comments (cloud gristle) have contained some useful suggestions, however.

By the way, I beg to differ with your friend, Polly Ethyl Lean, in her crusade to stop the slaughter of the naugas for their hides. I refer to her uninformed comment about 'placid herds of naugas'. *I* have a friend whose grandfather was *killed* by one of those placid herds. Stamp out the menace, I say!

V.

* * *

The banalities of Bangkok pound my brain like slugs made of cotton. It's over 4 months here now, but how ya gonna keep 'em down on Patpong after they've seen the forests? I'm Thaired of it.

Managed to learn a bit of the lingo in the last few months, what with a classroom situation and a good teacher, and expect, d.v. as they say, to leave next month for the hills of the North—no idea where yet, or maybe too many ideas—and be clear of the heavy vibes of Bangkok, where I've managed to do exactly no writing (hardly even answering correspondence, as you already have guessed), although I have learned to endure adverse conditions, in an intense form the jungle seldom offers.

I'd love to see what you're doing with *Bones*. No hurry—until I have an address mail will be held here at Wat Bovaranives for me—and expect to send you what I'm doing eventually, maybe even with *Bones*. Maybe we can both *rewrite* it simultaneously and then collate our efforts, you can do odd f pages and I'll do even # pages. What a collaboration! On the other hand, I may pick up *Getting Off*, in which case a collaboration would produce either *Getting Bones* or *Worthy Off*, I can't figure out which. *Track of Truth* needs some pottering too. I grow geranium alongside the roadway, wave to passers-by, snigger at their idea that they're going somewhere, at my own idea that I'm not.

Shit's good fertilizer. Shovel some on my geraniums. We all shovel our shit, of course, but few of us get paid for it, many of us pay for it, and pay and pay. I trust you're not being paid more than you're worth. Is the shit better (or even different), after all, from printer's ink? Or is it that printer's ink is *unused* shit? Lose a newspaper and find a farm?

*Worthy Bones*—love Mohel/Carmen/Jizi, stick with them, let them relate together, quarrel, see things same/different, love, let *them* be the story and let the bones be the background to their story. Let them seek truth between themselves, and learn the price of their illusions.

Love, brother

V.

* * *

In Bangkok I met with some friends who've been involved with the refugee camps, and they know a bit more about the country they're in. You may have heard of the 'voluntary' repatriation of the Khmer It was of course far less voluntary than the Thai government tried to make it sound like.

At Sae Keo camp, which is controlled internally by the Khmer Rouge, the government was expecting about 25,000 of the 32,000 refugees—soldiers, their families, and isolated family-less persons—to return to Cambodia to take up positions fighting against the Vietnamese. Much of the aid that had come into Thailand for the refugees has of course been used to provision Pol Pot's people. They're re-armed, rested up, given surreptitious training, and sent back to fight—a policy Thailand vociferously denies it is following—and only a small amount of aid gets to non-participant refugees.

A great deal is skimmed off the top by the Thai bureaucracy and higher-ups, and Thai villagers near the border are also demanding—and getting—aid: perhaps not unfairly, since they've suffered from both the war and the presence of refugees; but there is a great deal of anger and it has happened that Thai villagers have harassed the refugees and even fired rifles and thrown grenades into the camps. Every Thai has a vast store of armament. But what the villagers are doing in the Northeast is, apparently, child's play to what the Thais living on the Gulf islands are doing to this years crop of boat people: yes, there are boat people again, now that the currents and winds have become favorable again, though not in the same numbers as last year.

Anyway, the people I know have been working to provide the real refugees with some possibilities: training programs, language programs, etc., and of course a religious program. (The Khmer are a devout people, and all their monks were killed or forcibly disrobed many years ago. Quite a few of the men in the camp would like to ordain as monks, but the Thai government will not allow it, ostensibly for the reason that as monks they would have to be allowed to remain in Thailand and that the Khmer would be ordaining not out of religious motivation but from a desire to be free of the camps. Another reason, though, is that these men as monks would be useless as a buffer between Thailand and Vietnam. The whole point of Thailand's allowing the refugees in in the first place was to be able to support the Khmer Rouge as a buffer force.)

So... my friends were doing obvious good in the camps, and had an established position, and so they were watched carefully to make sure they didn't get out of line and were tolerated. (Once at the *wat*—temple—inside the camp—founded by them—a number of Khmer men shaved their heads and the Thai government got very upset, accusing them of plans to be secretly ordained in the night and the government needed to be re-assured that things weren't as terrible as all that and that at any rate the men's hair would soon grow back, which in fact it did.)

Then when this repatriation thing came up—because of the beginning of the wet season, when the heavy equipment of Vietnam is of less use against the Khmer Rouge—neither the Thai government nor the Khmer Rouge leadership inside the camp (this leadership is carefully controlled by the Thai government, of course) informed the refugees that the proposed repatriation was voluntary—as was insisted by the UNHCR, IRC, etc.—but simply that they would be repatriated, the refugees didn't know they had any choice in the matter. Therefore the government expected that some 25,000 would go, leaving only those who were too old, too young, or too sick to go. 'Going' meant, of course, not just going back to Cambodia but going back to Khmer Rouge-controlled Cambodia and fighting again, or supporting the fighters. So what was done was that Rob, an Australian fluent in Thai, wrote up a leaflet (in Khmer) informing the people that they couldn't be forced to go back to Cambodia, and he and Bent, a Swedish journalist, began distributing them, having first received the customary clearance from the camp commander.

The commander was immediately besieged by refugees declaring their unwillingness to be repatriated, and when he realized what was happening the commander flew into a rage. He ordered that Rob, Bent, and their leader, Peter, an American minister (and, also, the step-son of a former U.S. ambassador to Thailand), be arrested. Peter was arrested and held in jail five days, during which he was harassed and intimidated and some very heavy charges were laid on his head.

Rob and Bent managed to escape from the camp before being arrested, and made their way to Bangkok, where they hid out. Word came through that the orders at the camp were that if they showed up there they were to be shot on sight. After five days Peter's friends got him out on bail, but everybody was very upset, because now instead of 25,000 Khmer being repatriated from Sae Keo camp only about 8,000 went voluntarily, and fully 17,000 refused to go, all as a result of these leaflets

Rob and Bent distributed. They figure they probably saved about 10,000 lives, but the Thai government sees it differently: to them it's a betrayal of Thai security.

Rob, who was the prime mover in this particular incident—which none of them imagined at the time to be particularly significant or telling—has been in Thailand for some years (he can even *type* in Thai, a rare skill for a foreigner)—has had to leave the country and is now back in Australia. (Previous to the refuges situation he had been working, as a monk, with the hill-tribes in the North, doing social work.) Bent has been cleared and is still in Thailand, willing to go back to the camps if he can. Just before I got to Bangkok all charges against Peter were dropped and he too is now in the clear. The camp commander was fired—someone's head had to roll—and just before I left Bangkok Peter was on his way back to the camp to see if he would be allowed back in, and if so what he might still be effective at. I haven't heard anything further about this.

Because of all this, the Thai government has become even more uptight and paranoid than usual about foreigners messing around with their plans, and even though they would acknowledge, if asked about it, that foreigners such as myself are not relevant to their border problems, nevertheless their paranoia extends in all directions and affects the uninvolved as well as the involved. They have established a new rule with regard to foreigners connected with Buddhism: they will grant visa-extensions only to those who are monks.

After doing some running around in Bangkok I learned about all this, for of course they could never explain to me. Rather, the way it worked was that a) the World Fellowship of Buddhists, who had previously sponsored my applications for visa extensions, told me that Immigration no longer accepted sponsorship from them but rather required it now from the Department of Religious Affairs of the Ministry of Education. b) the Department of Religious Affairs maintained at first that they were still studying the regulations and would not be able to respond to my application for sponsorship for at least 3 weeks. When I pointed out that my visa expired in 12 days they informed me that I could leave the country and come back in 3 weeks. I told them that by doing so I would lose my Non-Immigrant visa status—which was no easy thing to come by—and would have to revert to Tourist status, which limits visits to 2 months. They said it was no problem, and of course it wasn't for them.

After further visits—during which the Director-General refused to even see me—they finally admitted that they were not studying the regulations and point-blank refused my application unless I ordained. Actually this was a step forward for me, for an application 'under consideration' is moribund even if its fate is known. Once it's refused then it becomes possible to explore other avenues. c) I then went to Immigration, who told me that they couldn't consider my application unless it had the approval of Religious Affairs. I told them that Religious Affairs had told me that they (R.A.) had been ordered by Immigration not to approve any applications by laypeople. So sorry, they'd like to help, but what can they do? Can't I see that their hands are tied? Who, I asked, has tied their hands by making this rule? The Police Commission, or one of the Police Commissions, or something like that, I was told: I don't understand the various levels of authority that were being discussed (and, perhaps, neither did they, though they knew what they didn't want: me).

Anyway, the upshot of it was that eventually I got to see a big-shot who I'd seen before (on previous visa application sojourns) and who was not unsympathetic to my plight. 'It's because of all the drug addicts,' he told me, as if laypeople living in temples was the source of Thailand's drug industry (the relationship of the government to the drug industry is another interesting topic). But of course he couldn't tell me it was because of the Cambodian situation, or more precisely because of the paranoia that has resulted from the situation, so he told me it was because of drugs. So I appealed to him on the basis of my past record in Thailand and long-time connection with Buddhism, and he looked sympathetic and said he would present the Police Commission, or whatever it is, with my appeal for an exception, and that he couldn't promise anything, but that he would do that, and he gave me a 2-week extension of my visa so that I could stay in the country until the decision was made (instead of having to go to Penang), and so I'm still here but on a very tentative basis.

* * *

Bangkok's not a healthy place. You walk around the city for a couple hours and you're covered with a gray film. The city strangles on its congestion, which it brought on itself by rapaciously robbing the countryside of its wealth and, subsequently, becoming filled with rural migrants who can no longer survive. (Farmers are required to sell their rice at government controlled and artificially low prices. This is only one of many techniques by which Bangkok middle-men get rich.) The result is that the city can't keep itself clean: the air is full of garbage, I invariably get minor ailments here, infrequently in the countryside.

If my visa hash is ever settled, and I'm allowed to stay on, I expect to find a fairly remote area, so some knowledge of Thai will be necessary. Consequently my intermittent and floundering efforts to learn the language have been revived. Unlike in Sri Lanka, it's rare to find any Thais in the country—side who are competent English-speakers; in spite of the fact that they are required to study English for 5 years in school, few of them seem to have progressed beyond 'Hey you', 'Was is your name?', and 'Where you go? Where you go?'—This question being, in Thai, the cultural equivalent of 'How are you?'—i.e. they don't really care where you're going, they're translating their form of greeting—'Pai nai'—literally, not understanding that to a Westerner they could be giving an impression of rudeness or nosiness, arousing suspicions in this bandit-plagued country rather than allaying them. Some countries—e.g. Pakistan—have exactly the opposite sort of greeting: 'Hey, you! Where you come from, huh?'

Thai script is incredibly complicated. Some of the complication is due to the necessity to indicate which of the 5 tones in Thai is to be used, but a lot of the complication is just plain complication. For example, there are 7 ways to represent the short vowel *a* (irrespective of tone) and the short vowel *a* is the most common vowel in the language. The various tone markers, or absence of them, affect different letters in different ways, and also the rules change according to what letter a syllable *ends* with as well as the letter at the beginning of the syllable (which is the letter that has *dominant* rule over the vowel and tone markers, although these markers are not necessarily written together with that letter. Got that? OK. Vowel markers are written before, behind, above, below, or in various combinations of these positions, and are sometimes not written at all. A final consonant can change the tone (and change itself; if it's a *d*, for example, it can change to a *t*). Also a low tone can be made by a tone marker. Etc., etc.

Probably there are exceptions and further complicating factors to these rules that I haven't learned yet, so I wouldn't place too much trust in the above brief explanation. Also Thai writing doesn't separate words, only sentences, so not only is it uncertain, unless one knows the words already (shades of Hebrew), where one word ends and the next begins, it's also uncertain, sometimes, which word, or which syllable within a word, a vowel marker belongs to. Does it follow the preceding letter or precede the following letter? There are 44 consonants. The number of vowels is indefinite, depending on how they are counted, but at least 9 and as many, perhaps, as 33, in addition to which are 4 tone markers. I'm trying to learn to write 'Which way out of here?' and to learn to read the directions.

Recently stopped off at the USICA library to see what's been happening in the world, and was shocked to learn of the murder by the Guatemalan government of a U.S. priest in the town of Santiago Atitlan, where I lived for about 3 months while in the country. It seems, from the report (in Time Magazine—hardly a radical rag) that the priest was put on the death list for having reported the Guatemalan army's previous murder of about 30 villagers (although *that* incident doesn't seem to have been previously reported in Time) for having 'wrong' political views. I've written, while in Guatemala, of the fear and repression I saw around me; it seems, though, that the situation is far worse now than it was then (at which time there was a change of power and a new president was just coming into office: though the various presidents are carbon copies of each other and there is only one political party with any effective power, a transition of of government every five years usually means a pause in the machinations of the powers-that-be). At that time there were about 4 political murders per day. Now, according to Time, the figure is about triple that. The situation in Thailand, though always tentative, doesn't seem so bad as that, though this country has to have one of the highest murder rates in the world (everybody seems armed). Even a town like Chiang Mai, with perhaps 500,000 people, has about 3 murders per day, and certainly individual police do a good share of the killing, they being by far the most corrupt people in the country; and yet none of this seems approved of and directed from the top, as it certainly is in Guatemala. When I leave Bangkok, by the way, it will probably be for a spell of wandering in the hills around the Chiang Mai area.

* * *

It's *always* too late. You can *always* write. I can *always* read. And, as if happens, vice versa as well. It wasn't the *Bones* that didn't want to get connected, but a *Bone*-crusher interceded in the matter. Sorry it cost you such a bundle to be parted for 6 months from the last third (knees down) of *Bones*. Just think how much it would cost you to be parted from them for a year? In any case, I never received any shin-bones, ankle-bones, or foot-bones, connected or disconnected. If you can give them another go-round, even by surface mail, I'd be willing to wait patiently (for about 3 months), but if you can't I'll still be willing to wait patiently, though in the end with much less to show for it.

What leads you to believe any Canadian publisher would give a puck about *Bones*? Something up front? Down back? I'm glad if it's true, and I'm glad if it's not, but some gladness is more equal than others. As for establishing the H/V Foundation,[1] it sounds as mysterious to me as the Foundations of Tibetan Mysticism, though presumably it's a foundation established on a different (though equal) footing. But the idea of investing what I don't have fascinates me. If I had it I might be less interested. Doing Business As? When I was a little kid with a new puppy my mother told me (and told me and told me) to train the dog to go outside to do his business as. There was a suitable place to do his business as. And it was okay to spread a lot of newspapers on which he could do his business as. You might consider whether the last third of *Bones* are enough papers to do business as.

This is Be Kind to Neutron Bombs week (Day? Hour? Minute? Millennium?).

Meanwhile, back at the monastery... I continue to hang on, but prospects remain (as always) uncertain, and though I'm ever being reassured that all really will work out for the best, there seems to be some perverse nugget in my gullet that makes me hack out a doubt or two, particularly when the sky is most blue. Besides, I can never really decide which course would be best for me. Perhaps it will be a misfortune to finally get the visa? ow can I ever know? Even getting it won't tell me, for I'll never know what wonderful, terrible, or totally mediocre things might have happened if the visa *hadn't* been issued (as it hasn't). And vice versa, as well. Which brings us full circle, and now we can go around the second time. But we always do go around a second time, don't we? Perhaps

1. A non-prophet organization stillborn for lack of sense—Hūm.

that's why it's always too late; or perhaps, again vice versa. Anyway, I see I've said nothing at all so far, and so without marring a perfect record, adding only that my own plans, such as they are, aren't—still not the foggiest what will become of me—I bid thee a fond one.

V.

* * *

Your *Bones* arrived, a Worthy supplement to my own narrow marrow. Not yet had time to do more than gnaw a bit on the joints, but it's my hope to have time (Time!) to swallow, digest, and shit them out again, to re-fertilize this old (Old!) earth. (!) What I have seen of them so far, they remind me of a fellow I once met in Afghanistan... who had a good story...

Glad you liked my story, *Vision*. I think it has a maturity and depth that much of my previous work lacks. And since I know exactly how and why it does so, it may be expected that future (Future!) work will have or strive for the same. But I write only when the daemons drive me to do so, or boredom, or (rarely) vast inspiration, and these days there is not much of any of those, so it may be a while before anything more turns up.

Your letter was even more Worthy than *Bones* (more Worthy and more *Bones*?). Indeed, I think you (and perhaps me too) are most lucid when your audience (potential audience, that is) is the smallest (for both of us our actual audience are about the same whether we write letters or novels). Nevertheless, John Barth seems to have killed off that genre (or at least laid it to rest for a while) as he did with the Great American Historical Novel (though the GAHN was done in with wit, humor, grace, complexity, etc., whereas the epistolary novel was bludgeoned with a long-handled solipsism that only an omphalophile could love.

Meanwhile, back at the monastery... we last left our hero he was striving, pen sharpened and at the ready, to do battle with the evil monster, Paranoia, and his scurrilous master, Chauvin. We remember how our beautiful heroine, Visa O. Lovely, was in danger of being done in by the monster: chained down, stripped to her bare essentials, and guarded by a Passport About to Expire... And our hero's friends, a motley (but lovable) crew of eccentric seers, visionaries, do-gooders, do-badders, do-nothings, and (zippity) do-dahs, were striving mite and maign to help our hero rescue his beloved from the maws of an Expiration Worse

Than Death… And how breathlessly we awaited the next installment of this thrilling (and seemingly endless) episodic soft-soap opera. Well, we're still waiting, we're still waiting, we're still waiting, 'cause nuttin' ain't happened yet. (Gorsh, maw, I can't hardly stand the excitement. Now let's go watch an ice cube melt.)

Well, it seems (Again!) hardly no trouble at all to fill a letter with the most pointless inanities and mealy-mouthed moronisms, so I can only conclude that in this case I must have slipped up and said something substantive, for I find that hardly halfway through the available (indeed, virtually obligatory) space of this aerogramme I have nothing more to say, and am forced to close. The rest of the paper will be fine toilet quality, void of black ink (with life as complicated as it is already, who needs a black asshole?) for the only thing left to say is, love you brother, and dig your trip and wish you a fine and error-free winter.

V.

* * *

(Atleast there were some bits of world-shaking news to pass the time, judging from the clippings stuck to his next letter. 'Even someone who falls off a 15-story building bounces a little bit when he hits the sidewalk'. 'Under Taiwan's martial law proceedings, defendants are not regarded as innocent unless proven guilty'. Visa problems, no doubt: 'The numbers of Sumatran rhinoceros are dwindling fast and there are only about 40 left in Malaysia,' 'There is no report of progress, but there is also no report of no progress,' said a spokesman for the union. 'We live in a complex world. Some may be saying, *We want out*. But this is 1981. The complications are the price of civilization as we know it. You can't get out.' ISRAEL FOR EVERYONE.—Hūm)

Yes, I'm still waiting for it (the f/Future!). How much longer, please? I remain in Thailand (as a *sāmaṇera*, by the way, got rid of some baggage in Bangkok, but picked up a new name—a lighter carrying-case—Bodhesako; where do I put it now?), but things are still precarious.[1]

My mother, who has been in poor and failing health for years, has now had to be put in a home because her mental state has deteriorated

1. He was ordained by Somdet Phra Ñāṇasaṃvara.—Ed.

and my father, exhausted, can no longer care for her. He is very pained by the whole situation. They (he, my sister, and presumably my mother) want me to return, perhaps for some prolonged (years?) deathbed vigil, and I am reluctant to do so, for obvious reason although I love them all and feel in many ways that I *ought* to go in *spite* of my own feelings that it would be a perilous journey—and one that would only add more pain and complications to the situation. I don't know what to do; it may depend on what pressure is put upon me. There's nothing they can say that won't make me feel guilty (even that they don't *need* me)—how cleverly we arrange our lives—but obviously some techniques are more effective than others. I'm not unhappy where I am, aside from this matter, and fear I'd be most unhappy, indeed, in L.A., but it's entirely possible I will go anyway. My father has given his all, and, I'm told, is aging rapidly. It's a difficult and painful matter, perhaps least for me but there it is. And my interests are divided so neatly in such a way that every decision seems to be the wrong one.[1]

Meanwhile, visa hassles continue but, because of the robes, may have a satisfactory resolution.

V.

* * *

What's a *falchah*? Choose one and only one of the following:

a) a Turkish sweet
b) a Japanese religion
c) a Soviet official
d) a species of ginseng
e) a Yiddish word meaning 'brother-in-law on the mother's side'
f) a Hebrew word meaning 'fields of grain'
g) a Swahili word meaning 'my neighbor's garbage'
h) the sound a person makes when he tries simultaneously to gargle and spit
i) none of the above
j) all of the above, including i

1. Bodhesako does not get permission from his parents to take higher ordination as bhikkhu.—Ed.

Any more questions?

Motto of the month: Gather ye hens' eggs while ye may,
for the clock it is a-tickin',
and that same egg ye seek today,
tomorrow will be chicken.

(A toss up between an Egg-McMuffin and Colonel Sanders.)

Rains. Wandering. Here and there. Walking. Sitting. *Carika* (in Thailand miscalled *thudong*—a corruption of *dhutanga*) in Northern Thailand. Hills. Cool. Soon rainy season retreat. Where? Up in the air. No, no, actually, I'll stay on the ground. But where? Still up in the air.

A few ideas keep arising, but instead of chewing on these old bones, I just let 'em fall.

Yes, sure, but... but what's it all *about*?

V.

* * *

Despite the Reagan shooting, and the endless instant replays on TV, riveting the nation, perhaps there's been some mention in the US papers of the trouble in Bangkok—practically on the eve of my departure for the North.

First there was the hijacking, ending in a deadly shootout, and then the attempted coup, which saw fewer fatalities, but a lot more excitement. The latter came close to a shootout too, but Sant, the usurping general, seems to have lacked sufficient strength and his troops, understanding that they were something less than a quarter of the army, and that neither the navy nor the airforce supported them, seem to have refused orders to fight Prem's troops (Prem is the PM) when several thousand of them actually entered the city.

That the navy and airforce were opposed to Sant was clear from the presence of some large warships in the Chao Phaya River, which flows past Bangkok not far from Wat Bovaranives, where I was staying, and from the fly-over of a number of F-5A fighter-bombers, who executed mock bombing runs over several of Sant's strongholds (all of which are within walking distance of Wat Bovaranives, which is on the 'government' end of town—the business end being on the East Side).

Nevertheless, even if fighting had broken out the wat would certainly have been safe, for neither side would endanger a place whose first 3 abbots were crown princes. (The King of 'The King and I' was a monk, as you know, before he was a king and he was, as a monk, the first abbot of this wat—the present abbot is the 6th.) So we had grandstand seats for a show that was better off not having happened. Still, there was a little nervous rush, what with the announcements crackling over the radio, sirens, sounds of distant gunfire, leaflets dropped from planes, etc.

The King of Thailand came to the wat the night before the coup attempt. Obviously he knew what was up and wanted to consult the abbot, who is his special adviser. He looked bewildered; now I know why.

Far from the King's bewildered face, I sit 350 miles north of Bangkok—not as far north as Chiang Mai, but most of the way—in a spacious cave in a limestone hill overlooking a forested valley. On the other side of the valley rise a fairly steep range of hills, running north/south, and on this side of the valley a lower range runs parallel. There are several caves in this hill, some as spacious as this one, but this one goes all the way through the rock and out the backside (maybe 250 feet), and, in this hot season, it's delightfully cool. Far better than the heat of Bangkok even with an electric fan. No bats seem to share this abode. The Northern RR line runs along the valley floor and I can see but only hear like a whisper a train at this moment. It's a 5 mile round trip to the village for alms, but I do it early in the day (leaving about sunrise) to get back before the heat. A small stream nearly dry each evening but fresh and clear each morning provides water. Since I'm unlikely to find another place as pleasing as this, not for a while, I'll stay here a while before heading north to Chiang Mai and beyond before I have to stay put for the rainy season.

* * *

First I went north about 40 miles to Kaeng Pan Dao, which you may recall, is the place I was staying at about 2½ years ago when I was robbed twice, and learned so much about how the police work in Thailand. Now, however, I found that since the abbot has left (about a year ago he went to France, which I already knew, where he now teaches) the place is totally deserted of resident monks. There were 3 *carika* monks there, out wandering like me, who'd been there about a week already, and so I stayed a few days and then left. The villagers didn't say anything directly about it, but I suspect they recognized me. I'd hoped a few of the monks from 2,5 years ago would be there, but as it was there was the chance to cover once-familiar ground and also to speak with the 3 monks, who gave me some useful 'tips for the road'.

After leaving, I headed west, and walked, in 3 days, about 50 miles over rolling scrub bush interspersed with buffalo grazing and cultivated plots; just clusters of a few huts and small houses on stilts passing for villages. As I went on the country got a more and more primitive feeling to it, until there was a very fine feeling to the land: the people seemed different, more open, more accepting, helpful but not pushy, and the land, on the verge of mountainous, felt fresh and clean, well irrigated, not overpopulated, smelling of the elements not oil fumes.

So I was very pleased to be walking through this country when, some days ago, I came to this place, Nam Pung Duat, which is on a dirt road about 3 miles north of the main (partly paved) road (which goes through Pai to Mae Hong Son, near the Burmese border—my destination), and there I've found what is to my mind the finest forest hermitage I've come across in Thailand. A hermitage, indeed: there's no one living here so I have the place entirely to myself. (I later learned it's used almost exclusively by *carika* monks, who come, stay for a while, then leave.)

The *wat* consists of 4 small bamboo cottages and one spacious hall, also mainly bamboo (though it has a corrugated metal roof and good timber in its framework). The bamboo around here can often have a circumference of over 12 inches. Used as whole lengths it provides a slightly springy base for a floor. Split lengthwise and opened up, it makes large panels which can be used for flooring or as walls. It's easy to sweep and comfortable to live on and around. The hall is very open (though it has an attached room which is enclosed where I've set myself up), with a fine view of pine forest, dominated by a verdant and precipitously steep mountain. Clouds like to pass across the belt of this mountain leaving its upper reaches exposed but no longer grounded, afloat in the clouds as it were; bamboo stands, wild banana plants in the lowlands, papaya trees around the hall, and no sounds other than forest sounds, and those muted and discreetly orchestrated.

Near the main road there's a village (15 houses) and another one about a mile north of here (10 houses) where the people are very rustic, with little or no formal schooling, but they are openly glad to have me here (they are careful to leave me undisturbed: they know the ways of wanderers, and I'm not the first *farang*—foreigner—to stay here), even though they know almost nothing about the outside world. Almost everything they have—even their rifles—are of regional, if not local, manufacture, houses are of forest material, they roll their tobacco in slices of cut and dried banana leaf (which, when dry, separates into thin layers), and even the women smoke large—10 inches long—conical cigarettes. They carry short jungle knives in unwieldy rattan cases on their belt and hunt with their front-loading rifles (i.e. they load it by pushing a bullet down the muzzle) small animals and birds, which seems to be the only game left alive in these parts. (In Ceylon it was unknown for a villager to have a gun, and Ceylon still has lots of large wildlife; in Thailand *everyone* has guns and the animal population has been decimated.)

About 2 miles north of here are some hot springs, small geysers, water churning as much as 10 feet into the air from a few of the pots, steam visible a long ways off, and a river of hot water running off of them. By going downstream until the water is at just the right temperature for me, I took a fine bath in a pond of hot running water (maybe a couple gallons/second-quite rapid). Nearby is a (cold) raging river, with impressive rapids and falls, and a pond, and a fine flower garden kept by an old man who, I assume, is in the hire of the government: a few facilities and sturdy bamboo bridges were paid for by someone—I suspect that when the main road was built, about 7 or 8 years ago, someone thought to make a park out of the springs, but since this dirt road is motorable (by Jeep, at best) only in the dry season (otherwise the river it crosses up near the main road is too deep for vehicles, though wade-able) the plan seems to have deteriorated, which means I've got the place pretty much to myself whenever I want to walk out there and get a hot bath.

I do have one new friend at the *wat*: a porcupine. He takes food from my hand and even lets me scratch him (a tricky business, let me tell you). He has no quills under his chin or around his ears. On his back I can scratch between the quills; his skin is baby-tender. He loves fruit, especially papaya and rambutan.

Another extraordinary thing about this *wat*: many fireflies at night. In front of the hall, in the clearing, where they can see each other, they tend to gather, and also tend to flash simultaneously. It seems to be line-of-sight, so sometimes different clusters will each have their own rhythm, but sometimes the different clusters get synchronized, and then it's quite extraordinary to watch.

The place has such a good and magical feeling to it I expect to stay for a spell. However, I haven't yet found a way to send mail from here and suspect there isn't any, so probably this letter won't get posted until I push on to Pai (another 40 miles), where there's a post-office.

* * *

Two days after writing the last letter, I was walking up the track to the hot springs when I met a Land Rover returning from there. The Land Rover had been rented by a group of Europeans. The person I talked with was a French photographer freelance but on assignment to do a photo article on the most difficult roads a Land Rover can travel. He told the car rental agency that he wanted rough roads and they told their driver to take him here. I was surprised that the river was fordable and even more surprised that they were able to get past two particularly bad points, one where a culvert—the only one on the track, had collapsed (but they managed to squeeze past it, going over a mud flat with 2 wheels) and another where a huge tree root covered most of the track (but they squeezed by, with 2 wheels going on a rather steep incline). The photographer took a few pictures of me, so perhaps in a few months I will appear in a French automotive magazine. And he also took your letter to mail.

In the month I stayed at Pung Duat there was only one other vehicle on the track, a Jeep which seems to belong to the son of one of the villagers—a rattletrap affair held together with wire and bubblegum—which for several days, at odd hours, carted odd goods from one place on the track to another. I don't know exactly what that was about.

And those were the 2 most exciting events of my stay here, which is coming to an end, for tomorrow I expect to continue on my way to Mae Hong Son, near the Burmese border. Either despite or because of its lack of eventfulness, Pung Duat has not only been very pleasant but very useful for my practice. I'd certainly stay longer, but as it happens I have to be back in Chiang Mai by the end of June if I'm to stay the rainy season at Wat Palad. I'd stay the rainy season at Pung Duat if it weren't that (I'm told) it's already reserved and the next most suitable forest hermitage I know of is Wat Palad. So I'll have a look at Mae Hong Son before I head back.

* * *

The mountain to the east of Pai (the provincial capital) is gorgeous: heavy jungle in parts, forest in parts, and parts of it like grassy parkland with enough trees for shade but no undergrowth. Wide vistas. Very steep in places—sometimes switchback roads pass the same viewpoint 5 or 6 times, each time from a higher vantage point, before moving on to the next hill.

The whole area from about 5 miles west of Pah Poe (i.e. about 10 miles east of Pung Duat) to the final downgrade of the mountains descending to the Pai valley floor (a very steep descent of 15 miles) is the finest country I've seen in Thailand.

Pai is a small town, about 3500 population, neither pleasant nor unpleasant, very ordinary, sleepy, old clapboard beside new concrete, tar roads needing repairs, an agricultural center of the only substantial valley between Mai Mali (where the westbound road began, 25 miles north of Chiang Mai) and Mae Hong Son (which is about 15 miles east of the Burmese border).

A night there at a temple, then over the next mountain on the most difficult day of the trip: walked 25 miles over the highest mountain in the area and through heavy rainstorm and clouds, simply because there was no place to stop, and the entire day there wasn't one single vehicle going my way (which will tell you how well traveled the road is, though there were 4 vehicles that day going the other way—I find it an invariable rule of walking or hitching that no matter which way I'm going there's always more traffic the other way). Anyway, I reached the summit and looked out on a magnificent view of range after range of mountains—I'm sure I could see well into Burma—and a valley before me, and after a 5 mile walk I reached a village of Lisu people about 7 PM and spent the night there in the school house.

The Lisu are hill-tribe people who wear very colorful dress, have their own language and customs (animistic), live in bamboo and thatch houses, quite large but without windows, smoke opium, are quite clean (which is no easy thing in the hills: their village, after the storm, was a quagmire), keep a lot of animals (pigs, dogs, cows, horses, but I saw no buffalo, and of course a lot of hens; I also saw several cats, an uncommon sight in Thailand), most of which roam freely. The boys all have their head shaved saved for a square patch, about 2 inches on the side, in the front center of their skull. The children all wear pullover dresses, boys and girls alike. The men wear baggy pantaloons and shirt, the women skirts (black), blouses of many colors, and a brilliant light-blue apron, long hair in a bun. They eat white fluffy rice, unlike most of the Thais in the north of Thailand, who eat brown glutinous rice, and meat of course, and I was given also some sort of root, not potato but not too different, fried with chili and some type of green all quite spicy and also quite dry, so I couldn't eat much of it and drank a lot of water (which fortunately was available outside the schoolhouse in a rain-catchment tank). The food also was quite clean.

The people were hospitable but, aside from the curious children, they left me alone unless I approached them. Few of the women spoke Thai and the men spoke with more of a Bangkok accent than the heavy and hard to understand Northern dialect—obviously they've learned their Thai in the school house (where the Bangkok dialect is taught, compulsory since various regions cannot understand each others' dialects), rather than through much contact with Thais. Also, their Thai is, in some cases, not even as good as mine, though a few can speak quite well. I saw one vehicle in the village, a Jeep pickup converted, as is common in Thailand, with two benches and a roof into a sort of jitney or small bus.

From a distance I saw some fields, but couldn't make out what they were growing—obviously not rice, which requires bottom-land—probably some poppies. The school was staffed by 3 teachers, all Thais from Chiang Mai who had no ties with the Lisu. The school had posters on the wall teaching the children to give respect and allegiance to the King and Queen, and to brush their teeth properly.

The village had about 30 to 40 houses, all on stilts about 5 feet off the ground in standard Thai fashion. This is very different from the Burmese style, which is to be found in the older buildings of Mae Hong Son (which, I believe, used to be part of Burma), where buildings sit flat on the ground. The old Burmese temples here, for example, rise in layers, like a square multi-layered cube, each level smaller than the lower one, with gingerbread fancy work on the eaves and other fittings, and ending, on top, with a spire or cupola. Navy gray de rigueur. Wood planks run vertically, not horizontally. Tin roofs always. (Thai temples all have tile roofs in a particular pattern of green, red, and yellow, and curlicue fancy work on the eaves rather than Burmese lattice-work.)

The tail-end of the trip was spent among the Shan people (who call themselves Tai-yai) who live around the border of Shan state in Burma.

Some of these people have been there many generations (the border used to be farther east, I believe), but some of them are recent refugees (in the last 10-15 years) from the fighting in Shan state, where they are faced with a hostile Burmese army on one hand and a collection of various political and opium—financed armies on the other.

The Burmese, who look upon the Shan people as inferiors, to be kept in their place and exploited, have been fighting a shifting panoply of revolutionary and mercenary armies since 1958, when Shan tried (as it still tries) to secede from the Union of Burma. (The Kayah state, south of Shan, also tries to secede, but though they have not succeeded either they are less harassed since they're not an opium-growing region.) The other armies, such as the Kuomintang, Communist Party of Burma, etc, control their various territories, collect taxes (mainly off the trade with Thailand, which profitably feeds a strong black market, and from the opium trade: the farmers have little left to give other than forced labor), but the Burmese army just takes over a town, confiscates all livestock and property, and tries to force the unwilling farmers to accept the government's socialist-collectivization plan, which is a tool for robbing the farmers and forcing them into a position of helplessness.

So some of the people have fled and settled in Thailand as refugees, living in remote border areas where conditions are very harsh (walking to one village the footpath was so muddy and tortuous that it took me 30 minutes to go half a mile; there are no facilities, schools, communications, etc, for these people; yet their life here is better than their prospects in Burma).

The one ray of hope in the situation of the Shan people is the Shan State Army, which seems to be, from what I can tell, to be a true people's army, with principles of democracy and freedom, and who are scrupulous in their relations with the people. They refuse to participate in the opium trade, so they are poor and poorly equipped, yet in the 10 or so years since their founding (mostly by disaffected students) they have grown into the second largest revolutionary army. (The CPB, funded by China, is twice their size, at about 15,000 men. The Burmese have 50,000 soldiers in Shan state.)

The refugees I've met (who sometimes return to Shan for visits) generally (but not always) speak well of the SSA, so if they can continue to grow in strength there may be a less than tragic conclusion to the Burmese uprising. Politics—no space left to remark on the appearance of the refugee villages, their social structure, the more settled groups, etc., nor to speak of the Kayah village I visited, which underwent 7 years ago a remarkable mass conversion from Protestant to Buddhist. Only to say I've been collecting medicine from various contacts I have in Thailand, which are passed on to the refugees from Shan state. As bad as the Cambodian situation was they still got some international aid. The Shan get no aid at all. Many have illnesses, including malaria and typhoid. So I'm glad to be able to funnel some medicines their way.

* * *

If you think winter was great, wait until you try a sweet-&-sour stringhopper: guaranteed to draw a fine line between (or is it around?) reality and illusion. Only trouble is, which side is reality?

What do you mean did I get the tail-end of *Bones*? If you mean did I finish writing it the answer is no; if you mean that you mailed me something more, the answer is still no, but with a question: what did you mail, when was it mailed, and where was it mailed to? And does the 'tail-end' suggest that you've mailed a middle-end and/or front-end as well (or would it be tail-middle and tail-beginning?)? Well, I haven't received any of that either, whether or not you've mailed it. That makes it serious. Waylaid by a brown-nosed coprophile (coprophobe?)? Hope not. Bless you and your 'feeble hawkings'. Spit for shit. That about sums up the selling of delusions. I'm especially interested in the negative commentary of readers and form letters which so carefully avoid saying anything in as few innocuous words as possible. So keep them cards and letters comin', folks.

So you woke up one morning laughing and nothing mattered in the slightest? Wunderbar! (But why laugh, then?) Did the woman appear because of, as a *result* of laughing/waking up/nothing mattering in the slightest? Or co-incidentally? Subsequently? Hyperspacially? (Land o' goshen, don't that beat all? Hyperspace would be merely an excuse for hypershit.) But then you say this woman wasn't actually there in the flesh. What *was* she there in? What is allowed now that wasn't before? In short, brother, whatever has or hasn't happened to you is all great and good (it's all perfect, it's all perfect), particularly so if I rightly interpret your statements as meaning that you have seen/do see Dhamma (it's all suffering, it's all suffering), but I'm not sure that that's what you mean.

(Perhaps you're not sure either?) But then again I'm not sure about a lot of things, but I *am* sure that it's time to start a new paragraph.

I'm staying outside of Chiang Mai, about a 1500 feet climb from alms round every morning—does my lungs and sweat glands a world of good, though it's hell on the knees and ankles—in a square but decaying *kuṭi*. The *carika* was very good, found some fine places, including one actually inhabitable, which I may return to, and lots of adventures and experiences ('But what's so great about adventures and experiences?' you may ask; to which I reply, tellingly, 'Well you may ask.') of no use to anybody, and more on the way. Why do I do it? Hell, I haven't even figured out (yet) *how* I do it. In fact, I'm only a shade on the side of thinking that I actually do do it, or at least that it's done (but not over and done; perhaps under and done).

I agree *Something Happened* didn't measure up to *Catch-22* (from an overblown wordiness, trying to tell too much, but not from a lack of trying). *Catch-22* is still, for me, one of the great influences on my life (an adventure and experience both?)

* * *

Still in Thailand, as you can tell, but also still only on the *edge* of Thailand, meaning the visa situation is not yet resolved, though I have some hope of a favorable outcome, since a number of people are helping me. It would seem that *something* has to work. For example, I know the 2nd-in-charge at Immigration, who has agreed to submit my application to the committee with last year's letter. (The problem is that I need a letter from a certain department before Immigration can officially give me a visa and that department has so far refused to give me one, for reasons which are too complicated to explain in a sheaf of aerogrammes, but they gave me a letter *last* year, and it's that letter that my friend in Immigration will use to see if it can slip past the committee which decides on all visa applications.) Also, someone who knows the boss of the man who refuses to give me the letter said he will speak to the boss (who is the Minister of Education)… But… enough of all this…

Bangkok is having its bicentennial celebrations, both of Bangkok as capital and of the Chakri dynasty as kings of Siam. This means that after a few frantic months of attempting to cover two centuries of filth with a coat of white-wash and patches of cement and plaster, there is now a hokey month of festivities, noise, crowds of tourists all trying to figure out what is happening (answer: nothing worth bothering about), and where it's happening (nowhere/everywhere), herds of hustlers all out for the main chance, and more traffic and turmoil and pollution than is normal even for a place like Bangkok, which, you may have gathered, is not my favorite place to be. Later this month the city will experience its annual floods, which submerge parts of the city in inches and sometimes feet of filthy water, so perhaps the parade will all float away like a bad dream (inspired by indigestion, no doubt).

The Thai *baht*, by the way, continues to plummet, and Thai upper-classes continue to seek foreign shelters for their (usually ill-gotten) gains. It may not be long before visas aren't worth very much. Meanwhile, the far-right-wing forces, under a general named Arthit, gather their strength. These are really vicious people, the sort who are quoted in interviews as saying things like 'I am bored with humanitarianism, very bored.' Not exactly the sort of people who would bridge the mammoth gap between Bangkok's very rich and the countryside's very poor (and, because of the encroaching technology of Bangkok, the countryside becomes poorer even without the rapacious rip-offs of the government forces). But then the very rich aren't interested in bridging any gaps in this country, only between themselves and the U.S. (or Australia, England, or whatever, but mostly the U.S.)

No doubt I could continue to struggle on in Thailand with short visa extensions; however, this would tie me up indefinitely in Bangkok, and I've had quite enough of that, so I'm more and more inclined to choose a country where, from all reports, these visa hassles don't exist, and that country looks more and more (for more than this reason) like my old isle of Serendip... Ceylon... Sri Lanka...

To bow out of society in style, this evening I shall be having tea with the family of a princess. English-educated, and though directly descended from King Mongkut—the King of the King and I—yet very remote from the present royal family. Her husband is English. She makes a living as a batik artist. I'll tell her about a man who looked like a fisherman in a Chinese painting: my teacher in Jogjakarta. Perhaps even demonstrate his silence.

* * *

Several glorious months up at Wat Palad, outside Chiang Mai, came to a sad end when my visa contracted what may yet turn out to be a fatal illness, terminal. Red Tape-itis. I'm in the middle of one of those interminal oriental intrigues, this one designed (by the Director of the Department of Religious Affairs) to kick out all foreign Buddhists without anyone who cares knowing about it. Some of us have banded together to try to Do Something about it, but Doing Something in Thailand is a very difficult matter, not at all like in the West, and though we're not defeated, we're rather stymied, after several months of fairly intensive effort, and it seems a possibility (to say the least) that a few of the most expendable of us (of which I'm at the forefront) may have to leave soon enough, the rest to follow in dribs and drabs as the Director, a xenophobe if there ever was one, can manage. It's a very long story, so naturally I consider writing it up. Difficult to start it, though, when it hasn't yet ended.

What is this about a publisher interested in *Bones*? A hell of a thing to mention it and to say no more. Well, say more. Please be less cryptic than usual. I know the world suffers from too much straightforwardness, too much prosaicness, too much detail, too little fancy, etc., but You have a Golden Oppy to add to the mess, and I'm surprised you would pass up the chance to leave your portion on the pile. Please don't keep me posted. The cancelling machines are hard on my fingers. But if you write fairly soon I'll still be in Occupied Palestine, oops, Siam, since I expect to hold out till the end of the year before giving up the visa—the modern equivalent of giving up the ghost—and transmigrating to Nepal, India, Sri Lanka, Sikkim, Bhutan, Bangladesh, or *Tavatiṃsa*.[1]

I always thought a Sooke[2] was *part* of a town; the part where they sold not Buddha bones but Mohamed hairs.

Yours in *falchah* shoveling,

V.

* * *

1. *Tavatiṃsa*: the Buddhist 'heaven'; a blissful, albeit impermanent, place or state of being; highly dangerous as it may sap the will to break through it to liberation, *nibbāna*.—Hūm.
2. A play on the Arabic word *souk* meaning bazaar or marketplace.—Ed.

(Culled from Thailand's English-language press, came the last news from that fabled land, as my legman was about to take up his new Sri Lankan beat. 'Khomeini objects to the bureaucracy because they are competent,' 'We didn't recommend it, we didn't approve it, we simply endorsed it.' 'No one told them what they had done wrong apart from performing official duties.' Former Prime Minister Moraraji Desai, 84, says the young generation should not feel discouraged, because India cannot get worse and the situation can only improve. 'We have kept going downhill for the past 2,000 years and now we have reached rock bottom. There is no way except to go up. So don't feel discouraged,' he told a meeting of his Janata Party youth section in Bombay.—Hūm)

Someone from Radio Thailand came through and asked me to write some 'Five minute pieces on Buddhism'. I bet he's sorry now!

## PEACE THROUGH SIMPLICITY

Can we be at peace? Not only with others but with ourselves? Is it possible? Or must we always make war with ourselves, always separating what we *want* from where we *are*? For a long time now we have been at odds with ourselves, restless and dissatisfied. For a long time now we have filled ourselves with praise and blame, attraction and aversion, love and hate. For a long time now we have found ourselves as if entangled, caught up and not free, and we haven't found any way that didn't lead to new entanglements, new bonds. *New* entanglements? Not really; just variations of the same *old* entanglements and bonds, the ways we've been confined all our lives. So: we haven't *even* found a way that didn't lead to *old* entanglements, *old* bonds. Can we do so now?

Can we do something *new*? Something truly new? Enough of the old: entanglements, loves, hates, dissatisfactions. All of that is just different ways of being filled with ourselves. Perhaps filled with ourselves to do good, perhaps filled with ourselves to do bad, but always full. Can we, instead, be empty? I don't mean empty of everything whatsoever: that's too difficult. Let's just say, can we be empty of ourselves? Everything that's not ourselves can stay: that's not our problem, we don't have to worry about what's not ours. Others can take care of that, or we can take care of it later. So first let's just deal with what *is* ours. And let's try a brand new way of dealing with it, something we may never have tried before. Okay?

Let's make things simple. Do just this. Let's close our eyes and empty our hearts of everything that has to do with 'me' and 'mine'. Nothing more than that. It's that simple. If we see a revolting sights—say, a decaying corpse—we can easily avert our eyes. If we smell a bad smell we cover our noses. There are lots of bad smells around, but when we can avoid them it's certainly more pleasant to do so. If we accidentally touch a hot stove we pull our hand back quickly! So let us turn away from these thoughts of 'me' and 'mine' in the same way, just as if we touched something burning, or smelled something foul, or saw something revolting. Do this right now, please: don't wait. In the next minute you may be dead. Then you will have missed the chance to do something truly new.

Close your eyes. That way it's simpler. Forget about what your ears hear. Pay no attention to smells, tastes, touches. If the wind touches you just let it be a touch. Don't take it to be *my* touch, 'Oh, the wind is touching *me*!' It's just wind touching skin. It's just a perception, just like a rock is just a rock. Don't make it more than that. Let it be simple. Any time you see a complication, watch out! That's a good hiding place for 'me' and 'mine'. 'Me' and 'mine' *love* complications, so if we are to succeed in this new thing we'll have to avoid complications. Wherever there's a complication, that's the old way. Leave it be! If you try to 'do' *anything* with it you'll just make it more complicated! Treat it like you would a tangle of barbed wire. Did you ever try to untangle a bunch of rusty old barbed wire? Hopeless, isn't it? So leave all that aside. It's hopeless, these complications, so let's empty ourselves of it all. We can do that; just let the mind turn away from it, let the mind turn away from *everything* that's the old way, the complicated way, the way of 'me' and 'mine'. Okay?

So... What's left? Is it like we expected or like we didn't expect? If it's like we expected, we've probably made a misjudgment, because what we expected is the old way. Only if it's what we didn't expect can we know that this is, for us, a truly new way, a way we've never before imagined. If it didn't work for you then try it again. Keep trying it until it does work. Keep trying, because there's really nothing else worth doing. Everything else is the old way, the way of dissatisfaction. Maybe even trying is the old way too, but if it works, then it won't be the old way any more, the way of dissatisfaction. Then it will be a new way. So keep trying.

Only one thing to remember; don't be like a man looking for silence. Everywhere he goes there's too much noise for him, and as he goes along he keeps shouting, '*SILENCE!*' at the top of his voice. But he can't find silence anywhere. Don't be like that. But then this man, one day he stops calling for silence, and he hears that it really is *quiet*… everywhere. That silence, that's not what he'd been expecting, is it? He'd always thought that silence had a voice. But it doesn't even have a name. Or if it has a name, it's a name that's not spoken. oR if it is spoken, it is said without echoes.

# PART IV

## Come Back a Long Way

Hindu mythology tells how a wrathful, avenging god set fire to a glittering pleasure city on the island of Ceylon. Today the exquisite island is called Sri Lanka and it is again aflame with violence.

The mythical demon-god of Ceylon kidnapped Lord Rama's wife from India and imprisoned her in what now is Colombo, and history records that on the island Buddhist Sinhalese kings fought Hindu Tamil kings from South India before and after the birth of Christ.

"... Heller presses his point home by telling us (on the same page) that Catch-22 is like the flies that Orr sees in Appleby's eyes.

'Oh, they're there, all right,' Orr had assured [Yossarian]... 'although he probably doesn't even know it. That's why he can't see things as they really are.'

'How come he doesn't know it?' inquired Yossarian.

'Because he's got flies in his eyes,' Orr with exaggerated patience. 'How can he see he's got flies in his eyes if he's got flies in his eyes?'

It made as much sense as anything else...

*Yathābhūtam na pajānāti*: he does not see things as they really are: the phrase—so typical a Sutta description of the *puthujjana*, the unenlightened commoner—is used here by Heller to illuminate precisely the characteristic of being entrapped in a situation. Not only does the *puthujjana* have flies in his eyes, he does not see that he has them, and he does not see this because he has them. His dilemma is that though he must find a way to see, yet he cannot find that way precisely because he cannot see. Indeed, he cannot even see for himself that this is his problem. And this is the dilemma which, at its most fundamental level, is the specific concern of the Buddha's Teaching. The structure of *avijjā*, the structure of *Catch-22*, the structure of 'having flies in one's eyes': they are one and the same. *Catch-22* is *avijjā*. The title character in both the novel and in our lives never appears and yet is omnipresent..."

Sāmaṇera Bodhesako, from *The Buddha and the Catch-22*

Bangkok

It's come down to the crux and so it's the end of the road here in Thailand for me. Next stop: Sri Lanka. Well, it's changed its name and I've changed mine, so we might still have things in common, even if they are uncommon things. However, I've still got a month on my visa, so I'm going to spend this time in the North backwoods country wandering, which is a complex form of walking and sitting. Complex, but not complicated.

This will be the first time I've returned to a country after a long absence (except for the U.S.), so it will be interesting from that point of view to see what changes have gone on there, and how conditions might have to be adapted to. And, of course, I'll be arriving with a rather different set of intellectual baggage—it's a good thing that the airlines don't charge overweight for that!—and be in a very different mind-set than 15 years ago too. (I like the way certain epochs of my life have worked out in round numbers. It makes accountancy so much easier. I *think* this is a gratuitous or accidental feature of my life-script. Act 97, Scene 16 finds us back in…)

3½ years in Thailand. Well, that's not a round number, but that's because Thailand (unlike Sri Lanka) is not a round country, nor is 3½ a whole or rational number, for the same relationship. It's a country fragmented into area vs. area, city vs. country, new vs. old, M16 vs. AK 47, and getting more fragmented. It seems clear that the divisive forces dominate over the cohesive ones, so Thailand, too, will come to the end of its road. Nor is it a rational country, even—I'm sure—by its own definition of 'rationality'. Emotions which cannot be expressed lurk beneath the surface of every relationship, an unseen motivator making situations forever irrational.

But my time there has been of use to me in a number of ways. It's a strong contrast to Sri Lanka, and so gives me a broader perspective of the way I can relate within different systems, a more coherent set of values about what is truly of value to me, and it's given me, until 6 months ago, the space (and time) I needed. Also some more difficult lessons, the one of the past half year perhaps the most trying, and still leaving much to be learned about it.

As for writing, I've mailed the lot off to Sri Lanka, including your conclusion to *Worthy Bones* (which I haven't had a chance yet to go over carefully). I think the book needs to be re-conceived in certain ways. (That's a new one, eh?) The characters need to be more human, less character-ish. The plot needs to be honed down. A lot of extraneous matters needs to go—e.g. Carmen's Israeli experience, a real shift for Jizi, and Mohel has to be less a Batman and more a real person with a problem related, somehow, to the matter at hand. The philosophy must emerge from the story, and not bury the story. And the tone, in the middle chapters, should be lightened up. We'll see what kind of set-up I can arrive at in Sri Lanka, and whether the space I'll be in there includes paper and ink. If so, I'm thinking of a few things—revising *Getting Off*, some short stuff, carrying on with my Dhammapada verses—here's a couple.

326. Once this mind fared as it wished, quite free
to wander where it lusted, as it pleased.
Today I shall restrain it properly,
as the mahout trains the rutting beast.

327. Be watchful of the mind.
For non-remiss aspire.
Rise above the unrefined
like a tusker from the mire.

'That life is worth living is the most necessary of assumptions and, were it not assumed, the most impossible of conclusions'—Santayana

How's the old sod near Sooke?

V.

* * *

Sri Lanka—BEAD

The flight to Sri Lanka was comfortable, a DC-10 half empty so plenty of room, with good Thai Airlines food and service. My first flight on a DC-10, which doesn't compare with a 747 in terms of impressiveness, although—in as much as it got me here—quite adequate. Adequate, too, is the word for Colombo's airport. Not only not air-conditioned, but not even ceiling fans. But Sri Lanka has always been a country that scraped by on frugal standards. Thailand, of course, is given to a sybaritic luxuriousness, and can afford to do so—atleast the Bangkok people can, because they ruthlessly plunder the labor and fruit of the countryside. But in Sri Lanka things seem more equitable. There are beggars, as in Bangkok, and poor people who live in hovels (these are, mostly, Tamils, Sri Lanka's oppressed minority); but not teeming hordes of them as in the squalid Bangkok slums and hungry countryfolk. Therefore Sri Lanka doesn't have the wealth (and perhaps not even the inclination) to indulge in the sensual crossness of Bangkok-style living.

Not that there haven't been changes. Many more cars (though Mercedes', etc., are still rare, not commonplace as in Bangkok, and many well-maintained old cars still ply the roads). Streets widened. TV arrived about 2 years ago, and the well-off all have color sets now. Such changes are found; but underlying it all is a sameness that is surprising: like a dowager aunt who has always had two biscuits at teatime, she is not going to change her habits in old age, nor even consider refurbishing all the somewhat tatty or shabby remnants of her old life just for the sake of appearances (as Bangkok has just done for its bicentennial). And, of course, the place is green. Unlike the brown of Thailand here there are palm trees in profusion, pleasant—perceptible even from the plane (which, by the way, took 15 minutes to fly over the entire island—distances that 12 years ago took me 15 days padding barefoot).

In company with the owner of a rubber estate, I took a trip about 36 miles south of Colombo to his place, and remarked on the stability of the country-side. He repeated the fact that other parts of the country had been much developed while this corner remained ignored—sounded promising—and ominous. I've also visited old acquaintances in Kandy and have taken the first steps towards finding a suitable place to stay in the upcountry. Kandy, having been a pleasant small town, with some sense of itself in style and history, showed more signs of 'development' than Colombo: construction despoils nearly every hillside, save the tall mountain to the Southwest. I went to the clearing where my old *kuṭi* used to stand, but the clearing had been replanted in pine and was so overgrown with dense stands of elephant grass that I couldn't even force my way to the old site to see if, perhaps, a wall might not yet stand... So much (or so little) swept away by time, the earth overgrowing our traces. A breath of relief, somehow...

As for mother... what can I say that I haven't said (and thought) so many times before? It grieves me that she should be in such a state; I'm only relieved that she has you to look after her, for no one else—let alone hospital staff—could do so with such love and care and attentiveness to what is needed.

* * *

Somehow I have the feeling I've been here before. I keep trying to analyze what it can be that gives me that feeling—maybe it *is* the string-hoppers, maybe it *isn't* the way I sweep up leaves—but the only result is that I suspect the feeling arises from trying to analyze it, and that if I stopped trying to figure out why I feel that way I'd stop feeling that way. But what would there be to do instead? Write indolent letters to exdolent friends, no doubt.

It's definitely a change for the better. Thailand has such a rigid hierarchical social structure, so unyielding, and so hostile to any with the temerity to not accept their proper place, let alone to not accept *any* place, and on the other hand so rewarding, materially, to those who do (I speak of *farangs*[1]—certainly the poor rice farmers get no rewards for being rice farmers)—for a loner like myself it was difficult in extremist, and that's why, of course, the twits gave me the old heave ho. Others may follow, but I was clearly the worst example of a bad lot—'the worst of hippies', as one writer styled me in a widely circulated Buddhist journal. I would have preferred 'the worst of late-blooming beatniks', myself, but we have to accept what we can get, these days, and be duly grateful.

Anyhoo, ol' S.L. is a breath of fresh, if rather damp, air, after the stifling mentality of Thailand (not to mention the pollution), and a green and beautiful place still, showing unfortunate signs of a disease called progress, but not yet infecting the whole of it, and there are a few odd corners left where an odd person can tuck himself away, and so, after completing the bureaucratic business of Colombo, I now find myself, or perhaps lose myself, in Upcountry, walking beneath cloudy skies down little-traveled roads, all of which feel like I've been here before. I feel like I've written this before. Or perhaps it's you who has written this before and I've read/not read it before—it's getting harder to tell who's to blame for what, these days, both of us shaping the same Carmen

1. *farang* (Thai) Westerner.—Ed.

Vipāka.[1] (I re-read W.B. before leaving Colombo, and must admit that it was funnier to write than to read. Still, it did evoke some smiles, one or two chuckles, and assorted wheezes and snorts. But yes, the thing is open to just about any potshot, fair or foul, one might care to heave at it, and it don't mean a thing 'cause it ain't got no swing—the shots, that is, not the book—but there too much, plotwise, to swallow easily, and possibly not enough, characterwise, to chew on. I say it what wrote it, or atleast what partly rewrote it, so it's said with some affection and love, and if a publisher says just the same without affection and love, that's his bag, but the mss. can be made into something, there's enough good stuff to be molded fairer and finer, amen.)

And you?

The Once and Future Present

V.

* * *

I left hot and humid Colombo for the cool, dry upcountry, but found Kandy, on the wet side of the hills, not so dry, so, after a few days poking around old haunts, took the train to the Eastern Part, to a town called Bandarawela. There I visited an old friend—a German monk—he was in Kandy when I lived there and helped in building my *kuṭi*. Unfortunately, about 2 years ago he developed poly-arthritis and since then has had a lot of difficulties, particularly since he's an active sort who previously lived alone in very remote areas. Now he's looking for someplace less remote. I may have found a place for him, actually, on one of my outings: in a small town called Ella, on the edge of Upcountry, where there is a view down to the plains 3000 feet below, a sweeping panorama, I found a small cottage empty, not far from town, on the edge of a tea estate on one side, rice fields on the other, a pine forest behind it, with water close by, and some land prepared for planting. A fine spot; if it's not too noisy—and that can only be known by living there for a while. I told him of it and he'll go to see it and decide. If he doesn't want it I might take it myself.

On another trip I went to see a place called Werakangama but missed

1. The name of the Israeli heroine of *Worthy Bones* is a pun on the Pāli *kamma vipāka*: 'ripening of karma'.—Hūm.

the way and wound up walking on a steep uphill path four miles and came, quite unexpectedly, to an enormous waterfall—790 feet high, according to a small and ancient signpost—which was in fine wild country just below the tea line. I've told Sinhalese about it but none of them (except those living in the area) seem to have even heard of it. Several of Sri Lanka's famous falls are much shorter. And then a local lad, as evening was approaching, invited me to stay in a bungalow. This usually means a well-made house, but I assumed he meant an ordinary shelter, but no, he led me to a fine brick house with glass windows—uncommon in the tropics, where shutters are usually considered sufficient—and a large stone fireplace and skylights in every room—including one door with a sign on it reading 'SILENCE—COURTLMARTIAL SITTING' which opened into a room with a Western-style sit-down toilet and shower fitted with a water heater. All abandoned years ago. Why, I couldn't learn, but because of the sign speculated that it might have been some Brit's retirement home, perhaps military, since all the doors had 7 feet clearance and were nearly wide enough for 2-abreast, perhaps someone loved Ceylon but was damned tired of always knocking his head on low doorways that had to be squeezed through and wasn't going to have that in his retirement home, which had a lovely view of the falls.

* * *

Well, I've moved in—for how long remains to be unseen—to the cottage I told you about, near the town of Ella, about 8 miles from Bandarawela. My German monk friend didn't want to stay here, preferring to be away from roads and RR tracks. He's found a place he likes about 3 miles away and will build something that suits him, which will probably take him 3 months. Some workmen have been here doing various work; clearing the yard, digging a hole for the pond, repairing the porch and the stone parapet walls.

Ella, as I described briefly in my last letter, is on the eastern edge of Upcountry, 3400 feet high, and there is a gap leading down to the lowland, which offers a fine view; also a large rock, certainly over 1000 feet high, with a eucalyptus forest on its side and top and a cave halfway up where, I'm told, Rohanna took refuge when his kingdom was conquered. Rohanna was the first of the great pre-Sinhalese kings, some 3 thousand years ago. The cottage looks out on this rock, and is bordered by rice-paddy below and to the right, a pine forest to the right and behind, tea on the left, and partly-wooded hills in front.

By co-incidence the manager of the estate (tea)—a Burgher—is a client of a Colombo man I know, and he has proven helpful in some ways. I occupy about an acre of hillside, not all at once, but such is life. A water channel from the tea above has been tapped and now there is a small 5 feet high waterfall going into the pond, and a tiny river running past my front door, over which the workmen have built a tiny stone bridge, for, presumably, a tiny Buddhist monk to cross on.

I'm about 150-200 yards back of a secondary road with little traffic but some noise, and at least double that distance from the RR tracks behind, from which comes at regular intervals a muted rumble. The tracks go around a hill, making a complete U-turn, west to east to west, before turning north for Badulla, the end of the line, about 12 miles up.

From the cottage the prospect sweeps over hills upon hills, dotted with dwellings here and there and several tea factories—large two-and-three story structures; they're all built on the same general plan, all have many small-paned windows, and all are painted white.

Very few mosquitos or other noxious pests here. The children can be pests (though are not noxious), but the first time they came I put them to work sweeping and clearing and they've tended to stay away since then.

Today a centipede fell from the ceiling to the ground only a few inches from where I sat, and proceeded to scurry onto my lap. I shook him away and he hid in the bedding, which I had to dismantle to find him and remove him. I'm told this chap has a very painful (though not fatal) bite, but I have some native oil that works amazingly well against poisonous bites. But such incidents are to be expected from time to time, as, in LA, close calls on the freeways are to be expected from time to time. Preferably while you're not eating, however, which I was.

Ella, by the way, seems to be perhaps the only place in Sri Lanka where they don't load up their food with enormous quantities of chilies. Also lots of vegetables are grown around here (some of the paddy field below is used for vegetables), so my diet suits me. But it's still uncertain how long I'll stay in this particular cottage—I too am not overly fond of trains, traffic, and neighbors (the nearest house is about 60 yards off) whose radios blare with Sinhalese music.

What do I know about President Jayawardene? Only that he's held in very high regard in Sri Lanka and considered their equivalent of, say, a Sadat or Nehru. I met his son once in Thailand, a very quiet and well-mannered boy about 20, but haven't felt inclined to contact him. Jayawardene is up for re-election next year. Since even the anti-government papers seem to keep hands off him I assume he will be re-elected. Obviously, he's not in it for the money. I don't know how much political power he has, if any, but I believe the position is more of a moral than political significance, as is India's presidency, for example, where the P.M.—Mrs. Gandhi—has great power and the president—J.M. Reddy until he died recently, don't know who's replaced him—has great respect. A reasonable division of the spoils.

* * *

Greetings from the edge. Restoration work continues, at about the same speed as demolition work. Unraveling stringhoppers and then raveling them up again. (Ravioli?) Good exercise for my amusing muse, whoever she be. (What *is* the Greek for this?) But which part is the restoration and which the demolition leaves me puzzled.

Things are here as always, changeless change, a bit for the better a bit for the worse, a bit closer to the grave, nothing dramatic to tell of—certainly no bullet holes through stump windows as you report. Nature's way of telling you…—except the excitement generated by the slow cultivation of boredom coupled with a gradual distaste for everything the world has to offer and some of the things it doesn't. The writing of this letter, for instance, is an Event in my life that I shall remember, review—oh, I could have said it *that* way, ever so much more clever, and I should have mentioned such and such, etc.—as I have anticipated and savored the prospect these last several months. TODAY'S THE DAY! Hi, Hum. Ho, hum. Something to DO. Contact (Roger Wilco) with another person. Well, it's not as great as I describe it, really. It has its mundane moments, such as the mundane boredom of studying Sinhalese—and such low-level low-count low-down kind of boredom if ever there was one—and such as the sensual high of food every day, but there's disadvantages to every profession, as well as every antifession.

As a bullet found its way inside your stump and plugged Mirotchka's sunflower painting, have you considered hanging it on the outside instead of over your bed? Over the bed sounds like a very tough shot, even for a great billiards player. Outdoors the flowers may get enough sun, air, and bullet holes to germinate.

Well, I'd love to write more now, but my muse, my very own moose, is calling me, so I think I'll go out on the porch now and be bored some more. Ah, Wilderness!

V.

* * *

The weather this month has been very hot and very dry, but the porch is cool and picks up cool breezes, off Ella Rock, I assume, which I plan to climb in the next couple weeks. Better do it now before the forest on top of it gets burnt to the ground—there have already been two fires up there (set by farmers burning off land—and a few trees—to grow crops), as well as several fires in the nearby pine forest. The philosophy around here seems to be, if you see a tree, burn it.

This cottage is curiously cool. Other tin-roofed houses I've lived in have been, in the hot season, unbearably hot at midday, but this one is cooler inside than out. Partly because it has a high roof, but that seems an inadequate explanation. It's dry enough so that in the afternoon my water trickle dries up and the level of the pond sinks down until, after sunset, the water starts to flow again. A minor inconvenience to me, but more serious to the farmer below, who isn't getting enough water to irrigate his paddy. (Even if I took no water he still wouldn't get nearly enough.) People say the NE monsoon is due to start this month. (The SW monsoon, just finished, affects this part of the island only in clouds and wind, not in rain.) We'll see what that brings. Nights have been noticeably cooler the last few days—if we can call night day.

So much fruit around, I'm on a high-fruit diet. Bananas, papayas, avocados, some citrus, lots of fruits I can't even name. Plus rice, bread, roti, and various vegetables—carrots, lettuce, and tomato salad the most easily identifiable. Lots of lentils. Some coconut. I keep discovering more stuff growing on this acre of land. 4 avocado trees. 2 naval orange trees. A lime tree. A coffee bush with nearly-ripe berries. (Coffee is very highly taxed on import, so it's definitely a luxury item, yet, until 100 years ago, Ceylon grew much of the world's coffee, no tea, and then blight and insects and planters' skepticism about their seriousness wiped out the coffee, and tea was planted as a substitute crop. Nowadays cautious attempts are made to re-introduce coffee, but with mixed results.) Anyway, I shall certainly make use of these coffee beans. Not that I'm such a coffee lover, but I love to use what's here. Along with what grows wild I have my usual failing flower garden. Main crop seems to be clover and some onions sprouted from old ones I tossed away last month. I wait for the jack fruit to ripen.

Two crows come to eat my left-overs, and are becoming less and less afraid of me. (Curiously, both of them are named Charlie.) Recently their 3 fledglings learned to fly and now appear here: they stand in front of a pile of (say) rice and caw and caw, demanding to be fed. They feel, apparently, that the world should be so arranged that they need only open their mouths and they will be fed. (We Buddhist monks *close* our mouths and get fed.) Their parents (Charlie & Charlie) sometimes feed them and sometimes ignore them. When ignored long enough they finally peck disconsolately at the food, complaining bitterly all the while at the injustice of it all.

Last night as I was standing outside looking at the moon (full tomorrow) a rabbit dashed past, not 5 feet from me. This is the biggest wildlife I've seen around here. He lives, no doubt, in the tea bushes, where small creatures can survive, and was on his way downhill to try his luck in the rice paddy, now all transplanted. The farmers are working their vegetables, spending most of the day watering. I should think they would have, by now, evolved a system to lift the water from the stream to the fields (a vertical distance of under 15 feet), rather than hauling it by hand in buckets. I've been tinkering with some Rube Goldberg designs using simple materials—bamboo for piping, etc.—that could ease their work considerably. Assuming, of course, it doesn't lead to quarrels over water rights, and presto! the modern world. Sometimes technology can have a devastating effect on cultural mores, as in the U.S., for instance, and in these utters it's best to proceed carefully.

* * *

Why the country calls itself *Sri* Lanka, I don't know. The Sinhalese alphabet has separate letters for an 'S' sound and as aspirated 'S' (also for B and aspirated B, P and PH, etc.), as do many Asian (Sanskrit based) languages. An aspirated 'S' is often transliterated as 'SH' (though the H is softer than in, say, 'should'—it is really a puff of air rather than a hard sound). Those who changed the English name from Ceylon to correspond more closely with the name the Sinhalese have always used for the country chose to transliterate it as Sri, but a case could be made for Srhi and, in other instances, is often used.

Climbed Ella Rock. 6 hour round trip. Good view. Bad day. Rain. Lightning crashing below, clouds doing weird dances as they hit the hot air of the plains just east of the Rock. Could see my cottage, a small dot identifiable by its location beside the pine forest. The climb wasn't hard, just long, up the backside (to go up the front-side—viewed from the cottage—one would have to be a skilled mountaineer, as it's partly very steep and partly precipitous.)

Getting ready for the rains. We've had a taste of it, but the monsoon sets in for real mid-October. Store of firewood in. Managed to obtain a sheet of corrugated plastic and now have a skylight, so I can batten darn when necessary and still have plenty of light. When it rains hard the pond turns muddy, so there is now a piece of bamboo across the roof to catch rain-water (the green bamboo hereabouts is quite large, 10-12 inches in circumference, and can grow 30 feet or more, though I need only 15 feet) and also a 55 gallon drum set up beside the porch to catch it in (lined with plastic to keep it clear).

Inside: A wooden table and straight-back chair. An armchair called, I'm told, a G.O.H. chair since it is the model used in the Grand Oriental Hotel. A sort of swing designed by myself—a length of cloth, poles at top and bottom, and four ropes to support each end of each pole—the most comfortable chair of all, and it rolls up and can be put in a corner when not in use. Some bamboo shelves I've built. And a bed of grass and pine needles. Nice smelling. I add fresh needles every week or so, and it gradually gets higher, but a long way from being too high.

A clover that grows wild everywhere here is not only edible but quite tastey lemony and sweet. A low-growing leafy plant called *gotukole* in Sinhalese (it was common in Thailand also, where it's called *baaybabaw*, but I don't know the English)—makes a good tea as well as a salad ingredient. The daily salad I make of these, plus tomatoes and onions, is not only delicious but healthy.

I'm also working on *The Track of Truth*—not on the translations so much as the notes, which will be at least double the size of the verses. They will consist of relevant extracts from related texts, my own commentary, and extracts from relevant contemporary writers. As not all this material is at hand, I must make many detours, working around what I cannot work through, and shall later have to do much backtracking, at a considerable loss of time, and perhaps some loss of accuracy. Frustrating; though the method, it seems, of every madness.

* * *

No doubt some magazines had articles about Bangkok's hokey 200th anniversary—hokey because there are a lot of ways of counting, and they chose this one simply for the sake of the publicity and tourist bucks. Last March, I think it was, I met a husband-wife team on a photo assignment for Town and Country magazine—he was gay and she was lesbian, so I guess they were a perfect match; they should get it about right.

Sri Lanka had an election about 10 days ago—no doubt you've heard more about it than I have, since I didn't inquire about the results and nobody bothered to tell me. There were a lot of fireworks the next day, so I gathered that somebody did win it, but remained in doubt until recently I went to Kolatenna to visit some friends and, passing through Bandarawela, saw much green bunting in evidence. Since green is the UNP color I suppose they were re-elected, and that would be the first time since independence that any government has been returned to office. Nominally they would be classed as the right-wing party, so no doubt Reagan & Co. expressed their pleasure; but the truth is that that division is unrealistic; it's really a matter of Sri Lanka's two most powerful families pitted against each other, and ideological stances are strictly secondary, a matter of convenience rather than conviction. I don't read the papers because Sri Lanka's papers are too dull for words, all Tea Board quotations and mundane provincial news, lacking balance, depth, or relevancy. Foreign reportage is equally ill-balanced, since the mentality is so provincial that they can't distinguish the trivial from the momentous. But the less I hear of it the more trivial it sounds when I do. The last paper I saw was in August, and I doubt anything much has happened since then—the football strike in the States was the international ordeal that day. (Last year, in Chiang Mai, I read Paper Lion, which I enjoyed in spite of its thinness.)

A brush with death can have markedly different effects on different people, you're right. Few, it seems, even after that, see the necessity of coming to grips with the fact of mortality, but rather something one's glad is behind one (which it isn't) and best forgotten about (which it isn't).

I'm pained that I'm unable to do anything as regards mother; but, pained or not, there seems little that can be done. You can know, at least, that which can be done you are doing.

* * *

The boxes of books arrived with newspaper packing—the LA News—which I read with some interest. I was impressed by the ads for fat people and for alcoholics—i.e. by the number of such ads—and by the ad for peppermint-scented hula hoops (a marital aid, possibly?). Puzzled by a letter to the editor expressing gratitude that the U.S. was a capitalist country, except for Santa Monica. What does this mean? Passed the papers on to some villagers, who have yet to comment on them.

On the way to Colombo recently, while stopping to eat, I drank some orange juice, which had a bit of a seed—I suppose it was—with a sharp edge that cut the inside of my throat. It only caused an annoying tickle, but then it got infected, so before returning to Ella I saw an MD in Colombo about it. Yes, he told me, my throat was red and my tonsils were swollen. Doctor, I told him, my tonsils were removed when I was a child. He had no comment to make, and gave me a prescription for tetracycline, which I took to the dispensary, where they gave me ampicillin instead. I was asked by neither doctor nor pharmacist if I had any allergies, etc. In any case, I took the ampicillin and am now recovered—with problematical thanks to the medical establishment. Another medical misfortune: we now seem to have entered into the season for a certain kind of caterpillar with thick tufts of black hairy fibers all over it. One fell on my head as I slept, waking me. I tried to brush it off, thinking it was just another cricket, which I get plenty of, but as soon as I touched it I knew it was no cricket. One day of intense itching, and about 3 more days of gradually diminishing itching. And then, a few days later, another one got in and got me on the arm. The best medicine I've found so far is preventive: a thorough wall-check before going to sleep each night—they, apparently, like to climb walls—though don't seem to be very good at it as they keep falling off.

This isn't only the caterpillar season—also swarms of small yellow butterflies, invariably flying southward. They haven't far to go before reaching the Indian Ocean and the next landfall (unless it's some secret butterfly island) would be Antarctica, so presumably the southern coast is now suffering from an infestation of butterflies and—unless they fly back at some later date—the north of the country will eventually be totally devoid of this species. Another of life's minor mysteries.

In the paddy fields they are now finishing transplanting rice shoots from the seed beds to the prepared fields, which is where I came in 6 months ago; but it's been a good show, so I'll sit through it again.

I can tell how hot it is by how melted my jar of coconut oil is. It solidifies every night, and on a warm day it will be cloudy liquid and on a hot day (or if I put it in the sun) it will become more and more clear. Today, it's liquid but very cloudy. But the solar heating system works well: a black plastic sheet covering a plastic bucket of water. Three hours in the sunshine and it's as hot as you would want it for bathing. On cloudy days I heat a kettleful on the fire. The rain barrel is empty, so I have to boil drinking water now.

Yes, as the Fiddler on the Roof said, 'If the rich could hire someone to die for them' they probably would. But they can't. Nobody can. This is morbid? Or the way it is? Morbid to me is the refusal to face this fact, and to morbidly insist upon living life as though it were eternal (except for those who have the bad taste and lack of discretion to die).

But who am I to convince you?

* * *

So Vanity Fair is back in bizness, eh? Enjoyed the Marquez piece even more than '100 Years of Boredom'—much more to the point and less 'diffuse, despite the horror-drawings. Looks like a high-class spread, some competition for the New Yorker.

Your WHAT[1] (me worry?) is obviously in a class of its own, without competition.

In the ethnic riot department competition is fierce on a worldwide scale, and Sri Lanka has little chance of carving out more than a minor niche for itself; but this is provincialism if anything is—in *that* department Sri Lanka stands high above every place I've ever seen, as the most non-significant country to care deeply and intensely what everyone

1. William Head Amateur Theatre—a long narrative poem of mine about a night out at a prison production of MacBeth.—Hūm.

is saying about it (nothing at all, usually)—and so there is a feeling of mixed dismay and pride that for a few days, at least and at last, they were able to get some play in Europe and U.S. rags. They believe, like Nixon, that the press is kicking them around; on the other hand being ignored totally—the usual case—is hardly an improvement. Ella, however, was unaffected save for the razing of one Tamil—owned tourist lodge, which sent the tourists fleeing in their nightclothes through the tea bushes. Nearby towns—Bandarawela, Badulla—were among the most seriously affected.

For reasons entirely unrelated to the riots, I must move. A site about ½ mile away has been tentatively selected, and provided the villagers get it together, work should start soon. I will be surprised indeed if I'm out of here before the end of the year, but early next year seems a reasonable bet, I thus will involuntarily maintain my record of never (in adult life) managing to stay in one dwelling for as long as 2 years. I'd be perfectly content to stay here—the owner wants the land back to build a house—and hope that with the next move I will live long enough (and that, in one place) to break this pattern. The move will put me several steps closer to the edge that I generally live on. (I may name the new *kuṭi* 'The Center for the Study of Peripheries'.) Like you, I'll have a river below me, but in my case it will be about 500 feet below, so fetching water would be a difficult task.

Meanwhile, I design an ever-increasing number of *kuṭis* only one of which (at most) will become reality. Higher than actuality stands possibility.

V.

* * *

I'm sure it's been a much more trying time for you than you say. I hope by now some of the emptiness has been worked through. Though, perhaps, it's never really, until or unless we see the source of it. As life goes mother had many good and full years; the end could have been longer and more painful than it was. You did all that could be done all these difficult years; at a not inconsiderable cost to your own well-being. Though I'm sure you don't see it that way; 'one does for one's own', as you say. Still, as you should accept the appreciation of your children, you should allow yourself some satisfaction in the knowledge that you gave what you could with such love and devotion. I wish I could say the same for myself so confidently. I hope, as time passes, you will tell me whatever is comfortable to tell. For my part, I am dealing with it by doing what I have been doing: trying to see the source of that emptiness. I believe there is nothing better I can do to honor my mother. Even from this great distance know that I share in all you are feeling.

love,

Bob

* * *

The most immediately obvious (though hardly the most profound) similarity between the Teaching and the novel is that both are deeply concerned with man's mortality. "Old age, sickness, and death" is a phrase that occurs repeatedly in the Buddha's Teaching, as recorded in the Pāli Suttas (and, indeed, throughout the later Sanskrit, Chinese, and Tibetan texts as well). A citation of even a small portion of such textual references[1] would be far beyond the scope of this brief discussion: the fact of man's mortality—a constant peril in an inconstant world—is a perception absolutely fundamental to the perspective of life presented by the Buddha's Teaching.

And in *Catch-22* the protagonist, Yossarian (a bombardier in World War II), is no less deeply concerned about old age, sickness, and death. The specter of their imminence is his constant dread. As his friend Dunbar puts it,

"Do you know how long a year takes when it's going away? This long." He snapped his fingers. "A second ago you were stepping into college with your lungs full of fresh air. Today you're an old man."
"Old?" asked Clevinger with surprise. "What are you talking about?"

..."You're inches away from death every time you go on a mission. How much older can you be at your age?"—pp. 38-9

As for sickness:

---

1. E.g.: As the herdsman drives his kine
with a stick to pasture-land,
thus decay and health's decline
drive out the life of man
Dhp. 135

Yossarian had so many ailments to be afraid of that he was sometimes tempted to turn himself in to the hospital for good and spend the rest of his life stretched out there inside an oxygen tent with a battery of specialists and nurses seated at one side of his bed twenty-four hours a day waiting for something to go wrong... Aneurisms, for instance; how else could they ever defend him in time against an aneurism of the aorta? ... He wondered often how he would ever recognize the first chill, flush, twinge, ache, belch, sneeze, stain, lethargy, vocal slip, lose of balance or lapse of memory that would signal the inevitable beginning of the inevitable end.—pp. 171-2

But even more than old age and sickness, it is the specter of death itself that haunts both Yossarian and the novel: "At night when he was trying to sleep, Yossarian would call the roll of all the men, women and children he had ever known who were now dead. He tried to remember all the soldiers, and he resurrected images of all the elderly people he had known when a child..."—p. 339. Yossarian is enmeshed in a killing war which is (as the novel's disclaimer makes clear) representative of a larger framework,[1] a war to which "there was no end in sight. The only end in sight was Yossarian's own"—p. 16. Nevertheless, Yossarian "had decided to live forever or die in the attempt, and his only mission each time he went up was to come down alive"—p. 29. Yossarian feels death hovering about him—indeed, even living with him, in the form of a dead man named Mudd, who was not easy to live with.

However, old age, sickness, and death are not apprehended merely as *things*, as objects in a world of objects, in themselves neutral. The fact of death changes Yossarian's world, as it does ours, radically, and Heller's insistence upon this point is the beginning of the novel's profundity.

In a world in which death is an unavoidable presence, "it made sense to cry out in pain every night"—p. 54. Indeed, the disorder that the awareness of death introduces into a world which, throughout

1. Perhaps it would be going too far to discover in this lager framework a reference to the Buddha's recognition of *saṃsāra*, the round of deaths and rebirths; but it cannot be excessive to relate the facts of birth and death to the minute and Learical apocalypse achieved in the vision of Snowden's death: "Man was matter, that was Snowden's secret. ... Ripeness was all."—pp. 429-30

our lives, we are forever trying to order, leaves us with neither simple order nor simple disorder, but rather with "a world boiling in chaos in which everything was in proper orders"—p. 143. Death, the great modifier, alters everything, so that for Yossarian "nothing warped seemed any more in his strange, distorted surroundings"—p. 402.

It is this strange distortion that is the keystone of the novel's humor—not merely that of its many throwaway jokes but also of the tragicomic perception which circles round and round the death of Snowden ("Where are the Snowdens of yesteryear?"—p. 35: what a poignant joker), drawing ever closer, while at the same time mockingly inverting that trivial sensibility which ordinary men use to deny the disorder of death: "the Texan turned out to be good-natured, generous and likable. In three days no one could stand him"—p. 9; "Nately had a bad start. He came from a good family"—p. 12; "Yossarian couldn't be happy, even though the Texan didn't want him to be"—p. 16; "strangers he didn't know shot at him with cannons every time he flew up into the air to drop bombs on them, and it wasn't funny at all. And if that wasn't funny, there were lots of things that weren't even funnier"—p. 17. But it is not merely the one-liners that are inversions of everyday logic: that everyday sensibility is twisted into various shapes, so that each character is seen to exist in his own uniquely topsy-turvy world, a world whose shape hovers somewhere between a wry smile and a teardrop.

Sāmaṇera Bodhesako, from *The Buddha and the Catch-22*

* * *

We're getting a sprinkle of rain just now—7:30 PM—which happens to be full moon. This is the first rain we've had since February, though it has yet to build into anything deserving to be called that, and of course no single rain could be adequate, for the fields are parched and cracked, and the rice shoots have been slowly dying back. But if the drought—which is nationwide—can be broken at least a part of the crop can be saved (due for harvesting in about a month), and of course without adequate rain no new crop could be planted. Neither do the cows have pasturage. Needless to say, it's been very hot. The town's reservoir ran dry about a week ago—up till then the taps can only an hour or so per day, gradually diminishing—and now everyone takes their laundry to any of several wells that are to be found in the forest, and carries water back for cooking.

In this respect I'm very fortunate, for although the small reservoir from which I get my water (it is not the town's reservoir, which is up the hill, but feeds a single paddy field in front of me)—although it is running low, it is nevertheless running, and my pond remains full (there are beautiful blue and gold water lilies in it now), except when I water my garden, which takes about 1/3 of it. My pond used to contain a frog I called Friendly Freddie, because he got so used to my dippings that he accepted me, and even allowed me to stroke his back as he floated (though not to pick him up); but he disappeared about a week ago and a few days later I noticed that the pond had a new watersnake in it. He hides in a little grotto, but he seems less fearful of me gradually; he likes to bask with his head on a rock and his body in the water. I saw him dart from his grotto once and snap up a grasshopper who was having a swim (doing a sort of crawl, not quite dog-paddle), and I assume that any snake that eats grasshoppers can't be poisonous, though the theory has not been tested. But as you know I've had many close encounters with snakes (of the 2nd kind, and something 2½th kind), so he doesn't worry me, though I admit Freddie was the preferable neighbor.

The snake, however, is preferable to some: there's been a spate of petty thievery, which has now (I hope) ended. A trap was laid and three kids—teenagers—were caught. They live near the RR tracks (which side I can only surmise), where there are about a dozen families squatting on government land. The police gave the kids a warning (I had already given some general warnings myself), and in Sri Lanka, unlike Thailand, they treat petty theft quite seriously—if it had gone to court they could have gotten 6 month sentences—so now it has stopped. I really didn't mind the stealing so much—it was petty enough: fruit, soap, and little things that could be easily replaced—as the vandalism that was accompanying it (tearing down the fence I'd built to discourage the cows from helping themselves to the garden); and if they'd been content with just taking what they did I would have done nothing.

My garden hasn't been invaded by cows but by termites, who eat the manure that has been mixed into the soil, and thereby kill the plants the manure was supposed to fertilize. Termites, in Sri Lanka, are called 'white ants', so you might say I've got ants in my plants.

My neighbor, Mr. Henry, who owns the Sutherland estate, spoke of the film 'Gandhi' the other day (have you seen it?)—he had seen some poobah or other on TV (since the start of this year TV is broadcast island-wide, as it has been in Colombo for 4 years past, with programs from 6-10 PM alternating between English, Sinhala, and Tamil—one channel) holding forth about it and seemed enthusiastic to see it. However, Mr. H is not very successful at managing his estate and will probably lose it before 'Gandhi' ever gets to Colombo, in which case he would probably migrate to Australia (not only to see the film). He keeps getting his workers angry with him, and production is down. His is the only privately-owned estate left in the area, aside from a few small holdings (he has 140 acres), so that also puts him in a difficult position, for the government-owned estates (taken over during Mrs. Bandaranaike's reign) are doing things for the workers—new housing, bonuses, etc.—that he can no longer afford to do, compounding his problem. Too bad; his great grandfather pioneered the estate when this country was still thick jungle.

Some people, it seems, like to get things arranged the way they want them and are then content to leave them there, or to try to do so (things *don't* always stay put) while others prefer to keep things in more or less continual motion, a sort of juggling act, and are content when things don't stay put (but this is both exhausting and endless). You might think that I am of this sort, but actually not. I would be quite content to arrange things the way I want them—that's the hard part—and then stay put ('Things', of course, doesn't mean just physical things.) That's what I've been trying to do since 5 years ago. I would have been content to stay in Thailand, but the visa hassle got to be too much, and now I will be even more content to stay in Sri Lanka (a country much more to my liking than Thailand ever was), and in Ella (which is a nice place, offering hospitable people, suitable climate, enough elbow room, and a stable situation; people say the place hasn't changed much in the last 25 years and, aside from an increase in the number of tourist guest houses—there are 6 now—will not likely change much in the future), and even in this cottage. Unfortunately, for this last point, the landlord is now making moves that will make me make moves. Nothing has been said directly, but the unmistakable message is that he would like his land (and his house) back. I am not being pushed out precipitously, but need to look around. So in the next few weeks I will look around—first in the vicinity—for another place to put myself. On the other hand, before selecting I might as well see more of the selection, so my look farther afield. In any case, I intend to make long-term arrangements at my next stop.

Two weeks ago was the annual Sinhalese New Years celebration, but the last couple days, judging from the crackers, shooting, and goings-on, sounded like a repeat performance.

Today I have learned that it is the custom to celebrate a girl's first menstruation—'coming of age', it's called—and that's why my Tamil neighbors are having the two-day shindig, loudspeakers blaring music that sounds to me like Bob Dylan must sound to you. But this is the only disturbance they've made in the year that I've been here (363 days today) and even if speaking about it would do any good (which it wouldn't) I wouldn't do so, for they've been good neighbors. Asian people in general are more polite-spoken than Westerners, but Tamils seem to carry this to an extreme. It is common for them, when speaking to Westerners to use terms of extreme respect—'Master', being a common one—but recently one Tamil visitor (he wanted me to help him prepare for an exam in management, which he was studying in English medium) went perhaps as far as one can go in this direction by persisting in calling me 'god'. 'Please don't call me god,' I asked him. 'Yes, god' he replied. Maybe he was hoping for more help than I could give him.

On books, as it were, I'm looking for a gardening book. One for someone who knows nothing, has no equipment, and grows on poor soil in tropical highlands. No doubt no such book exists—like all the necessary ones. Available locally are mainly travel guides-cum-pop philosophy, *In the Footsteps of the Buddha*, and other such titles, which aren't for growing a thing. After interminable niggling and hemming and hawing, by the way, the Buddhist Publication Society in Kandy has agreed to publish a long essay of mine *The Buddha and Catch-22*, more or less as I wrote it. It will be out sometime next year. Not a guide to grow anything either.

* * *

(Late '83 I started a 'Peace Run' from British Columbia to Southern California; knees—40 year old knees—and logistics gave out; but it was worth the try.—Hūm)

I think it's a great idea. You can run. You want peace. Therefore, you can run for peace. It may not *work*, of course. It's at least conceivable, arguable, that at the conclusion of your run there will be no more peace, no less contention, in the world, any way you describe the world, any way you quantify or qualify peace/non-peace. But, of course, *that doesn't matter*. You do what you can/must do; to expect results is already to do violence to the present—i.e. the world. Therefore you run not to *bring about* peace; you run *for* peace. 'Folks, I'd like to dedicate this next mile to peace in... let's see... peace in Zimbabwe, okay? For the next mile we are running for Zimbabwean peace.' And who knows? Even without expectation, without hope, who can possibly deny the *possibility* that... Stranger things have happened. The pebble has given birth to the avalanche. If there is any movement to be initiated, your movement may be the... but even if not, it is *still your movement*. It is not a movement *towards* peace. It is a movement *for* peace. Being such, it is its own success, and whatever follows, or tries to follow, or fails to follow, doesn't matter. Your movement is, in itself, complete, like a strong dose of castor oil (as I'm sure you've thought yourself already) produces a complete and very purifying movement.

I think it's a great idea. But I can't run worth a damn. 50 miles a day? Every day for a month? 'One day, on *carika*, I walked 23 miles (in 10 hours of walking time), and was totally done in for the next 3 days. Normally I'll do 8 to 10 miles and be proud, and that's for all day. Running's not my thing. But I can fart. When I consider my various talents (almost entirely non-marketable) I conclude that the best thing I've got going is flatulence. Not that I'm in any world-class competition, mind you. No; but of an evening, down at the local health food bar, I can harmonize and odorize with no fear of being shown up as a Johnny One-Note. Yes, I can fart. And I too want peace. Therefore, I can fart for peace. For the next month, entirely due to your *inspiring* example, every expulsion of gas will be for peace. Of course, these days I'm not into actually *organizing* anything. But *ideas* occur. These ideas—who knows how far things might spread? Part-ins. The Pass Gas for Peace movement. ('You know in your bowels that it's right.') Giant balloons can be filled with collected farts and floated over the skies of the world—whoops—there goes another one, right now, dedicated to peace. Tonight, I predict, will be—whoops—big one that time—tonight will be a time dedicated—whoops, long thin one, trifle malodorous, but for peace, for peace, just like all the others—yes, tonight will be a time, whoops, brief crack of a fart, it was—a time, I say, a time dedicated to peace in our hearts, in our minds, in our bowels, in—whoops, good satisfying one that was—yes, peace in our hearts, in our...

(The edge of the aerogramme wafted with peace, which may have lasted a month, to judge by the next aerogramme from him, picking up the scent, as it were.—Hūm)

... My own backward and long-winded efforts, inspired by your example, to make a contribution towards peace, continue apace—not exactly striking a blow for peace, perhaps, but a blow nevertheless, and certainly a clarion-call (to myself—ain't nobody else around to hear it, but that don't matter no nevermind) for all we believe in. As you say, all we have is wind and poesy, so though it was a one-man effort—I invited some friends to join me, but they thought I was cracked—nevertheless your slogan Plutonium Piles Are Hard To Sit On was the inspiration for my expiration, the Pass Gas for Peace Movement. For one month every fart I farted was, with a song in my bowels, dedicated to peace...

I too prepare for winter—the NE monsoon will hit with full fury next month—the termites have already done so, as you can see by the bites taken out of this aerogramme—and huff and puff, but, I hope, will not blow my little house down. But what makes it interesting is that I can't be sure. People keep telling me not to live on top of hills, but what, then, is Upcountry *for*? So I go down to the pine forest below, where the village women illegally pull down branches, and I gather the small sticks that they don't think worth carrying. Pine burns great. The needles go into the bed, which thus gets fractionally higher each day. Soon I shall be *above* the top of the hill and beyond the doubts of my distant neighbors and supporters. (Sometimes, at night, I see rabbits—or one rabbit several time running past, so there must be rabbit holes about the place. Moon-lit, he looks rather... well... *white* and seems in a hurry.)

Here's a few more Dhammapada renderings for thee.

Let go of the future; let go of the past;
let go of the in-between and surpass
existence. When freedom of mind is attained
then to birth and decay you will not come again.

If its root is firm and stout
a tree cut down will heal and grow.
With craving's base not rooted out,
again, again, will sprout this woe.

People who are biased, moved,
exult in what's engaging,
though bent on ease, though seeking good,
they undergo but birth and aging.

The blemishless man who's gained freedom from thirst.
untrembling, the one who's accomplished the aim,
for that man the dam of existence is burst.
This is his final frame.

V.

* * *

Ella, Summer '83

Even a few months ago I was hearing stories of 'troubles', of 'difficulties in the North'; but I've heard a good many rumors in a good many countries, and have learned that whatever basis they may have in fact they usually come, in the end, to little or nothing. (One notable exception was the Sri Lanka insurrection of '71.) But—so I gathered—there had been increased terrorist activity (against government forces and Sinhalese) in the Tamil-dominated north of the island, by the 'Tamil Tigers' (TT), who for some years have been waging a campaign for 'eelam' or partition of the island into a Sinhalese nation (in the South) and a Tamil nation (in the North). I had also heard of (well-publicized) instances of the government making reparation to Tamil families who had suffered in one way or another at the hands of the army or police, and been struck on occasion by the barrage of government-originated publicity decrying 'eelam' as 'asking for the moon'.

But the first news I had of the present situation was the morning of the 26th, when I asked three brothers who live nearby why they weren't in school that day. 'Because the Tamils killed 13 soldiers,' they told me. I've heard better reasons for staying out of school, and I've heard worse, so I questioned them further. The killings had taken place in the

North of the island, not in Upcountry (which is well to the South), and the brothers were unrelated to any of the victims; so those were not the reasons for staying out of school. The schools, it turned out, were closed. So too, it seemed, were the banks and all government offices. Finally they told me that it was not in mourning for the soldiers but because of a Sinhalese reaction to the killings which had resulted in anti-Tamil riots—hardly the first, there having been a number of them even in the year that I've been back in the country (all local and quickly put down by the government).

The Sinhalese and the Tamils have both occupied the island for several thousand years, and there is a long history of tensions, as well as innumerable wars. Since independence in '47 there have been scattered outbreaks of disquiet caused by competition for what wealth exists, by differences of view and lifestyle, and so on. But this outbreak, I learned, was widespread, and for that reason the schools (etc.) were shut down for the day. But they felt that all would be well by the morrow, the schools would re-open, and peace would be restored. So I went about my business and didn't concern myself further with what seemed to be distant troubles. And indeed on Wednesday I didn't see the boys (or anyone else), and assumed them to be in school.

Thursday morning I went into town, and was informed by the AGA (Assistant Government Agent—who is the highest government official in the village, a genial portly chap from Kandy side) that curfew would take effect that afternoon at 2 PM and would be in effect until 5 AM Saturday. 'Oh, then I won't be able to go to Bandarawela,' I said to him, although I had not in fact any plans to go there in any case. 'You shouldn't go to Bandarawela,' he advised me. 'There's fighting there. It's very dangerous. Many shops have been burned.'

Well, Bandarawela is the nearest town of any size—maybe, what? 10,000 people? and only 9 miles from Ella—so it was about then I first began to get an inkling that the situation might get serious enough to affect even me (although, as you know, it would not be the first time that I've found myself in the middle of big-screen-drama situations; in fact, it might even seem that I have a propensity for them). So I finished my business in town and returned home where, shortly afterwards, one of my Sinhalese neighbors, Suntil, came to call on me.

Suntil looked very upset, face puffy from lack of sleep, and he said the whole country was in flames, arson, riot and looting going on in much of the South by Sinhalese against Tamils and in much of the North by Tamus against Sinhalese, and that he didn't know what would happen to this country. Since he is a sensible fellow who has not previously been given to alarms I had to take him seriously. His brother, he said, had just returned from Colombo and reported the city devastated. The whole city, he said, would have to be rebuilt. Obviously not every single building had been destroyed, so I had no way to judge from such a statement how extensive the damage actually was, but I knew that in the capital there were no ethnic quarters, Tamils living alongside Sinhalese, and that most of the homes are old, i.e. made of wood (the Sri Lankans have never taken up the idea of tearing down the old to make way for the new).

Tamils are a significant minority in Colombo, as in fact they are also in most Upcountry towns, including Bandarawela and Badulla, which is the district capital (and rail head), about 15 miles away, with about 50,000 people. I believe it's the largest town east of Kandy. Most of the Tamils who have settled in Upcountry towns are traders and professionals. They are also all 'Jaffna' Tamils, Jaffna being the main city in the North of the island, as distinct from the Estate Tamils. The JT's have been in the country for about as long as the Sinhalese, whereas the ET's were imported during the last century by the British as cheap labor to work the tea estates (or, before the blight of the 1890's wiped them out, the coffee estates). The JT's look down on the ET's, and even speak a rather different sort of Tamil dialect, like uppercrust Oxford English and Cockney, and there is virtually no intermarriage between the two communities, which therefore maintain separate identities.

Around Ella itself there are not JT's, but of course there are hundreds of ET's who work on the tea estates which surround Ella, still fulfilling the role for which they were brought in from India. (And still working for base subsistence wages, presently about $1/day). So the Sinhalese do not fully identify the two groups with each other. But obviously they also have some things in common, so they are partly identified together. The danger, then, was that the ET's might also be attacked, in which case Ella would become involved, and, with ET's and Sinhalese about equal in number locally, the situation could become serious. Suntil told me a few horror stories, probably true, of what the Tamils had done to some of the Sinhalese in the North (the TT's seem to cultivate a bloody-handed image); no doubt similar stories can be told of what some Sinhalese have done in the South, though I haven't heard any such tales myself.

That afternoon it was very quiet: I've accustomed myself to the modest amount of traffic on this road (a road less traveled by), but for the first time I became aware of how much I'd had to ignore. It was a very pleasant afternoon, though, and the troubles were still at that time remote enough that I could indulge myself in reveries of supporting whichever side promised to maintain the curfew, etc. Even then, although I appreciated that the situation was difficult, I still regarded it as not more than a larger-scale version of the local incidents that had affected various towns from time to time. Multicultural nations have many advantages over unicultural nations (such as Thailand)—e.g. a greater ability of the people to accept, and to understand, different ways, a greater ability to adapt to changing conditions, a more diversified pool of talents, etc.—but there is a price to be paid for it in the form of communal tensions. These need not result in riot, but they all too easily do.

Such were my reflections on Thursday afternoon, and in the evening as well. The few shops and houses visible from my place had their lights out, and it was pleasant to take the night air without their lights glaring (frequent as they are, power failures come all too seldom for me). But about 8:30 at night I noticed to the west a bright red glare which could only be fire. It died down, then flared up a minute later, then again died away. Well, I'm east of Ella, so I speculated on what the light might signify.

Most of the ET's live near me or across the road and into the estate—away from town—but there are a few of them living in old housing near town. These people do not work for any estate, but survive on odd jobs and so on. I believe the housing is left from a failed estate; and the people are mostly elderly and mostly quiet and religious; by no stretch of the imagination could they be supporters of the TT. They are also extremely poor. So I hoped that nobody had been so foolish as to set their homes on fire. Another explanation was the tourists. There are 6 guest houses in town, from the high-class government-owned Ella Rest House to the ones that attract the backpack crowd. During the season (now) they do well on people who come usually for a night only, look at Ella Rock until they get bored with it, and leave the next day, since there's nothing else to do here except walk around. One of the owners had mentioned that morning that he had 12 tourists—a full house for him—that day; and perhaps they had become bored with the curfew and lit a bonfire. I've seen more foolish behavior than that by travelers, e.g. during the

Guatemalan earthquake, during the Cambodian refugee crisis, during the Bangladesh refugee crisis, etc. I listened for a long while, but heard (and saw) nothing else—no cries of distress, no screams (or bumps) in the night—and so finally concluded that whatever the flare had been, it had not spread. With that I went inside for the night.

The next morning—Friday—there were buses on the road, and a train on the tracks, so I guessed that the curfew had been lifted. Even if it hadn't I would have gone into town; there are footpaths through the woods. But instead I went by the car road. In town I learned that curfew would start at 5 PM and also that the night before the firelight I had seen had been the initial flare-up of a fire that had destroyed the Sunnyside Lodge, the guest house just beyond the other side of town (more than a crow's mile from me, the farthest buildings before the tea estates start again).

The lodge had had half a dozen tourists at the time, who fled into the dark injuring themselves a bit on the pointy ends of the tea bushes, but otherwise unharmed. I knew the Sunnyside was owned by a Mr. Joseph, who I had thought to be a Burgher (of European or part-European descent), since he is a supervisor on one of the estates the previous government had nationalized, and because of his name (Tamil names are usually long and difficult—for us—to pronounce), and because of other impressions. But non I learned that I had been wrong in this belief, that he is a JT. I had been told that there were no JT's living in Ella, which is true: he lives on his tea estate a number of miles away; and that no shops were owned by JT's, which is also true. But I hadn't known the Sunnyside to be owned by a JT.

A I also learned that a rumor had been circulating—false, as it turned out—that a number of JT's from Bandarawela were hiding at the Sunnyside, refugees from the riots and killings in the main towns. So it is entirely possible that people from Ella set the place on fire to 'get the Tamils'. It would be easy enough to do, since it is out of Ella, surrounded by tea and a small fruit grove. But other explanations are also possible: it could have been Sinhalese from one of the outlying villages, which look to Ella as their commercial and government center. These are villages up in the hills, where I had heard of occasional difficulties between Sinhalese and JT's in the past. (The JT's there all moved away during the last few years.) Some of these villagers are rather rough-cut (though there are certainly some locals who would be quite capable of splashing some gasoline and lighting a match). Or it could have been from the neighboring tea estate, for they and Sunnyside had been having an acrimonious dispute about water rights, an important matter in this dry area, particularly so in this year of drought. I don't know the management at that estate, so I can't say whether this is or is not likely. But certainly it is possible. Or it could have been Sunnyside's competition. I've heard it said that the (Sinhalese) owners of some of the other tourist joints felt that Sunny sideways getting an 'unfair' amount of the trade (whatever that means). And the owner of one of these guest houses is a person who would be up to such an opportunistic act (none of the others would be, I think). Or it could be something I haven't even thought of (just as the fire itself was accounted for in a way I hadn't thought of). There's no telling.

The place, though, was totally destroyed. Stone walls waist-high still stood, and the walls at each end of the tourist building, which supported the roof structure, still stood. One of them had a window with a glass unbroken. But otherwise there was only ash and stench and fire-whitened zinc roofing sheets, and a couple of chairs too burnt to be repairable-perhaps they had been outside. The black char on one wall seemed to indicate where the gasoline had been poured (it was the light of the gas flame I had seen; the light of the burning building was not intense enough to light up the sky for me to see it over the hill that lies between my place and the Sunnyside). The other building was also totally destroyed; it was the dwelling of the cook/caretaker and his family, and he had lost everything he had put together in his life (he is in his 50's, I would guess). It was impossible to tell what material—wood, bamboo, or whatever—had formed the walls of either building above their stone base. One large roof beam, only half burnt, still smoked. A garage had not been burnt.

On my way back through town I met a villager who had just been to Ballaketuwa to sell some produce. This small town—one or two hundred people, the same as Ella—is about 4 miles from Ella, 3 miles from my place, and is therefore the closest town to Ella, aside from the villages which—5 or 10 houses each—lie wherever there is farmland. He told me that at Ballaketuwa one of the Tamil-owned shops had been set afire and was burning even while he had been there. And then on my way back home I heard from someone else that all the Tamil shops at Ballaketuwa had been set afire—maybe 4 or 5 shops, I'm not sure, for I've only been there once—and that the Tamils, not content with the situation, were fighting back. With fists? I asked—or with weapons? Not with fists, he said. But he wasn't sure what sort of weaponry was involved. Were the Estate Tamils involved? He wasn't sure, but he thought so.

I decided then not to go directly home. I consulted Suntil (who is the most influential of the younger Sinhalese in Ella, not only because he runs a shop and owns much land and comes from a large family, but also for reasons of character), who told me that he was storing in his house the valuables of the ET's from the Sutherland lines ('lines' meaning the row buildings where the ET's live, one family to a room), Sutherland being the estate closest (it is the only private estate in the area: I've mentioned before the owner, Mr. Henry, a Burgher), for the ET's there were now very worried, and had been making arrangements for the women and children to stay in the more remote lines while the men were prepared, if necessary, to defend themselves. One block of these lines lies directly in front of (and below) my place, a few hundred yards away. So I told these people that if there was any trouble, they could come to my cottage, where they would be safe. It is quite certain that no Sinhalese would harm me, and—Suntil agreed with my assessment—almost as certain that they would also not make any trouble for anyone I put under my protection. This is particularly so for the Ella people, who all know me. So the ET's knew that they could find safety nearby. Suntil was also worried for his own safety, for if the Ella people learned that he was protecting (the goods of) the Tamils some of them might cause him trouble, particularly if they thought there was a chance to do some looting. He is the youngest child. His last sister was married just last month and now only he and his mother are in the house (though one brother—the one who had returned from Colombo—lives with his family nearby).

I then went on to Mr. Henry's bungalow—estate bungalows, built during the days when the British owners were making fortunes, are always substantial structures that could hardly be duplicated nowadays—to inform him of what was going on and also to phone on to the Newburgh office (although Newburgh tea lies just above my cottage, the office, bungalow and lines are a mile or so away, and I'd already done a lot of walking) to inform those people that there was a safe place for them, if they needed it, and could get to it. The phone wasn't working just then, but Mr. H said he'd call later. I also learned that the Newburgh

Tamils were taking a more militant attitude than the Sutherland Tamils, making large knives (firearms, if any were to be had, were not spoken of: it would be rare in Sri Lanka for any average person to possess such weapons, unlike in Thailand—or the US) and preparing a defense. There had been rumors that some JT's were taking refuge there, and whether true or not the rumors themselves were enough reason to be concerned: witness the fate of Sunnyside.

Mr. H had also hired a number of Sinhalese—roughnecks, I assume—to keep a patrol on his land, including the lines, during the night, and no doubt the same had been done at Newburgh (which is government-owned). He told me what he knew of the national situation, from radio and TV, which largely centered on government proclamations, suspicions of 'foreign' (i.e. Indian) support for the Tamils in general and the TT in particular (many of the ET's are still legally regarded as Indian citizens, even though they may have been born here: there is no doubt that, like many minority groups in the world, the Tamils have grounds for perceiving inequality of treatment), and also revelations of much that had been previously kept secret. It seems the killing of the 13 soldiers had not been a singular incident: something far more serious had been developing for some months, approaching in the North, a full-scale insurrection. Loss of life on both sides (army/Tamils) had been much higher than reported; in particular army losses had been concealed, much to the disgruntlement of the army. And it was in fact a group of angry soldiers who finally told the press about the 13 slain that blew the lid off the government cover-up. (The government had tried to ship the 13 bodies to Colombo in the dead of night—so I was told, and it may be true—without informing the next-of-kin, this last detail being a particular grievance of the army dissidents, as well as the payment of reparations to some Tamils but not to army next-of-kin.)

The government had kept all these troubles quiet, of course, hoping the situation would blow over and fearing that exposure would result in rioting—a reasonable fear, as it turns out—and then just got sucked in deeper and deeper until the situation could no longer be hushed up. By then rumors were so rife—many of them true, it was being discovered—that the rioting when it came, was beyond the government's capacity to control.

All of this was interesting, of course, but this story—the national story—was in certain ways quite divorced from the immediate situation in Ella; on the national scene we were only spectators (with seats in the bleachers, yet) whereas on the local scene there was a situation that was very dangerous. Therefore after checking with Mr. H, as to his preparations, I went back to town, and talked to the people there, telling then basically that it was not a question of Tamil/Sinhalese, that such a view would only lead to more trouble, but that it was a question of right action/wrong action. Then as evening came on, I went back home, along an empty road.

The night was tense: that was clear. It was always possible that people—Sinhalese or Tamils—might come from Ballaketuwa. We didn't know how the fighting had gone there. Or they might come from farther away, particularly the Tamils, either seeking refuge or—TT's or their agents—come to stir up troubles. Occasionally vehicles went along the road. I could recognize the government jeeps on patrol; but because so many vehicles, especially trucks, had been put to the torch many owners had turned their vehicles over to the army and police for official use as well as greater safety for the vehicle. So most of the vehicles were not jeeps, but whether they were army/police patrols or something else I couldn't tell. One car stopped, about 8:00, at the entrance to the lines, paused a minute, then returned towards Ella. I kept watch, but nothing happened, and I learned the next day that this had been a police-driven car taking one of the ET's (who for some reason had been in town) back to the lines.

That was the most dangerous time, that night, and it is fortunate that nothing happened, for there could easily have been a spark struck that would have left Ella in cinders as were Bandarwela, Colombo, Kandy, and other towns (though, of course, on a smaller scale). But Saturday morning when I went into town I learned that there had been locally no further trouble. However I also learned the sad story of Badulla, the district capital.

Badulla is an entirely ordinary town, neither beautiful nor ugly, but since Kandy is not really considered quite Upcountry, being only 1600 feet elevation—Ella is more than double that—Badulla is the biggest town in the tea area. Tamils, like any minority group in the world, must specialize in order to survive as a group. Thus the JT's tend to be better educated and more industrious, and dominate the business community and play a big role in professional capacities. ET's survive as a group by doing work that no one else cares to do, and doing it for less than anyone cares to do it. The Muslim community, on the upper-side, control a substantial amount of the gem trade and, on the down side, are often fishermen (these are of Moorish descent, the last Moors left in the world). The Burghers are often in managerial positions. The JT's have been attracted to Upcountry towns because (aside from good climate) outside of Colombo and Kandy most of the coastal Sinhalese are too hostile to them for the JT's to wish to settle there. It was in coastal towns that most of the isolated troubles of the last year occurred. Also, of course, they will have better business opportunities among the ET's even if they do not mix culturally or socially. And Badulla is large enough to offer the professionals—doctors, engineers, accountants, etc.—a chance to establish themselves. So in Badulla there are a lot of Tamils from the North. (I also have the impression that there are larger-than-average sized Muslim and Burgher communities.)

The TT, it seems, had a plan to take Badulla in the hopes—quite possibly justified—that if they succeeded the ET's of the entire district would rise with the JT's. Since the ET's can hardly be expected to be content with their position, economically, socially or otherwise, it is not an unreasonable notion that if they thought there was a good chance of success they would join the JT's.

Accordingly, at least 50 Tigers had been in Badulla, where aside from raising money from the Tamil merchants, they had also been stocking large quantities of weapons. When the riots began in the country they prepared themselves and laid their plans. The police seem to have had some idea of what was going on, for they arrested some of the TT before they could escape. Somehow—perhaps from the arrested Tigers—it was learned that the Tigers had made plans for a general attack on the Sinhalese, and somehow—perhaps from the police—the news became known to the Sinhalese in Badulla that the time for the attack was but two hours away. It took no more than this for mobs to form. Every Tamil shop and most Tamil homes were put to the torch. As the shops burned explosions from inside revealed that stores of bombs had been concealed in them. Naturally the flames spread. The Tamils tried to hurriedly mount their attack, and fired upon the Sinhalese, but the Tigers were not organized, and after a bloody fight they finally surrendered to the police/army.

One person who had been there said that in one schoolhouse he counted 55 bodies. In other schools Tamil refugees were guarded by police against the Sinhalese—about 3000 homeless—and elsewhere hundreds of captured terrorists were being held. (I'll bet there was no school in Badulla that day.)

The town, I've been told repeatedly, has been destroyed, flattened, demolished. In Bandarawela I'm told that though few houses were burnt, all Tamil shops were destroyed and some Sinhalese shops as well. Looting was rampant. The army, which could hardly be expected to look kindly upon the Tamils, is said to have told people (unofficially, of course) that they could kill and burn, but not to loot. On the other hand, soldiers went out to Ballaketuwa, stopped the fighting (which, it turned out, had not gone farther than stone-throwing), recovered from Sinhalese homes what looted goods they could find and restored them to the Tamil merchants, and warned the Sinhalese not to make more trouble or risk arrest (for looting, I assume).

In Colombo there are about 50,000 homeless refugees and perhaps another 25,000 in the rest of the South. I have no idea whether the death toll is still in the hundreds or has mounted into the thousands, nor do I know the situation in the North. Ironically, the coastal towns—Sinhalese-nationalist strongholds—suffered less than Upcountry, because most of the Tamils had already fled those places due to previous troubles. In the area north of Upcountry but below the Tamil area—Anuradhapura is the main town—there seems to have been little trouble.

Some people who tried to get to Kandy said they were turned back at Nuwarm Eliya—the foremost tourist town in Upcountry, the one homesick British like so well (though homesick Americans would not concur, there being no McDonald's)—due to mobs and flames. Parliament has passed some new laws, about what I'm not quite sure. A minister from Mrs. Gandhi's cabinet has flown in to assess the situation. And opportunists of every stripe and spot have taken what advantage they could of the situation to benefit themselves, most commonly by looting or taking revenge for wrongs done to them, real or fancied. But in Ella, that Saturday, all was peaceful and the situation felt less tense (shops opened half their shutters rather than a quarter of them, though the small fruit stalls were closed). But the roads were still uncertain, and there were no trains, so some of the tourists were getting itchy. Saturday night passed peacefully.

Sunday morning was very quiet—no vehicles, no trains, no pedestrians. So naturally I went into town to see what was up. All shops were closed and I was told that the night before the government had declared

Sunday to be full curfew island-wide. Some of them thought there was still trouble in Colombo while others opined that Saturday night the government, having realized in a flash of intuition that the next day, being Sunday, was not a normal business day, had decided to celebrate their acumen by declaring full day curfew. Certainly all was quiet in town, although the police in a jeep which passed me (raising no objection to my being out and about) were heavily armed with rifles and shotguns. I was also told that the chief of the local constabulary had been sheltering some Tamil refugees in his own home, upon their payment of a very sizable incentive, and that someone had pasted a letter to the door objecting to this, though whether the objection was to his sheltering refugees or taking protection money or both was not made clear. At any rate, so I was told, the chief took fright at this notice and ordered his wards to leave at once, though whether they were able to recover any of their payment I did not learn. I did not learn where they might have gone, and heard no further rumors of JT's being given protection by the Newburgh ET's. So much for Sunday.

Monday morning there was traffic on the road and no curfew until evening, and a feeling the tension was now relaxed and that, for Ella at least, there would be no further troubles. This feeling was maintained into the afternoon. At about 5 o'clock a private car with a policeman at the wheel drove along the road, came to a stop, did a clumsy reverse, nearly backing into a ditch, and after an unnecessary amount of unskillful maneuvering, managed to reverse itself. Then a jeep came tearing along the road with several policemen, came to a screeching stop beside the private car, and held a hurried consultation. I happened to be at a house by the road at the time, getting one of my sporadic Sinhalese lessons and therefore I was able to learn that the policeman in the private car had decided to give himself some practice in driving and had borrowed the car—which was in the care of the police so that it would not be burnt—without telling anyone. The police in the jeep, having suddenly realized that their comrade and one car were missing, had rushed out to rescue him from whatever dire fate might have befallen him. He claimed that he had only gone out to get some tea and sugar for the boys (although there were at least 6 shops between the cop shop and where I observed the incident); they advised him to get back to work. They left and he haltingly followed after. And with that Keystone cops episode the uprising can be considered to be over.

Curfew lingers on, as it did in '71, long after what gave rise to it has finished, just as a cough can linger on after the cold is cured. But otherwise, in Ella, all has pretty much returned to normal (it is now Thursday, the 4th of August, a week since I first heard of the curfew). And now what remains is to pay the price for the past week. ('Riot now, pay later.')

Economically it can be calculated: so many buildings to be rebuilt, so much production lost, so much to be made up for or forgotten, etc., etc. So much goods destroyed, to be replaced or done without. Food distribution will be the first priority. Probably no one will go hungry (or if anyone does it will be the Tamils), but some things are already scarce. Even here, where no shops were burned, they can restock themselves only from the government co-op in Badulla (which is farther from here than is Bandarawela), and not all things can be had there. In Colombo, I hear, a coconut—formerly Rs. 2.50 (figure 23 rupees to the dollar)—is now going for Rs. 12. A kilo of beans up from Rs. 3 to Rs. 50. Because of the transport shortage all goods that need to be moved are now very expensive. And though, as tie-ups get unsnarled and profiteers put down, prices will drop, it's unlikely that they will drop to their former level. This will be a very difficult time for many hard-pressed people who have already been suffering much from the inflation which is a concomitant of the present government's efforts to tie the country more strongly to the international economy.

Such a tie-in inevitably benefits urban people at the expense of the rural—the demand for rice, after all, will not rise as fast as the demand for the flood of electronic goodies now pouring into the country, mostly from Japan—and therefore hurts my neighbors, though they usually have other ideas, or no idea, about the source of the present inflation.

With much of this year's first rice crop failed due to drought the food situation will worsen. The second priority will no doubt be construction material. Not only is the demand great, but existing supplies of many materials will have been destroyed—timber, zinc sheets (which can be ruined by an intense fire), etc.

This will affect my own plans, though as yet I can't say how: my landlord clearly intends to carry on with his plans to tear down this cottage and build himself a house, though whether the increased price of goods will convince him to wait until, the demand going down and supplies coming in, the price reverts to something more reasonable, I can't say, and perhaps he can't either. He has made up the plans, however, and showed them to me recently. The dining room is at the opposite end of the house from the kitchen, which he planned to make 5 feet by 9 feet, 'Will that be big enough for your wife?' I asked him, 'I didn't ask her,' he told me, perhaps surprised at the notion. I suggested to him that if his wife were consulted, and if a space suitable to her needs were allotted, he might get better meals than otherwise, and if he put the kitchen next to the dining room he might get hotter food as well. Perhaps some communal strife can be avoided. Though whether he will act upon my suggestion remains to be seen.

The burden of making reparations will not be eased by the disruption of communications networks in general—in some cases power facilities damaged, many vehicles to be replaced or done without, etc. What the final cost will be I can't say, but I can say it will be more than this poor country can afford.

Also more than it can afford will be the non-economic cost-the loss of trust and co-operation between people who, a decade ago, were not at loggerheads, the greater dissatisfaction among those who already find or invent grounds for dissatisfaction, etc., etc. Certainly the Tamils have now learned that the Sinhalese have the will to keep the island as one undivided nation, and since they are a substantial majority the Sinhalese will succeed. Diehard Tamils will still resist, but most of them will now realize that for the present 'eelam' really is 'reaching for the moon'. What sort of agitation will persist I don't know, but it should be, if at all, on a much reduced level—for the time being. That's perhaps the only 'lesson' drawn from the past week, and it's a lesson for which this country has paid dearly.

* * *

> ... And yet, by the very fact of being part of such a world one cannot be completely sane; and to be not completely sane is to be not sane at all. But if one tries to escape is that not then evidence of a spark of sanity? Perhaps so; but the problem is that when we try to escape we discover that we *can't*: every effort to free oneself from (in Buddhist terms) involvement with craving, aversion, and delusion or (in the novel's terms) the war—every effort apparently brings one back to the same dilemma, and results only in making the problem more urgent (and perhaps also more evident), as will be recognized

by anyone who has ever tried to extirpate the root of craving, and failed. Is it not madness, then, to try to escape?

And yet, if to do nothing is regarded as less insane, still that too does not lead to disengagement from a mad world. This is the very crux of Yossarian's dilemma, and ours as well: a dilemma illuminated in experience by the effort to practice the Buddha's Teaching and in fiction by Yossarian's effort to escape from the war. Heller puts it this way:

"Can't you ground someone who's crazy?" [Yossarian asks the flight surgeon, Doc Daneeka.]

"Oh, sure. I have to. There's a rule saying I have to ground anyone who's crazy. "

"Then why don't you ground me? I'm crazy.... Ask any of the others. They'll tell you how crazy I am."

"They're crazy."

"Then why don't you ground them?"

"Why don't they ask me to ground them?"

"Because they're crazy, that's why."

"Of course they're crazy," Doc Daneeka replied. "I just told you they're crazy, didn't I? And you can't let crazy people decide whether you're crazy or not, can you?"

Yossarian looked at him soberly and tried another approach. "Is Orr crazy?"

"He sure is," Doc Daneeka said.... "I can ground Orr. But first he has to ask me to."

"That's all he has to do to be grounded?"

"That's all. Let him ask me."

"And then you can ground him?" Yossarian asked.

"No. Then I can't ground him."

"You mean there's a catch?"

"Sure there's a catch," Doc Daneeka replied. "Catch-22. Anyone who wants to get out of combat duty isn't really crazy."—p. 45

Thus Yossarian's efforts to establish a rational basis for being grounded must fail. Logic is an inadequate tool to deal with the human situation, for whenever we apply logic there is always a catch. This is not to suggest that logic is not *necessary*, but rather that it is not *adequate*. In this computer age we could hardly manage without logic. Let alone computers, without logic we could make neither mathematics nor music nor marmalade. But whenever we try to deal with the fundamentals of existence, with the forever unanswerable question, "Who am I?" (or any other question concerned with "me"), we find that logic neither answers that question nor shows us the way to stop asking it.[1] ("'*Why me*?' was his constant lament, and the question was a good one"—p. 34.)

And the reason for this, the Buddha informs us, is because of *avijjā*, or ignorance. But *avijjā* is not a mere absence of information; it is a refusal to see what is at all times there to be seen. It is not failure to see one particular thing among other particular things, but a radical refusal to see the way all particular things are, and in this respect it is as great a modifier as death—indeed, the two are (so the Buddha tells us) inseparable. The dependent arising formulation says, in summary, "With ignorance as condition, aging and death, sorrow, lamentation, pain, grief, and despair come into being."

The deluded person, in refusing to see the nature of all things, refuses also to see the nature of his refusal to see (which is also a thing). That is, he refuses to see delusion. Thus, by denying itself delusion sustains itself. This is stated in the Suttas (e.g. Sammādiṭṭhi Sutta, M. 9) as follows:

Friends, that which is non-knowledge of suffering, non-knowledge of the arising of suffering, non-knowledge of the ceasing of suffering, non-knowledge of the way leading to the ceasing of suffering, this, friends, is called ignorance.

For after all, what is "the way leading to the ceasing of suffering"? It is (the Suttas tell us) the noble eightfold path. And what is the first factor of this path? Right view. Ignorance, then, involves non-knowledge of right view. And right view is knowledge of the arising of suffering; that is to say, knowledge of ignorance. Right view is knowledge of right view, and also knowledge of wrong view, whereas wrong view is non-knowledge of wrong view, and also non-

1. It is for this reason that the Buddha's Teaching is said to be *atakkāvacara*, not in the sphere of reason or logic. (*Catch-22* is not the only well-known book which asserts the insanity implicit in being in a situation. In *Alice in Wonderland* the Cheshire Cat tells Alice: "We're all mad here. I'm mad. You're mad. You must be or you wouldn't have come." Indeed, *Catch-22* contains a number of very specific allusions to the Alice books.)

knowledge of right view. And this structure of ignorance is, in fact, Catch-22 at its most fundamental level.

Sāmaṇera Bodhesako, from *The Buddha and the Catch-22*

* * *

The water situation became critical: the amount coming from the reservoir was insufficient to reach me—it got absorbed by the mud in the channel—and I had to trek to the well for bathing and washing, hauling back for drinking and to keep alive at least part of the garden. Finally yesterday we had a good rain, which refilled the pond—it had emptied to within a few inches of bottom, which I left for the benefit of the tadpoles (who will turn into mosquito-consuming frogs)—and there are a few inches of water in the reservoir, which I open for an hour or so a day, giving me perhaps 30-40 gallons: enough now to keep things going (the garden—most of it managed to survive—consumes the bulk of this.) With luck and care it should last about 2 weeks. The monsoon normally starts (gradually) about the middle of September. So if it is not late, or if we get another good shower, we'll make it. It's very difficult for all the people, most of them more than me. Some women have to walk a long way for water, and usually have to haul it uphill, even for their cooking. And of course tea production also goes down, with loss of income to the estate and to the workers. This is one of the driest years on record.

I did manage to save all the vegetables, and in fact have just harvested my peas. I planted 15 seeds (all that I had), and 3 months later harvested 105, all of which I will use for further planting. This is a 7-fold increase in 3 months, a very substantial return on my investment. If I were to continue at this rate for another 3 years I would have approximately 1,383,936,400,000 peas. This is more than 250 peas for every man, woman, and child in the world. If each of them were to plant their 250 peas and replant their 7-fold quarterly increase for two years, then 5 years from now every person on the planet would have 1,641,200.20 peas enough to solve the food crisis for decades. It's amazing that no one has thought of this yet. Or perhaps a very few geniuses have tried to indicate where the future lies, but only by indirect suggestion. Tolstoy, for example, in his classic novel, War and Peas.

Recently the curfew was advanced to as early as 6 PM, due to some incidents in the North—relocated Tamils attacking isolated Sinhalese—apparently coinciding with the one-month anniversary of the outbreak of the riots. But there have been no further incidents in Upcountry or Colombo. About 10 days ago I was passing through Bandarawela and saw the extensive damage; perhaps up to 20% of the shops I saw were empty blackened shells, exactly like WW2 bombed-out buildings. Elsewhere it's business as usual, or nearly so. Steps have been taken against hoarders and profiteers, so most goods are available and prices for staples are now about the same as before the riots. Many Tamil shopkeepers, forewarned by reports from elsewhere, were able to remove some of their stock to safe places (and to claim insurance loss on it afterwards as well).

A friend from a village just outside Bandarawela says one Tamil couple was killed in his village. One night someone threw a rock through their window and the Tamils, who it seems owned a shotgun, fired upon the person (missing him). A Sinhalese crowd gathered and set fire to the house, which burnt to the ground. He doesn't know whether they were burnt to death or killed while trying to escape. Only a few hours before this incident my friend had had tea with the couple.

Judging from what I witnessed and the reports of others during the riots of '71, government estimates of casualties, homeless refugees, etc. will be off by a factor of 8 to ten fold. For example, at least 50 Tamils accused of being terrorists were massacred in prison when—according to the guards—Sinhalese prisoners overpowered the guards and killed the Tamils, the guards being helpless to intervene. The government seems inclined to accept the guards' assertion without a serious investigation. And I have heard private estimates of reliable eye-witnesses that place the Bandarawela and Badulla tolls at well above the official numbers, as well as reports of isolated incidents that almost surely did not get included in the government figures. So I think we can safely assume that at least 3,000 people were killed, and that at the height of the riots there were at least 200,000 homeless refugees. These figures don't approach the '71 figures. But the property damage is much higher than in '71.

Every Tamil I've spoken with says he has friends who have died and I've heard numerous tales of narrow escapes. The Tamils are still very much afraid, and most of the Estate Tamils hereabouts continue to sleep in the tea bushes rather than in the lines—the drought continues, so they keep dry—and to keep their valuables hidden. At least 75% of the ET's seriously intend to return to India, where they—or more often their parents or grandparents—came from. As difficult as their lives are here economically, they will be yet more difficult in Tamil Nadu (the South Indian state where most of them would go, and which is poor even by Indian standards); but there they will at least be among their kin (who may not be overjoyed to have them, but could not refuse) and will no longer need to fear from outraged Sinhalese mobs. That there will be other fears no less fearful is, at present, not of importance.

Obviously the tea industry—Sri Lanka's biggest earner of foreign exchange—depends upon a superfluity of cheap labor, and if even as quarter of the workers go the situation will be very difficult. If anything like 75% leave the estates will be devastated. But herein Sri Lanka is in a difficult position, for the government has steadfastly maintained for decades that the Estate Tamils are legally Indian citizens, not Sri Lankans, and has encouraged their migration by making things difficult for them. A superfluity of labor is needed, but there has been an over-abundance. Now it will be difficult for the government to prevent vast numbers from leaving (though they will not allow to leave those few who have obtained Sri Lanka citizenship).

The tourist industry is also hard-hit. There are *no* tourists in Ella these days (normally August is a prime month, for French and German workers take their holidays in August and it is mid-winter in Australia). The expectation is that the trade will take 4-5 months to normalize.

The government seems to have hastily forced through an amendment to the constitution making it illegal to advocate separatism. Since it is of the essence of freedom of speech that even the most unpopular views may be espoused (and that only physical deeds, not verbal ones, can be made illegal) this means that Sri Lanka now has taken a step away from liberty and towards authoritarianism. Since separatism is a view espoused by a significant minority—the TULF (Tamil United Liberation Front) is—or was—the largest opposition party in Parliament and separatism was (is?) their major plank—the step is a large one. It can be argued that nothing less would have sufficed to quell the outrage of Sinhalese at the effort to divide the island and that had this not been done the damage would have been much worse, but it can be replied that damage to property cannot be compared with damage to the principles of liberty, and undertaking such a serious change while influenced by the heat of the moment is a rash method of administering a nation, and that in any case to muzzle opinion only drives it underground, where roots can spread and deepen, resulting in eventual difficulties which will prove more costly than what is supposed to have been saved. Which is not to suggest that I think partition to be a sensible move—it makes no sense geographically, economically, culturally, or esthetically, and would not correct the injustices of which the JT's complain but only perpetuate them in an altered guise (it would tip the scales of Injustice who, as we know, is blind)—but only that to do outrage to such a precious institution as freedom of speech is yet less sensible. But people seldom appreciate such freedoms until they lose them.

Two further problems will be involved with the military and the Parliament. The reason the Sinhalese were enabled to do as much damage as was done was firstly because of the half-hearted effort of the army to stop them (even in Diyatalawa—just beyond Bandarawela—where both army and airforce have major bases, every Tamil shop was razed), understandable in light of their long-running battle against the Tigers, though not therefore condonable, and secondly because the army is divided along political lines, and many officers and enlistees who oppose the UNP government saw the riots as a possibility to topple that government. These soldiers either abetted the rioters or at least did so little to stop them that their actions were correctly taken as a green light.

The riots can only further fragment the army and raises the possibility of the government control over the army weakening, which leads to further future danger of the country being beset by a coup, or an attempted one.

The situation in Parliament compounds the danger. Traditionally, the two major parties have been UNP and SLFP, which alternately won elections. But the SLFP became fragmented due to internal quarrels (the Bandaranaikas run the SLFP as Mrs. Gandhi's clan runs India's Congress Party, and the parallels, including those between Mrs. B's son and Mrs. G's, are striking) and the SLFP was soundly trounced in '77 due also to their having manipulated a two year extension of their term. UNP obtained a 5/6 majority, enabling them to do as they wished, and the TULF became the major opposition party.

Earlier this year the government forced through an amendment to the constitution enabling it to hold a referendum on the question whether to extend the life of this Parliament for a second 6-year term. They won—it was the first time any government in Sri Lanka has been returned to office—due to the popularity of the President (Jayawardene)—far more popular than his party—and the lack of a viable opposition, and therefore by a majority vote retained a 5/6 majority in Parliament.

Now the TULF, because it advocates separatism, has been made illegal, and its members cannot sit in Parliament (nor, if they are individually convicted of advocating separatism, would they retain *any* civil rights, including the right to practice a licensed profession which, of course, includes law).

And three other minor parties (including the communists) have been accused of fomenting troubles and encouraging rioters, apparently, hoping to topple the government. Warrants have been issued for the arrest of their leaders and deputies—some have gone underground—and so those parties too are probably destroyed.

If the government has presented any evidence for these charges I am unaware of it, though I've heard and read statements by a number of ministers making such charges without offering evidence. Therefore it seems that Sri Lanka is now in danger of becoming a one-party state. UNP and SLFP are ideologically more differentiable than say, Republicans and Democrats; but even if they were not, the danger of a one-party state is that there is simply no incentive to govern for anyone's benefit other than their own, whereas a two-party or multi-party system, even when it's just a case of Tweedledum and Tweedledee (or is it Tweedledee and Tweedledum?), generates a concern for the electorate out of simple self-interest. If a one-party state should befall Sri Lanka the country's hopes for improvement will be lost in a quagmire of corruption and mendacity.

And of course there is still the problem of the Tigers. Since the Tamils tend to regard themselves as the victims of Sinhalese hatred and infighting (their view of themselves is myopic, as are most such views) we can expect new recruits for the Tigers, and further activity. The only possible way in which Sri Lanka could be partitioned would be if India intervened (as she did against Pakistan in '72, leading to the creation of Bangladesh), and India would only intervene if it were forced to do so (at least as long as the present government rules in New Delhi; other governments my be less fastidious about such matters, and obviously Mrs. Gandhi will not rule forever). And the only way India could be forced to intervene would be if the Tamils were to come to such a pass that there was no political alternative to military intervention. This would mean the slaughter of thousands or tens of thousands of Tamils and it may be the strategy of the Tigers to commit such outrages as to provoke the Sinhalese to embark on such a slaughter. It sounds like—and is—madness, but the world has seen crazier things. Therefore, the Tamils who support the Tigers may be paying to have their throats cut.

Oh, one thing I forgot to mention about the aftermath of the riots is that the government has said that it will help rebuild industries and homes—nearly all Tamil-owned—destroyed by the riots and fires. But (here's the catch) it will thereby become part owner of all such industry (the exact percentage to be determined by—of course—the government), and under the guise of establishing an architectural coherence to the reconstruction—a joke, but a bad one, since 1) Colombo is a hodgepodge architecturally. 2) Tamil houses are found scattered amidst this hodgepodge, not in a ghetto-like area. 3) No such plan exists nor could such a plan be produced in a reasonable time—they have declared themselves to be temporarily the owners of all property under repair, so that they can ensure that all reconstruction proceeds according to their plans, and owners will be billed according to whatever the government sees fit to charge for its services and can recover their property upon settlement of the bill. The Tamils, naturally enough, think that the government is trying to get what the looters missed. I hope I have misunderstood this, because if I have not, and it is as I report, then it's an incredibly stupid act which will have serious repercussions in the future.

* * *

Greetings from the rabbit hole of the March (or so) hare. Perhaps with no way to go out of, I have either simply gone a long way and come a long way, or complexly come a long way and gone a long way. Or vice versa. A recent newspaper clipping (recent to me, that is; the newspaper itself was last year's model) has given me just the right phrase to describe what I am doing in Sri Lanka again: I'm here to *restore a new order*. How paradoxical! How ironical! How religious. Well, parody and irony are very well as a religion, provided you know to *hūm* you are praying and on whom you are not praying. Paradoxically, such a religion is not at all ironical. Ironically, it is not paradoxical. For some reason it reminds me of dancing with my shit. Dat take a *long* way.

Glad DAMAGED IN TRANSFER (or is it TRANSPERRED DAMAGE?) arrived safely damaged (General Delivery's doing, no doubt—you don't get busted *to* General for nothing): our latest bicentric biographic bigolly co-creation, unpublishable if anything ever was. Though totally unreadable, it's actually quite brilliant, provided it remains unread. But WB VI (or is it VII?)—sounds like a Leon Uris title—is just as well out of the hands of grimy publishers, who are only interested in it (if at all) in the same way that sex-starved drilling crews are interested in oil rigs. If you could glue two pages together with a paste of Krakir's Crapper[1] that would give them a rise. But otherwise we should remember it as a toy we both played with (and may play with again)—AND NOBODY ELSE! Nevermind its flaws. It starts off like a metronome—ticking away furiously, lots of energy and juice but not characterization, then runs down gradually from presto to lentissimo, then—your entry again—suddenly gets plugged into a wall socket and—not being wired—fizzles and jumps all over the place in an orgy of mixed tempos until it's simply all gone. But nevermind it floss. Itl's a nice toy. Quite unmarketable, and tinkering will only make it (if possible) more so, but a nice toy. Unmarketable? There's one remote long-shot chance. If you could devise a board representing Samadhi,[2] and added dice, markers, and 'chance' cards, you might be able to sell the package to Parker Brothers. Then *everyone* could play with it, in groups of 2-5, ages 10 to 100. But as a book? Who reads books?

My mother died in January—I'm not sure exactly when (rather like Mersault, though I hope not to end up like him)—after a long painful and losing decade battle with mainly, Parkinson's. The last couple of years were, apparently, pure ordeal, spent mostly in a sort of semi-delirium. I heard of it too late to return with any good purpose to the States. My father and sister are, it seems, handling all matters as well as can be expected. For which I'm thankful—and about as aggrieved as relieved. Something irreplacable lost—the mother who loved one; yet, as long as one draws breath, not gone—the love that mothered one. And—womb in tomb—it's not so easy not to see where one's going… The most moving remark, a year or so ago, was my father's, who said

1. In *Worthy Bones*, Sri Krakir is a shadowy Hindu scientist who's concocted a microbe—Krakirls Crapper—that eats—and shits harmlessly—oil slicks.—Hūm.
2. *Worthy Bones* transpires on Samadhi (Sk. meditation), an island in the mouth of the Red Sea.—Hūm.

that sometimes my mother would emerge from her semi-delirium into a sense of reality, and then begin to cry.

I'm settled into my own hillside, a squatter like you, save that I didn't build the house (except the one wherein I squat), and now have no plans to leave here unless/until I'm told to go (which, I'm told, will happen when the owner's son has saved enough money to build a house—and tear down this cottage). However, there's always the bright side: I may die before that happens. So good cheer.

V.

* * *

Since WW2 the driest year in Sri Lanka has been 1983. The drought, of course, was not so bad as it was in Africa; but bad enough. Still no less solar energy striking the earth's surface, and presumably about the same amount of water evaporates from the oceans, so *someplace* must be getting an excess of rain, unless it just falls back in the sea. One theory is that the whole drought is due to some inexplicable 'hot spot' that developed over the last few years somewhere in the South Pacific Ocean, only a few degrees above normal but over a large enough area to affect the world's weather. Dump that on the theoretical pile.

In any case, the drought has ended...with a *vengeance*! It was assumed the rains had come and gone, only half filling the reservoirs, and promising continuing power-cuts in the foreseeable future. Predictably, the clouds gathered, and we had 4 weeks of rains, during which time it rained a little or a lot every single solitary day, and there was almost no sunshine. The plains had floods; the people were evacuated and helicopters flew emergency supplies to them, but of course in the hill country there is no chance of floods. A lot of crops were damaged or destroyed. The rains ended (again), and now the weather is dry (the doors don't stick anymore) and crisp, though it's probably too late for a real winter season like the cold one of last year.

However, the rains went on a bit too long for the *devale* which is just up-hill from me. A *devale* is a place for the deva, or local god, in this case a two-room building, one for the god herself (I'm told she's female), and one for the occasional visitor, a few a week from what I've been able to see. The god is a stone statue about 18 inches high of curious proportions, the head being as big as the torso, but otherwise unremarkable—only the usual number (usual for humans that is) of arms, legs, and heads. I don't mean that this statue is a representative of the god. It is, I'm told, the god herself. Anyway, the day after the rains ended the roof (tile) collapsed and took the wall with it, or perhaps it was the wall (adobe) that collapsed and took the roof with it; in any case it fell downhill and took a chunk of my roof with it too, though nothing that can't be spared; overhang and verandah. My roof (asbestos) fortunately managed to not get broken over my room. But a big mess, a day's work to clear up, and then a workman had to dismantle much of the rest of the *devale* before (today) 3 workmen began rebuilding it. They are paid by the owner of the *devale*, which is not the god herself, who is only resident, not owner, but I'm not sure whether the *devale* is owned by one man or whether he is a front man for a committee of owners, or what the arrangement is. Perhaps, I'm like the god herself in this regard.

A few days ago I walked into the nearby village, as I often do, and saw there were flags up, and a banner on a rope overhanging the roadway, and other signs of festivities. The reason, I found, was because a deputy minister was coming to give a speech that day to inauguratethe installation of a telephone in the village's sub-post office. It's a grey dial phone, which one can hire by payment to the sub-postmaster (I suppose he's called). All calls must go through an operator. A great day in the life of the village.

A few days before that there was a *shramadana*, which is when all the villagers get together to do some public work. In this case it was clearing the weeds from the dirt road which connects up to the main road. Lots of people out with hoes, someone hooked up a tape deck to a loadspeaker (at full volume, naturally), a banner on a rope overhung the car road announcing the work. The road needed it, for the sides, by the water ditches, were quite tall with weeds. The road is motorable only about half its length, the last half being blocked by landslides; but there are signs that there are plans to asphalt the road its full length, which is maybe 3/4 of a mile. These signs—gravel piles, etc.—have been there since at least last December. Considering the work the villagers were putting in they don't seem hopeful of its quick realization.

One time in the village I passed a house where a woman was sitting outdoors in a sort of bamboo frame, curtained on three sides, but open in the front. Before her several men dressed in very elaborate costumes—brocaded sarones, the first time I've ever seen men wearing them, and what on a total would be called a middy blouse, but is in fact a traditional sort of men's blouse worn on ceremonial occasions—were dancing furiously in front of her, while several other men were wailing on flutes and beating drums. This was an exorcism of sorts, for the woman was ill (fever and so on), and the dancing was intended to cure her. It was a bit difficult to discover this, for when I asked different people everyone seemed greatly embarrassed, and they gave me slightly different explanations of the goings on, as they wanted to soften the truth of the matter. I guess they supposed I would dismiss the whole thing as primitive superstition, as they themselves were half-inclined to do. However, when I later inquired of the woman I found that she had in fact recovered. If she had died there would have been a stronger basis for dismissing the whole thing as primitive superstition (as opposed, no doubt, to the sophisticated superstition of the Western medical tradition). But it sure is a lot simpler to take two aspirin and then call the doctor in the morning (particularly since there is now a sub-phone in the sub-p.o.).

Recently I listened on a short-wave radio to one of those hot-gospel American stations that beam around the world. I've noticed before on these shows a propensity for the archaicism 'that which is', which can sound quite strange when combined with modern usage. For instance, the broadcaster said something like: 'The main book, Get All Excited, Jesus is Coming Soon, as well as The Destiny of America and the Time-Line Chart that tells you what all is happening and the order of events in which it will happen, over 100 news items in Bible references, is yours for just t̤15, that's right, send just $15 to Today in Bible Prophesy. God bless you, we want you to know that which is happening.' Well, the phrase 'that which is happening' struck me as odd, so I also noticed another 'that which is', when I heard on the same program, 'Just in case Russia strikes first our submarine can release that which is in them that can make a cinder out of Russia. Bless your hearts, we've got 19,000 nuclear warheads aimed right at them.' Of course, with stuff like that going out (and giving every appearance of having private U.S. sponsorship, even when not broadcast from US soil) one begins to think Radio Moscow tirades are not so paranoid as might be at first assumed.

The local schoolmaster has naw informed me that there are 'talking cars' in America. If true, I wonder what they say when you push the horn? 'Get off the road, you SOB!'? And no doubt they're programed to say, on a monthly basis, 'Have you mailed in your payment this month?

If not, then when Nissan executives push a button, I will drive myself back to their office.' Or, 'I am the computer working for X corporation, and according to my records I have no registered any payments from you for the last three months. So far you and I are the only ones who know about this, but if I do not receive a payment from you within ten days, then my program requires me to inform a human...*unless* (heavy computing) you happen to know a nubile young piece of software...'

These days I'm reading a quite extraordinary book called *Gödel, Escher, Bach: An Eternal Golden Braid*, which is an exploration of intelligence, both human and artificial, and therefore talks much about the principles of programming a computer. It does it with considerable wit, play, and lightness, but, though written for the newcomer, it requires careful attention to follow the mathematics, and since it's 750 large pages, I shall probably continue to be-reading-it for quite some time. I disagree with much of what he has to say, but enjoy working out exactly what my disagreement is, and thereby clarifying my own views on the nature of mind.

* * *

Kolatenna Hermitage, Bandarawela

Fooltide greetings ('Tis the season filled with folly...'). Another Xmas, another residence. I don't seem able to spend two consecutive ones in the same place, indeed I'm lucky (I guess) to be able to be in the same country. *Move thy wastes*? It's all of me, why not move all of me, that gets the heave-ho from Papa Time every time the spirit (of waste) moves him, not just the wastes, excepting one adopts the perverse view (truth will out) that it's all waste, even the part that doesn't get wasted. So here I am, never made it to the Center for the Study of Peripheries, though it warn't a half-bad notion. Still, I suppose I should be glad (or is it *sad*? I keep forgetting) that I'm *any*where for Xmas, or at least not nowhere. Not even on the edge of it, but smack dab in the middle, rainy season just ending in time for the downpour of year's end. All of which is to say, I hope you're making it well, brother, and I'll be glad to hear about it if you want to tell.

Love ya,

V.

* * *

As for the prequel to *Worthy Bones*, although you have mentioned that Our Hero was born one stormy night in Chattanooga, neither of us have charted the ins and outs of his early days.

Mohel had a very confused childhood. Although his father chewed tobacco, drank beer in his undershirt, cussed, and avoided attending the Baptist church, he was a very sloppy housepainter, who frequently came home with a red shirt collar and a blue neck to the family's embarrassment. His mother (whom his father married for the sake of a small inheritance which was soon dissipated like his father) was of Jewish stock, but she had radical ideas which turned out worse than her cooking. The matzoh balls and black-eyed peas which made their way, via his bloodstream, from Mohel's stomach to his brain, left him so uncertain of his identity that he could never quite recall whether he had any brothers or sisters.

In high school he developed an interest in the theatre and began by doing stand-ins for fallen stand-up comics. Then the civil rights movement came along, and he turned to doing sit-ins, until one day in Moscow, Georgia, he had a run-in with the local KGB, was beaten unconscious, and for the next several weeks did a lie-in.

Having thus completed his education, he enrolled in University where he neither fell in nor stood out. On the day that the last of his savings ran out he read the lines of Kenneth Patchen you mentioned ('a cowboy went to college/somebody spilled ink of his horse'), and decided to drop out.

Necessarily, the next several years were all downhill, during which time he became skilled in mankind's oldest crime, that of writing poetry. Only when his conscience (which lay in his guts) most sharply pricked him did he atone by shoplifting at the local Spend-Thrift or by impersonating the local agent for the Society for Hearing-Bar Parrots for deaf people.

He lived alone in a ramshackle old cabin in the Ozarks, built by himself upon architectural principles learned from Nature ('nothing level, nothing square') until one day in midwinter it caught fire and burned to the ground while three feet away a barrel of water stood frozen solid.

Leaving his one-man ghetto in ashes, he emigrated to Europe, where he starved, and recalled the warnings his mother had given him in the distant past ('Eat your food, Mohel: don't you know there are poets starving in Europe?'), and read Peregrine paperbacks, and peregrinated until one day in Spain when he was trying to peddle some recently-minted ancient Hebrew shekels at a synagogue in Madrid, when in quick succession he met HMV, who was seeking a suitable agent to *shul*-lift an unimportant pre-Inquisition mezuzah, and then Carmen... And there our story begins...

I continue my homeless existence. How can I found anything if I can't find it? A calling? Or a being-called? I think I may have an uncalling. I don't hear a thing (like Reagan). I hear the Russians (a.k.a. the Americans) are finally getting rid of some of their missiles, by moving them somewhere else. If that's not hearing nothing, then I don't know what ain't.

V.

* * *

Dear Rev. Sir,

I must apologize for having left you so suddenly and without farewells. This, I think, was a mistake. I hope it was not a serious one. or course, the light in that tunnel was very poor, but I don't want to blame that, I want to tell you what happened later, and how I came to be here.

I fell, I think, for a long time, although I can't be sure about this. In fact sometimes, I suspect that I'm still falling: even though I stand on solid ground unfortunately my two feet are unable to cover it all. But what I do remember is finding myself *wedged*—most uncomfortable, although possibly better than falling—between two rocks, while my feet dangled free. It was very dark, I long since dropped the Crapper. Indeed, I was so frightened of my position that I had also dropped a crap. So you see, I am your true disciple.

Then something a little bit out of the ordinary happened: a rabbit bounded past me and into a nearby hole. I was so excited to see a rabbit that without thinking about it I followed him, and found myself in another tunnel. I think this happened just in time, for behind me I could hear strange hissing sounds. I ran as fast as I could. Somehow I could see, as if all the air was aglow, as if the Crapper had taken over. I don't know how long I ran—a long time, I think. I felt energized with every breath I took. Then I heard a deep deep rumble behind me and a roar like the end of the world, and I ran and ran, but could not find the rabbit anywhere.

What I finally found was a warren, out of which many tunnels emerged, and in the centre of which was a pile of what appeared to be stringy discs. I examined one, curiouser than ever. It smelled good, so I nibbled at it. It tasted good, so I ate it. I ate many of them. Then, as I picked up the bottom disc I saw one piece of stringy stuff ran out of it and down one of the tunnels. So I followed it. This tunnel was dark, but the string went on and on, until finally I came to the end of the tunnel, and crawled up a very ordinary rabbit hole and found myself in this land.

I know you won't believe me, but people here speak very peculiar English indeed. Many speak no English at all. Isn't that amazing? But they are very nice people who treat me well, and they grow rice and tobacco (although in truth I myself have certainly lost all interest in smoking—perhaps you can understand why) and live on the side (near the top) of a big long hill with a view of many ranges of hills, and the sun rises *every* morning and sets *every* evening, which is very commendable, I think, and the people laugh and smile when they see me, I don't know why, so I try to preach to them *your* doctrine ('It all comes out in the end'), which they like very much to hear, and they show me great respect because of this and give me many stringy discs to eat, so I think I'll stay here for a while and see what happens, or doesn't.

Your devoted disciple,

Saṃsara[1]

* * *

Dear Mr. Hūm,

Please excuse me for having read your letter to Mr. Sam, but when you have read this letter I hope you will forgive me and understand my reason for having done so. I am very glad that we have finally found one of his friends, for we have no knowledge of his family or friends in India.

Mr. Sam appeared here one morning in the middle of a paddy field, unable to account for himself or how he got here. Indeed, he seemed as bewildered about his appearance (which was rather shabby: torn and

---

1. In Worthy Bones Samsara was Sancho Panza to Mohel's Don Quixote. *Saṃsāra* in Pāli means 'running-on', or becoming (from existence to existence). *Nibbāna* ends it.—Hūm.

dirty once-white robes, scratches and bruises, etc.) in our village as we were, but he seemed so harmless and good-natured that we took him in, where he at once took to going from house to house insisting upon doing the washing-up, all the time muttering strange things about either rabbis or rabbits, nobody here was quite sure. Some of the women were very happy to feed him, and soon discovered that he loved above all else our native food, stringhoppers. 'Why do they call them stringhoppers?' Mr. Sam often asked me (excuse me, I should introduce myself, I am Ven. Bodhesako, one of the village monks). 'Because they look like they're made of strings,' I told him. 'But do they *hop*?' he would ask, to which I had no answer.

Mr. Sam was so fond of stringhoppers that it was inevitable that he should eventually want to learn how to make them himself, after which he extended his services to the village beyond doing the washing-up, and went from house to house looking for opportunities to make the family stringhoppers (and, of course, to share in consuming them), and it was this that led to his downfall. As you may know, Mr. Sam, being an Indian, wore the 'lucky string', a length of black thread that had been blessed by a swami, around his wrist. What happened was this: one morning while making stringhoppers for one of our neighbors his lucky string became entangled in the strings that were being woven to make a stringhopper. Before he noticed it the lucky string (which, in retrospect, may not have been so lucky after all) was thoroughly enmeshed in a stack of stringhoppers, and in attempting to extricate himself Mr. Sam only found himself becoming more entangled. This was his mistake. He could have cut the string, but this of course would be looked upon as terribly unlucky, or he could have called for help, but he delayed until it was too late. First his hand disappeared into the stack of stringhoppers, then his arm, and by the time he called for help there was little of him left. Despite all our efforts we couldn't save him: he disappeared.

Two days later at a neighboring village a woman was preparing her family's meal when she noticed, in the stringhoppers that were being made, a black thread. She attempted to remove it and throw it away, but found that when she pulled on it a hand began to emerge. She screamed and fainted and when her husband came running in to discover the hand he pulled on it and eventually a wide-eyed and bewildered person emerged who, it was eventually discovered, was in fact our Mr. Sam. Now Mr. Sam does nothing except eat stringhoppers all day long—he won't touch anything else, not even other foods he used to love—and he won't do the washing up or anything. When he moves he doesn't walk or run, but makes a strange rabbit-like hopping move. And he now is unable to say anything at all except one sentence: 'Now I know why they're called stringhoppers'—a phrase which he repeats about two hundred times a day. Please, Mr. Hum, what does this mean? And please tell us what we should do with Mr. Sam. How can we help him?

With all friendship,

Bodhesako

* * *

...In the end, perhaps due to the exigencies of the novel's form, Heller does suggest a solution to Yossarian's dilemma. Whether this solution works artistically is not of concern to us here. Rather, we need to understand why this suggestion of a solution is incompatible with the Buddha's Teaching.

The Buddha's Teaching is concerned with letting go of what can be surrendered within the sphere of the unenlightened (namely, sensuality, hatred, lethargy, agitation, and doubt—the five hindrances) in order to allow for the possibility of seeing what might be let go of beyond that sphere. This further perception can be indicated by one who has already seen for himself, and must be initially accepted by the practitioner as an act of faith, until he too comes to see it. At that point it is possible for there to be a further letting go, a giving up of what can be surrendered only outside the sphere of the unenlightened, namely, all beliefs concerned with selfhood (*sakkāyadiṭṭhi*, *attavāda*) and, eventually, the conceit "I am" (*asmimāna*). Thus the Buddha's Teaching is a course of practice concerned fundamentally with renunciation. Without giving up the world to the limits of one's ability to do so one will never be able to extend those limits: one will instead remain entrapped within the world...

Sāmaṇera Bodhesako, from *The Buddha and the Catch-22*

* * *

Udamadura, '84

I'm not surprised you couldn't find Udamadura on your National Geographic map—it's just a farming village. It's unknown to Sinhalese except those who are locals—most Sri Lankans don't even know where Nilandahenna is, which is also not surprising, since it's just a fork in the road. Udamadura is on my one inch map (i.e. one inch to one mile scale)—it takes several dozen maps to cover all of Sri Lanka, but I have just a few sections that cover part of Upcountry, (and which cover half of one of my walls). But since Badulla is on your map, Udamadura is exactly 12 miles northwest of Badulla in a straight line (but about 50 miles by road!), and Ella, where I used to stay, is 8 miles south and very slightly west of Badulla.

Tonight I hear the villagers drumming and singing for the future tobacco crop. It's quite beautifully abloom. The flowers are rather like morning glory, only a third that size, and grow in clusters at the top of the stalk, which is usually about 3 feet tall, though some giants get up to 6 feet.

The villagers sound inspired by another flower as well. The flower of the kitul tree is pressed for its sap (one flower stalk can produce a few quarts of sap), which is fermented to make toddy. Fresh the sap is sweet and tastey, boiled down it makes jaggary, a fudge-like confection. Fermented, because of its high sugar content, it's a potent punch. There are many kitul trees here as well as eucalyptus forest which is owned by the Ceylon Tobacco Corp. The eucalyptus wood is apparently used as fuel to cure tobacco leaves. The government has been trying to discourage tobacco growing; not from any consideration of public health, but because tobacco growing causes heavy soil loss, which runs down and silts up the reservoirs, which have been redredged. On the other hand, it may have nothing to do with this either, merely another of the interminable intrigues between the Government Agent, the Forest Service, and the Ceylon Tobacco Corp.

While in Colombo last week to get some much-needed dental work done (two root canals—without proper equipment—though he seemed to know what he was doing; in any case, the choice was between his treatment and having the teeth out at once—I once read an interview with Joseph Heller in which he was asked if he believed in an 'afterlife', to which he replied 'no', though imagined if there was it was something like 'root-canal therapy'), the news came that Tamil terrorists had blown up a police station in Jaffna killing 25 people. In the following days there were several 'bomb scares' in Colombo, and one that went off harmlessly. One Tamil shop was burnt, but things didn't get out of control. Nonetheless, many Jaffna Tamils have gone back to Jaffna, though from all reports things are less safe there than in Colombo (at least for as long as there is no outbreak of violence in Colombo and there continue to be killings by the army in Jaffna, as well as the inconveniences of curfews, etc.), but perhaps they just prefer to be among familiar surroundings, ways, and peoples regardless of the actual danger—or rather that they perceive greater safety surrounded by what is familiar even when that perception may be false.

More troops were evident around town; some road barriers were set up with armed soldiers checking ID, etc., but they seemed cheerful and relaxed, not the nervy sullenness of imminent danger. The press, of course, blasted away at its usual bugaboo 'anti-social elements' (lead? manganese? fluoride?) and the papers had half-page ads placed by the army advising what to do if 'unattended parcels' were discovered (unattended *how long*?). What I liked best about my time in town was reading the comics in the papers. The comics in Sri Lanka papers—atleast the imports—exist in the 1950's exclusively. Mutt & Jeff, the Phantom, Blondie, Bringing Up Father, etc; that's the current crop.

Not able to resist the real low-brow stuff, I noted in Time that the U.S. has constructed a 'fallback' position in the Philippines on the island of Saipan. This answered my own question as to exactly where Saipan was, for, on occasion, I've caught a SW broadcast on KJOI, an all-rock station with no commercials or identification of proprietorship, and they sometimes announce that their transmitter is in Saipan. It also made me wonder whether their failure to identify their ownership might not indicate that they were not simply a group of philanthropic rock-lovers determined to bring rock-music to a hungry world, but might not be, instead, a CIA front. They seem to have their main offices or studios in Canoga Park. So I wonder if you would be interested in phoning them and mentioning that your son reports that he's heard their broadcasts round about 0700-1000 GMT (which is early afternoon here) usually a bit faint but usually clear (fading in the early afternoon and being lost in atmospherics by mid-late afternoon), in Sri Lanka, and that they might be interested in a reception report, and that by the way he was wondering how the station manages to support itself, since they have no commercial content and seem to have no religious affiliation (the Jesus stations are obviously supported by the faithful) nor government affiliation. I'd be interested to know what they say. Sometimes there are peculiar blips and beeps which previously I ascribed to the normal dirty atmospherics that creep into some broadcasts, but now I wonder if these might not be code signals to operatives. (They always come between songs.) By why rock? Is that supposed to be a good cover these days?

Maybe I've been reading too much Le Carré. I just finished his latest novel (at least the latest I know of): *The Little Drummer Girl.* I've admired much of what he's done in the past, particularly the Smiley trilogy—but *The Little Drummer Girl* is the best of all. It concerns Israeli Intelligence's plans to neutralize (I believe that is the correct phrase these days, sort of like a stomach that is slightly acidic and needs to be set aright)—to neutralize an Arab terrorist/freedom fighter (choose one). Astounding powers of characterization and a story that pulls no punches in its ethical viewpoint. For a view of the Israeli/Arab situation that you wouldn't get from any journalistic matter, I can certainly recommend it.

I spent a few days in Kandy before coming back here, and while there visited a friend who has a TV and we watched Mrs. Gandhi's funeral (I'd heard the BBC bulletins when she was shot, and managed to pick up an All-India Radio broadcast to follow developments on the day of the assassination, just before I left Colombo). What a wretched affair. Poorly organized, 3rd class all the way. Nobody knew what to do next. When the murners poured ghee on the pyre they poured it from a 4-gallon metal drum in which it is shipped, instead of having one of India's elegant brass urns filled. The army trucks had a few wreaths on the hood but otherwise were undistinguished. Even the TV camera work was atrocious. Instead of focussing (at least at some point) on the various dignitaries present and identifying them, a few quick pans without commentary was all we got, together with meaningless shots of soldiers' berets, of other unidentified goings-on, etc. Rajiv seemed to stand aloof from all the confusion, which is better than being involved in it but not as good as ending it—I predict such will be the nature of his leadership—and he was trying, I suppose, to look Prime Ministerial. He looks like a nice fellow, but Indian politics is vicious.

In Colombo I also heard the debate between Reagan and Hondale from Kansas City, about our foreign policy you know (if Rodgers and Hammerstein will forgive me). Reagan seemed to have trouble even remembering names like Beirut. His stumbling was made all the more apparent by his 'set pieces'. Well, Mondale won't get my vote either. The ballot I'd like to see would read: ☐ yes or no, ☐ yes and no (check one). I expect we'll be saddled with another 4 years of Reagan and Bush (As H.L., Mencken said: 'Democracy is the theory that the people know what they want, and deserve to get it good and hard.')

After sunset, in fact through the night here, there's a rather curious twilight, though not in the west: our very own 'northern' lights. 15 miles north of Udamadura is the Victoria Dam on the Mahaweli, the biggest river in Sri Lanka, and the glow in the northern sky is from arc lights at the project.

Infinitely more impressive, however, was a sunrise I saw about 3 weeks ago. The most amazing I've ever seen. The sun rose into a long black cloud which hung a few degrees above the eastern horizon, and was hidden. But to the south a large fluffy cloud hung alone in an intense pale sky, like one usually sees only in high mountains in winter. And on this cloud was a patch of intense brightness as brilliant as if the sun was rising there instead of about 20 degrees to the north, and on the left-hand edge of this brilliant patch were bands of intense orange, red, brown, green, deep blue, which shimmered as if they were a light source rather than reflected light, absolutely brilliant. Meanwhile below the black cloud, between it and the mountain, the sky remained a deep and fiery orange for an amazingly long time. What I theorize is that although it was a normal morning at my altitude it may have been unusually cold in the high air (as the intense pale color suggests) and the cloud my have contained frozen ice crystals which caught the sun—and could stand out so brilliantly because of the dark cloud hiding the sun. The green color was especially remarkable.

As I blow out the lamp, listening to distant drums and trills of flutes, it occurs to me that a local money-lender, one of the honest ones, who charges merely 10% interest a *month* (which, you can figure, in a year makes a peasant farmer into an indentured servant for life), has been very ill. Perhaps the celebration is for it—or against it'?

Did you know George Bizet wrote an opera set in Sri Lanka called the Pearl Fisher?

Love,

Bob

* * *

BEAD

Is I is or is I ain't? Well, I is and I ain't, though what I is and what I ain't wouldn't bear thinking about, much less discussion. Actually, I did reply to your letter in a letter dealing with the on-going (…and going and going but never quite gone) sad saga of Sam who, it seems, has got himself into a stringhopper. This letter was sent to your old chap (apparently retired or dead; to be sadly missed) POB. Perhaps it will be forwarded to you by this General Delivery fellow (what *are* you doing mixing with this shadowy military type these days?). Or, perhaps, not, I also sent you, via slowboat to China, care of departed Mr. POB, a booklet, *The Buddha and Catch-22*, which should arrive, if it is to arrive, later than sooner. Let me know if there is any spooky communication between Mr. POB and General D. (What could *they* be up to?) If not I'll send another booklet, and perhaps also a repeat of the latest gossip re. Sam.

Speaking of gossip, Our Carmen of the Snows dropped me these lines: 'I'm down from my tottery Himalayan perch, umgnificent though it was, but I understand now I can no longer pay the price for getting high off someone else's magnificence, even if that someone is no one—shades of *Ayin*[1]—the wrong roof for this fiddler. It's just too bright for my dark Semitic soul.' Ergo, her pan-Asian search for panacea proceeds apace… Perhaps you've got more details?

And you? What is and what ain't. Don't be coy. Your last missive made the most passing of references to some bloody great accident, but (even without the gory details) failed to cover the ground (is that the phrase?) in the least comprehensible manner, leaving me quite uncertain as to what is—perhaps, though, that makes 3 of us? Are you still in your stump, or have you been uprooted?

V.

* * *

(And then the rains came—and came and came! The Upcountry of Sri Lanka had further to fall than the lowlands of the Negev—though it was not even the second time the ground didn't stay put under Bob's feet—for him, even the Flood's twice—Hūm)

1. The Non-Existent; her name for God—Hūm

Ella—January '86

For days we were in very thick cloud much of the time, raining almost continuously, atleast as a drizzle, swept by winds. As a result the parapet wall which fronts the verandah became increasingly drenched. Now, on this wall are 3 posts which support that part of the roof which covers the verandah and cantilevers several feet in front of the parapet. About 9:30 at night this parapet collapsed, in part, taking with it two of the posts which were holding up the front of the roof, causing that half of the front of the roof to tilt at a strong angle. I made an effort to shore up the beam but found this impossible. In fact, a support was torn from my hands as one of the cross-beams cracked. The inside was unaffected, and I contemplated staying the night there, moving over to the half of the room that was away from the tilted roof, but when another roof beam cracked I thought that although I might make a bed, and I might lie in it, it was unlikely I would sleep in it.

So I grabbed a bag, stuffed with a few things, donned a poncho, took the lantern, and was about to leave—when I was delayed by two hours. First I discovered that a mouse and her pups had taken up their domicile in my bag. Perhaps to distract me from her sleepy pups not inclined to move, she jumped out and darted around the room until I finally caught her under my alms bowl. I took her and the pups a decent distance from the cottage and let them find a new home. When I came back and opened the door, a kind of robin, a black robin, flew inside. There was no catching her, except by giving up. I left the door open and she finally flew out. I heard several roof tiles fall off the roof. They're quite heavy and could be dangerous. The whole house seemed ready to collapse. Even walking into a storm at night seemed a safer place to be.

The gully by the bus road was in half flood, but I was able to leap it, and then went to my nearest neighbors, about 200 yards away, but it seemed they had already left their house—a brand new and well—constructed building—for the schoolhouse, since they thought it was safer. However, my next nearest neighbors were in and they gave me shelter. Their house is tile-roofed from the front to the peak, but shingle and thatch-roofed down to the back—they are not well-off and probably haven't yet been able to afford the additional tiles—and the back half of their house dripped into numerous pots and pans through the night.

About 5 AM the rain became torrential for an hour or so, and at first light I could see the gullies—not the little one I have to cross to the road but the much bigger ones that run year around—in a raging torrent that reminded me of the flooded wadi mt Ein Gedi in '65, though the Ein Gedi flood was far more substantial since it was at the bottom of the riverbed systems rather than well up the mountain. You might think that since we have passed the winter solstice that sunrise would be coming earlier each day, but repeated observations through the years convinces me that in fact the sun continues to rise ever later until late January or so, and if the days do truly become longer (and it's not just a scientific hoax) that it must be due to the later sunset. Therefore it didn't get light until after 6, and then, once the gully to my place receded enough to be negotiable, we were able to survey the damage by light.

Of course, I hadn't known, as I lay awake much of the night, what I would find in the morning—complete devastation or no further damage—but it turned out between the two extremes. From the front wall forward every tile had fallen to the ground, many broken, and the third front roof support had collapsed, and he whole front part of the roof tilted down, lacking support. But without tiles it was no longer so very heavy and therefore the roof over the room held firm aside from a few tiles which were out of place, perhaps due to the roof tilting forward, dropping a load of tiles, and then resettling.

The verandah was blocked so that rainfall was trapped and running backwards under the door frame into the room, but most everything in the room was still dry. Since there is a problem with termites, before I leave I always pack the books and papers into the emptied rain barrel and a few buckets, so there wasn't a lot to do to pack up the contents of the room, and various neighbors came and helped remove everything to the house where I had spent the night, and to put up some temporary braces to hold up the front of the roof frame, and to cut a channel to drain the porch. Almost the whole parapet wall had collapsed and there were no tiles before the front wall to protect the top of it, but I didn't think it safe to start climbing up on the roof to put up tiles, so left that to stand or fall as chance would have it.

A repair job is possible, but not for a long time, since new tiles are needed and they are expensive and would have to be brought in by truck, which cannot be done until the road is repaired, which will take months. This road was built about 10 years ago by hand, without any heavy-machinery available for its repair. Once I had seen a round near Bandarawela being built by hand and I talked to the supervisor, who told me that in terms of cost there was little difference, except that when construction was manual the cost went mostly as wages to poor local people whereas when construction was by machine it went mostly to Japan for heavy equipment, wasting valuable foreign exchange. The only disadvantage to manual building is that it's so very much slower.

Naturally I was told I could put up with one of the villagers until the rains were finished, but this would be very inconvenient both for them and me, so I decided to go at least to Nilandahenna to learn the condition of the main roads. Since I didn't want to leave my things in the house where I slept (too small and also too leaky) we then arranged to shift everything to a closet in the schoolhouse some distance off. This was completed about 10 AM. All this time the rain had ranged from steady to drizzle. The road, I was told, was no longer passable even on foot—I didn't believe this at the time but later when I saw the Randy road I could easily believe that the Udamdura road was indeed impassable even by foot.

However, several, villagers had to go to Nilandahenna, one of them being a a man I knew well, and they were going over the mountain, so I decided to join them.

It could have been a terrible climb if it had been storming and windy, but fortunately the whole climb was done in a light drizzle without wind, so it was merely difficult. In some places the way was very muddy, sometimes boulders had slipped across onto the path, obliterating it, but when I had climbed in the past it had been hot and sunny and this time at least it wasn't hot but cool, so that discomfort was eliminated.

I went as fast as I safely could, but still the villagers went slow for them to let me keep up. It was perhaps a 45 minute climb, with lots of leeches near the top, but we had a bar of soap, which when applied to the feet will instantly change a leech's intentions from bite to flight.

Along the top of the plateau there was a lot of laterite to deal with, which is extremely slippery when wet, and the down side was mostly stony. I found that the gully that we needed to negotiate was not crossed but rather descended along for several hundred yards, so it is extremely fortunate there were no heavy rains, since muddy water would obscure the rocky and uneven bottom, and its pressure would inevitably cause a fall. But the gully had only a few inches of water running and was negotiated safely and carefully.

While descending we met a village family going up, the wife had been in the hospital near Watumulla having a baby when a mudslide endangered the hospital and forced evacuation of all patients. Since they were poor people there was no place for them to stay, so they had to return to Udamadura. So the wife was carrying a 3-day-old baby while the husband was lugging all their goods plus a jerrican of kerosene up this rugged hillside—and the side we were descending is about 4 times the length of the side toward Udamadura. Until the road is repaired this will be the only way the villagers can get supplies from the outside—kerosene, food, medicine, building material to repair their houses, etc. It will all have to be carried over the mountain.

Near the bottom it started raining hard, but a few minutes later we were among tea bushes, and in another few minutes had arrived in Nilandahenna. I went to the post-office to give them a change of address to the monastery in Colombo where I usually stay when in the city. The post-master told me all roads were blocked, even to Watumulla, the next town towards Kandy, 4 miles away, and that I would have to stay in Nilandahenna for at least a few days until the roads could be cleared. I thanked him and left. Then I met the G.A. (Government Agent, top man in each district), who also told me that the road to Watamulla could be walked but not driven. I said I'd walk. He tried to discourage me. As we discussed the matter the van which plies this stretch of road pulled in from Watumulla and discharged passengers. End of debate. I got in the van and when they collected a full load we set off for Watumulla.

The road was indeed in bad shape, and there were many places where there was just barely enough clearance between the edge and the mud, or as fallen tree, or boulders—many kinds of obstacles. But the road was motorable and we made the 4 miles in about 30 minutes. From here I set out on foot, but my writing hand is giving out so I'll continue later.

Later—So I set out from Watumulla on foot. I'd been told the road was closed as far as Rikilikasgada, 18 miles away, but that from there I could get a bus to Kandy, but I had the idea that I might get lucky along the way, for example meeting some earth-moving equipment which might give me a lift.

About a mile out of Waatumulla I met a bus coming the other way. It stopped and the driver told me that the road was motorable for only another 3 miles or so and that he would return if he got enough passengers, but I decided to keep walking, and if he came along then fine and if not I was better off moving.

The weather was drizzly to dry. I was now on the west side of the big range of hills that form the first barrier to the NE monsoon (Udumadura is on the eastern side), and as I learned later this was in fact an effective partial barrier. Also, this stretch of road offers views of some of the most spectacular variegated, and dramatic country in Sri Lanka, and I'd never seen it before it as walking pace, so it was actually quite pleasant.

Again there were narrow places and some ankle-deep mud, but with sandals off this could be managed without difficulty. So after a while I came to the end of the motorable stretch. There were people walking here and there most of the way, generally going short distances, but I met one person who had begun walking that morning from Rikilikasgada (coming from Kandy), and who warned me that there were many places that were difficult or dangerous.

The first few places that were not motorable were relatively minor—a couple of men with shovels could have cleared them sufficiently for a car in a few hours—but then I came to a place where large boulders blocked any possibility of motor traffic. Many earth slips, and a couple places where part of the roadway had collapsed into the deep valley below. But certainly the worst of all was a place where mud about 2 feet deep covered the entire road up to the very edge, and the only way across was to plunge in. It was thigh-deep, and each step involved pulling out one leg and swinging it forward and plunging it into the mud. Only about 30 paces, but it took 30 minutes, and was very exhausting. Of course, there were plenty of small stream where I could wash off, but the mud was smelly and I noticed bright pink splotches on my legs as I cleaned myself off. These remained with me until Colombo, and I've been treating them with a cream since then with some relief—they can itch fiercely for short periods of time—but they will no doubt go away in a few days.

The sky remained leaden, with a light rain on-and-off through the day—not unpleasant walking weather, and since the road was a steady slight downhill grade this was also nice; and by evening I'd covered about 9 miles from Watumulla, leaving me, I incorrectly calculated, another 6 to go to Rikilikawsgada, when I came to a village where I asked about shelter.

I was told the schoolhouse (apparently built to be a refuge not only for the mind in these small villages) was completely filled with refugees who had fled endangered houses, but I pointed out that I was also a refugee, since my house had, indeed, collapsed, so I was taken to the schoolhouse, where I was recognized by someone from the Nilandahenna area as the foreign monk who lived in Udamadura, and the outcome was that eventually I was taken off to a private house and given a bed to sleep on—a result which was very pleasing and very kind of my hosts, but in Sri Lanka not really at all surprising. You would be correct if you supposed that I went to sleep right away, although the sleep was neither as solid nor as long as I would have liked due to the itching of my legs.

Wednesday AM

I forgot to mention yesterday that while walking, on that first day, in late afternoon I heard loud motor sounds and shortly afterwards a convoy of road-repair vehicles came along, heading toward Nilandahenna—a jeep, dumpster, backhoe (with those huge 4 feet high balloon tires), and road gang. They gave me a cheery wave as they passed. Too bad they weren't going my way, but I reflected first that it was conceivable that they could clear the road as far as Nilandahenna that night, in which case it was possible that the 6:30 AM Kandy bus might run the next day, and secondly that even if that didn't happen, at least the road would likely be clear now of any more major obstacles ahead of me, and in fact this was true the rest of the day—nothing more than ankle-deep from then on.

So when I set off the next morning shortly after 6 I was still quite tired, but hopeful that perhaps a bus or van would come along or that atleast there would be no obstacles ahead.

After about 2 miles of walking in fact a lorry came from behind me, having started I don't know where—the first vehicle since Watumulla, except the road gang—and gave me a lift. They said they were going to Kandy, so I started to feel very lucky, but my luck didn't hold. After a mile or so we came to a place where a bridge had been washed out and a way had been cleared for vehicles to go around and through the streambed—boulders as large as houses lay about and the way went around these. But apparently during the night there had been further earth-slippages and mud-slides and the way was blocked.

We cleared some of the stones by hand and then the driver tried to bully his way across the rocky terrain, but he became stuck on an iron girder from the bridge, and after a lot of pushing it was apparent that he (and anything that might come behind him) had gone as far as he was going until heavy equipment arrived.

So I set off walking again. I could see two sets of caterpillar treads on the road, one coming and one going, so I assumed the way past the broken bridge had been cleared by a treadled vehicle, and in fact after a mile or so a Jap version of a D-9 or D-10 came along, obviously to clear the landslide of the night before—all heavy equipment in Sri Lanka is of Japanese origin.

I figured there were about 2 miles left to Rikilikasgada, and was disappointed now to be told by several different people that there were in fact 5 miles to go. I was tired, and had developed a few blisters, and would have been glad to stop, but was determined to get on with the trip.

However, after 2 miles I did come to a town where in fact a CTB bus was parked and just about to leave for Rikilikasgada—apparently it had been mrooned there for some days and the drivers had enjoyed a paid holiday which they were now obliged to end. So I hopped on and stretched out while we jangled the last 3 miles Rikilikasgada, where a Kandy bus was due to leave in 10 minutes.

I was told there were no further roadblocks and that traffic was running freely, so I thought that at last my difficulties were over—a dangerous thought, as I soon found out, for a few miles down the road there was a sudden loud hissing sound, the bus started listing and bouncing to a stop—flat tire! It's never over I decided, and sat down to wait until, about 20 minutes later, another bus came along and went into Kandy without further incident.

From Kandy, in a pouring rain, I got the Colombo express, which plies the 72 mile route (for 20 rupees—about 72 cents) in a mere 2½ hours—a fantastic speed from my point of view! By the time we reached the plains the rain had stopped and I could see blue patches of sky—the first in over a week—and when we arrived in Colombo it was warm and sunny and people were walking about doing their shopping and it was obvious to me that none of them had the slightest notion of what had been happening Upcountry—oh, they heard the news and read the papers, but it might as well have been on Mars, they didn't relate to it (except perhaps to wonder why I would go about town looking so scruffy and dirty—even for a monk). A genuine refugee, unnoticed in the throng, though perhaps not unsmelt. But I have no plans to register myself with the UNRWA.

Since then a few people I've spoken with seemed genuinely interested in what had been going on in Upcountry, but most listened only out of politeness or stupor—it meant nothing to them. And why should it? The next day, Sunday, was sunny and I wondered what conditions might be like up there, but aside from a few newspaper reports it was for me too becoming just a somewhat remote incident. I don't even know whether the rains have ceased yet—no way for me to find out.

So here I am, contemplating my next move. They say that getting there is half the fun. I can't wait for the other half.

* * *

If any character in *Catch-22* comes close to accepting the Buddha's advice it would be Dunbar, who tries to increase his lifespan by cultivating boredom, on the grounds that when you're bored time passes slower. His idea seems to be that if only he could achieve a state of total and absolute boredom he would be, for all intents, eternal. This sounds like a rough literary approximation to meditation (although we must remember that the Buddha, unlike many Eastern teachers, quite explicitly stated that meditation by itself is an insufficient condition for enlightenment).

Dunbar, given to cultivating boredom, to seeking eternity, lies motionless in bed: he goes so far in his efforts that at one point Yossarian, looking at him, wonders whether he is still alive. This will remind us of the story of the Ven. Sañjíva who, we are told (M. 50: i,333), was seated immersed in the highest meditative attainment when some cowherds, shepherds, and ploughmen, passing by, saw him and thought, as did Yossarian of Dunbar, that he was dead. They collected grass, wood, and cowdung, heaped it up about the Ven. Sañjīva, set his pyre alight, and went on their way. The next morning Ven. Sañjíva emerged from his meditative attainment and went wandering for almsfood. His would-be cremators were astonished at seeing him alive and gave him the name by which he became known, Sañjīva, which means "with life." Dunbar seems to have lacked the Ven. Sañjīva's meditative abilities, but each sought to escape death (Ven. Sañjīva, the Sutta tells us, successfully), and each came thereby to be taken as dead.

It is common, of course, for beginning meditators to be assailed by boredom (as well as the other four hindrances); however, this does not justify equating boredom and meditation: on the contrary, boredom is an enemy of meditation. Despite the story of Ven. Sañjīva, then, we must regard any effort to equate meditation with the cultivation of boredom as tenuous, and as being further weakened by the episode in which Dunbar becomes *a fortiori*. However, we must also note that it is immediately after Dunbar becomes convinced, upon re-encountering the soldier in white, that (p. 358) "There's no one inside! ... He's hollow inside, like a chocolate soldier"—thereby perhaps suggesting something of the Buddha's teaching of *anattā*, of not-self—that Dunbar is *disappeared*. We never learn the meaning of this cryptic event ("It doesn't make sense. It isn't even good grammar"—p. 359), but if the parallel with meditation is accepted then the further parallel that would be suggested here is with *nibbāna*, extinction. After being disappeared Dunbar is described (p. 360) as being "nowhere to be found", which is exactly how the Suttas describe beings who have attained full enlightenment (*arahattā*).[1]

Perhaps a literary parallel of an achievement that transcends literature (let alone literature, *nibbāna* transcends *bhava*, being) could not be more closely described; but in any case we cannot allow that the parallel is more than a suggestion, and (no doubt inevitably) an inaccurate one at that. And in any case to be disappeared sounds, from Heller's description of it, far less desirable than extinction, from the Buddha's description of that. (Still, it would be interesting to know how much acquaintance Heller actually had, if any, with any school of Buddhism during the seven years in which he was writing Catch-22.[2])

Sāmaṇera Bodhesako, from *The Buddha and the Catch-22*

* * *

---

1. The phrase occurs frequently in the Suttas. See e.g the concluding lines of the Vakkali Sutta (SN 22:87). At Dhp 180 we find:
   That tangle of snares by which he'd be penned isn't found anywhere.
   His range has no end, that Buddha awake.
   What track can there be to trace one who's trackless, craving-free?
2. This question was put to Mr. Heller. The reply was that he knew "not an inkling." The range of the *puthujjana*, it seems, is more extensive than commonly supposed.—Hūm.

(In Colombo Bodhesako picked up a box of books and manuscripts he'd requested which had been shipped from the States. He needed the material for the annotation and commentary of his verse translations of the Dhammapada. But what he was again faced with was the manuscript of Ñāṇavīra Thera, which had so deeply instructed and haunted him for twenty years. He realized that it was finally *his* responsibility to prepare the manuscript for publication, and he also realized that would not mean merely editorial duties. With only a small fund available for the project, the only way he could see that it could be done properly was to electronic type-set it himself. So, having never touched a computer in his life, he began looking around for a suitable word-processing system, and also a place to do the work: i.e. a dry, stable room with electricity and few distractions. Also in the box were a bundle of my old letters to him during his former sojourn in Sri Lanka. He sent them back to me with a note.—Hūm)

A warning about going down old rabbit holes. You can *never* tell what you'll find in them. Rabbit shit. Rabbit food. Rabbit nests. Maybe even rabbits. This stuff turned up (incredible what people will squirrel away, isn't it? Or should I say, what people will rabbit away?). Now it's turned over. Perhaps it will be turned out, or in. Down, not likely. (You don't get down off a rabbit anyway; you get down off a goose.)

Anyway, I introduce you to yourself—Hum, meet Eric, meet Jungne, meet Fred & Nelly, etc. Also some old friends, such as Vināyadhara & Ñāṇasuci. I could go on. No doubt I shall. But not here. Let you dig into it now and watch karmic juices get squeezed back into their fruit.

V.

* * *

I believe I mentioned the Congreves when I was staying at Ella—they are the friendly couple who were managing (the husband, at any rate) one of the large tea estates near to Ella. Now he has retired and they have moved to their own tea estate—about 40 acres—a few miles the other side of Bandarawela. They will be setting aside a small part of their bungalow for me, and that will be (I hope) a more suitable place than where I am now in a number of ways, particularly for the work I shall be doing. (By the way, in Sri Lanka the word 'bungalow' is used to describe the single-story palatial residences built mostly during colonial times for estate managers. In those days the owners were usually in England, and since they knew that their managers could easily rob them blind, the usual strategy of defence was to give them everything they could possibly want anyway, leaving them with little incentive to cheat. An estate bungalow is typically built from granite blocks, expensive hardwoods, etc. with generous proportions and set on a carefully tended lawn with lavish gardens. Even today they are almost all kept up and retain their English atmosphere.) There are, it seems, several foreigners staying there (also a 'guest' bungalow, a smaller affair with four rooms, which is rented out—though I've been told that if I would pay for the electricity I use the Congreves expect no rent from me), but I haven't met any of them and have been told that everyone keeps very much to himself, which is fine with me. Unforeseen problems could arise, of course, but it could turn out to be just what I need presently.

But before I move to the estate a trip to Colombo is necessary to have some corrections made to this word-processor which by now you will have realized that I have. A computer, actually, coupled to a printer, with a word-processing software package. Therefore it can be used for many other projects besides word-processing. But there seems to be a problem in that the software will not communicate certain commands to the printer, and therefore it can't do all the things it is supposed to be able to do in setting text to look like a professionally-set book. My requirements are for as text-setting ability, since that is its primary purpose (though I admit to having quite a bit of fun with it already and have written some basic programs myself). The computer is an Epson QX-11 with a monochrome green monitor and dual disk drives, and the printer (the Spinwriter ELF 350) is made by NBC. Epson, I learned only yesterday, is owned by Seiko. NBC is the telecommunications giant, Japan's answer to AT&T.

Everything goes slowly in Sri Lanka. I ordered the system when I was in Colombo in January, but since some of it had to be 'got down' (as Sinhalese English puts it) from Singapore I didn't actually take delivery until my trip to Colombo of about six weeks back. So, knowing about delays, it would not surprise me if the software problem did not get corrected this trip.

The book I will be publishing is that of my teacher, Ñāṇavīra Thera, a typescript of which you saw about 18 years ago. I'm not the only one involved, but am the principal editor. I've also written some things and there is the possibility that they will be published under the same imprint—we are setting up an entity called Path Press to handle legal matters, though there is no plan for it to be a full-function publisher. But one thing at a time. After this book we'll see what, if anything, comes next.

I suppose you'd only find giardia[1] listed in a medical dictionary, since it only occurs in tropical climates. It's an intestinal infection characterized by loose motions and frequent belching, often with a foul taste. Though I've never had it before now, it's, apparently, not uncommon, and is not regarded as dangerous but it is persistent and difficult to get rid of completely. However, I have been free of symptoms for a week or so and a stool test shows no parasites, amoebas, etc., of any kind. But it's sapped my energy, at least; at most, it's a discomfort and hindrance to concentration.

Well, that's the second time I typed the preceding. I got that far the first time when there was a power cut of about a half second and everything got totally erased. This time I've recorded it to disk so that that can't happen. Hardly a day goes by without a power cut—usually brief, but occasionally lasting several hours. So it's necessary to get into the habit of saving a disk every half hour or so. (There are some word-processing programs that will do so automatically, but not this one.) Then it would not be possible to lose more than a half-hour's work (though I doubt it took more than either half an hour or half a brain to compose the preceding).

The Kantalee dam—as you ask—is far from here. (This is Upcountry—dams are a feature of the plains.) It is in the Trincomalee area, a place where there is a lot of fighting going on, and it may be that the dam was sabotaged, as claimed by one group. I doubt the rains had anything to do with it, else there would have been earlier warnings of its being breeched. I believe it's one of the ancient earthwork dams constructed 15 centuries ago at a time when major irrigation schemes were the kings' pride for several centuries. It may have been strengthened in recent times, though these old dams have been found to be very well engineered. No doubt you also heard about the plane being blown up at the airport. Although the political situation seems worsening, there is no reason, however, to believe that it will affect Upcountry (except in

1. Perhaps, not the first symptom, or misdiagnosis, of the herniated bowel, which eventually took him to his death-bed in the hospital in Katmandu.—Hūm

indirect ways, such as economic), and however disastrous it is to those unfortunate enough to live in the north of the island it is to me so far only a nuisance (e.g. the army's main training camp is only a few miles away, and their target practice, which is clearly audible, has increased considerably since I was first involuntarily introduced to their 'fusillade symphony' when I settled in Ella). But, where are there no troubles? (E.g. The rain in Ukraine is a radioactive bane.)

* * *

May Flours

May flours are the best for making stringhoppers and glue for aerogrammes without a glue.

I've now returned from my wanderings to distant lands (like Colombo and Dodanduwa), where I write several novels in my head; such as an action-packed soy thriller with high-governmental intrigues and international consequences that just happens to be set not in modern times but in India, 2500 years ago, in which a certain ascetic who has attracted many disciples, and for whom certain extraordinary claims are being made, happens to play a role which, though minor, turns out to be vitally crucial to the denouement? Howzat for a guaranteed worst-seller? And then there was the one about the very first European who ever became a Buddhist monk (that we know of), who happens to be a Greek at the time of King Asoka (he—the Greek—is mentioned in the Dipavaṃsa)—how he came to India (as a spy for the Persian emperor who, having heard of the death of Bindusara—Asoka's pa—and foreseeing a power struggle sees a chance to regain territory lost by his grandpa to Asoka's grandpa, Chandragupta—perhaps as a spy disguised as a merchant who gets into the court and participates in the power struggle and learns about India—maybe he was a Stoic back in Athens, from which he's now exiled—and maybe… but that would be telling you my plot, and maybe you prefer to invent your own, or none at all, and, in fact, due to a power outage of no longer than a hiccup, it—unrecorded to disk in my head—has disappeared into an mnemonic black hole forever… Just as well, I could never get up the steam to actually *write* it…

Yes, it must be getting difficult to know how to address me by now—I know it's not easy figuring out how to sign off at the end of a letter. Indeed, I shall soon run out of letters in the roman alphabet and shall have to turn to some other alphabet—fortunately no shortage of them, either ancient or oriental, to choose from—and shall eventually become first unspellable, later unpronouncable, and in the end, dead.

Yes, love,

um...well...B?...no, V?...no, how about RES? CDE? BEAD? QED?

(Dear Postmaster of Sooke, B.C., Please be advised that the addressee of this letter is a criminal of the worst sort, who refuses to believe the popular lie and will not bow down to Mammon. Obviously he deserves the harshest penalty society can possibly offer him, which is to entirely ignore him, I trust to your good offices to see that this is achieved. He informs me, without ever complaining, that you have been reading his mail. The nerve of him, to have neither righteous indigestion nor wrongeous indigestion. Please horsewhip him, if you have a horse. Or dogwhip, catwhip, or canary whip him. On second thought, he would then no longer feel ignored, so better not. Instead, just put his name quietly on file with the KGB—North American HQ in Moscow, Georgia. Your friendly spy, X.)

* * *

Tell you what, if I die before you then you can have my body, give you all the opportunity to see me again that you could ask for. Sure, I'd love to see you too, and not only you but a whole trainload of people I've enjoyed in my own way, but also every morning I wake up and see my robes and almsbowl and give a cheery wave and say 'Hi there, friend', and I just couldn't face the prospect of parting from my dearly beloved (not to mention loving my dearly departed). Of course, you'd always be welcome to hop out here and join me—if your brotherly twinge can ever find its way outside those big black parentheses, that is—and I'd even be willing to arrange for some robes, a bowl, and a stump in the woods. But maybe your nearly departed, the ever-departing HMV,[1]

1. In *Worthy Bones*, HMV was the representative of the English 'collector', Sir Makepeace Gravenhenge (SMG), who, perhaps, 'more than represented him' and hired Mohel to pinch the Buddha's bones; he was also the author of the novel and now and then in his dotage dashes off notes of bone—dry humor to former agents and god-knows who else.

might object as vociferously to your departure as my nearly parted robes (oy, have they got patches—but the rains-retreat ends in a few weeks and next month I get a new one, wot cheer) object silently to the thought of mine. So here I sits.

You'd like some local color for what disappeared down my black hole? Mauve, magenta, burgandy, chartreuse? We got 'em all. But which one fits into a book you ain't writ yet I couldn't say. So instead of sending you a lot of paint buckets which you might not even be able to use at all, would it not, pray, be better if you sent your quasi-historical rag to me and then let me suggest where specific touches of specific shades might go well? I'll be a sort of interior decorator. (I've always fancied starting a firm called Sky Ghost Writing Services.) Send me your novels, your poems, your essays and potboilers, I'll turn them into spiffy scenes you'd be proud to have your friends in for dinner parties. Meanwhile, back at the typer, I think your idea of a novel about the famine in Ethiopia has to be a sure-fire winner provided that you write it as a well-ordered garden rather than as a dense, impenetrable jungle. Publishers just are not handy with machetes or pruning shears, and tend to fear meeting up with a libelous lion who has become a publisher-eater.

I'm not the sort to attack dying people, even though we're all dying, where the devil else you think we're heading, particularly when they're as busy dying as old HMV seems to be these last years, but he seems to have latched on to the peculiar notion that somewhere or somehow the Buddha teaches the Truth, and he seem to have the further notion that there ain't no such thing. Well, if that's his truth... But actually, I'm not aware of anyplace in the Pāli Suttas where the Buddha makes any such suggestion (though all sorts of people, starting probably with Nagasena, make that claim on his behalf). He claims to teach something quite different from Truth, or so I read it, so the question of how messy the universe is actually misses the point. The point is that man is perpetually unhappy with the, as he sees it, mess, and is always trying to neaten it up, which as HMV says is poetry. But what the Buddha says is that all this ordering of the universe to be other than it is, poetic as it may be, is just *dukkha*;. To give up *dukkha* you have to see that to give up *dukkha* you have to give up poetry. I'd like to see you nuke that one rhyme. Whatever ol' buddy HMV sees in the Buddha is all in the eye of the beholder. It's not a question of how much can be or cannot be known, but of how much can be or cannot be groan. Like nearly everyone, HMV seems to be doing his best to miss the point. But since HMV thinks the Buddha is finally poetry (or the poetry of no poetry), then I'm very pleased to know he's not a Buddhist. I'm not either (as Stan Laurel once remarked).

Ven. Dukkha[1]

* * *

... The upper slopes were closed all morning by heavy snow. When the clouds lifted around noon, I was one of the first on the just-opened lift and at the top there was miles of untouched powder snow. My skis sank ankle deep, giving incredible support, but the snow was dry so speed was possible, and everything was so quiet and pristine. After speeding down a slope I came to a rise which ant the top (as I discovered when I got there) was cut away sharply. There was no warning, no chance for planning, just the automatic reaction as for 15 yards I sailed over the snow and made a perfect landing. It was such a rush I knew why people risk their necks to do those incredible hundreds-of-yards jumps... This was one of the most vivid dreams I've ever had in my life—not a fantasy, but a memory—perfect recall of an event I'd all but forgotten. The jump with synchronous perfect recall...a suggestion, perhaps, of what I'm trying to do with my life?...

My stay in Colombo was much longer than I'd have thought possible, but all's well that ends well (enough), for I finally got the basic software problem sorted out. I had to return the computer to the people who sold it to me, since their model couldn'd handle the software I needed. They weren't very gracious about it, but in the end they had no choice, not only because legally I was in the right but also because I know a few people who could make my position stick, and the computer company knew it. So I got a different computer, a Taiwan-made CAF, which is simply an imitation of the IBM PC, mistakes and all (the better compatibles try to put right some of the things IBM did wrong). But it runs the software I need to use (and makes my printer work up to its capacities),

1. In *Worthy Bones*, Ven. *Dukkha* (Pali: un-satisfaction) was the Buddhist Patriarch of the island of Samadhi and possessor of the relics. In the original draft he was called Ven. *Tanha* (Pali: desire, craving).

and also the people who sold it are reliable and will always go out of their way for me, and that makes a big difference in this country. For instance, I paid for 256KB RAM (random access memory—the amount of data the computer can keep in its own memory, the more of which the more software it will be able to run and the faster it will be able to run it), but they gave me a computer with 640KB memory, remarking that the additional memory chips (worth about ṭ̤100) were already soldered into place and it wasn't worth their while to remove them. Obviously, there was only one possible reply I could make to this, namely, 'Thanks for the memories'.

A video game called 'Demon's Forge' intrigued me. In most games one knows the rules and wins by skill within the confines of the rules: in this one only a few of the rules are given, and one has to discover, by experiment, what the remaining rules are. They could, perhaps, re-name this game 'Life'.

I remember as a kid the only sort of entertainment comparable to video game was the pinball machine—put a nickel in and get five balls and two or more flippers. Well, it's more expensive now—in video: costs a quarter to play, but since pushing 'Q' earns me two bits a push I can manage. Extremely realistic, with flippers, etc. exactly like the mechanical versions of old. Only thing is that it's hard to remember that to 'jiggle' the machine certain keys have to be pushed: the tendency is still to try to jiggle the table, which achieves nothing (except jiggling the table). And if you push those jiggle keys too much, you go tilt. On the other hand, with the electronic version it's possible to change virtually any of the parameters at will: bumper action, flipper response, scoring system, etc. The curious thing, however, is my reaction to winning a 'free' game. In the arcade version there is always the rationale that a 'free game' means additional playing time for my money, but here obviously the plays don't cost me anything at all, except wear and tear of the keyboard: why, then, should there still be the same emotional response of satisfaction at winning a free game, even when it's only by matching numbers at the end of play?

Then I tried the 'Flight Simulator' and was eventually successful in bombing Kraut factories and shooting down a, number of Hanse-Brandenburg DIs, Albatross DIIs, and Fokker DVIIs. I learned something about the controls, including the radar and radio, and managed a few daredevil stunts. However, I couldn't land successfully. When in the

Chicago area, it is from Meigs Field that I fly, by the way, and the tall building into which I frequently crash is, therefore, the John Hancock building.

I also beat the computer in chess: quite badly; it was probably embarrassed.

This all plays well with my sense of satire; generally unwelcome in polite society. But I'm not the first to be misunderstood when irony is intended: it's a risky undertaking. Even Swift had some trouble, I believe, when he made a modest proposal of his own.

While in Colombo I read a report on the results of a match in the recent World Cup games which observed that the 'Lebanese marked the football victory in traditional fashion, blaring car horns and firing machine guns.' I also learned that the word 'optimism' was first used in 1737, and of the invention of a new unit of measure called a 'helen', which is the quantity of beauty sufficient to launch one ship. (Helen of Troy is of course the standard measure, at 10 kilohelens.) I also heard a few BBC programs on the radio. I enjoyed the Vienna Boys' Choir; in particular a solo version of 'Ave Maria' done to a counterpoint from Bach's Prelude to a Well-tempered Clavichord—I forget the number of the Prelude but you know which one I mean, the one that's made up almost entirely of arpeggios: I used to play it on the piano. The BBC was also running a series of readings by Garrison Keilor on Lake Wobegon Days. I chuckled (and twinged considering my dental problem, which I have yet, as the Sri Lanka idiom has it, to 'do the needful by) the retired dentist who went fishing all the time and, having snared a sunfish, prepared to remove the hook from the unfortunately creature's mouth by remarking, 'Open wide now; this may sting for a moment'.

A couple peculiar remarks were made on a news broadcast. A person being interviewed, a partisan for a particular cause, said, 'There would be no violence if these people would just get out of the way!' He happened to be a Muslim fundamentalist (not one of my favorite charities), but the remark struck me as summing up so much of the world that it is virtually a sociological paradigm. The other remark was a report on the Gulf war, in which I clearly heard: 'A new offensive by Iran is definite for October, which is the start of the tourist season.' This puts a whole new perspective on what the war is all about. The six-year-long equivalent of a professional football game? Killing your neighbors for fun and profit? Seeing the world the hard way? It occurred to me that perhaps

I misheard, and what had been said was 'the start of the terrorist season but that interpretation raised even more questions, and seems no more probable than my first understanding. Perhaps, in an irrational world, we cannot expect news reports to be both accurate and rational.

Have you ever felt an elephant's tongue? It is very soft and moist, and also very large. It does not seem to be a very flexible tool. In the municipal park across from the Colombo monastery where I stayed was a very friendly elephant who likes to be patted and rubbed, especially on her concave jowls, and who, if I approach her with food in my hand, opens her mouth and expects to be fed like a baby ('Here comes the choo-choo!'). Only reluctantly will she take food with her trunk (inside is just like a giant pair of nostrils-she doesn't like me to touch the tip of her trunk at all) and feed herself. A whole loaf of bread is a modest mouthful. Bananas go at about 4 to a bite. I just shovel it and she looks at me with a very gentle long-lashed eye. As a pet she would be an expensive white elephant, even though she is gray (with pink spots on her mottled ears, pink tongue, pink nostrils, a few brownish molars, no tusks) and—so I'm told, I can't judge for myself—pregnant. But who done it?

* * *

Some month or other (or else not)

Dear HMV,

I've been out, or out of it, for a long time, sort of half involuntarily. Well, o1' Ma N told me it was time to get out of that *kuṭi* (BAM! SMSH! well, yes ma'am, I see your point) and until a few days ago I've been loose upon the world. Though I must admit that sometimes it seemed the other way 'round to me.

Not that anyone's tried to do me more harm than, say, sprinkling some chili sambol over a mess of stringhoppers—terrorism comes in an infinite variety of forms—but eventually I had enough of that way and with—I hope—Ma N's tacit consent have once more become settled down, albeit in my own unsettled (and perhaps even unsettling) way.

Your letter of some month or other (or else not) arrived, as did your birthday (the Buddha's, not mine, and probably not yours either) greeting, and will be celebrating (or mourning) its own soon, so let this be a greeting to it as well as to you. Hi there!

As you will have noticed by now, in all likelihood, I'm writing this letter using one of those newfangled word-processing machines. Never be as good as ola leaf, goose quill, and carbon black ink, will it?, but then what can we expect in these degenerate times?

The thing is, it's not only letters what can be written on these infuriatingly versatile critters, but books as well—they can be formatted in what is a fair approximation of electronic typesetting, and that, it seems, is exactly what is about to happen to *Notes on Dhamma* and the rest of that shmegegga to be known collectively (unless something better comes along) as *Clearing the Path*.[1] The whole to be printed by something called photo-offset, if you believe everything you hear.

And it occurs to me that it's only a few months shy of 20 years since I first started, in fits and, working on Ñāṇavīra's manuscript in much the same way that your 20-year sentence (or was it life + 20?) has been, or is being, served upon *Worthy Bones*. Or vice versa. And since you promise that you won't send me a copy I'll get even with you by promising that I will send you one. After all, fair is fair. But I warn you, it's a thorny work, as anyone who tries to use it for toilet paper is liable to discover.

Keep those gentle catastrophes coming. Yes indeedy, *metta* to all tarsals.

V.

* * *

(
Few Buddhist monks have probably had this affliction: computer problems. First Bob couldn't get in Sri Lanka the particular 'thimbles' or daisy-wheel-like print elements for the diverse typography of the book's text, then Spinwriter ELF blew a gasket… er power distribution chip… even Singapore didn't have them in stock, so it had to be 'got down' from Japan… and fickle local electricity filched floating memory.—Hūm)

While my days have been spent for the most part, east of the subroutine and west of the monitor, the trip to Colombo, even Kandy, kept getting bumped into the future, till I realized it might just stay there…

Unlike here, in Kandy there is daily evidence of security: armed soldiers guard main intersections and sometimes stop cars, the road past the Temple of the Tooth is closed to traffic, although there seems

1. He succeeded to have it printed in 1987.—Ed.

little danger of an attack on the Temple: this obliged me to frequently make a long detour around the other side of Kandy Lake to get to and from town. When news was heard of the killing of the 32 monks in the Eastern province, almost all the houses and shops in town flew yellow flags in mourning and protest. This got a big play in the paper which, however, virtually ignored an inter-religious peace march of about 500 people from Kandy to Anuradhapura which started while I was there. (I walked in it for a few miles.)

Then on to Colombo, where my printer was finally repaired, after nearly 3 months to get a single part from Singapore! My order for fresh ribbons, placed 2 months ago, had still not been filled, so obviously attempting to get thimbles would be as futile exercise. My teeth have taken about as long to repair with about as much satisfaction. I still may end up losing the molars with the root-canals, because a low-grade infection seem to stay with them which nothing but antibiotics can check. I usually get some other bug in the city that I'm spared in the country. This time it was more serious, however: paratyphoid. It's a water-borne virus from contaminated water. I usually am very careful, but such things are a monk's occupational hazards. Atleast, it was mild case, from which I'm mostly recovered. I had it once before 15 years ago; worse, as I remember. The latest plague in the city are the virus' infecting computer software, I have learned. The virus' are encoded in the software turning it to gibberish on unaware command. Almost all software is pirated here, even that which is sold by established firms at list price. Unlike imitation watches, it is, except for the label, indistinguishable from the original, being-an electronic copy. The virus' are employed as protection against piracy, for piracy, and by piracy. Except through the most reputable agents I'd be very leery about purchasing any more software locally.

I saw some destruction in Colombo: the burnt hulks of buses and other vehicles alongside the road, stretches where telephone poles were broken, the wire missing, black patches in the road where tires had been set alight. Some telephone exchanges are totally destroyed, and I've been told other tales of destruction of many millions of dollars of government property, in protest against the recent peace accord signed by Jayawardene and Gandhi.

The accord is basically between Sri Lanka and India, not between Sri Lanka and the Tamil separtists. The Tamils are granted some concessions, but it is not entirely to their liking since it doesn't give them the separate state for which they have been killing and dying, and the unification of the Northern and Eastern provinces is contingent upon a referendum, which the East, it seems, will probably reject. But they have no real choice in the matter, since the accord offers, in exchange for Gandhi's promise to deny the separtists a base in India (without which they would have no possibility of being a credible presence), a de jure recognition of India's de facto dominance in the region, guaranteeing strategic concessions (a non-militarized Trinco bay, etc.) which India has long sought.

It's probably the best deal that any of the parties could have hoped for, but some Sinhalese in particular are unhappy about it, regarding it as a sellout. And the JVP (the radical party that was behind the '71 rebellion) will no doubt use it as a rallying cry for sympathisers, who are very nationalistic and anti-Tamil, The Indians are quite pleased about the pact, mistakenly regarding themselves as having successfully brokered peace between two factions: what they've really done is to have agreed, for a price, to stop supporting one of those factions.

But it has yet to actually be implemented: very few weapons have been surrendered, parliamentary debate will surely be stormy, even within Jayawardene's own party, and there was quite a bit of rioting and some killing when Gandhi came to Sri Lanka to sign the pact. Perhaps you saw the video clip of the Sri Lanka sailor trying to knock off Gandhi's head—he'd have succeeded if there hadn't been an alert officer at hand who deflected some of the blow. I heard the live commentary of the proceedings on the radio, but the announcer made no mention at all of the incident and I didn't learn of it till later. I don't know if he failed to see it, though that seems unlikely, or was too stupid to think it worth mentioning (a distinct possibility: Sri Lanka Broadcasting Corporation is an outfit of incompetents if there ever was one), or was afraid to speak of it without official approval, also distinctly possible. Anyway the coming weeks or months will tell whether the accord, still just a piece of paper will become anything more than that.

Another project I'm involved in presently, apart from the book, is called, among the few of us who are taking it up, the Hopelessly Poor, and its purpose is to find, among those who are hopeless because of dire poverty, individuals who if helped might be able to earn their own living instead of being dependent on begging. These people, who are a small minority of the hopelessly poor, would be trained in whatever skills they would like to learn and which we can arrange for and would be lent funds (which we will be contributing collectively) and whatever else is necessary to get them going. When they are self-sufficient they will be expected (without bated breath) to repay (without interest) what has been lent them, so that these funds can form a revolving account. Only when they have repaid the money will they be considered rehabilitated. However, we will continue to make contributions to our kitty for as long as is necessary or useful. We are doing this quietly, privately (although a few government people have been informed so that we will not unwittingly get ourselves into unforeseen difficulties with suspicious bureaucrats), and experimentally. I don't know how it will turn out but I think it's a worthwhile thing to do with the income being generated now from my share of the LA property (as I also think the publishing project to be worthwhile).

Three Dutch students are staying at the estate for a few months (in the quarters of the Dutch Catholic priest, who is away), partly to do some engineering on behalf of 'Uva Spice', the non-profit spice exporting unit that has recently been established by said priest. They want to be sympathetic to ideas which are new to them, but I find it interesting to see how difficult this task is for them. Several times I've talked to them about a perspective to which they are unaccustomed—once specifically on the Buddha's Teaching, but the other times on more general cultural perspectives—and I discover that even with reasonable good will on their part, they aren't really able to see what I'm getting at. Always, they put my words into their own perspective, which automatically prevents them from seeing any perspective other than their own. (And since they are, all of them, committed to Christianity, our more specific discussion produced even less comprehension. They could not fathom that what seems important to them is, from another point of view, irrelevant; and try as they might to understand, they kept missing the central point, however directly—or indirectly—I stated it.) Curious to think that at one time I was in their position exactly. Even the most sympathetic Westerner, bound to his Western perspective, is bound to sympathetically misunderstand the Third World and any point of view with which he is not already comfortably familiar.

Fortunately, due to my weakened condition, I had an unusually comfortable ride back to Ella from Colombo. An Englishman who lives on the estate with his wife happened to be coming up at the same time I was: in a big chauffered air-conditioned car belonging to his company. And since getting back to my kindly hosts, the Congreves have been looking after me to the small extent that I need.

I'm sorry about the rather poor quality of the printer. The ratchet which holds the thimble steady when a letter is printed has become partly worn and can no longer do its job. As a result some of the letters tend to be a bit out of place It's just a little plastic bit that fits in with a c-clamp, but until a new one can be got down from Singapore we'll both have to put up with it. Still beats a typewriter, though.

Well, if they've added color to Casablanca I assume they will also have changed its title to Casarosa. Did you know that Ronald Reagan was one of the candidates for the lead part in the film? He didn't get it then, but some 35 or 40 years later he nailed down the translation rights. Just goes to show the translation is never as good as the original.

Love,

Bob

* * *

(A tape cassette arrived from Wye Estate, and after General Delivery vetted it, I spirited it away to my stump in the woods. I was appalled at the poor sound-quality of the tape—practically inaudible—and, after reeling the tape between my fingers very attentively for some time, I finally gave up and took it to a friend in the village who had a tape-recorder, with results which were much more satisfactory.

The tape begins with a rendition of the Negro spiritual, Zem Bones, beamed to me by the Sri Lanka Broadcasting Corporation and performed by—if their sound had names—Kingfisher and the Breawthless Sisters, to the clanking accompaniment of cymbals, cowbells, and, perhaps, rattling bones, and as the song fades out in ecstatic moans and wails, a familiar voice, at first black-faced then assuming the complexion of a tranquilized Woody Allen, fades in.—Hūm)

... Yeeesss, boss...how you doin', man?...remember those talking records when you were a kid?...well this here's...this tape machine's here...so I thought I'd send you a talking letter so instead of reading me you can hear me, huh?...and I want you to know right off that I hear you when I get your letters 'cause I read them over and over again and

I love what you say and I love how you say it...I want you to know that I thought your last letter was really moving about when you were with your dad in his last days...it was special for you to share that with me...but, hey, but you started off that letter by saying something about my loving *hard rock*, huh? ...wow, I don't remember that!...what I remember was when I was in the States, when I got back to the States, was right away I loved *Mozart*, man!...I used to play his horn concertos over and over again...now I haven't heard any of them for donkey's years, but I can still hear it in my head, you know...some of that stuff... mostly I think maybe because of that Flanders & Swann parody...you know the one that starts off, how does it start off...? (sings) 'I once had a whim and I had to obey it to buy a French horn in a second hand shop, I polished it up and I started to play it in spite of the neighbors who begged me to stop!'...well, I'll stop before you start begging me—and from now on I promise this is just a talking letter not a singing one... unless I maybe just get carried away...because you can never tell about that...but Mozart or hard rock or wherever it is...a lot of that stuff you know it never vanishes does it?...You know I remember another thing I always loved was, flying...even in those big commercial planes which really is like sitting in your living room...but one time I was...the one time I was really ever in a small plane that's when my cousin married a guy who could fly...he had a...he had a small plane...that was really a trip...in fact it was a trip all the way from Albuquerque to Los Angeles... and I remember how I used to...in fact I still do...I...I dream about flying...I mean it's not in a *plane*, man...like I mean I don't need a plane when I dream about flying...I just sort of stretch out like...like superman and *off* I go, huh?!...a friend of mine he told me that when he dreams of flying he does it *cross-legged* which...which right away struck me as a *weird* position to fly in, huh?...and oh I got to pay careful attention...! have to be *very* mindful all the time when I'm flying because if I don't *constantly* keep willing myself to stay up in the sky then I start going into a sort of *dive*...and once I...one time I can...I can remember I got a little careless and I came really close to some power lines...and that scared me...almost woke me up...I woke up later and I could remember that part of the dream really vividly...so when I dream about flying now I have to really be mindful...and...a...another thing about flying I read about once...was...was that there's this kind of glider that comes in a kit...but you don't need to be towed up into the air by a powered plane 'cause it's got a little engine...and what it...what this engine actually is is...get this...it's a lawn-mower engine with a propeller attached...and the whole thing...what it is is it's an enormous set of light-weight wings with that lawn-mower engine behind it and a way to fasten yourself in and a strap to sit on and what you do is you get into this thing and you start up the engine and then you RUN LIKE HELL DUWN THE RUNWAY!...and if you're fast enough and if you're going into a headwind you can really get up enough speed to take off...(softly) and then you just circle around and climb and climb and when you pick up a thermal and when you're high enough...*you turn off the engine* and just...(breathless) soooooоaaaaaar...and glide for as long as you like...of course, I never got that one together but...but I remember some fantasies I had of gliding through the Himalayas...and I *know* that idea has to blow your mind because you've been there and you know how incredible those mountains are and I remember you once said something about flying always being a fantasy of yours...so when this...this flight simulator program came into my hands, man, I just had to give it a spin on the old disk-drive...'cause..'cause I could fly without even needing a plane, without even needing a lawn-mower, man, I didn't even have to sleep I could be wide-awake and now I've...I've flown all around Chicago, I've circled lake Michigan, I've circled the Statue of Liberty, and I've flown *under the Brooklyn Bridge*...and then there's this WW I Ace option—and then this whole story sort of spun out from there like how to tell it dramatically...and I figured you'd really dig that 'cause also I thought it was pretty good writing and then I know you get off on good writing...so I was surprised you didn't get off on that fantasy flight letter I sent you...but anyway don't worry about my getting addicted, because you know it's, it's not really a question of getting like addicted or not getting addicted, it's really a question of like getting *unaddicted* or *not* getting unaddicted, because we already *are* addicted and it's just a question of what the object is of our addiction...I mean like how many years now have you been writing your...your sort of jungly prose novels?...and...what are you going to tell me, that...that you can quit any time, that you just don't want to??...well, better if you tell me it's a way...you're hoping it's a way, of putting the addiction to an end...and I'm sure you're doing it with clarity and love...or as much clarity and love as...as you got, which is a lot...and that's fine and there's no criticism of it...but...a...well, I'm not going to pretend that that flight simulator has anything to do with Dhamma...but the real purpose for the word-processor, for the computer, is to get Ñāṇavīra's writings into print and about that Dhamma...now that I don't need to make any claims for because you know how I feel...and it's been like what?...it's been like nearly 20 years since that manuscript first came into my hands...and that's long enough time for something to finally happen... (*beep, beep*)...that's the beeper...it's 10 o'clock at night now...I've borrowed this tape-machine from the people where I'm staying...and it's... it's my little electronic clock that beeps on the hour you can probably hear that in the background...so anyway it's been like 20 years and I want something to finally happen and so when this possibility arose I took it and I have no regrets about that...and so most of my time I spend in front of the monitor I don't spend flying over Europe shooting down...you know, the Red Baro...I spend most of that time putting the book together and I hope it's for the last time because I've done it a few times before, you know...and I won't pretend I don't get a lot of pleasure out of that...in a lot of ways it's more fun than shooting down the Red Baron...it's not like it's something I have to endure. I do it because I want to do it, and because I want to see it done, and because I think it's probably good for me, and maybe it'll be good for other people too, and it's good work to do...you know I had to modify the soft-ware program to get it to do Pāli and to get it to do the italics and diacritical marks and columns and all that kind of stuff and for somebody who's never even touched a computer before this year...I have to say I think that's doing pretty good...'cause some of it is pretty technical...and the so-called soft-ware experts I talked to in Colombo they all told me they could do it but they wouldn't want to because it would be too arduous for them...which really means they couldn't do it, at all, and I figured out how to do it, and there's a lot of satisfaction in working out all those technical problems—and achieving soma really high-quality print-outs... pretty close to a professional level, or I should say a *high* professional level, because it's already at a professional level...you know the monks at the BPS (Buddhist Publication Society)...the Ven. Ñāṇaponika and Bhikkhu Bodhi they've seen what I'm doing and they think it's so much better than the quality of print that they're getting they're going to copy the system and they've been out here and...well not Ven. Ñāṇaponika... he's 86 and he doesn't go anywhere, but Bhikkhu Bodhi came out with one person from the board of BPS and they looked at the system and watched me do it and talked about it for a lon[illegible] cided they're going to get it themselves...'cause it [illegible] low priced...and...they've got...they've now got th[illegible] ing...but that's pretty expensive stuff...that's 10-12 th[illegible] a system and...a...there was this fund made available [illegible] Ñāṇavīra's stuff...and it's a few thousand dollars to pu[illegible] together and then all you need after that is just to pay the pri[illegible] what's already been type-set and that's like photo-offset and in [illegible] they do that pretty cheap and they do good quality too...so I thi[illegible] you might remember those Ajahn Chah booklets I sent you once [illegible] that was done in Thailand and you might remember that that was reasonably good quality stuff, so that's what I'm expecting to get when it finally happens which will be sometime next year, maybe the middle of the year, maybe a little bit after that...so anyway I've agreed to teach the BPS how to get the special effects that I've developed...so it turns out that what I've developed is going to be of use to others as well... but, you know, *addiction*?...that's something I dabble in a bit but I don't think it'll ever come to more than that...even with that morphine you know all those years ago, 20 years ago, 21 years ago, even with that that's all it came to really was dabbling, and I was never really that heavily into it...so anyway enough for that trip...so I'll tell you the way this whole tape trip came together is that last month I had to go down to Colombo to get a new passport—oh, hey, you know those new passports are for ten years now and that means that the next passport I'm gonna need I'll be *57 years old*!...that's *astonishing*!...*an old man* me?...*never*!...so anyway they told me I had to wait for a few days while they called Washington to find out if they maybe wanted me for something like if I was a fugitive or they wanted to ask me questions about like gun-running to Nicaragua or maybe selling arms to fanatics like the Ayatollah Khomeini...or maybe about fiddling with secret Swiss bank accounts...so in the end it turned out they didn't have anything to ask me about that...but I had to stick around Colombo for a few days and it happened that at the temple I was staying at I had to share a room with a monk who had a radio...and he very kindly kept tuning in the English language programs on my behalf...like even without me even asking for it...and it happened like one evening he tuned into a program where they were rebroadcasting these old half hour BBC dramas...and the one they happened to be doing that night...was a play called *A of Retreat* and it was by this guy named Robin Maugham… out incredible serendipitous coincidences!…though maybe after ear the play you might think that serendipitous is really the wrong rd…'cause the play is really an act of hate…still it's good for a few ughs 'cause we know who the model for…for his monk is and we know how…we can see ourselves how totally off-base he is but anyway it's…you know it's like something I had to do I went down to the Sri Lanka Broadcasting Corporation—like the SLBC—and I asked them if I could get a copy of the tape and so right away they grabbed me and they said that the party they were supposed to be interviewing for one of their Buddhist programs hadn't shown up and I was *just in time* and would I come this way to the studio please and here we were and we just have a few questions for you and it won't hurt much and it will all be over in a few minutes…and so we did this interview and…and then after that they agreed to give me a copy of the play and they stuck a copy of this interview on the tape too…I guess they copied it when they broadcast it…I didn't hear the broadcast myself…I went back a few days later to pick up the tape and I guess it was all done…so all that stuff anyway is on the other side of the tape…and if you ever want to listen to it then it's there, and so I still had this one whole side of the tape left and I was wondering what to do with it when I was back at the temple and this monk's radio was on…I think that this time he didn't turn it on I think my hand must have accidentally hit you know the *on* button or something…and so anyway there was this…there was this music show…so the radio announcer said that he was going to play 'Bones', man, and I just hit that record button and *away we went*!…and then the whole tape just turned out to be just like sort of like *ordained* for you…I mean like…like dedicated from the start, you know…I mean like I realized when they played 'Bones', man, everything was coming together so much that if was just *meant for you*…and so here it is man and I just want you to know that I love you and I *really* respect what you're doing with your life and this tape is just my way of telling you just that…OK?…*sukhi hotu*,[1] man…(whisper) yeah…(voice fades out humming, 'Zem bones, zem bones, zem dry bones…now *here's* the word of the lawd…')

---

1. *sukhi hotu*: (Pāli) 'my you be happy.'

(I flipped the cassette over and listened to *A Question of Retreat*, Robin Maugham was the grandson of Somerset Maugham. His grandfather told him a story he had heard of an Englishman living alone in the jungles of Sri Lanka. The young Maugham, a journalist, searched out Ven. Ñāṇavīra who, perhaps with the odd qualm, granted the young man an interview. For his courtesy, the monk was slapped with an unflattering portrait in a London rag as well as the disparaging play.

Following the play on the tape was the radio interview with, according to the announcer, Ven. Bodhesako *Thera*. The mistaken title of *thera* was, in fact, ironically fitting. A monk who has taken his higher ordination is a *bhikkhu*. A *bhikkhu* with atleast ten years as as *bhikkhu* is a *thera*. Although Bob had once been a *bhikkhu*—Ñāṇasuci—in his last stint as a monk he chose to not take his higher ordination, preferring to remain a novice or *sāmaṇera*. However, all his years as a monk toted up to atleast twelve; the *thera* ten plus. The interviewer called him 'Ven. Bodhesako *Sāmaṇera*', but the announcer, at the conclusion of the interview, called him 'Ven. Bodhesako *Thera*' again. Also the interviewer introduced him as 'from Thailand', where he *was* ordained, but over the radio one wouldn't assume that someone 'from Thailand' had been born in Detroit and had a Jewish grandfather from Russia named Morris Medvedovsky; perhaps, they all looked the same to the interviewer.—Hūm.)

> Announcer: The time is 10:45 AM and you are tuned to the national service of the Sri Lanka Broadcasting Corporation. Ven. Bodhesako Thera is heard in conversation with Alec Robertson in our weekly program 'Buddhism and You'.

(Though to one with an ear to hear Ven. Bodhesako says some enlightening things, such an ear, apparently, does not belong to Alec Robertson, as he keeps answering his own questions, quite content to be in dialogue with himself. The comic effect is compounded by Mr. Robertson's singsong tenor, as if he were parodying himself. An excerpt from the interview may give something of its unique flavor.—Hūm)

> AR: It is indeed a pleasure and an honor to have with us today Ven. Bodhesako Sāmaṇera from Thailand to take part in this short discussion. Venerable sir, you have been a monk for the last six years and

you take a very keen and enthusiastic interest in the study, practice, and publication of the teaching of the Buddha. In fact you have written a book on…a Buddhism which has been published by the Buddhist Publication Society…kindly…entitled…a…the…

B: *The Buddha and Catch-22*.

AR: Yes…a…now, reverend sir, with regard to the doctrine of *anattā* or no self, one of the most abstruse teachings of the Buddha. Westerners find it most difficult to understand and comprehend this teaching. What is the reason for it?

B: Well, I think that any person looking for an explanation is going to take this doctrine and use it to fit his own needs, desires, whether it's in accordance with the teaching or not. And since people have always been looking for answers to questions, they've always been looking for resolutions to situations, and this is not only today, not only Westerners, this is true of all times and all peoples. People have always been looking for answers to questions—now somebody comes to this teaching and they are told that the Buddha said that wherever you look you will see nothing that is self or pertains to self and they look for an explanation they can understand within their own frame of reference and so because this teaching is so different than what Westerners are accustomed to they will try to adapt the teaching to their own framework. What they need to do is not adapt the teaching to their own point of view, but their point of view to the teaching—this is called *saddha*—or trust—to give oneself to the teaching even if it is contrary to one's preconceived notions of the way things are. That means instead of looking for answers, what they need to do is examine this need they have to ask questions—and this is what the Buddha teaches—that we must examine ourselves; that when we need to ask questions we must discover the root of this need and to find out what it is that gives rise to it. If we put our attention on the question instead of the answer then we will be practicing the Buddha's Teaching.

AR: Yes…now with regard to the doctrine of *anattā* or no self…

(After AR gives a little spiel telling us all about meditation, he asks, by the way, B what it is.—Hūm)

> B: Meditation is simply facing our existence, living in the present, seeing things as they are, instead of seeing them with a lot of glitter. You may see some of these display windows where they're trying to sell merchandise; all these glittery things are strung out in the window to catch your attention. But when somebody is really attached to something you don't need to string out the glitter—the glitter is in his eyes and he will see things with glitter—mindfulness and meditation is freeing oneself from the glitter, becoming disenchanted.
>
> AR: Yes...as you said meditation helps one to...
>
> Announcer: That was Alec Robertson in conversation with Ven. Bodhesako Thera. The time is exactly 11:00 AM. You are tuned to the Sri Lanka Broadcasting Corporation.

* * *

Why do I love your awful writing, you ask? Really, it's very simple: your writing isn't just awful; also, it's aweful, and for aweful writing—writing that has a sense of awe, wonder, generosity, touching (but not squeezing), and waking-up joyfulness—I'll forgive just about anything. Of course, if it was good writing as well then it would be all the better, because it is, what I've seen of it, also pretty awful as writing (I haven't had a chance yet to get into your Ethiopian epic; maybe *The Falasha's Choice* will be great writing—if the drought's pruned the jungle), I think the reason for this is that, as you say, you really get into what you're doing, so much so that you can *only* see it from the inside—or, rather, you *choose* only to see it from the inside, since it's not really a question of can/can't—and *from its own perspective* it is, of course, great writing (because it's aweful writing), and nothing else matters. Only later, when you become distanced from the creative act, are you able to see it from a partly different perspective, and to appreciate that difference.

If you would be willing to make a great sacrifice and choose to be able at will to distance yourself from your writing while you were writing it I believe you would develop a different sort of critical faculty, one which would allow you to recognize bad writing as it was being written, and through which you would learn to write not only awfully but also well. (I, for example, can write very well, but very seldom awfully: good writing can be learnt, but awful writing just has to be in you, and in me it's not-hence, I believe, the sense of weightiness you often find in my work, whereas yours, even when stylistically it's a ton of bricks, still has a kind of motion that I love.) I know it's a lot to give up, but it doesn't have to be all given up at once, and in fact I think it probably can't be all given up at once, since giving it up has to be learned, bit by bit!

But the learning, and the giving up, are immensely rewarding and the long-term result is an incomparable gain. You don't lose anything, because you can still be totally within your writing; rather, you gain the ability to flash back and forth between being in it and being out of it (sort of like gliding, maybe), and while in it you can see what needs to be done to make the conception stronger, strong enough to truly support the conception, the feeling, the essence without which the best writing is merely a well-executed pratfall. More work for poppa, of course, but on the other hand, what else is there? Hell, you know all this anyway.

Your tape, on the other hand, wasn't awful at all, and maybe you should turn in your typewriter for a cassette recorder, and start putting out talks for people to listen to while they're driving to and from work. (Though I must admit that as much as I enjoyed your tape I didn't enjoy it so much as to go completely bonkers and get a job so that I could afford to buy a car so that I could drive to work, listening the while to your non-existent tapes.) Meanwhile, my 'affordable desktop printing' strategy continues to be improved as I learn more about computers: just the other day I learned, at last, how to break into the tables which control the software so that I can modify any value or relationship at will. But learning this is sort of like discovering the entrance to Carlsbad Caverns: there's still a whole heap of exploring to be done. While interested not at all in marketing this, I'm willing to freely share the info with anyone who will also freely share it with anyone who will also...(the infinite hierarchy strikes again!), and I shall probably compose a small tutorial telling the good folks how to go and do them likewise. When I get the time. And when that'll be, only the non-existent good lord knows.

However, I've finally found the time to finish, just the other day, a long-planned paper doing some theoretical physics (Buddhist physics, actually)—*The Big Bang: A Modification*—my first venture back into science in a long time. Nothing awful in that one at all, of course, but it's now being studied by a physics prof to find out if it's awful. Mebbe so: when it comes to science I'm like you when it comes to writing: me critical faculties be a tad undeveloped, and I have yet to make the choice to develop them. Of course, I won't be doing physics every day for the rest of my life, so there may not be the same incentive, but anyway we seem to have come full circle now, and 360 degrees ought to be enough for anyone.

V.

* * *

(The next—the last—tape Bob sent I didn't reel between my thumbs and complain but took straight to the friend's tape-recorder—and complained. If anything it was poorer quality than I imagined the first tape to be. In fact, it *looked* like a type-writer ribbon spool with the ribbon itself made out of bits of paper scotch-taped together and would around the spool. I even imagined there were *words typed on the ribbon*. Fortunately, a second after I put the tape on the recorder and switched it on, I had an uncanny premonition that in *two* seconds the splices would break and bits of tape would fly apart, so I switched off the machine and was content to reel the 'spool' between my thumbs imagining I was listening to—or reading from—a real made-in-Sri Lanka cassette.—Hūm)

Wow, thanks for another tape. I really enjoy hearing your voice. The reading of your new novel shows a marked shift in your style, out of the jungle, so to speak, and into the garden. There are many kinds of gardens, both formal and informal. In yours there are many pollen-gathering insects busying around, and all of them are going, 'Hum-mmmmn, Hummmmmn.' Hmmm. The section you read was actually interesting and enjoyable, and didn't take that great effort of will and concentration necessary to pick my way through your earlier stuff, tripping over vines and long words, a dictionary for machete, never sure whether I was heading right and lacking a guide. Now I feel like I'm on a well-conducted tour: hey, look at the bougainvillea, watch your step around the hollyhocks, and now we're coming to the secret jewel of the scarab beetle (or is it the dung beetle?), and just ahead… What I mean is, I could understand the situation, I could understand the trip your protagonist was on, it was all vivid. Good stuff.

Yes, you are right, there isn't much to say, and a blank 60 minute tape is sure a way of demonstrating it. Still, we keep finding new ways to say it, don't we? And, I suppose we'll keep finding new ways until we get it right.

By the way, how do you like my latest invention? A tape that doesn't need a machine to play it? If I can keep coming up with 'em like this, the world will surely (or is it surly)? beat a path to my door, and then I'll have to beat them back. (I could never understand why anyone would want to trap better mice.)

Flash: this is my favorite time of the year: sun basking warm, light breeze just chill enough to offset the sun, sort of tactile sweet-&-sour, a real tropical pineapple sun instead of the northern white sugar type. Nights blanket-bundly steamy-breath cool. This season lasts about a week, if I'm lucky. If it lasts less, it's not enough; if it lasts more it gets boring. A week is just about right. And this is the third day.

A copy of *Clearing the Path* has gone off to you, and should make its appearance in Spring, along with the daisies, artichokes, hay fever pollen, brambles, and Spring. Actually I suppose it should make its appearance in Sooke. I'm not sure where Spring is. (The daughter, Alice, has immigrated to Australia, I'm told.)

And now I'll read you part of my latest work. It's called 'The Silence'. Just keep turning the spool and you can hear as much of it as you like. Meanwhile, love you. Other side of this tape is blank—use it if you like. The Silence:...

* * *

Sorry to hear you had such trouble playing the tape I sent you. Actually, as I said, it was a new invention of mine, designed to be played without the need for a machine. Like all early prototypes it has its faults. It takes generations, sometimes even years, for a product to reach the pinnacle of perfection of, say, a perfect stringhopper or a perfect rabbit-hole. However, vast improvements have been made and I have now developed a tape which not only does not need to be played on a machine but also does not even need a spool on which to wind it. You are, in fact, holding this invention in your hand at this moment.

I have yet to give it a name, since I feel only a good snappy term will have a chance of catching on in today's marketplace. I showed it to one friend who suggested I call the invention 'paper', but obviously such a name has no pizzaz and would never be a commercial success. I've been working on a line of related ideas for transcribing thoughts on to this new medium, which I'll call paper until a better term can be invented. Instead of using an electronic printer, as we have all been doing since time immemorial, I am now working on a system which is independent of electronics. My dull-witted friend has termed the device a 'manual typewriter'—clumsy oaf, to think such a mouthful would get anywhere. And even beyond that there is the hope of someday creating a system which will be so compact that it can be held between two fingers, and yet, incredibly enough, so versatile, that it can form characters in any script, can do drawings, perhaps be available in different colors, and yet be so inexpensive that if damaged it need not be taken in for repairs but can simply be thrown away. I call the system 'writing'. The major problems yet to be overcome is to invent a material which can make a suitable mark on the 'paper'. My friend tells me this is a pure nine dream. If God wanted man to write, he says, he would have put ink in our veins. I wonder what he means by 'ink'?

Glad *Clearing the Path* got to your stump. I find that in a coherent book form it is easier to use, to understand, than it was in typescript. But not everyone who has used the typescript feels it makes as much difference as I do. Perhaps that's why it was I, and not they, who took the trouble to see to its publication.

Path Press has been going great guns, and the camera-ready copy of *Change* (which you saw in typescript) is with them. Path Press will now be taking a three or four month holiday from wordsmithery in favor of the practice of silencesmithery before resuming operations at the same old stump.

I loved hearing you read your stuff, even though I couldn't make heads or tails what it was about. Seemed like a lot of flashbacks/flashforwards/flashsideways. Is it really necessary to demand so much of your readers? I try to make it as easy as I can for the poor ninnies and still get accused of making them work for it. But I sure admire the way you can turn it out, day after day. Me, I've got so many blank days I could pass as a snowstorm. And to get an entire page written in one day! The feeling of accomplishment, of self-worth, it instills in me! And then I look at the stack of your typescripts that rest on my shelf, and next to it are my two pamphlets and a few folders and envelopes of incomplete perhaps uncompletable stuff, I do admire your persistence and inventiveness, and if I can't figure out what the invention is for, why, I guess you'll never guess the latest use I've discovered for this stuff called 'paper'. I'll give you one clue. It will be a saving of soap and water'.

V.

* * *

I went to the professor of my Colombo dentist, at the Peradeniva campus a few miles from Kandy—my first time on that campus; rolling hills, attractive buildings, surrounding greenery, very upmarket for Sri Lanka.

The professor looked at the molar X-rays and showed me how the bottom half of one of the roots was dark, whereas the other root-and-a-half were white (Was? When does plurality begin? At two, to be logical? Or at the tiniest fraction above one, to be mathematical? Or at some foggy and indeterminate place near the middle, to be psychological? Sinhalese verbs make no distinction as to person or number, so presumably this sort of question would not occur to a Sinhala.) This, the professor assures me, meant that my dentist had not filled the bottom half of one root with whatever sort of stuff they fill it—cotton wool, or sawdust, or some exotic polymer. And it was why, he said, I've been having recurrent infections in the gum around the tooth, requiring courses of antibiotics every three or four months for the last several years, ever since the root was canalled (a Venice of the mouth).

Furthermore, he added, he could not understand why my dentist should have attempted the work without the proper tools, since the equipment *is* available on the campus, and he would be glad to redo the work properly and put an end to these infections, but at present it was between semesters and as I must have seen when I came in he was not actually seeing patients during this time, since he had to supervise the between-terms maintenance of the school equipment, which was therefore inoperative, and in addition he had so many committee meetings and important conferences in Colombo, and he began rattling off a lot of names that meant nothing to me. I was more concerned, actually, about his hands probing at my teeth since, you see, when I came in he had had a drill's innards on the table and the oil had not been as thoroughly washed off his hands as I would have liked. But he was as sensible as he was garrulous, and kept his greasy thumbs off my shiny molars, only probing and tapping with tools, handed to him by his dumpty nurse like in an operating theatre. He would name a pick or mirror or whatever, and she would slap it into his hands. Once she handed him something which he then realized wasn't what he wanted. He threw it to the ground and told her, 'Don't give me what *I ask for*. Give me what *I need*.' She did.

As for the dust jacket of *Clearing the Path*, it was done by one of the best-known artists in the country. Personally, I find it too romantic. However, as usual my opinion seems to be a minority view. And among those who disagree with me is the Sri Lanka Printers' Assn., for they have just awarded it first prize in their annual contest. It's an ink drawing. All those color plates don't come cheap, and then there was a lot of work examining the printing work to make sure the colors and other details were right. Amazing the number of things people will get wrong if given the chance. In any case, the book seems to be doing well, though I can't say how long this will continue, already more than a quarter of the first printing has been distributed, mostly outside the country.

Our street people project has made only slow progress, having net with both anticipated and unanticipated obstacles. Now the government has announced that it will launch a project which more or less duplicates (and undermines) ours. If they actually do it, that's fine; but chances are it will accomplish little other than to provide sinecures for a few relatives of politicos. Aside from reviving their sporadic 'get the beggars out of sight of the tourists' campaign (though they don't call it that) it seems aimed primarily at sideswiping our project. Why? I can only guess it's because we are not part of any establishment and nobody is getting anything out of it (apart, that is, from the street people, who don't count).

Weather has been erratic—evening or afternoon rainstorms very welcome to the electricity board, a bit less so to farmers since it's well out of season. But days are hot and sunny. There's an experimental solar dryer here, for drying the spices which are packed in the spice factory, and the temperature in the dryer has gone to over 150°F. The thing was built late last year, so this is its first real test in optimum conditions. (In cloudy weather, of course, it doesn't do so well.) The spices are sold mainly in Europe and the U.K. but there are plans for expansion, both geographically and into related projects. The Dutch and Canadian governments are providing some assistance for the project (which is non-profit, its purpose being to provide a fair market outlet for small spice growers and employment for the village people), but basically it is expected to pay its own way.

I'm afraid to use the computer when it's raining. A few weeks ago during a thunderstorm, when the computer happened to be off, lightning struck somewhere close by, and the light bulbs snapped and fried. Then, a few days later, it happened again, with the computer off. I don't know what might have happened had the computer been on, and I don't want to find out, so this means I only work when it's clear, assuming there are no power cuts, or power failures.

The political situation in the North is mostly unreported, but the information reaching me is that the Indian troops, who are trained for a conventional war, are ill-prepared to engage the Tigers, whose leader apparently prefers war to peace (those who have met him describe Prabhakaran as a militaristic fascist with no interest in, ability for, or understanding of peaceful processes). The Indians, it seems, are given (or taken) to looting and pillage (the ships that bring in relief supplies of food and medicine return to India, I'm told, laden with booty), the civilian death toll is certainly in the thousands (the official Indian figures are in the scores but the press is permitted to report estimates in the hundreds, since the official figures are Indian, not Sri Lankan), and the people in the North, though now disillusioned with the Tigers, hate the Indians even more.

Meanwhile the JVP spreads its tentacles over more of the South. There are now areas of the southwestern low country that are no-go areas, semi-officially, and considerable territory where travel at night is no longer safe. But the government seems bent on making the situation worse, partly through corruption and ineptitude, and partly through the JVP having a certain amount of sympathy in some government circles and a strong page within the army (which is supposed to be putting them down). A Catholic priest who worked with the poor of that area and preached non-violence—both very dangerous things to do—was murdered last week, the victim either of the army (the common supposition) or a cabal of narrow-minded landowners. There will certainly be no meaningful investigation of the murder.

Concern is increasing Upcountry, but, for the time being, there's little trouble here.

I've been a bit under the weather—perhaps the weather has something to do with it. Not bed-ridden or anything, just a spell of tiredness, headache, and general malaise. I think I've made some connection to tea, and then to sugar. (Is there any diabetes in the family?) I stopped all tea, coffee, and sugar and in a couple days the headaches eased, and I was less tired. Experimenting, I've found I can take a small cup of slightly sweet tea daily with no problem, but must limit myself to this. I've also gained considerable weight in the past few months, though I haven't changed my diet.

Perhaps, I've just become an old man. About two weeks ago (so I'm still new to the business of being an old man), when I got a pair of bifocals for reading. They certainly make print a lot clearer, but they are a nuisance to wear, and I still find myself trying to look at distant things through the reading portion or trying to read through the plain-glass portion, and they give me a headache (on top of the headache I've been having; a sort of duplex?) I prefer large print, but unfortunately many of the things I must or wish to read are in small type (not to mention my own handwriting). Until I got the specs I used a magnifying glass, but it was always reflecting the lamp bulb and other things and was no solution. Guess I'll have to learn to live with glasses.

While reading Herman Wouk's *War and Remembrance*, which I thought very well done, its scenes of Russia and of East European Jews pricked my dormant interest in the family tree. So you've been collecting anecdotes yourself? Thinking of making a book of them? I, for one, would be an interested reader. Today's a particularly good day for memories, I suppose: it's been five years since mother died. Do you also often think back on grandma and grandpa and the stories they must have told you about the Old Country? I know I never asked you much about your growing up in Chicago, and I'm not even sure what part of Russia grandma and grandpa came from; I'd be glad to hear any stories that you remember.

Well, I've got a new passport and visas onward, and soon I'll be departing for India. I may spend some time in South India, then possibly Nepal, possibly Burma, and on to either Thailand or Singapore to catch the flight to the States. I won't know until I hook into the travelers' grapevine in India. But you can expect me to show up in LA some time in late August, I expect—only for a few weeks before returning to Sri Lanka, but *after* ringing in your 80th birthday! Well—and well—into your next three score and ten! I hope my presence will be a little icing on the cake. (Ahead of me, I also hope, will arrive a box containing the broken carriage of my printer, which I'm sending airmail. The step motor seems to be defective. Repairs are impossible here, but may not be in the U.S.)

I leave you with a Buddhist joke:

For twenty years Suntil, a village Buddhist, had been cook to Father Carolis, the priest who ran the church attended by the upper class folk. One day, while they were in the river for their daily bath, the priest said to Suntil, 'You've been my cook for twenty years, and you're still a Buddhist. That doesn't look right. People wonder what kind of priest I am when I can't even convert my own cook. Now the Bishop is honoring me by coming to lunch this Friday, and I've decided to baptize you as a Catholic so that I can present you to him as my latest convert.'

Suntil protested that he was content to be a Buddhist, and didn't want to be a Catholic, but Father Carolis would have none of it, and without further ado he pushed Suntil beneath the water, declaring, as he did so, 'Thou art Samuel!' When Suntil surfaced he declared, 'I am Suntil!' But the priest pushed him down again, with the words 'Thou art Samuel!' A second time Suntil declared himself to be Suntil, whereupon Father Carolis pushed him under the waves a third time, and held him so long that when Suntil surfaced he could only sputter and gasp for air.

On Friday the Bishop showed up, and the priest seated him at the place of honor for lunch. Suntil brought in lunch, the main course in a covered salver. When the priest lifted the lid his face grew red with anger. 'Samuel! what is the meaning of this? For twenty years you have been my cook. You know perfectly well that we don't eat meat on Fridays. And now, with the Bishop himself before us, how dare you to serve chicken? What does this mean?'

'Oh, but that isn't chicken,' replied Suntil. 'That's fish.'

'Fish? How can you say such a thing? I can see perfectly well, and I say it's chicken.'

'Oh no, Father, That's fish. You see, before I cooked it I took it down to the river, and three times I pushed it under the water, and each time I said, 'Thou art fish, thou art fish, thou art fish! So that isn't chicken, it's fish!'

Love,

Bob

(Our Dharma-bum banter about 'black holes' during his last sit on my stump apparently went on in his head until, a decade later, it got somewhere: *The Big Bang: A Modification.*—Hūm)

> 'The universe,' the ethnologist was told by his native informant, rests on the back of a giant turtle.' And what, the ethnologist wanted to know, does the giant turtle stand on? 'Another giant turtle,' his informant asserted. And that turtle? 'Ah, I know what you're getting at, and it's very important,' said the informant, 'but it's no use: it's turtles all the way down.'

## SUMMARY

Obviously a great deal more could be said on the subject of the birth, evolution, and death of the universe; but what has been presented here should be sufficient for a preliminary draft.

Since the universe is now expanding there must exist a repulsive force which operates on a scale sufficient to have started that expansion. There is no evidence that such a repulsive force is presently operative, at least on a sufficiently powerful scale, to counteract gravitational attraction, so it must have been operative under conditions which do not presently prevail. Those conditions existed during the first minutes of the universe which is described in the Big Bang view, when there was a mass of sufficient density to create a pressure-opaque era. However, this era could only have emerged given proper antecedent conditions. Those conditions could have been the collision of two black holes such that their combined mass was sufficient to initiate a region of the universe wherein a pressure-opaque era could arise. And the condition which allowed black holes of such mass to form are those which are operative even today. Despite the absence of the absolute proof that our presently-expanding universe will eventually begin to contract, there is a great deal of indirect evidence to support the notion; and if this single assumption is allowed we find that it is possible to describe a cyclical universe, wherein the questions of beginnings becomes meaningless.

Furthermore, such a view allows us to address a number of other unresolved questions and either to propose solutions to them or at least to suggest that this cyclical view of the universe allows of approaches to solutions where previously no approach was apparent.

A number of ways—by experiment, by survey, by mathematical calculation—have been suggested whereby the views presented in this paper could be tested.

> 'The universe,' the ethnologist was told by his native informant, was born out of the collision of two gigantic black holes.' And what, the ethnologist wanted to know, were those black holes born from? 'From the previous universe,' his informant asserted. And what was that universe born from? 'Ah,' said the informant, 'that too is very important; but it's no use: it's black holes all the way down.'

Late note:

Unexpectedly high amounts of deuterium have been detected recently by satellite and radio telescopes. This indicates that the Big Bang must have been less massive than formerly supposed, for otherwise the deuterium (which is hydrogen with a neutron in its nucleus) would have been fused, in the additional heat of a great Bang, into helium. This, it has been argued, means that the universe is less massive than earlier evidence indicated and therefore also very much younger. This, of course, contradicts the existing evidence for the age of the universe. But the contradiction is resolved if we reject the assumption that the Big Bang involved *all* the matter that exists. If, instead, we allow, as this paper suggests, that the universe contains considerable matter which did not directly participate in the most recent Big Bang then we can acknowledge the validity of these recent measurements without being obliged to conclude that it is in contradiction with earlier findings. Indeed, in the model suggested in this paper such a finding would be expected, and can be taken as supportive evidence for the views put forward here in support of an oscillating universe.

* * *

> "...And if any character tries, however ineffectually, to understand the real nature of his situation, it is not Yossarian but the chaplain. The chaplain (he was named Shipman in the hard-cover edition, but for some reason the name was changed in the paperback edition to Tappman—not his only identity crisis), who has an open mind, is continually

'... wondering what everything was all about.

... There was no way of really knowing anything, he knew, not even that there was no way of really knowing anything. *Was* there a single true faith, or a life after death?

... These were the great, complex questions of ontology that tormented him. Yet they never seemed nearly as crucial to him as the question of kindness and good manners. He was pinched perspiringly in the epistenological dilemma of the skeptic, unable to accept solutions to problems he was unwilling to dismiss as unsolvable. He was never without misery and never without hope...'—pp. 262-3

In the chaplain's tale the human dilemma is presented from a different point of view; it is not a question of sanity or insanity but, in Kafkaesque terms, one of guilt or innocence. Because it is the nature of beings that they are continually trying to establish an existence that continually eludes them[1]; their existence is perpetually in doubt, and they exist, if at all, in a state of guilt. This, it would seem, is the basic perception of Kafka's *Trial*: Joseph K. arrests himself by recognizing that his existence, being unjustifiable, is essentially guilty. And the chaplain (for whom the question 'Who am I?' becomes acute when he is formally charged with 'being Washington Irving'—p. 378) is also in this situation...

And later the chaplain's identity crisis and dilemma of existential guilt is expressed in the same terms that were used earlier to describe Catch-22:

'I offered it to Sergeant Whitcomb because I didn't want it.'

'Why'd you steal it from Colonel Cathcart if you didn't want it?'

'I didn't steal it from Colonel Cathcart!'

'Then why are you so guilty, if you didn't steal it?'

'I'm not guilty!'

'Then why would we be questioning you if you weren't guilty?'—p. 377

Thus each of us faces the question of our basic unjustifiability in a purposeless world. Some, of course, flee from these questions and

1. Thus the question 'Who am I?', whether or not it is answerable, is recognized at once to be vital and fundamental to the epistemological dilemma we each face; indeed, it is thus that there is the concept of such a dilemma at all.

deny them (by indulging in sensuality, hatred, lethargy, agitation, and doubt); but the questions return for so long as their root, the conceit 'I am', exists, and the verdict is inevitable: Guilty.

'Chaplain,' he continued, looking up, 'we accuse you also of the commission of crimes and infractions we don't even know about yet. Guilty or innocent?'

'I don't know, sir. How can I say if you don't tell me what they are?'

'How can we tell you if we don't know?'

'Guilty,' decided the colonel.

'Sure he's guilty,' agreed the major. 'If they're his crimes and infractions he must have committed them.'

'Guilty it is, then,' chanted the officer without insignia…—p. 379

And guilty it is for all of us, if the charge is the fundamental one of being possessors, or even of simply 'being': being *what*?

And thus Heller repeatedly and ingeniously offers us brilliant literary expressions of the dilemma of existence. The formulations are lucid and compelling and they fully take account of the circular and self-sustaining nature of the dilemma. For this we can praise *Catch-22*, and perhaps find it of use as a tool in keeping to the forefront of our awareness the nature of our problem. But it would be asking too much to expect the novel to offer the means of resolving that dilemma: for that we must turn to the Buddha's Teaching.

Sāmaṇera Bodhesako, from *The Buddha and Catch-22*

* * *

(Shortly after Bob's death in Nepal, a Sri Lankan journalist, Maureen Seneviratne, published an article about him: COMPUTER MONK REMEMBERED.—Hūm)

'… Ven. Bodhesako will no more walk the roads and paths of Ambegoda, a village near Bandarawela on the Welimada Road. Every morning the monk descended from the hillock where he lived on his round to collect his alms-food for the day. He walked the gravel roads barefoot, his begging bowl in a sling… Still, American remained the Sāmaṇera till his last days. You could see it from his gait. His feet carried his stocky body at a speed higher than an Asian monk on his begging tour ever would develop. So he returned with his bowl carefully but efficiently carried. For who has an eye for it, even the way he wore the monk's garb was not fully Eastern. A misfit in a Sinhalese village? Had the villagers known that the only piece of furniture in the monk's room, apart from bed, bookshelf, table and chair, was a word-processor, they might have been stingy with their alms!...

I had a long interview with him on the spacious verandah of the hundred years old bungalow of Hubert and Connie Congreave at Wye Estate...

Once, he said, he had possessed everything (in a material sense) he had wanted and had never been satisfied. It was for 'layman's reasons' he had 'gone forth' and thus he had found out the 'monk's reasons' for being a monk. He had had like many others to shed 'all romantic and flowery ideas' of being a monk and face and understand the 'true reasons'. He had used the Teachings as 'the raft for crossing a river' as the Buddha had said. Now he was still learning to use the 'raft'...

'Peace can only start with and within the individual,' I remember he told me, adding that Buddhism was not out to change the world, but the individual—give him right knowledge and understanding—and every individual transformed goes to make a better world, he said. Self-understanding alone would lead him to the inner peace that can exist for an individual even in the midst of strife and conflict...

...Ven. Bodhesako died in Nepal, close to his favorite temple, on a meditation pilgrimage, shortly before he would have attended the 80th anniversary celebration of his father in California. I imagine that Robert Smith—for that was his name from birth in Detroit, Michigan U.S.A.—had grown his hair and donned civilian clothes fitting the California climate for the occasion. But perhaps also he would not have done so. What does it matter? Would he have gone a-begging in California?... One can take for granted that such musings were thought unnecessary and even irrelevant by Sadhu, as the monk was called at Wye Estate...

...This computer word-processor was Sadhu's pride and worry. If anything in his life has been illustrative of the basic truth—not only of Buddhism—that all is transient and therefore needs to be handled properly, it was this electronic machine.

It took Sadhu almost the time he needed to learn how to meditate to find out the refinements he could utilize to print his book. Or was this his way to meditate? Surely he should not be considered to be a Western Buddhist for the sole fact that he worked a word-processor. For him it was nothing more than the stylus monks at Aluvihara near Dambulla cave temple even today use to print the ancient texts onto ola leaves. They also need ink. Who thinks of a word-processor as a higher being should never buy a newspaper either. For Sadhu probably handling this machine was of the same quality as being aware of one's breath in meditation.

And how it tested his patience! Not only because finding out its skills and moods was almost as volatile an exercise as scrutinising one's subconscience. It also liked breaking down…

…No, Robert Smith was not a Western Buddhist because he handled this intricate machine nor was he a Sinhala Buddhist because he walked Ambegoda's gravel roads barefoot. He remained American to the hilt. American stamped by the revolutionary 60's and the meditative 70's. His way of Buddhism was as contemporary as that of the Buddha himself in his days. For everybody has to go it on his own or her own, here and now.

Then why stayed Sadhu in Sri Lanka and why on Wye Estate? Because he found his Sangha there. Hospitality received from Hubert and Connie Congreave in an annex of their own house was their permanent *dāna* to him and his computer. Connie provided him with tea, gently placed outside his normally closed door. Sadhu had his perfect solitude woven into a relaxed but intimate relationship with the elderly couple. Would Robert Smith have found such a setting in his home country? The sensitivity for each other's privacy and need for communication developed in the 'Wye Hermitage' can be called unmatched and reason for Sadhu to settle down there. For though he died in Nepal on his way to America, Hubert Congreave meanwhile was doing up Sadhu's simple abode to have it ready for his return. For days they could hardly believe that he would never return. They would have believed any villager saying that he had been seen on his swift morning round. However, that is what Robert Smith would never do… He was a man of consequence. Someone who can handle a computer in a contemplative way also knows how to switch off.

A Western Buddhist by historic conditioning, lives among Christians. Different from what Eastern Buddhists might think, that can be an inspiration. Both ways, of course. That is what made Wye Estate Sadhu's

Sangha. All inhabitants are Christians. To their company the Buddhist monk Robert Smith wanted to return. Not for high-flown discussions, since there were none. Simply for the living, leaving each other alone but not lonely. Is not that a perfect definition of a monastery?...A mirror of what humanity as a whole is or should be.

*Clearing the Path*, the writings of his teacher, the Ven. Ñāṇavīra Thera, was really Sāmaṇera Bodhesako's magnum opus... There is no name of the editor—in the great tradition he chose to follow. It is notable that in his foreword he claimed the book 'is meant to be lived rather than read and set aside'. It is what he himself endeavoured and achieved in the way of life he adopted as his own...

* * *

(What I wonder, were his thoughts and impressions training up the subcontinent to his Himalayan destiny? Once again making his Indian rounds? Or had he somehow broken the circle in his own mind? Were the sights—and insights—somehow fresh, touched with some wonder and grace? When came the first pain, the first premonition of something very wrong, the realization of dying? Were some last thoughts cast to California? Wafted to the Sooke hills? At least that was not the end of his journey, even with the last period in this book. I doubt if that would have been news to him.

Finally, what is a father, a friend, a brother in Dhamma, to say? Perhaps, no more than the Pāli word *evaṃ*: it is as it is. The Buddha said, 'Be lamps unto yourselves, and work out your salvation with diligence.' The Buddha was called *Tathāgata*: He who has come and gone. None but a Buddha wholly comes and goes. Robert Smith devoted his life to homing on that wholeness. May ours be as well. Perhaps, this is ending in the middle as well.—Hūm)

THE END

Sooke, B.C.—December, 1989

COLOPHON

Typeset at Path Press Publications
in Stempel Garamond SouthAsia (MacCampus)
using Adobe InDesign CS5.5 on Mac OSX

PRINTED AND BOUND IN THE NETHERLANDS